NEW THEATRE
AND FILM 1934 TO 1937

NEW THEATRE AND FILM 1934 TO 1937

AN ANTHOLOGY

Selections Edited and with Commentary by
HERBERT KLINE
Foreword by Arthur Knight

Harcourt Brace Jovanovich, Publishers
SAN DIEGO   NEW YORK   LONDON

HBJ

Copyright © 1985 by Herbert Kline

All rights reserved. No part of this publication
may be reproduced or transmitted in any form
or by any means, electronic or mechanical,
including photocopy, recording, or any
information storage and retrieval system, without
permission in writing from the publisher.
Requests for permission to make copies of any part
of the work should be mailed to: Permissions,
Harcourt Brace Jovanovich, Publishers,
Orlando, Florida 32887

The publisher thanks Mrs. Marion Shaw for
permission to include *Bury the Dead* © 1936
by Irwin Shaw.

Library of Congress Cataloging in Publication Data
Main entry under title:

New theatre and film, 1934 to 1937.

Includes complete text for the play Bury the dead by
Irwin Shaw.
1. Theater—United States—Reviews.   2. Moving-
pictures—United States—Reviews.   I. Kline, Herbert.
II. Shaw, Irwin, 1913–   . Bury the dead.   1985.
PN2266.N46   1985   792.9'5'0973   85-815
ISBN 0-15-165457-3
ISBN 0-15-665507-1 (pbk.)

Designed by Margaret M. Wagner
Printed in the United States of America
First Edition
A B C D E

*In memory of my brother
Mark Marvin*

Contents

Illustrations   *xiii*

Preface   *xv*

Foreword by Arthur Knight   1

THEATRE

"1984" Flashbacks to Half a Century Ago   7

The Awakening of the American Theatre by Clifford Odets   13

Marching Song: Flint, Michigan, and Brimmerton, U.S.A. by Albert Maltz   16

Lawson Crosses the Class Line by Lester Cohen   18

Our Hall by Mark Marvin   20

The Scottsboro Case and the New Theatre Movement   23

They Shall Not Die! by Ben Blake   24

Peace on Earth by Jack Shapiro   26

How Archibald MacLeish Joined Our New Theatre Movement   27

Theatre against War and Fascism by Archibald MacLeish   30

The Hope for Poetry in the Theatre by Archibald MacLeish   32

ANOTHER MAJOR *New Theatre* DISCOVERY, JOHN W. GASSNER   35

Broadway Tries Again BY JOHN W. GASSNER   36

Perspectives—Past and Present BY JOHN W. GASSNER   39

HAROLD CLURMAN'S TOO FERVENT YEARS   44

Interpretation and Characterization: A Theatre Workshop Discussion BY HAROLD CLURMAN   46

PAINTER TURNED DRAMA CRITIC   50

The Quest of Eugene O'Neill: From the Moon-Drenched Caribbees to the Foot of the Cross BY CHARMION VON WIEGAND   51

A PANORAMA OF THEATRE ACTIVITIES   75

Eva Le Gallienne—Ten Years BY WALTER PELL   75

Memorandum on Hedgerow BY MARY VIRGINIA FARMER   79

Idiot's Delight, Anatomy of a Success BY DAVID SHEPPERD   83

Black Pit BY HERBERT KLINE   85

The Artef BY SAMUEL KREITER   89

Anti-Nazi German Theatre in Yorkville, N.Y. BY MOLLY DAY THACHER   91

Footlights in Filmland BY RICHARD SHERIDAN AMES   92

Pins and Needles BY BEN IRWIN   95

A "BACKSTAGE" RELATIONSHIP WITH HALLIE FLANAGAN   97

A Letter from Hallie Flanagan BY HALLIE FLANAGAN AND HERBERT KLINE   98

Contents

A Statement BY ELMER RICE   102

A Scene from the Censored Play BY ARTHUR ARENT   103

The Federal Theatre Presents BY JOSEPH MANNING   105

The Living Newspaper BY MORRIS WATSON   107

INVITATION TO A HARLEM PARTY   112

From *Uncle Tom's Cabin* to *Stevedore* BY EUGENE GORDON   113

On the White Man's Stage BY AUGUSTUS SMITH   117

Trouble with the Angels BY LANGSTON HUGHES   121

A *New Theatre* GREETING FOR ADOLF HITLER'S FLAGSHIP, THE SS *Bremen*   126

Shifting Scenes   128

Bury the Dead BY IRWIN SHAW   130

A THEATRE TOUR TO EUROPE DURING THE TIME OF HITLER'S GROWING POWER   165

Reinhardt Hails a Popular Front Play BY ELIZABETH MEYER   172

Impressions of Nazi Drama BY H. W. L. DANA   174

François Villon in Prague BY CHARLES RECHT   181

Soviet Diary BY HAROLD CLURMAN   185

It Makes You Weep: An Interview with Stella Adler on Soviet Actors BY JANET THORNE   188

Spain Says "Salud!" BY ANGNA ENTERS   190

DANCE

New Theatre AND THE MODERN DANCE WORLD   199

Whither Martha Graham BY EDNA OCKO   201

Texts for Dancers BY EDNA OCKO   204

The Fokine Ballets BY BLANCHE EVAN   207

LINCOLN KIRSTEIN: FIFTY YEARS AGO IN *New Theatre*   210

Revolutionary Ballet Forms BY LINCOLN KIRSTEIN   212

Men Must Dance BY GENE MARTEL   220

FILM

Gorky on the Films, 1896   227

THE GROWING ROLE OF *New Theatre* IN THE WORLD OF FILM   231

The Movie: 1902–1917 BY ROBERT STEBBINS   234

D. W. Griffith BY RICHARD WATTS, JR.   237

Billy Bitzer, Ace Cameraman BY PHILIP STERLING   241

Little Charlie, What Now? BY CHARMION VON WIEGAND   245

Louella Parsons: Hearst's Hollywood Stooge BY JOEL FAITH   254

THREATS AND NEWS FROM INSIDE THE HEARST PRESS EMPIRE   259

John Ford: Fighting Irish BY EMANUEL EISENBERG   267

The Films Make History BY ROBERT STEBBINS   271

Month of Bounties BY ROBERT STEBBINS   274

Reinhardt's *Dream* BY CHARMION VON WIEGAND   279

Contents

The Animated Cartoon and Walt Disney BY WILLIAM KOZLENKO 284

The Movie "Original" BY WILLIAM LORENZ 289

Notes on Hollywood BY JORIS IVENS 294

A New Approach to Filmmaking
BY RALPH STEINER AND LEO T. HURWITZ 300

DOCUMENTARY FILMS IN *New Theatre* AND IN MY LIFE 306

Robert Flaherty's Escape BY IRVING LERNER 307

Too Much Reality BY FRIEDRICH WOLF 310

The Plow That Broke the Plains BY IRVING LERNER 313

Redes BY ROBERT STEBBINS 316

THE FOREIGN FILM, YESTERYEAR AND NOW 320

The Films of René Clair BY LEWIS JACOBS 321

Parade-Ground Art: The German Film under Hitler
BY CARL DREHER 327

HOW HITLER AFFECTED THE LIVES OF TWO *New Theatre* CONTRIBUTORS 337

Der Kampf BY MAX OPHULS 341

A Letter to F. Ermler on *Peasants* BY G. W. PABST 343

A FILM DIRECTOR HERO OF THE SIEGE OF LENINGRAD 345

Dovzhenko's *Frontier* BY IRVING LERNER 346

The Youth of Maxim BY V. PUDOVKIN 350

THE RISKS OF LIFE ON THE LEFT 352

Who Speaks for Us? BY ROBERT FORSYTHE 355

AFTERWORD

The Beginning of the End of *New Theatre*   363

TABLES OF CONTENTS for *New Theatre* (1934–36) and
New Theatre and Film (1937)   369

CHRONOLOGY of Selections in this Anthology   383

Illustrations

In the Text

Our Hall
Phil Bard
20

The Puppet Master
S. Bunin
102

Drama under the Swastika
Phil Wolfe
175

Drawings for *François Villon in Prague*
John Groth
180

New Dance Group in *New Theatre Skit*
Norris
199

Cartoon, "*Hollywood Extra!*"
James Kelly
260

Drawing of Katharine Hepburn
Aline Fruhauf
272

Drawings for *Who Speaks for Us?*
John Groth
356, 357

Drawing of John Howard Lawson
Phil Wolfe
364

INSERT *Following page 224*

New Theatre Cover, March 1936
Miguel Covarrubias

New Theatre Cover, April 1936
George Grosz

New Theatre Cover, June 1936
William Gropper

Living Theatre Montage
Hosen

New Theatre Cover, July 1936
Augustus Peck

So You Want to Go into the Theatre?
William Gropper

New Theatre and Film Cover, April 1937
Lewis Jacobs

Preface

I DEDICATE this book primarily to my late brother, who used the stage name Mark Marvin and who was and remains the main influence on my life and work. Although other deserving coworkers will receive appreciative credit throughout, I am especially grateful to Ben Blake, who, as founder of *New Theatre*, started me as an editor in 1934 on three of the best years of my life.

Main credit for urging me to do this book is due David Shepard, special projects officer for the Directors' Guild of America in Hollywood. David also brought me together with Donald Knox, senior editor for Harcourt Brace Jovanovich. I had thought that my job would be only to make selections from thirty-six issues, but Don convinced me that publication today required fresh context, which I should supply as personal reminiscence about experiences I shared with contributors and close friends among the magazine's coworkers.

I was dubious initially about using parts of the book for my recollections, worrying that the space could be better used for more articles. But Don proved skilled at such matters and elicited one intriguing remembrance after another, encouraging me to bring into sharp focus that time long ago. And I also want to give credit to Naomi Grady, Don's assistant, who helped edit my commentaries after they were written.

Even harder than the new writing was selecting a representative sample of the many wonderful articles and play excerpts. I apologize here to the fine contributors, living and dead, for not including everything of value. Also, to make room for as many articles as possible, I shortened some, but I have been careful to preserve the essentials of what was originally written.

I am happy for the opportunity to revive knowledge of *New Theatre*, original copies of which are almost impossible to locate except in a few major libraries. Preparing this book put me simultaneously in two eras—the present and the past of a half century ago. I hope readers will find that, for them, our old struggles against domestic injustice and foreign fascism still reverberate in the courageous activities of those presently trying to prevent the mad and terrifying holocaust of nuclear war.

HERBERT KLINE
New York City
March 1984

Foreword

A PERSONAL NOTE

by Arthur Knight

NINETEEN THIRTY-FOUR wasn't a great year for high school graduates. The Great Depression was in its fifth year and still clinging tenaciously. There were breadlines and Hoovervilles, and on street corners all over New York ragged and even well-dressed men were selling bright red apples for a nickel apiece from improvised fruit stands. The labor market was glutted. Even so, I felt that I had some slight advantage; at least I knew what I wanted to do. Ever since junior high, when I began writing reviews for the school's literary magazine, I had wanted to be a movie critic. Now a graduate, I wasn't so naive as to think I could march into the *New York Times* and offer to replace its current critic—even had I known then that the late Bosley Crowther was already his apprentice. But I would gladly settle for a starter job—copyboy, file clerk, runner, anything that would bring me close enough to the city desk that one day I might get a tryout.

Accordingly, I began making the rounds of every newspaper and magazine in New York and Brooklyn that evinced the slightest interest in the arts. I didn't get a single interview, not even with a clerk in an employment office. And then one day I climbed the stairs to the shabby headquarters of *New Theatre*. They couldn't afford an employment office; instead, I was introduced directly to the editor himself, young Herb Kline, a big, disheveled man who listened sympathetically to my youthful aspirations, then turned me over to his newly appointed film editor, Robert Stebbins (better known as the late filmmaker and teacher, Sidney Meyers).

Sidney was a marvelous man—warm, funny, perceptive, and with an enormous fund of Jewish stories to fit every occasion. He didn't exactly *hire* me; as Herb Kline points out in his introduction to this volume, *New Theatre* operated on a bare-bones budget. But Sidney did *employ* me. He sent me out to do lobby interviews sampling audience reactions to certain films. And he asked me to research pieces that he was writing, or to check the accuracy of articles that had been submitted, which became my introduction to the extraordinary resources of the Theatre Collection at the New York Public Library and, of even greater consequence to me, the Museum of Modern Art Film Library, which had only just opened its doors at 485 Madison Avenue. Jay Leyda, Sidney's good friend and a contributing editor to *New Theatre*, was then its assistant curator, and Jay became my mentor. A few years later, when the building on 53rd Street was about to open, I was invited to join the staff—my first paying job in the movies. (Ironically, the first film article that I ever sold went to *Theatre Arts*, *New Theatre's* liberal but more conservative rival, for a princely $40!)

As the following pages attest, New York in the thirties was a rich, heady place to be. The theatre was flourishing—and even on Broadway you could buy a gallery seat for as little as fifty cents. The Group Theatre brought us Sidney Kingsley, whose *Men in White* became a Broadway hit, and Pulitzer Prize winner Clifford Odets, whose *Awake and Sing* marked a new era of social drama in America, and probably the finest ensemble acting of any company in America. Down on 14th Street, the unabashedly Left-oriented Theatre Union had recently displaced Eva Le Gallienne with a series of vivid social protest plays. The WPA Theatre Project was just getting under way, bringing us Sinclair Lewis's stirring, antifascist *It Can't Happen Here*, its innovative Living Newspaper productions, and sponsoring the talents of a very young Orson Welles as director of an all-Negro *Macbeth*, a full-bodied mounting of Marlowe's *Dr. Faustus*, and the controversial *The Cradle Will Rock* (which managed to rock the entire Project). Down in the Village, such artists as Martha Graham, Doris Humphrey, and Charles Weidman gave Sunday dance recitals in their respective studios, while nearby the "revolutionary" New Dance League performed for the *New Theatre's* exciting benefit nights, often in tandem with such one-acters as Odets's *Waiting for Lefty* and Irwin Shaw's *Bury the Dead*. Tickets went for fifty cents to a dollar, and the benefits were invariably sellouts.

Movies, too, were being recognized as a vital art form, a fact duly noted when *New Theatre* eventually changed its title to *New Theatre and Film*. The Little Carnegie was generally acknowledged to be the flagship of the art houses; but the Filmart, on West 58th Street, kept us abreast of the French imports and the Cameo (now the Bryant) on 42nd Street served as headquarters for the emerging Soviet cinema. But I also attended (I think in 1935) a daylong showing of about a dozen of the greatest Soviet silent classics at the historic Fifth Avenue Theatre (on Broadway; it was the theatre that had housed the first Gilbert and Sullivan productions in America), while the tiny Fifth Avenue Playhouse (at 12th Street) harbored such offbeat items as *The Fall of the House of Usher*, *The Cabinet of Dr. Caligari*, and, at least once a month, Jean Cocteau's

Foreword

surreal *Le Sang d'un Poète*. For the true film aficionado, however, the town's biggest bargain was the Apollo, a 42nd Street grind house that differentiated itself from its grubby fellows on that once-glittering thoroughfare by offering double bills of outstanding European films (mostly French) for a mere fifteen cents admission (later raised to seventeen cents). Elsewhere, mostly in union halls and at political meetings, the leftist Film and Photo League offered its primitive documentaries and social protest shorts as an alternative to Hollywood's glossy features and escapist frame of mind. Admission to these events was generally free, although a small donation was expected.

These are the times, this is the world reflected with startling immediacy in the following pages, often reported by the men and women directly responsible for making it all happen, or the people it was happening to. I found an enormous poignancy in Angna Enters's attempt to remain unbiased in her eyewitness account of the outbreak of the Spanish Civil War in Málaga, despite her obvious outrage that Franco's fascists, abetted by foreign mercenaries, had been brought in to crush the newly won democracy of the Spanish people; and also in Carl Dreher's precise, unemotional recital of the effect that Hitler's National Socialism was having on the once-great German cinema. I was reminded of the courage that it took to speak out against war and fascism, lynching and vigilantism in those days, or to take a public stand favoring unionization and the civil liberties promised in FDR's New Deal. As editor, Herb Kline had a unique perception of what was happening on the artistic frontiers of theatre, film, and dance in the thirties, and the ability to cajole major artists and critics to write about it for free. That many of them did so under pseudonyms, denying themselves even the ego satisfaction of a byline, is at once a comment on the strength of the repressive forces of that day and a testament to Herb's enormous powers of persuasion.

All of this took place at a time when liberal artists and intellectuals were being drawn together by a glowing concept called the Popular Front. Not a political movement per se, the Front was the name given to all liberal, antifascist, antiwar organizations (including the early CIO) that were united by these ideologies. No one questioned for a moment that Communists, Socialists, and other American radicals were part of that Front, even though this made it more vulnerable to attack from reactionaries. True democracy demanded nothing less, and *New Theatre* became one of its strongest cultural voices. Soon after Herb left the magazine to volunteer for Loyalist Spain, however (and unexpectedly wound up as a filmmaker), *New Theatre and Film* went into decline, to be replaced by the glossier *TAC*, the publication of another Popular

Front organization known as the Theatre Arts Committee. *TAC* continued to support liberal leftist movements in the arts until the disillusionment following the infamous Nazi-Soviet nonaggression pact caused a sharp split in its membership. In a remarkably short time the entire Popular Front was torn asunder as the Communist elements persisted in their pro-Soviet stance. This split marked the beginning of my political education, just as *New Theatre and Film* importantly influenced my critical awareness of the social and artistic power of the motion picture medium.

The thirties were an era of tremendous change in this country, change that had its roots in the Great Depression. One can't read this book without sensing the anger and frustration of the period, but also its idealism and hope. Social historians, looking back, may give a more balanced perspective to those years, but these pages convey vividly the sense of how it really was to those of us fortunate—or unfortunate—enough to have lived them.

THEATRE

"1984" FLASHBACKS TO HALF A CENTURY AGO

I AM WRITING these words in this Orwellian year of the fiftieth anniversary of *New Theatre*, but please don't think of us mid-1930s survivors as yesterday's news. Many of Clifford Odets's generation have passed on. However, many continue working in films, theatre, TV, and teaching: Elia Kazan, Orson Welles, John Houseman, Albert Maltz, George Sklar, Jules Dassin, Martin Ritt, Cheryl Crawford, Stella Adler, Sandy Meisner, Ben Blake, Oscar Saul, Perry Bruskin, Peter Frye, Bobby Lewis, Vincent Sherman, and Sidney Kingsley. In dance: Martha Graham, Anna Sokolow, and Lincoln Kirstein. Still active in documentary filmmaking: Leo Hurwitz, Lewis Jacobs, Joris Ivens, Ralph Steiner, Willard Van Dyke, Arnold Eagle, Leo Seltzer, Henri Cartier-Bresson, and myself. Our numbers have dwindled, but not our spirits. Despite disillusionments about the better world we envisioned and worked for, many of us are still activists now as then, especially in opposing the nuclear arms race.

As for myself, this "Remembrance of Things Past" relates to what I tell my son, Ethan, and daughter, Elissa, now in their twenties, when they ask, "What was it like then, Dad?"

For now, 1984, try to imagine that *you* were like us then, impassioned participants in the theatre arts renaissance that *New Theatre* helped generate from 1934 through 1936. Three rebellious, creative, challenging years of dramatizing the harsh realities of American life and the imminent dangers of fascist-triggered wars. Also three years of growing faith in America's future, in Franklin Delano Roosevelt's "New Deal" presidency after suffering deprivations in the most terrible depression in our nation's history. Difficult, dangerous years in which our colleagues included many different political opinions and allegiances from left-of-center Democrats, unaligned radicals, Socialists, and Communists, a popular front against reaction and fascism. Our beliefs were a kind of all-embracing humanism stemming from the American Revolutionary ideals of Democracy, but strongly and openly Leftist.

Our idealism about helping forge a better world often led to violent attacks: police repression, censorship, arrests and jailings of writers and theatre artists of our New Theatre League groups. We resisted criminal attacks on performers in plays like *Waiting for Lefty* and *Till the Day I Die* by German-American Bund members, who even smashed newsstands selling our magazine.

We fought back in the mid-1930s with a spirit comparable to that of later generations, of 1960s civil rights marchers and 1980s antinuclear protesters. Only there was no television to acquaint the public visually and dramatically with the harassments and violence we withstood. Our theatre and dance groups reached an enthusiastic but limited public, and the beginning efforts of the Film and Photo League failed to reach mass audiences. Radio and press gave some social struggle coverage, but their presentations were often biased, like newsreels and *The March of Time*. Major Hollywood studios and Broadway commercial theatres failed so badly in dealing with grave social problems that Brooks Atkinson, the eminent drama critic of the *New York Times*, commented:

> If there is any trend in today's theatres it is the vigorous advance of the drama of the Left. The revolutionary theatre is forging ahead. It is becoming increasingly dynamic and is no longer a skirmish on the fringe of the theatre, for it has a coherent program and is inflamed with a Crusader's zeal. The Broadway theatre has no program and no convictions; and in the midst of vast social upheaval, it has no comment to make.

Audiences grew rapidly as the revolutionary theatre was encouraged by similar recognition from Richard Watts, Jr., Robert Garland, Heywood Broun, and drama critics in other large cities.

We had strong "convictions" and edited *New Theatre* with "Crusader's zeal." Leading American and European writers contributed even though our magazine could not afford to pay them. Staff work was done gratis by talented, part-time volunteers, especially Molly Day Thacher as drama editor, Leo Hurwitz as editor of the film section, and Edna Ocko as dance editor. We had only five low-paid, full-time, overworked, dedicated staff members: myself; George Redfield, our efficient, scholarly managing editor; two young business aides, David Crystal and Bob Steck; and one office manager, Jin Stern.

Somehow we managed to get by on subsistence wages of twenty dollars a week from magazine sales at ten cents a copy and subscriptions at one dollar a year. Unlike our chief rivals, the well-established and well-financed *Stage Magazine* and *Theatre Arts Monthly*, we had no funds for sales promotion and very little return from advertisers. But we believed in what we were accomplishing and had wonderful responses from readers, theatre people, and audiences for our New Theatre Night benefit performances.

We won over to our cause distinguished converts, such as poet Archibald MacLeish, who was also a highly paid journalist and editor of *Fortune* magazine; and in academic circles, Vassar's Hallie Flanagan, who was staging theatre of social protest (I particularly recall her production of *You Can Hear Their Voices*) long before she became the controversial head of the Federal Theatre Project. We also made inroads in the Broadway theatre through the influence of the Group Theatre, headed by Lee Strasberg, Harold Clurman, and Cheryl Crawford; and Group Theatre members worked during their spare time teaching professional skills to the Workers' Lab Theatre, the Theatre Collective, and other New Theatre League school groups.

Once Alfred Lunt invited me to his dressing room backstage at *Taming of the Shrew*. As often happened with people at that time, Lunt reacted to my youth. "Oh, you're so young to be editing such an exciting, important magazine," he said. "I feel like quoting Voltaire, that I may disagree with so much you radicals say but, for the theatre's sake, I'll defend to the death your right to say it. Here's fifty dollars from me and fifty from Lynn [Fontanne], as we agree your *New Theatre* is doing a great job stirring things up on Broadway."

Soon after, Burgess Meredith, the young star of Maxwell Anderson's *Winterset*, invited me to be his guest. I thought his performance was brilliant and admired the play more than our drama critic, John Gassner, had. Afterward, Burgess said, "I don't enjoy your critic's review, but I'll be magnanimous as I do appreciate the magazine's role in the theatre today. So here's seventy-five dollars to help pay the printer."

Little did either of us dream then that almost fifty years later, in 1982, Burgess would join me going to the Moscow Art Theatre, the Peter Brook Theatre Bouffe in Paris, the Dublin Abbey, and to American and English theatres for a new documentary film, *Great Theatres of the World*.

So it went with occasional unsolicited donations, the largest of which came from Bennett Cerf, a $500 check sent with an admiring letter for "the best theatre magazine in America."

We appreciated such expressions of support from major celebrities, but our main objective was the discovery of unknowns. In retrospect, I consider our two greatest achievements publishing and presenting, on New Theatre Night Sunday benefits, Clifford Odets's *Waiting for Lefty* and Irwin Shaw's *Bury the Dead*, months before their remarkable talents won them worldwide fame.

In the 1980s, long after the start of my second career as a filmmaker, I returned to the New York theatre world where I had begun my work in 1934. While writing and directing a documentary, *Acting . . . Lee Strasberg* (which was filmed just before Strasberg's death), young crew members questioned me about "the past" Lee and I reminisced about between camera moves.

"Tell us, Herb," they asked, "what was it like to know great writers like Odets and Shaw, and directors like Kazan and Welles when you were all in your twenties and just beginning your careers. Were your lives as exciting, radical, and romantic as those of Barbra Streisand and Robert Redford in *The Way We Were?*"

I answered them as I had answered my own two children when they had asked me similar questions about those long-gone times. I said it was a marvelous experience to get to know such major artists in early friendships based on common beliefs. But our lives were not like those pictured in *The Way We Were*, especially in the romantic and sexual aspects my young friends were so curious about. I explained that we young people of the midthirties Left had come along a decade after the 1920s "lost generation" of Ernest Hemingway and Scott Fitzgerald. Unlike Edna St. Vincent Millay, we didn't "burn the candle at both ends." To us the "sexual revolution" had seemed already won. We were much more committed intellectually, emotionally, and politically than most of the midde-class characters in *The Way We Were*, who lived on a far costlier scale than we could afford. Our League members supported themselves with low-paid side jobs, having to "get by" doubling up in small, overcrowded apartments in New York City's Greenwich Village or Queens, or equivalent quarters in other cities. Even many professional actors of the Group Theatre company on Broadway and the Fourteenth Street Theatre Union struggled on salaries far below Broadway levels. Living on the working-class Left was hard, for we had no "Broadway angels" and, despite accusations from various quarters concerning "paid propaganda," no "Moscow gold."

But we did strike a different kind of American gold in late December of 1934 that changed our lives. Clifford Odets, a tall, handsome young actor of small roles in the Group Theatre, submitted a play about the New York taxi strike to our One-Act Prize Play Contest. Molly Day Thacher brought *Waiting for Lefty* to us from Boston, where she had accompanied her husband, Elia Kazan, on a pre-Broadway Group Theatre road tour. She explained breathlessly how Odets had holed up in a hotel room for three hectic days and nights to finish his play, rushing to meet the contest's deadline. There were only a few hours left, so on Molly's urging we passed the pages around, all reading with intense excitement. For our staff, and later for the jury, it was a "no contest" win for Odets. We decided to pull articles lined up for the next issue of *New Theatre* and publish *Lefty* instead. We also decided to rent the Theatre Union's Civic Repertory Theatre for Odets and his Group Theatre friends —among whom was a future major Hollywood film star, young Jules, later John, Garfield—to stage *Lefty.*

We booked the theatre for Sunday, January 6, 1935, but had to pay $300 in advance by Friday the 4th. After a wealthy businessman promised to lend us the money, all seemed set; but the "backer" backed out Friday noon. He was almost in tears for letting us down and admitted, "I can't risk my name being bandied about as supporting Left causes."

My brother, Mark Marvin, who had just moved to New York to head the New Theatre League, came up with an idea I agreed to carry out, although both of us felt guilty doing so. We would not tell our Theatre Union friends, Albert Maltz, George Sklar, and Paul Peters, that we couldn't pay the cash in advance, but would give them a check after the bank closed and pray the performance and the expected $900 in box-office receipts would not be rained out. So I wrote a bad check to rent the theatre and managed to act surprised when told I'd come too late for the money to be deposited before Monday.

Of course, with that cliff-hanger scaring us all, it rained. But over 1,400 people came through the downpour to pay ninety cents and less a ticket and pack the house. Several hundred more had to be turned away.

The audience went wild with enthusiasm. Sandy Meisner, with Odets's aid, had staged *Lefty* brilliantly. The challenging poetic dialogue rang true in one exciting, deeply moving scene after another. As Kazan recalls, "The balcony, like a Niagara, seemed to roar down on the audience below."

At the conclusion of the play, a taxi driver leaped onstage shouting the bitter, tragic news that Lefty had been murdered by the bosses' goons. The Group cast, led by J. Edward Bromberg as Agate, turned their heart-rending mass grief into a flaming call to "Strike! Strike!" The audience rose en masse, many shouting "Strike!" as if part of the performance, which indeed it had become.

That was half a century ago, but it remains as if yesterday in my memory. In a scene I filmed five decades later for *Acting*, Lee Strasberg recalled, "That first performance of *Waiting for Lefty* was the most thrilling night I have ever spent in the theatre." Harold Clurman called Odets "the most significant new talent since Eugene O'Neill." We knew we had witnessed the birth of a new era in American social drama and the emergence of a major revolutionary playwright.

The proscenium arch had disappeared: We the people shared the dramatic life on stage. As Harold Clurman wrote later, "When the audience responded to the militant question from the stage, 'Well, what's the answer?' with a spontaneous roar of 'Strike! Strike!' it was something more than a tribute to the play's effectiveness, more even than a testimony to the audience's hunger for constructive social action. It was the spiritual birth cry of the thirties. Our youth had found its voice."

At a quickly arranged follow-up New Theatre Night performance of *Lefty* at the Fifth Avenue Theatre, audience emotion ran so high that it affected the actors on stage. Suddenly we heard a sharp blow. Morris Carnovsky as Harry Fatt, a treacherous leader of the taxi strikers, staggered. Tony Kraber, playing a striker, had punched Carnovsky so hard that blood spurted from Carnovsky's broken nose. Phoebe Brand, Morris's actress fiancée, started to rush to his aid, but he waved her off and gave a marvelous performance, bravely stemming the blood flow with handkerchief to the end. Later the "class enemy" received a special curtain call for his courage.

In the next four feverish days and nights, the young actor-turned-playwright prodded himself to complete a powerful and timely anti-Nazi one-act play, *Till the Day I Die*. We hastily organized a special New Theatre Night. The new play's premiere on a double bill with *Lefty* scored another success. The Group Theatre executives, who had long had doubts about staging Odets's full-length play, *Awake and Sing*, put on a beautiful production, directed by Harold Clurman, that subsequently gave them a Broadway hit. With three plays on Broadway, an unknown small-part actor had given his company its greatest recognition since Sidney Kingsley's Pulitzer Prize winner, *Men in White*.

At the New Theatre League office, Mark and his two main colleagues, Ben Irwin and Alice Evans, were almost overwhelmed with phone calls and telegrams. Theatre groups sent advance royalties and demanded rights to rush the Odets plays into production. Odets was thrilled and insisted on low charges for the workers' theatres. Soon the successes of the Odets plays stirred the formation of many League theatres throughout the country. Magazine sales that had been only 2,000 in late March 1934 tripled to 6,000 by September, then doubled again to over 12,000 for the *Waiting for Lefty* issues we hurried to put out late in January. Demand was so great we could have sold 25,000 if we had had the credit with our loyal, but long-suffering, printer. Subscriptions poured in from all over America and from abroad. Productions of *Lefty* and *Till the Day I Die* scored hits in London, Paris, Montreal, Mexico City, and Moscow.

Soon we were able to move our offices uptown to 44th Street in the heart of a Broadway that we had "invaded" successfully. Commercial theatre ads began coming in. Subscriptions kept rising. George Redfield, Mark, and I were able to draw $25 a week and afford apartments in the Hell's Kitchen area west of Eighth Avenue—years later the location of the Actors' Studio.

But back in 1935, along with the astounding public response to Odets, there was also ugly hostility. The "hate Roosevelt" reactionaries couldn't attack the national government physically, but they could act against us, often with the encouragement of local authorities. Armed "Friends of New Germany," the California Nazis, broke up an Odets New Theatre

Night in Hollywood. Incensed by *Till the Day I Die*, they kidnapped and badly beat actor-director Will Geer. Will managed to escape and thus saved his life. He came out of the hospital and staged Odets's anti-Nazi play and *Lefty*, this time with guards armed with baseball bats. Often police stood aside while armed fascist vigilantes blocked performances; and some officials and judges issued court injunctions to stop performances. Soon Clifford Odets became the most violently attacked and censored playwright in the history of the American theatre.

Theatre artists, writers, actors, dancers, film people, critics, and even many who did not believe in Odets, or our leftist ideas, joined in nationwide protest. Democrats, Socialists, Communists, even liberal Republicans, formed a popular front against illegal censorship laws and acts. Our New Theatre League groups and the magazine led well-organized, union-backed struggles against the reactionaries. *New Theatre* ran editorials and feature articles condemning censorship as a vicious violation of fundamental constitutional rights. We prepared a dynamic anticensorship cover designed by our part-time, volunteer art editors, Cipe Peneles and Bill Golden. Odets's face was featured on the cover along with those of other writers, artists, and actors, past and present, whose works had been censored, such as Ibsen, Heine, Tolstoy, Barbusse, Joyce, H. G. Wells, G. B. Shaw, Mark Twain, Walt Whitman, Eugene O'Neill, and Sinclair Lewis; also film stars recently attacked by the Legion of Decency —James Cagney and Charlie Chaplin. Like the taxi drivers of *Lefty*, we had struck hard against the vigilantes of the mind, the censors, their police, and their judges.

For us, the Constitution of our country was the best defense as we fought and won battles for "the land of the free and the home of the brave."

The Awakening of the American Theatre

BY CLIFFORD ODETS

IN THE BOOM days of our country, lots of young and old people slept fitfully in the night. They wanted "art." They had money and all the implements of prosperity but no "art." It troubled them. They got out of bed and ate a roast chicken, sometimes two. But they didn't sleep. So they finally started the little theatre movement. They got their "art."

By the time the big dark days came, they discovered that art wasn't very important. Banks were crashing, men fell off roofs, Hoover lost more hair; and art and the little theatre movement drifted away empty, smoky, evanescent. What was the use? What did it have to do with life? Besides money was scarce. Bye-bye little theatre.

All this was true of the big-time Broadway theatre too. A rash of art broke out all over the street. Art was a paying proposition! Anything stuck on the stage was a paying proposition! Lots of talented playwrights were bothered. They got paid for their bother! Mr. Ford, the Bishop of Detroit (since replaced by the Bishop of Royal Oak), promised Americans the gold stream would not stop. But what is man? Man proposes, God deposes!

With the first thunderclap it was all over in the home, in the garage, and in the theatre. The Columbia Burlesque circuit gave up the ghost. Many Broadway producers took to the Riviera. A few playwrights went on bravely. They discussed the problems of 1492 and 1669. They earnestly examined their navels and told audiences what they had found. On the West Coast Mae West got to be America's favorite tootsie. Overnight she became America's symbol of the good old days. Daring went, and no one could look 1929 in the face.

Yes, it looked black from wherever you sat. Everyone was saying the theatre was dead. Some blamed the movies. Some the radio. Others said it was the Gulf Stream's fault. Nights were growing longer. People were wishing Teddy Roosevelt would come on the scene and straighten things out with a big stick. (Still going on!)

Then a curious thing occurred: Certain small groups of theatre people began to concern themselves with 1929 and the years to follow. These isolated groups said art must be about something. It must be hot and spiteful, and it must probe the future with reference to the past and present. Yes, it was an early spring that year, and out of the bloody earth a lone pale flower was growing up. It grew stealthily at first, quietly, underground, unnoticed. It sucked in fresh air. It was cultivated tenderly. It happens to be a forest of healthy trees at present!

The record of the growth of this theatre is the concern of Ben Blake in his fine pamphlet, *The Awakening of the American Theatre* (63 pages —issued by Tomorrow Publishers—and 25 cents buys it). You will find compactly stated the history of a whole genuine theatrical renaissance. Abundant and vital are good words to use for this new theatre, which concerns itself with a sincere critical examination of life. Most of our theatre is gangrened tissue on an ailing body. This will drop off of its own weight even before the surgeon of economics gets to the scene. The live tissue of the American theatre is the subject of Blake's writing.

The Awakening of the American Theatre

Yes, you will find this booklet is about what is referred to as "the propaganda theatre." (A few eminent conscious propagandists: Euripides, Aristophanes, Dante, Molière, Byron, Shelley, Hugo, Tolstoy, Zola, and Ibsen.) How did this theatre begin in America? What people spanked the baby to a fuller breath? How was the baby kicked around, and who did the kicking? Lots of interesting facts like the answers to these questions are found in *The Awakening of the American Theatre*.

And how talented men like Lawson, Maltz, Saxe, Rice, Peters, Sklar, Odets, Wexley—lots of others—how they grew and developed upward with their various theatres and groups.

The whole question of groups is very well brought out here. What it means for actors and writers to work for audiences which actively participate in the stage life. Why New Theatre League plays are immediately produced from coast to coast in town and hamlet: *Waiting for Lefty* plays in 104 American cities in eight months!

And censorship! plays banned, actors clubbed, policemen pushing, overalls and evening clothes joined in protest—and riding clear and high over all, a new consciousness of what the theatre can and must mean in our country today! The love of our people for the theatre! The disjointment of price and desire set right! Coal miners, dockworkers, spindle girls—all catching fire from the same plays which startle and entertain Broadway. Hard-worked critics first amused, second bemused, next amazed! The whole shebang looking forward eagerly to promised production of these new plays.

Ben Blake has done a good job. His booklet was badly needed. But don't forget with the amazing growth of this new theatre movement came the magazine you are now reading, the one in your hand. This NEW THEATRE magazine, its very name is significant. Those pages are filled every month with a content plucked from the mouths of very good people, Americans, Europeans, first-rate artists of every theatre front. World-famous names. Men busy with the great stuff of modern life.

And all their good ideas and works thrown back through this magazine into the new theatre movement. Where they are eagerly seized on, chewed up, rejected, accepted, worked—all for the continued growth of this new vital theatre which is as healthy as the fruit on Florida trees.

Marching Song

FLINT, MICHIGAN, AND BRIMMERTON, U.S.A.

BY ALBERT MALTZ

FLINT, Michigan, is a town of a hundred and sixty-five thousand people. A few weeks ago, I stood on a street corner in a shabby part of the city where the houses are old and the side streets are of dirt, not pavement. It is one of the districts in which employees of General Motors live—the machine men, the tool men, the men on the assembly lines who have coined a name for their work—they call it the "chain gang."

It was nine thirty at night. A siren suddenly sounded in the distance. I had heard it before. I had been hearing it since early morning. It was a police squad car, but its siren was different from the ones we have become accustomed to in the movies. It was less dramatic, more like a deep, steady locomotive whistle. It was coming closer and it was coming at a terrific speed. My companion had been talking but he stopped as the car swung around a bend in the street. It burned past us about seventy miles an hour down a half-mile straightaway. Then it flashed under an underpass alongside of the immense Buick plant and disappeared finally into the darkness.

What was that car doing?—Nothing! Where was it going?—No place! It was chasing its own radiator cap! The police cars had been doing that all day—burning the road five miles in one direction, then turning around and chasing right back again. The purpose was panic—they were trying to create the impression that the town was convulsed by rioting, that there was trouble here and trouble there—that in general everybody better pray for the state militia to come in as quickly as possible. The state militia came in the following day.

And in that police car, in the shabby houses on one side where the auto workers lived, and in the immense, concrete, walled fortress of the Buick plant on the other side with its green mercury lights and the steady pound-pound of presses working the night shift, storing up parts against the threatened spread of the strike—in those things you have the picture of Flint, Michigan. From those things could be traced everything I had seen and been told in the previous two days. I had been told that General Motors owned the *Flint Journal*, the only newspaper in town. On Monday night I saw a policeman in shell vest and gas mask take careful aim and fire a gas shell through a restaurant window where wounded strikers were waiting for ambulances; and the next day I read in the *Flint Journal* that an unidentified civilian threw an unexploded gas bomb into a restaurant. I had been told that the courts were owned by General Motors and forty-eight hours after I had arrived in Flint a General Motors judge issued twelve hundred John Doe warrants entitling a General Motors district attorney to arrest anyone he chose, on charges from criminal syndicalism to kidnapping to inciting to riot, and to hold him as thirteen union men with bullets in their flesh were already being held—incommunicado—unable to see wife, lawyer, friend or, as one striker put it, "Jesus Christ himself." I had been told about George Boysen, ex-G.M. employee, leader of a vigilante group which was masquerading under the name of the "Flint Citizens Alliance" ("for the protection of our homes, our property, our jobs"). I had been told about Caesar Scavarda, former strikebreaker in Calumet, Michigan, former chief of police in Flint removed from office for too intimate connection with the vice and liquor racket, at present rewarded for his long record of citizenship by a captaincy in the state police which was being called in to keep order in Flint. . . .

A dozen bits of information like this crowded into my head and suddenly I thought: "My God, can this be the *first* time I've been in Flint? Haven't I seen this town before or a town just like it?" Yes, I had. I remembered then. Flint was Brimmerton. Brimmerton? Brimmerton was in rehearsal! Brimmerton was an idea, it was blue prints on a scene designer's desk, it was actors in a cold theatre; Brimmerton was theatre benefits being sold in advance, it was a man called Lawson, it was a play called *Marching Song*, which the Theatre Union had been working to produce since last summer.

No, art wasn't following life here. Life seemed almost to be lagging behind. Six months before my arrival in Flint I had read a highly dramatic and highly poetic typewritten manuscript. Now, in the middle of January, in a real town, in Upper Michigan, I found myself watching a series of events that seemed half familiar; I was unconsciously interpreting a struggle in the light of something previously known; I was witnessing a complex clash of social forces, a bitter foment of naked brutality and of almost unbelievable courage—and all of it I seemed to have known before in a play called *Marching Song*.

Yes, but with what difference and with what tribute to the author! A town of a hundred and sixty-five thousand in which a strike is being fought is not a flowing stream with a middle, beginning, and end, with a forty-five-minute first act and a dramatic curtain to the second. It is a boiling sea with a thousand eddies and a thousand streaks of color, with a thrust and swirl of current and crosscurrent. It is people and social forces churning each other at a frenzied, confusing pace. To bring real clarity to that is an artist's task. To give it meaning, order, and beauty, to treat of all things not by statement but through the human tragedy and aspiration of living people and of sensitive flesh—that is an artist's task and a hard task and that is what Lawson had done.

In the mythical town of Brimmerton, in the setting, at once symbolic and highly dramatic, of an abandoned factory left to rust, left for a hideout for broken men, Lawson has created the whole flow and beat and struggle of a town and its people. It is the play of a town, of the automobile industry, of a sit-down strike—yet it is not a play about any one of these things but rather of the varied people and groups of a community who have been captured from a real world to live more fiercely, more vividly, in the two-hour world of a stage play.

John Howard Lawson and the Theatre Union are presenting Brimmerton, U.S.A.

Lawson Crosses the Class Line

BY LESTER COHEN

JOHN HOWARD LAWSON, Broadway playwright, was picked up in a Birmingham, Alabama, court last week, jailed, grilled, ordered to leave the state.

Why?

Because he crossed the class line.

Funny thing. Just yesterday—Lawson was a respected citizen, an honored artist of our time, his plays appearing in Broadway theatres (two of them this winter), his pictures shown in the movie palaces of the world, his position in Hollywood exemplified by his unanimous election to the presidency of the Screen Writers' Guild, his associations indicated by his being asked to participate in the formation of the NRA code for motion pictures.

And today, John Howard Lawson is a seeming disturber of the peace, an exile from the fair state of Alabama—a public enemy.

Why?

Because John Howard Lawson crossed the class line, because the range of his interests extended beyond ordinary respectabilities.

He heard of the terror directed against workers and sympathizers in the present strike of the Tennessee Coal and Iron Company properties. He didn't quite believe the things he heard, he thought he'd go down South and see.

He did. Didn't see much. Didn't get a chance. As soon as he started to ask questions, as soon as he seemed appalled at company-thug murder masquerading as deputy-sheriff legality—he was picked up, jailed, cross-questioned, told to get out of the state.

Why?

Isn't a playwright to interest himself in such matters? Isn't a playwright to have a social conscience? Isn't a playwright to have a point of view on murder when committed by corporations? And who is to tell a playwright in what to interest himself—a company thug, a police court judge, or a one-way ticket out?

The answer rests with Lawson, with other writers who are experiencing the mass life and mass problems of our time, the writers who will give us the living literature and the living theatre of the modern world.

And to get it—they have to cross the class line.

Our Hall

BY MARK MARVIN

IN winter the Hall stands out prominently among the decaying frame houses and the sagging signboards that no longer attempt to entice the passing motorist. The Hall is old, and its age is reflected in its sway-backed roof, its rotten undertimbers, its treacherous steps, and its weather-beaten windowsills that soak up the cold winter rains. The Hall has been standing a long time, but its reason for existence has changed with the changing years.

Once our Hall was simply a hall, like thousands of others throughout the land—a place to meet one's friends and talk and dance and drink. When the factories began to appear in the neighborhood and poor Jews, Negroes, and industrial workers settled in around them, the hall became

OUR HALL   *Phil Bard*

the property of the Arbeiter-Ring, a group of Jewish workers and petty merchants who met to discuss socialism somewhat as a philistine discusses heaven after a good dinner among friends. But the Arbeiter-Ring lost its appeal and its following and disappeared.

The Hall is situated in the midst of a rich city crammed with food, bristling with powerful, creative machinery, fine modern homes, sunlit hospitals, stores piled high with warm blankets and clothing, and large theatres with modern stages used only as bases for the silver screen of Hollywood. The Hall lies two miles west of the million-dollar Elks Lodge with its marble floors, its spacious leather-cushioned lounging rooms. And not two blocks away is Washington school—rickety, drafty, and overcrowded with students. Stone Island is one of the large industrial centers of the Middle West but half of its factories are permanently shut down. Grass grows in the streets in front of many factory gates in the summertime. Like recently discovered Mayan cities of Yucatán, Stone Island is growing back into the wilderness. Soon, if things continue like this, Stone Island might again become recognizable to those sturdy pioneers who murdered the Fox tribes and took their lands away.

Now there is a large sign over the weather-beaten door of our Hall which reads:

NEW THEATRE
Stone Island, Ill.

Our Hall

Outside of the movie houses the only theatre in town is the New Theatre. Before 1929 there had been a little theatre which did some very interesting work. However, admission was granted to subscribers only and, since subscriptions were very high, only well-to-do people could afford to go. When the crisis came these patrons of the arts decided that drama was a useless luxury, and they allowed their little theatre to go bankrupt and disappear. As if to justify this attitude, the members of the school board discharged the teacher of drama at the local high school a year later, claiming that dramatic instruction was a "frill" which the taxpayers could ill afford.

Inside our Hall there is a small stage that was built by the Arbeiter-Ring, in the last year of its possession of the Hall, and left unwittingly as a precious legacy to us. The long Hall is crammed full of secondhand theatre seats and long benches fashioned roughly by sympathetic carpenters years ago for the crowded meetings to protest the murder of Sacco and Vanzetti.

The theatre group is at work. It is cold outside, and there is little heat within. Young men and women are working on a scene from Paul Peters's play, *Dirt Farmer*. Three of the cast have walked seven miles in the bitter cold to attend rehearsal. They do this four times a week unless by chance they bum a ride over. A tall, gaunt coal miner from out near Atkinson is speaking. He has the part of Joe, the militant farmer who leads the march on the town to obtain food for the starving farmers denied adequate relief. He says the lines simply and with great power:

> "Listen everybody. We're going to Elmira now. The thing to remember is that we're going to force them to give us food, all the food we can get. To do that we got to stick together. If we separate, if we go one by one, they'll cheat us, they'll tell us we ain't starving ..."

The director, the discharged dramatic teacher referred to before, interrupts him with a sharp "Stop!" Joe listens closely as she criticizes his interpretation of the role. The criticism was just and again they go over the scene, for the twentieth time perhaps.

They will get it right and when they do they will have achieved the full significance of the quotation painted over the proscenium: *THEATRE IS A WEAPON!* Not a blunt instrument, not a blackjack, but a fine, beautifully wrought art that recreates life and shapes its course. They will take *Dirt Farmer* into small towns along the concrete ribbons that wrinkle the surface of the prairies, and toiling farmers will observe and learn and return home to talk about a theatre that really concerns itself with their lives. And as they bury their surplus hogs and cattle in quicklime they will recall line after line from the play which makes militantly articulate their previously incommunicable plight.

In the back room a class is on: it is the Theatre Workshop, where those not busy in current productions study the social basis of the theatre, stage technique, play writing, scene designing, etc. An attractive blonde girl who works by day in a bakery is talking: she is comparing bourgeois naturalism with revolutionary realism in literature and drama. Our realism, she explains, as in *Dirt Farmer*, reflects day-to-day life but it contains the dialectic of struggle out of misery and points a very concrete way to improvement. The young bakery girl is on fire with her idea—she does not speak in the polished evenness of suave radio lecturers. Her speech is ungainly, some of her arguments a bit too schematic, but every word is charged with intense conviction.

Out in front again a different cast is working on an election skit. This is the weapon that the workers will use against the national radio hookups and the reactionary press. This skit is an uproarious comedy to be performed not on the stage but on the floor of the theatre in the midst of the audience, on street corners, or before factory gates. A pill vendor sets up his stand and in a few minutes he is selling the fake pills of the demagogue to a dubious audience. Everyone listens carefully, for every sentence is close to home, the charlatan's promises of past campaigns are exposed in their proper light, and the hypocrisy of the NRA, of rising prices, of falling wages, becomes apparent.

With the election skit and several short plays the New Theatre toured many small towns bordering Stone Island. Many workers saw legitimate theatre for the first time, and they rejoiced in a theatre which could make drama out of their lives. In one city members of a little theatre who attended the performance came backstage to find out where they could obtain such an interesting repertory. Out of this contact the little theatre—which had been producing Barrie and Pinero—began production of the antiwar play, *Peace on Earth*.

Life in and about the New Theatre is not all heroic, not all on a pitch of single-minded effort. Petty intrigues hamper the work. An occasional love affair disrupts rehearsals. There are those who appear to work awhile and then, dismayed by the steady discipline, drift away. These last are more than compensated for by those who remain to develop their talents and the theatre. It is these hard workers who have built and made secure the future of the new theatre.

Back at the hall the work goes on steadily. Finally eleven-thirty comes and those who do not have to go home early so that they can get up in time for work the next morning adjourn to a neighborhood restaurant and talk into the small hours over cups of coffee.

As the last ones leave our Hall and it is left black against the cold winter night, it seems isolated from the rest of life in Stone Island. No telephone wires run into it. The street before it is unpaved. The attendance is still comparatively small. But from our Hall an invisible current runs into nearly every worker's home in Stone Island. Our Hall seems isolated—but only to the blind, for it is linked with similar halls all over the earth.

Downtown in the shadow of the courthouse the movies disgorge their patrons. Men and women come out of the darkened houses rubbing their eyes and stretching their cramped legs and their minds, which have been held as in a vise by the fast-rolling frames of Hollywood's latest confection. As they step out of the lobbies they find themselves flung back into the world of reality—of cold winter winds and shoddy clothing, of high-priced groceries and low wages. Perhaps some, as they recall the picture they had just seen with its lovely actress suffering the pangs of love amid the luxurious furniture of an expensive penthouse, will say softly under their breaths, "It's a lie, a rotten lie with which they beat down our strength." Perhaps they will recall that one of their neighbors has told them of a theatre down near the John Stagg Plow Company's plant where plays were to be seen that dealt with their own lives, their own problems, and not with the sex lives of the Hollywood playboys and playgirls. Perhaps one will recall that his shopmate said his kid was spending all his time down at a hall working in plays that gave the lie right in the teeth of those who say that people on relief must be grateful for being treated like dogs, that showed how youths were unable to marry and live decently because they couldn't get jobs. . . . What was the name of that place, New Theatre?

THE SCOTTSBORO CASE AND THE NEW THEATRE MOVEMENT

JUST as the Sacco-Vanzetti trials aroused American and world protest in the 1920s, the nine Scottsboro boys became symbols of injustice and a rallying cry for human rights in the 1930s. A number of agitprop plays of varying merit were written and performed by workers' theatre groups the country over. I wrote one, *Free the Scottsboro Boys!*, for the Chicago John Reed Club in 1931, which was performed in a public square before

30,000 people during a May Day protest. None of the Scottsboro agit-props equaled the brilliance of Al Saxe's Workers' Laboratory Theatre version of *Newsboy*, V. J. Jerome's poem on corruption of the press. The plays served, rousing mass support that succeeded in stopping the executions of the youths. Later they were proven innocent after one of the white prostitutes, supposedly raped in a boxcar by the young black boys, confessed that the so-called rape was a frame-up a racist sheriff, threatening imprisonment, forced on her and her companion.

Before the frame-up was finally revealed, one American playwright, John Wexley, had the courage and talent to write *They Shall Not Die*, which was produced by the Theatre Guild. I have selected the following review from a number of reviews Ben Blake wrote that I admired, as I did him as a person and an editor. After the review appeared, John Wexley came to the magazine office and told Ben he agreed with the criticism that the play should have portrayed the mass support, which in the end saved the Scottsboro boys. But Wexley also pointed out that, if he had done so, even a liberal organization such as the Theatre Guild would probably not have risked producing it. The time was not ripe for such a "propaganda play" to win either drama critics' acceptance or wide Broadway audience support. We agreed with the playwright that the audiences on the left could not pay ticket prices to support such a costly production. We also agreed with Wexley's positive point of view that though our New Theatre League movement was still in a difficult struggle for existence, we had reasons for optimism about the future.

They Shall Not Die!

BY BEN BLAKE

Review of a Theatre Guild production of the play
by John Wexley, author of *Steel* and *The Last Mile*

SO RAPIDLY do events move in the theatre (as elsewhere) today that whole periods of development are often encompassed in one or two years. Only two short seasons ago, the Siftons' unemployment play, *1931*, burst like a bombshell on Broadway, inaugurating a new dramatic trend. The bourgeois critics declared it was "propaganda" and therefore not really a play. Now the Theatre Guild, most respectable of Broadway producing organizations, stages *They Shall Not Die*, John Wexley's revolutionary drama of the Scottsboro case.

In *They Shall Not Die* John Wexley has brought to powerful artistic life two of the three major aspects of Scottsboro. His first act, one of the most stirring scenes ever presented on the American stage, is a brilliant dramatization of the social attitudes and terrorism by which the Southern white ruling class seeks to keep the Negro down. The last act shows the machinery of "legal lynching"—the court, determined to burn the innocent Negroes despite the overwhelming weight of the evidence—in order to keep the Negro people down.

The main weakness of the play lies in its scanty treatment of the third and most dramatic aspect of Scottsboro—the struggle outside the courtroom, the organization of mass pressure, with millions of Negro and white workers all over the world making known their determination that the Scottsboro boys shall not die. Whereas Wexley has presented the first two aspects in terms of human character and social viewpoints in conflict, and though he has clearly brought out through the speeches of his characters the role and work of the International Labor Defense (in the play, the "National Labor Defense" or "NLD"), yet the third aspect is relegated to a few speeches and not presented in terms of dramatic action. The result is that what is probably the best revolutionary play thus far to achieve professional production in this country just misses being a truly great drama.

Though the Theatre Guild was no doubt influenced by the widespread interest in the Scottsboro case, it was nevertheless a courageous thing, from the commercial viewpoint, to stage the play at all. The Guild produced it handsomely, as is its custom. A fine cast was assembled. The production was faithful to the text.

But—and here is the most important point about the production—the Guild gave a revolutionary play the same kind of treatment, stylistically, that it gives to a drawing-room comedy or a *Strange Interlude*. "Realism," the production board, with Phillip Moeller directing, decided. And to them realism means literal faithfulness in the representation of characters, locale, tempo, and so forth. And thus the sets seek to give a picture of the jails and the courtroom as perhaps they really were (but Lee Simonson has managed to prettify them, and has, for example, made Lucy Wells's poor-white home a high-walled, spacious place where the directions called for a small, cramped shack). And since the director's imagination ran along conventional channels, he did not sense what is obvious to those who have been in contact with the revolutionary theatre in any country—that whether or not they are included in the script, this play artistically as well as every other way demands the significant utilization of the masses who play such an heroic part in any great social struggle like the Scottsboro case.

A Piscator would have done it. Any revolutionary director with a bit of imagination would have essayed it. And of course such a conception would have resulted in an entirely different type of production. The play would have abounded in dynamically staged clashes. The action would have shifted rapidly from locale to locale on sets with several playing levels, with rapid mass actions on the upper ones alternating with the action below in the courtroom. (Mordecai Gorelik's projected designs for *They Shall Not Die*, reproduced in the February numbers of *Theatre Arts Monthly* and *New Theatre*, give a good indication of what could be done along this line.) In short, this revolutionary play would have had a revolutionary production.

One other point about this production is very important. There is a tremendous potential audience for the play. But this audience cannot afford to pay prices that begin at $1.10 and go up. If the Guild is wise, it will quickly make special arrangements with labor and other organizations enabling their members to see the play at special prices.

Peace on Earth

BY JACK SHAPIRO

Review of a Theatre Union production of the play
by George Sklar and Albert Maltz, at the Civic Repertory Theatre

SOMETHING new and significant has made its entrance upon the American stage with the launching of the first production of the Theatre Union, *Peace on Earth*. The authors of the play have virtually plunged into the social-political whirlpool and have emerged to say something vitally important—a rather risky procedure for those who would invite the plaudits of the average reviewer.

Peace on Earth is to some extent the story of Peter Owens. It is more properly an incision into the threatening war situation, from which it derives its real significance. The scene of the play is a New England college town. The workers on the waterfront are on strike against a shipment of munitions. The struggle penetrates the college. A student gets into trouble through an indiscreet speech. A movement for free speech develops in the college. Peter Owens, professor of psychology, becomes involved despite a manifest reluctance and some amusing notions on his part as to the proprieties of professional conduct.

Once involved, however, ensuing events and his own basic honesty conspire to draw him further and further into the antiwar struggle.

The last act is unusual. Peter Owens is in his death cell awaiting execution. War is imminent. But with it all comes a clear triumphant note, a revolutionary prophecy. For, as he is being led to his death, an antiwar demonstration of workers is heard outside, clear and uncompromising.

Peace on Earth is therefore more than the story of Peter Owens. It is the drama of social problems and forces of momentous importance—the story of greed-enmeshed capitalism, of sterile, hypocritical pacifism, of impending war, and of revolutionary determination to struggle against it. It has no pretensions to being a detached work of art, and its grim forecast (the time of the play is "in a year or so") is something to ponder seriously.

There are many splendid individual performances. But often in the play there was a diffusion of dramatic means—which we can't go into here and now. The revolutionary theatre and drama are still in early stages. There is no doubt that toward its further development *Peace on Earth* is an important contribution.

HOW ARCHIBALD MacLEISH JOINED OUR NEW THEATRE MOVEMENT

THE most frequently asked question about my editing years was about *New Theatre*'s involvement with Archibald MacLeish. How did the famous poet move from a right-wing position, as author of *The Young Men of Wall Street* and editor of *Fortune*, to join the "cause" our magazine represented?

Here's how it happened. The phone rang at my 14th Street office, and a man's voice said, "Mr. Kline? I'm Archibald MacLeish."

I felt like answering, "Yeah, and I'm T. S. Eliot," but I refrained and asked, "Really? You're not Sol Funaroff putting me on?"

Sol was a talented young poet friend of mine who had met MacLeish at a poetry reading. Sol had failed later to convince me that MacLeish had wanted me to call him and arrange a meeting. Now here was the editor of *Fortune* calling the editor of *New Theatre*.

The voice continued, "I gather you are wondering why I'd call you. Our mutual friend Sol convinced me you would take time to consider what I have to say."

I agreed to see him, and he invited me to his home for dinner. Although I didn't want to sound rude, I was skeptical of his attitude toward me and remember asking if he would be embarrassed as a *Fortune* editor to meet me in a public restaurant. He laughed and quieted my suspicions by saying he would like complete privacy for our first meeting.

Soon afterward I was at his elegant apartment. In MacLeish's presence, I saw he was a man even more handsome than his photographs. He was still slim and graceful of movement, as he had been in his days as an Ivy League football star halfback, and held himself ramrod straight from his military service as a World War I hero. He made me feel welcome as he poured some wine, explaining he was making dinner, but that it wouldn't be ready for another half hour. I felt like asking, "What, no servants?" but I held back, determined not to show any hostility toward this writer who had long been under attack in the leftist press for being a reactionary.

He came right to the point. "I realize you mistrust me," he said.

I nodded yes, and he went on, "I've read and admired *New Theatre* for months now. On our mutual friend Sol's encouragement and from your articles, I felt you were an open-minded man who could understand that I could be deeply moved—and convinced—by your writers, especially by Clifford Odets and *Lefty*."

"Are you crediting Clifford, *New Theatre*, and me for changing your politics from right to left?"

He reached for a sheaf of papers in an open binder and said, "I didn't invite you here to make political statements about what I've felt since our awful depression—while my work and life have been mostly with the people you consider the reactionary rich. But let me read you a few scenes of the play I've just completed that I call *Panic*. Perhaps by the time we get to dinner you'll understand how I feel and mistrust me less."

In his marvelous deep voice, he began to read from his poetic drama of the Wall Street crash. His gestures were so restrained that Lee Strasberg would have approved his acting. His sincerity was convincing, and his words were those of a man baring his soul. I realized this was an experience with a truly great writer which I would never forget.

Then MacLeish looked up, like a schoolboy who has read his term paper for a teacher's approval, and asked, "Now would you trust that I am not a right-wing enemy but your friend? And would you consider publishing these scenes as my first overture to your theatre of social protest?"

I took only a few seconds to decide.

I said yes I would, even if I had to face a revolt of my staff members, who considered him a reactionary as did most *New Theatre* readers.

Then I asked him about *Fortune*, "Wouldn't you be likely to lose your prestigious, high-paid position as editor, the way Hiram Motherwell was fired from *Stage?*" (Motherwell, a former editor of the commercial *Stage* magazine, was dismissed the day after he appeared at a symposium where he stated "*New Theatre* is the most exciting, important theatre magazine in America today.")

"Probably," MacLeish said. He continued talking as he took the dish he called Vermont Style Baked Chicken from the oven and served it with the vegetables and salad he'd prepared. "I'd resign tomorrow if I felt I couldn't express my opinions without censorship, as I've done in *Panic*, dramatizing what I think of as the symbolic death of capitalism."

Then he invited me to a private performance of *Panic* costing five-fifty a seat for his wealthy business colleagues. He also asked me to bring John Gassner along as the *New Theatre* critic, and explained that John Houseman was producing the play with a nineteen-year-old actor named Orson Welles made up to play the leading role, an aging Wall Street figure facing the despair of financial failure. Then he added ruefully, "I'm afraid a wealthy conservative audience will hate my play. I wish I'd have it appear before one of your wonderful New Theatre Night audiences. I confess I sneaked in surreptitiously one night to see Odets's marvelous plays from your standing-room-only view and was swept up in the crowd's enthusiasm."

What MacLeish said gave me an idea. Since I had already met both Houseman and Welles, I suggested a follow-up performance of *Panic*. *New Theatre* would guarantee to sell out the house at our lower, not-over-one-dollar-a-ticket prices. My suggestion appealed to MacLeish, and over a delicious dinner we also agreed to hold a symposium after the play in which he would take part.

The *New Theatre*–arranged performance was sold out, and we had to turn people away. Welles and the cast were wonderful and said afterward that our audience stirred them to even better performances. Then came the symposium, where a variety of leftist viewpoints were expressed. The participants (in addition to MacLeish) were John Howard Lawson for *New Theatre*, Stanley Burnshaw for the *New Masses*, and poet V. J. Jerome (author of "Newsboy," the poem used for the agitprop play), who was considered the "cultural commissar" of Communist intellectuals. Years later in *Run Through: A Memoir*, John Houseman wrote of Jerome's effort to trap MacLeish into a pro-Communist position. But as I remember, most of the discussion dealt with the play on an artistic level—how, dramatically, MacLeish had captured the tragic life and death of his Wall Street antihero.

The "politics" came later when MacLeish expressed himself in *New*

Theatre in an article he asked me to publish as a statement of his convictions. He helped our staff choose the title, "Theatre Against War and Fascism," in which this great poet passionately affirmed his new beliefs, but always within the basic democratic traditions of American radicalism. With this statement, MacLeish joined other major American writers—Theodore Dreiser, Sinclair Lewis, Ernest Hemingway, Thomas Wolfe, John Dos Passos, James T. Farrell, Waldo Frank, and Langston Hughes—all of varying political opinions, who had become members of a worldwide alliance against war and fascism, a Popular Front, which was headed by the French activist writer, Henri Barbusse.

Theatre against War and Fascism

BY ARCHIBALD MACLEISH

TWO NIGHTS ago I read in the paper that *Waiting for Lefty* was to close. I went to see it again. It was a sweltering night—air you could hardly breathe outside and inside a slow, sweating breathlessness. There were no more than half a dozen theatres open in the city and those few barely filled. Even the gentlemen who live by having (and publishing) one dramatic reaction regularly every day like bran flakes for breakfast had given up: they were filling their news columns with personal items about parties in Hollywood. The theatre was dead—the theatre as Broadway and Broadway's intellectuals understand the word. There wasn't enough life in it to justify the ads.

That was outside the Longacre. Inside the Longacre it was also hot. Every time the curtain went down the temperature of the room went up. There was no more breeze than a hat would make hanging in a closet. But no one, after the first minute, noticed. Because inside the Longacre something was going on which made heat and air and almost everything else irrelevant. You can call it anything you like. If the word *theatre* means the kind of thing the Pulitzer Prize judges recognize and the kind of thing the critics of the one-a-day approve, then it wasn't theatre. But if it wasn't, then so much the worse for the word. And so much the worse for those who use it.

Now the point I am trying to make is not that Clifford Odets is a good playwright nor that his work is better than anything else in New

York. The first fact is pretty widely known and the second is obvious. The point I am trying to make is that Clifford Odets and the Group and a crowded sweltering audience created among them something moving and actual and alive. And the implication I am trying to suggest is that this moving, actual, living thing existed only in the Longacre theatre and not in the theatres where the regular seasonal offerings familiar to the trade were wheeling through their mannequin ceremonies.

In that point and in that implication lies a truth which American writers, revolutionary or not, cannot continue to ignore. The truth is this: The American theatre is dead and the American theatre is now alive. The American theatre is as dead as we have been saying it was for many years and the American theatre is more alive than it has ever been in its history. What is dead is the commercial theatre with all its appurtenances, all its critical and promotional paraphernalia, all its tricks, all its grimaces. What is alive is the workers' theatre with all its lacks, all its poverty, all its meagerness—and all its passion, its eloquence, its insolence, its force. The workers' theatres offer a stage and a hearing for the best work and the most honest work any writer of verse or prose is capable of doing. For the first time since I have known anything about such matters there exists a theatre in which dishonesty is not demanded, in which hokum is not a compulsory ingredient. There is offered, in other words, a theatre for art.

And there is offered also something more. There is offered an opportunity to affect the life of our time. No serious artist, no matter what he might pretend—no matter what the conditions of importance of his life might force him to pretend—has ever doubted that his art would have fundamental meaning for him only when he could feel the impact of his art not upon the appreciation of an audience, not upon the judgment of a critic, but upon the life of the generation of which he is a part. There is no greater persuader than art when it is permitted to touch the vital nerves. There is nothing more frivolous than art when it is denied access to the sources of life. In the workers' theatres art may touch and reach. It may be more powerful than the possessors of power, more serious than the creators of knowledge, more persuasive than the actions of armies.

Now, sooner or later, it is probable that the people of this country will be faced with a choice of which one alternative will be fascism. The appeal of fascism, since it has no intellectual content and no economic logic, is purely emotional. Against emotion only emotion, in the great masses of men, can fight. Against the false and journalistic emotions of fascism the real and human emotions of art must contend. There therefore exists in the workers' theatres not only an opportunity for an honest art and not only an opportunity for the impact of an honest art upon the life of this generation but an opportunity for the delivery of that impact at the precise point where it is most essential that the life of this generation should be influenced. In support of fascism, when the time comes, there will be enlisted all the forces which money can buy—the press, the movies, the commercial theatre. They will be lined up as they were lined up during the war. Their power will be overwhelming. Against them will stand the artists whom money cannot buy. And yet, and despite the discrepancy in numbers, in wealth, in everything else which creates discrepancies, the conflict will not be unequal. No power on earth can outpersuade the great and greatly felt work of art when its purpose is clear and its creator confident.

The Hope for Poetry in the Theatre

BY ARCHIBALD MACLEISH

THE PHRASE "Poetry in the Theatre" means two very different things. It is impossible to discuss it unless it is clear which of the two is intended. To some people—to most perhaps—it means a stage on which people speak in poetic language. Poetic language in this connection means elevated language, lofty language, flowery language, beautiful language. In this meaning of the phrase I have no interest. If people want elevated and flowery language on the stage they can very easily get it. Nothing is easier than the composition of such language. It is much easier to dress language up than to strip it down. There are probably several hundred thousand Englishmen and God's own quantity of Irishmen, who can write such language as against a very few men who can lay it bare. No one who wants to hear poetic language on the stage need wait very long. In fact he need not wait at all. He can hear it on Broadway in any season. There is only one thing he must not do. He must not confuse what he hears with poetry.

The other meaning of the phrase is at once much simpler and much more complicated to understand, for it means exactly what it says. It refers to the possibility of a theatre in which *poetry* shall be presented. The difference between poetry and poetic language is too obvious to discuss. Roughly it is the difference between bridge building and interior decorating. A poem is not a poem because it has a surface of poetic talk but because it is a poem in its conception, in its construction, in its whole and in its parts. It is an entire experience. Its whole quality consists in its power to present entirely, immediately, and essentially what prose can only describe or explain from the outside. Nothing could possibly be farther from poetic language than a poem.

The difficult question then is the question of finding or creating a theatre for poetry in this strict sense. It seems to me that such a theatre is becoming possible. It also seems to me that the reason why such a theatre is becoming possible now is closely related to the reason why such a theatre has not existed in the immediate past. A true poetic theatre requires for its success a community of emotional understanding between audience and stage. Precisely because its function is *not* to explain or describe but to present, poetry must make many assumptions. It enters any emotional situation at the crisis—at the third act. If it is obliged to spell out the early scenes—the background and derivation of that emotional crisis—it is lost. It is clumsy and self-conscious and lost. But if it is permitted to seize at once and directly upon the emotional crisis it is infinitely more lucid, because it is infinitely more immediate and more inward, than prose. It is for this reason that all the great poetic dramas have been dramas dealing with situations as familiar to the audience as to the poet. The situations of the great Greek plays were threadbare with familiarity. So were the plots of most Elizabethan plays—where they were not familiar, the verse, carrying too great a load of explanation, has long periods of an incredibly prosaic dullness and awkwardness. It is the essential condition of poetry for the stage that no scaffolding, no extraneous preparation, should be necessary: that the audience should be ready for the essential discovery of the verse: that the audience should be willing to believe in the emotion upon which the poetry moves.

It is this community of assumption and understanding between audience and poet which has been lacking in our society. The great common experiences carrying the great common emotions have raveled out, leaving sexuality as almost the only universal. But the emotions of sex, although they are universal, are not *common* experiences. They are, on the contrary, exceptionally personal experiences: although all men have felt the same thing they have not all felt it together. A sexual play is a communication not between the playwright and an audience but between a playwright and a roomful of individuals—a thousand whispered secrets. A theatre based upon sexuality as its one universal is a theatre in which poetry is impossible—a theatre which must itself very shortly decay—a theatre which can only take refuge in sexual perversions. For unlike the great common experiences out of which the creative emotions of love and hate and triumph and revenge may be produced, the experience of sex produces only the emotions of sex. And the emotions of sex are essentially banal and must be spiced with variety to be frequently palatable. It is this disease which has attacked the commercial theatre and which indicates its senility and the senility of the society which it reflects. Not only some of the worst but some of the best of recent Broadway plays have been plays in which sexual perversions have been desperately used to restore the vitality of a theatre which has no other life.

The basis for hope for a new dramatic poetry lies in the fact that gradually over a period of years a new community of experience has been established, a new common ground of fact supporting a new commonly felt emotion. Social injustice is no novelty in this world. Indeed it is quite probable that there is less social injustice in this century than in the last: the most academic description of an English mill of the early eighteen hundreds will make the most exciting story in the *New Masses* sound mild. What is new is the *recognition* of social injustice; the recognition specifically that it *is* injustice and that it is hateful. People a hundred years ago and fifty years ago refused to know what they knew; and people who knew it very well in their blood and in their anguish were taught that what they knew was natural and to be expected and the will of God. But with time a part of that has changed. A larger and larger number of those who suffer have come to believe that they should not suffer, and a larger and larger number of those who observe have come to see, whether they wish to see it or not, that what they see is intolerable. There is again in the world a body of experience—of facts, of names, of cities, of human suffering, of human hope—which is held in common. There is an emotion distilled from that experience which is also common. These are the elements of poetic drama.

Until that common experience is more widely shared the audience for such poetry of the theatre must be limited, as it is limited now, to groups connected in one way or another with the political Left. But as long as that common experience is so limited those who do not share it must continue to take their theatre in a rotting house and to miss altogether the delight and the excitement of the building of a new.

ANOTHER MAJOR *NEW THEATRE* DISCOVERY, JOHN W. GASSNER

ALONG with Odets and Shaw I rank as our magazine's third great discovery the drama critic who began with us and rose to national and international fame. When John Gassner joined *New Theatre* he was known as a play reader for the Theatre Guild but not as a critic. We had corresponded, and I had appreciated his criticisms sent to me in my hometown in Iowa. He had invited me to visit him at the Theatre Guild if ever I made a trip to New York City. If any of you reading this fit what *Variety* calls "Hix from the Stix," you can guess what encouragement from a Theatre Guild professional meant to a young, would-be playwright far from the bright lights of Broadway.

A few months later I visited John at the Guild. He was a small, chubby man who greeted me with warmth and took me to lunch at a good Broadway restaurant. He guessed I was near broke and needed a job. He suggested I call Elmer Rice, who had asked John to recommend a young writer as an assistant. We agreed such a job with the author of *Counselor at Law, The Adding Machine,* and *Street Scene* would be a good way to learn my craft. This led to an appointment with Rice, who treated me with consideration but explained the job would have to wait for a month or two while he was on a trip away from New York. He suggested that, if I didn't get another job before his return, I should call him again.

I was excited by the possibility, and determined to find temporary work somehow until I'd end up with the author whose plays I so admired. However, fate intervened a few days later. I have often wondered since what my life would have been if not for meeting the Group Theatre's set designer, Mordecai Gorelik. Like Gassner and Rice, he was friendly to a rather lost midwesterner and recommended me to Ben Blake, who was looking for a managing editor to aid him at *New Theatre,* a magazine founded in the early 1930s by leftist theatre groups and formerly called *Workers' Theatre.* Ben and I hit it off from the moment we met and remain friends to this day. When Ben resigned to return to playwriting, one of my first decisions as the new editor was to ask John Gassner to become our main drama critic. He came downtown from his Theatre Guild office to our comparatively crummy magazine headquarters on 14th Street to discuss his doubts that he was the best choice for this responsibility. I finally reassured him, but explained we couldn't pay contributors. Even with our rising circulation and subscriptions, we barely made rent, printing, and living money for the staff. He accepted anyway, joking, "Work now, and no pay later, huh?"

John's reviews lived up to our highest hopes and raised the prestige of the magazine, especially among Broadway professionals and in academic circles. John ended up an internationally acclaimed authority on modern drama. He was a joy to work with, always bringing his reviews on time and asking cheerfully, "Who is cutting my overlong sentences today—Molly, George, or Herb?" Then he would sit with us and edit, welcoming "criticisms of the critic" but usually improving on suggested changes. The following selections are from his contributions, which won high recognition for *New Theatre*.

Broadway Tries Again

BY JOHN W. GASSNER

AFTER an inconspicuous beginning with an Italian *Abie's Irish Rose* and an allegedly humorous melodrama, Broadway is at last well on its way through the annual game of stimulating a few people and fooling a great many. It is to be noted, however, that the beginning of the season is not without redeeming features. When one reflects upon the condition of the stage in Germany and Italy, and for that matter in England and France, a theatre that has room for several arresting efforts in a single month is not to be lightly dismissed. It is not surprising, of course, that the country which is the strongest outpost of a declining civilization should be the one to record the most energy on that sensitive social barometer, the theatre. Just as it is unavoidable that this civilization's problems and confusions, let alone hesitations, should become apparent in its art.

Symptomatic is the awakening of the theatre to the live issues of war and peace; two antimilitaristic plays within a month is something of a record. Though they cannot possibly be mistaken for masterpieces, their vitality and sincerity are beyond question. *If This Be Treason*, considered elsewhere in this issue, burns with indignation against the profiteers and politicians who play shuttlecock with men's lives, and entertains a dream of how good will may be made to prevail on this earth. Sidney Howard's dramatization of *Paths of Glory* bares the inhumanity of militarism. Both plays support their thesis with some effective playwriting. *Paths of Glory* dawdles through military maneuvers that Hollywood can present ten times more effectively than Arthur Hopkins. But once the play pulls itself together it presents a second half that commands mounting interest. Where these plays fall short of achieving a maximum effect is largely in their thinking.

Paths of Glory is ineffective insofar as it lacks a tragic heightening of its action. This can only partly be attributed to the fragmentariness of its early scenes. Basically the play falls short of tragedy because of its overcautious objectiveness. As a result the dialogue does not sing with pity and anger, the execution of the three soldiers as scapegoats for their battalion, which failed to advance under fire, becomes a special case instead of a basic indictment, and the play has no tragic release. Objectiveness is a greatly overrated virtue when the material demands a definite stand, and it is that very stand that is being consistently avoided in the play. The isolation of the scapegoat tragedy as a unique, unrelated event is almost one hundred percent complete. Not only does the execution of the soldiers depend upon the egotism of one nitwit general, Assolant, but the war itself is treated as a kind of act of God, instead of as a product of distinct and eradicable factors. Therefore the war is accepted fatalistically while thousands of lives are being wiped out and a grave travesty of justice is being perpetrated under our very eyes. Even a posy for Gandhi like *If This Be Treason* is far more challenging. If ever a play cried for the catharsis of passionate rebellion it is *Paths of Glory*. The novel by Humphrey Cobb was similarly deficient, but the fault was bound to be much more glaring in the theatre.

Maxwell Anderson's *Winterset* belongs likewise to the living theatre and is similarly defeated by its inconclusiveness. This gifted playwright has been riding two differently colored horses for a long time. He has alternated between the full-blooded romanticism of historical tragedies like *Elizabeth the Queen* and *Mary of Scotland* and the sober realism of *Saturday's Children* and *Both Your Houses*. It was in the cards that he should try to fuse the separate facets of his playwriting, to amalgamate the poet and the prose writer, the romanticist and the realist. The effort was made in last season's *Valley Forge*, but the romanticist and the realist did not mix well. In *Winterset* they do not mix at all.

In the winter of his discontent Maxwell Anderson has returned to an old wound, the Sacco and Vanzetti case, which outraged his sense of justice and drew from him that spirited, if confusing, collaboration, *Gods of the Lightning*. In his new play he is still indignant. He brings his most competent dramaturgy and his most ringing poetry to bear upon the judge whose guilty conscience has unsettled his mind and the embittered son of the electrocuted man who would clear his father's name. But Maxwell Anderson is not content to treat a contemporary theme; it is his ambition to move on to the eternal verities, and he falls back upon one of the staples of the poetic trade, "pure love," with the customary sprinkling of noble sentiments. Rightly enough, *Winterset* sees the futility and hollowness of personal revenge. The corroding single-tracked bitterness of "Vanzetti's" son is an impasse that must be broken through. Therefore, the play provides him with a vapid and melodramatic love affair for the good of his soul, at the conclusion of which he dies grandiosely and self-sacrificingly—and vainly, in a Romeo and Juliet aura! The result is a play that labors like a volcano and brings forth—a mouse. The conclusion is irrelevant; it is more than that—it is an evasion of the logic of the play, which demands that "Vanzetti's" son should substitute social vision for private hatred. His newly found love might help him to find this solution but must be subsidiary to it. We may speculate on the mote in the playwright's eye which prevents him from seeing this clearly. Is it not an aversion to the social struggle and a desire to rise above it even at the expense of logic?

The author and his apologists evade the issue when they defend the use of verse in *Winterset*. The theatre can most certainly use exalted and colorful speech for the expression of significant experiences. The trouble with *Winterset* is not its manner of saying things but what it says. Content naturally affects expression, and Anderson's dialogue is weakest when its dramatic direction is weakest, just as the characters become wooden whenever they are steeped in a miasma of poetic sentiments in which the direction of the play is forced and needlessly complicated. Incidentally, Mr. Anderson shows a surprising ignorance of working-class people, and the Communist in the first act is an inexcusable caricature in a play that purports to be a fair-minded idealistic drama. *Winterset* is half masterpiece, half pretentious melodrama and romance. Like last season's *Within the Gates*, the play is significant as a landmark in a very talented playwright's search for meaning in the world. There should be room in the theatre for this search, especially when it is so ably supported by Richard Bennett, Burgess Meredith, Jo Mielziner, who has designed excellent sets, and Guthrie McClintic, who has directed the production as well as it was possible without altering the text.

Bright Star, Philip Barry's newest play, makes a less ambitious effort to treat with social realities. Barry's forte has always been his treatment of domestic situations which have given him free play for his moderate talent for neat dialogue and sharp, though narrow, characterization. But even this favorite playwright of the elite has not been immune to the pressure of a troubled world. Essentially, a study of an egotist and social climber who marries without love and is destroyed by his sense of guilt, *Bright Star* does show the operation of his egotism in the larger field of social relations. He sells out to the conservatives, whom he supports politically, abandons his utopian industrial project, and sells the newspaper that was to be the organ of his social ideals. This play has the makings of a forceful analysis of the false messiahs, the unsteady idealists and careerists who litter the American political arena. But Barry does not follow the line of analysis that would give his play importance and dramatic force. Instead, answering the call of his early success, he finds shelter in the rarefied atmosphere of an aristocratic New England home, and contents himself with a picayune domestic tragedy. His egotist, overplayed by Lee Tracy, breaks the heart of his pure-minded starry-eyed wife, a negative woman negatively portrayed by Julie Haydon, who looks like one of Marie Laurencin's wraiths and threatens to melt into thin air while you are looking at her. A fundamental weakness of conception waters down a play that might have had power. It is becoming distressingly evident that Philip Barry's star is all too steadfast in its loyalty to his early work, which was far less bright than his admirers once seemed to believe.

Perspectives–Past and Present

BY JOHN W. GASSNER

MAN'S inhumanity to man is an eternal verity of the theatre. But the perspective changes; evil ascribed to one cause in a fourth-century Athens becomes evil ascribed to another cause in sixteenth-century London or twentieth-century New York. Nor is there any guarantee of uniformity of perspective within a given period; especially in one which, like our own, is torn by conflicting and shifting allegiances. To choose a perspective is to determine the direction and meaning of a play. To discover the perspective is to understand the play. Such decidedly divergent plays as *Bitter Stream*, *St. Joan*, and *Murder in the Cathedral*, three of the most provocative productions of the closing season, make sense only when viewed in the light of their objectives.

T. S. Eliot's object in *Murder in the Cathedral* is primarily devotional; Shaw's approach to Joan of Arc is sociopsychological; Victor

Wolfson's (like that of his model, Ignazio Silone, author of the novel upon which *Bitter Stream* is founded) is plainly sociological. Eliot is attesting the drama of religious faith; Shaw, the conflict of the progressive individual with a declining social order; Wolfson, the tragedy of a class. Correspondingly, the dramatic effect varies from the religious fervor of *Murder in the Cathedral*, to the explorative analysis, the precise diagnosis of *St. Joan*, to the hot indignation of *Bitter Stream*. At the same time, the force of the plays depends upon the relevance of the point of view. How intimately can we be involved in a drama of faith or historical investigation or immediate protest? Much depends on the workmanship, but a good deal also depends upon the playgoer's own perspective. It would be stretching a point to say that many of us will find the conflict between the medieval church and state—the issue of T. S. Eliot's play—of vital concern, though the simpler problem of faith might prove illuminating. Shaw's drama, while drawing the attention of all intelligent audiences, would find its staunchest following among persons still enjoying a measure of neutrality in the conflicts of the day. Wolfson's drama about fascist dictatorship should impress every thinking individual, but would ring the tocsin loudest in the ears of the working class and the intellectuals. This fairly distinct stratification of interest indicates little more than that the world in which we are living is a divided one. But the division is a reality that a playwright reflects as inevitably as he breathes; that the theatre reflects *so long as* it breathes. And the situation is further complicated by the fact that the playwright, like so many of his fellowmen, is more often than not divided against himself. But this, too, is an aesthetic as well as general reality, to be gauged and adjudicated before his work can be understood.

There is no inner or outer uncertainty about *Bitter Stream*. Victor Wolfson knows a wrong when he dramatizes one. His viewpoint is definite and direct. His dramatization strikes at the heart of the Fascist order in Italy when it exposes the plight of the simple, unpolitical peasants of Fontamara. The regimentation of thought which the play ridicules so acidulously is of concern to everyone who prizes the erect posture which distinguishes man from the lower animals. Fascism, however, has too often boasted its contempt for the intellect to be vulnerable in the cerebral department. But it has always vaunted itself the one-and-only defender of the little man. Yet the play makes it abundantly clear that while Fascism has been only too ready to stuff his mouth and ears, it has had no such plans for his stomach. The Italian peasants, being damnably insensitive to fine logic when they are threatened with hunger, rise in spontaneous revolt. Their uprising is crushed, but they have learned the truth about their government, and are groping for a solution when the play ends. "What must we do?" they ask themselves.

Bitter Stream makes a vivid and vastly appealing drama. That it should achieve so much power is a tribute to its vital exposition, born of a perspective that embraces the laboring masses rather than the special classes. It has the clarity and definiteness that always follow when a playwright knows what the fight is about and who the fighters are. Would that it also enjoyed the dramaturgic and directorial skill it deserves! Unfortunately, despite a rich variety of moods and situations, the play is uneven and often labored. Its first act becomes wordy and diffuse. Its satire, though effective in ridiculing regimentation of opinion, blunts its blade with too much caricature. Thus, the mayor of the village and the police official are too idiotic to be effective as villains. Here, as elsewhere, the direction is stilted and insensitive. In spite of fine characterization by Manart Kippen, an appealing performance by Lili Eisenlohr Valenty and appropriate spurts of strength by Albert Van Dekker, the Theatre Union has not given the play its full complement of theatric investiture.

But, conversely, the production would have benefited from more fully considered play writing. Though the second act is utterly moving, one misses the dramatization of such exciting events as the revolt of the peasantry, mentioned but not seen, and the diversion of the stream, merely indicated offstage. Though the conclusion makes poignant use of the groping of the peasants engrossed in composing their first underground paper, it does not constitute a fully dramatized scene and is hardly the most forceful climax one would imagine. The new social theatre sometimes evinces a fondness for leaflets as a dramatic device which I cannot share. Logic is on the side of the leaflets, and they may well play an important rôle in history, but not all of us find paper on the stage exciting. It is, further, regrettable that Berardo's self-sacrifice, comprising the bulk of the final act, should be developed so rigidly and scantily. He assumes the blame for distributing incendiary leaflets, sacrificing his life in order to save an organizer of the underground movement whom he considers more important than himself. The latter accepts the sacrifice too easily. There may be sound logic in this idea, but it requires more emotional motivation. Intellectual motivation is inadequate unless dramatized at sufficient length, as Shaw knew when he devoted two of the most rounded scenes of *St. Joan* to historical matters. Moreover, Berardo has loomed so large in the earlier scenes as a potential leader that his dismissal from the play as an individual of secondary importance is open to misconstruction. The play might almost imply that a peasant like Berardo is incapable of leadership; an implication not intended by the playwright, and contradicted by the building of an underground movement among the peasantry after Berardo's death.

Nevertheless there is no gainsaying the effect of the play. In its simple, rugged manner it unrolls a tragic situation applicable to large sections of the world and of equal importance to America. It should sound a warning against the demagoguery that is straining every tear duct with generous pity for the poor whom it intends to gag and mulct. The story of the Fontamarans is history charged with lightning immediacy.

THE CASE OF BERNARD SHAW

Wolfson and Silone are expressing a protest; Shaw, when he wrote *St. Joan*, was carrying on an investigation. The dozen or more years that have elapsed since its initial production have increased the possibility of understanding its place in Shaw's repertory. Not only has the experience of the world added much necessary clarification, but the author has come to our assistance with several later plays and a number of pronouncements. So, in a sense, has the current Katharine Cornell production, one of the most lucid as well as affecting examples of modern theatre art.

The production, no field day for a star like Miss Cornell, who belongs to the highest firmament, but a marvel of collective effort, throws the emphasis where it is most appropriate—upon the history. Each character is individualized and yet related to the institution he represents. Brian Aherne is not only Warwick, but in his palpable assurance and worldliness, he is the entire feudal order. Ciannelli and Byron are not merely priests of God but the very reason and order of the medieval church. Miss Cornell is not solely Joan of Arc, but the simple, partially masculinized womanhood of all the peasantry, as well as the very incarnation of youthful revolt against age and lassitude and caution. If, quite against Shaw's prescription, her femininity is never quite suppressed, neither is it too obtrusive. Above all, we are grateful that there is no villainy in the performances, not the faintest caricaturing of the Archbishop and the Jesuit. Joan's antagonists condemn themselves solely by the principles they exemplify. Only the slight buffooning in the court scene mars the production, but not radically. Altogether, Shaw's word becomes flesh without ever becoming carrion.

St. Joan deals with an injustice, but with reference to an individual rather than a class. Joan wins impassioned sympathy, and her persecutors a measure of opprobrium, but in line with Shaw's spirit of inquiry the drama revolves around a series of questions. What was the secret of Joan's success on the field of battle? Pure hypnotism or mental suggestion, is Shaw's reply; she breathed courage into the defeated troops. Why was she done to death? Of course the British, whom she was driving out of France, wanted her out of the way. But why did the French allow her to perish, and why did the Church that later canonized her order her to be burned at the stake? Shaw concludes that she was the victim of a profound, if still undefined, social conflict, the first phase of the struggle between declining feudalism and emergent capitalism. She was guilty of both political and religious heresy when, reflecting the new spirit of the people, she exemplified the progressive tendencies of her time—namely, nationalism and Protestantism. Her self-assurance told her that she, a child of the people, could confer and collaborate with the central authority, the king, without the interposition of the feudal nobility, making the latter superfluous. By the same token she would communicate directly with her God without the help or so much as the guidance of the Church. She could be acquitted on a dozen or more popularly understood charges which were not fundamental, but the Church could not forgive her Protestantism.

Shaw's analysis is a masterpiece of intellectual construction, in dramatic terms so powerful as to refute forever the notion that reasoning and argument are alien to drama. He has often been derided for his borrowings. Shaw, however, borrowed shrewdly in *St. Joan* when he ignited his imagination with a spark from the Marxian theory of history.

But Shaw has also borrowed from Shaw! One notes his preference for quips which we must sometimes forgive him, his gift for oratory which one admires in him, and, most considerably, his fondness for the exceptional individual. His own brilliance, his Fabianism (with its socialism from above!), his scorn for the Victorianism of his youth, and his sizable borrowings from Europe's most confusing philosopher, Nietzsche, have disposed him in favor of superior beings. His supermen and superwomen have notably enriched the field of comedy, but in none of the other plays, not even in *Candida*, is there so warmly, so humanly conceived a brilliant character as Joan. The other characters have been largely remote figures, sports of nature, mouthpieces of a very voluble dramatist. It is otherwise with the peasant girl from Lorraine. She is bright but not infallible, superior to fools but not wiser than wise men, merely more bravely young. Hers is the collective intelligence, the superior common sense of the common people. We are in love with her because she is one of us—so high and dazzling and yet so near in her simplicity, so frail in her person and yet so strong with the strength of the common man who has held his own through long dark ages of struggle with natural and man-made evils. In *St. Joan* there is a synthesis between the private individual, upon whose infinite appeal depends the surging personal emotion of the play, and the collective phenomenon, the struggle between an old and new world. It is understandable that Shaw should have reached the summit of his art here; he reasons and feels at the same time as never before.

Masterpieces, however, do not as a rule merely flatter their creator; by shedding light upon his work as a whole, they are as likely to reveal his vulnerability as his strength. How easily could Joan have become just another Shavian character just too clever to be alive? How easily could her drama have become an over-simplified Shavian conflict between intelligence and a consistently stupid world? The epilogue in which her antagonists confess their error, though otherwise eloquent and beautiful, verges on this error. Burning obscuring incense to Joan the superwoman, the epilogue, with its sentimental afterthought of pity for all superiority in the world, detracts from the body of the play, which needs no addenda to its splendid analysis. The epilogue causes no basic damage because the architecture of *St. Joan* is too strong to be shaken; but it throws a revealing light on Shaw, who is for socialism on Mondays, Wednesdays, and Fridays and for fascism on Tuesdays, Thursdays, Saturdays, and Sundays. Worship of the superman, along with Fabianism, has left the grand old man stranded in a world which mere intelligence has been unable to save.

HAROLD CLURMAN'S TOO FERVENT YEARS

I WILL always admire Harold Clurman for his great contributions to the Group Theatre, and remember his warm relationship with *New Theatre* and myself from the day we met at a Group rehearsal. Throughout 1934 to 1936, Harold took time from directing and other activities to write for our magazine and, up to my departure for Spain, we met many times, both professionally and personally. But the strangest meeting was at his favorite restaurant, the Russian Tea Room, adjoining Carnegie Hall on Fifty-seventh Street, where years later he invited me to lunch.

This was shortly after publication of Clurman's *The Fervent Years,* which, despite certain unfortunate omissions, ranks as the classic history on the Group Theatre period. Over the hot borscht I avoided a cold response to Harold's query how I liked his book. I responded that it lived up to everything I expected of him except . . . He interrupted in his usual volatile manner, "Except the way I chickened out about *New Theatre?*" I shrugged as he continued, "I asked you here today because I want to apologize, Herb. I realize how you must feel about my avoiding mention of the role of the magazine, the New Theatre League, and all of your cooperation with Lee, Cheryl, and myself in the Group Theatre. But my publishers insisted that I should avoid being open to 'red-baiting.' With my consent they cut an entire chapter about you, your brother Mark, Molly, Kazan, even my participation with Clifford and you in the early *Lefty* days."

"You were the author, Harold, you didn't have to give in," I replied. We discussed matters Harold had left out of his book: how he, Strasberg, Crawford, Kazan, and Meisner had joined Mark in forming the New Theatre League School, where Harold, Kazan, and Meisner had taught classes that were forerunners of those at the Actors' Studio.

Harold nodded and said he hoped I would understand that congressional committee terrorizing of writers and theatre and film leftists had frightened him as it had his publishers. He felt the important thing was to get *The Fervent Years* published with its main story of the Group Theatre.

"I guess you regret now being 'too fervently Left' then." I recalled the titles of some of Harold's fine articles in *New Theatre*: "Interpretation and Characterization," "Soviet Diary." Then I reminded him of his article calling Mark's and the New Theatre League's publication of *Theatre Workshop* "a signal event in the development of a theatrical culture in America."

I'm afraid neither of us enjoyed this tense luncheon very much, but we talked awhile, as theatre and film people do, about present and future projects. We were interrupted several times by mutual friends, but made no mention of our self-censorship discussion. We met again and again, especially at Harold's fascinating lectures on play writing and directing at the Actors' Studio. But he never mentioned plans to publish the missing chapter and he never did. Otherwise, I remain a fervent fan of the great talents of Harold Clurman.

Interpretation
and Characterization

A THEATRE WORKSHOP DISCUSSION

BY HAROLD CLURMAN

WHEN I returned from the Soviet Union last June, New York had a strange effect upon me. Nothing had changed in the eight weeks of my absence, yet everything had somehow altered its meaning. To sum up my impression: my whole environment—my good friends and intimates, the plays I saw, the books I read, the newspapers I scanned, the conversations I heard—all seemed a bit mad! People complained about woes that were mostly imaginary, overlooked conflicts that were immediate, belied their thoughts by their acts, explained their acts by ideas they professed to scorn. Many spoke of saving and spent beyond their means, others talked of sacrifice to ideals and wasted their time, still others clamored for things they had no real interest in, and waxed skeptical over struggles that were essential to their happiness.

When I came to direct Clifford Odets's new play, *Paradise Lost*, the contradictions that are at the base of almost every scene became clear to me through my own experience of a few months back. This crazy world that Clifford Odets had wrought out of sheer artistic perversity, as some might believe, or out of a desire to emulate the great Chekhov, as many have said, or even out of a "Marxian prejudice," as the ignorant would have it—this crazy world was simply the world we live in—or to be more exact the middle-class world of our daily experience.

All the characters in *Paradise Lost*—excepting only Clara Gordon, the mother, and two of the workers from the shop delegation—are a trifle "touched." This does not make them "exceptional"—on the contrary, it makes them like us—but it was my job as the director to make the characters' madness clear not merely as "realism" but *as a comment*. Beyond this, there was the problem of making an audience feel what it was that all these characters were doing in their madness, what possibly caused the madness and how it was connected with the life of the spectator. The main problem in the direction of *Paradise Lost*, in other words, was the problem of finding characterizations that were true to the individuals yet part of an organic conception which made their world, despite particular differences, a common one.

Why are the characters in *Paradise Lost* funny? Why are they bewildered, tragic, grotesque, violent as the case may be? They are all looking for reality in a world where nothing is altogether real, where there is something insubstantial and dreamlike in the most ordinary processes of behavior. The world of the ruling class is real in the sense that the rulers know where their interests lie, work hard and fight systematically to protect them against every possible enemy; the world of the working class is real because its struggle is so primitive and plain that there is no mistaking or avoiding it. But the middle class carries out the orders of the ruling class with the illusion of complete freedom, and it is sufficiently protected from the terror of material nakedness to believe in transcendental explanations of human woe that keep it "calm" without really satisfying it. There is no "enemy" in the middle-class world except an intangible "fate"; there is no fight except with one's own contradictions—and real life (the life that both the upper and lower classes know in their opposite ways) enters upon the scene like a fierce, unexplained intruder.

Though this interpretation may be regarded as "personal," it is the director's job to proceed from some such general conception to the minute details of the production. A more Chekhovian—that is, a less social view—might be taken of the play which would tend to make it "sadder," more fatalistic and generally "true to life" in the meaningless sense of the word! The "reading" I have given the script gives the play a definite *line* or what certain reviewers would call a propagandist slant. Also the comedy has been made organic with its tragedy, whereas in relation to the rest it might easily seem a forced whimsicality. Certain tragic characters like Leo have been treated more humorously than the text indicates; the musician Felix has been made less "sympathetic" than the author intended, the daughter of the house is taken a trifle less heroically in the production than in the script. In the following notes I sketch some of the character interpretations, but a comparison of my statements with the published book will show throughout the addition of "business" and motivations that are distinct from, though compatible with, the play's lines. The text (the author's work) and the subtext (the director's treatment) in these remarks are given as a unified whole.

Leo Gordon, the "hero" of *Paradise Lost*, is an unusual man only in the sense that few middle-class people are so aware of their own subtle misery or so fervent in their desire to cure it. He is always trying to remedy the suffering he sees about him, but being typically middle class he does not know how to do it. He would like to make war on injustice but does not know what weapon to use and any weapon more concrete than ideas frightens him.

How do we portray such a character in the theatre? We see his kindness not only in the actions given him by the author but in such a detail as his instinctive caress of the girl worker whom he wants to reassure. We visualize his confusion before simple objects and his inadequacy even in trivial situations. When the workers come to visit him, he is embarrassed and clumsy: He offers one of them a chair when there is none to sit on; at another time he serves brandy, which he thinks is the same as wine; he dashes after his partner to convince him that wages in the shop must be raised, but he hesitates at the last moment, retreats to his own apartment, sits down, rises impetuously again, hammers his resolve on the table, and then proceeds to get drunk! He traces imaginary figures in the air as he listens to memories of the past; he rarely completes any movement. As each act develops, the character becomes soberer and more direct. Only in the end do we establish a stronger tone for him—something to suggest that now at last he may become an integrated person. Yet even his eccentricities in the first two acts are made to arise from a vital sensibility, a capacity for love.

Marcus Katz, Leo's partner, written with a certain comedy explosiveness, is given an even more tragic interpretation in the production. He wants to be loved, but everyone hates him. Why? In order to exist as a small capitalist he is forced to do ugly, shameful things. Leo concerns himself only with the "artistic" side of the business, but Katz himself must do the dirty work, and for this he earns nothing but scorn or suspicion. He questions everybody. "Why are you better than I? I do the things I have to do in order to provide the wherewithal which enables you to cultivate the airs of a fine gentleman. Why then am I the most despised of men?" The answer he gives himself is that because he does the terrible things that business demands he is actually better than anyone else. This is the source of his madness.

Gus Michaels, the family friend, fights imaginary battles and boxes with nonexistent contestants, cries apropos of most of his grievances because he wants to assert his right to live even though he has never been able to earn a living. The man who fails in our middle class is generally looked down upon; unless he is strong he will always hanker for that degree of "respectability" which is denied him. So Gus vacillates between his true nature—an imaginative, sensitive one—and the stupidities of the bourgeois world he would like to feel part of. His greatest satisfactions are in his dreams and his memories of the past. I have tried to visualize all this in production by numerous small details which make clear both the positive and negative side of the character.

The equivocal Mr. May, the man who arranges fires so that troubled businessmen may collect insurance, is also a seeker after reality! He knows his little occupation is an illegal one, but if a fine "front" is put on it, if his vocabulary shows a degree of refinement and "ethics," what he is selling will find a buyer in the middle-class world. To sell at a profit is real—it is almost the only reality which is universally accepted in our society! So that the most "ordinary" character in the play, the one whose mental process is most "average" and most "normal"—the dull salesman of the play becomes in production the most insane, the most stylized figure of all. The details of dress, of makeup (the actor's hair does not naturally grow red), the conjurer's mannerisms, the sweetened speech is the director's way of making a theatrical comment on the scene, a means of saying: "What the author has written here is the grotesque and tragic farce of our class life."

And in each character, whether "sympathetic" or not, I have tried in a similar manner to create through a definite quality of behavior or through special imagery the salient contradictions—the craziness!—of these middle-class types. Mrs. Katz knows the secret of her husband's tragedy, she protects him at all times, following him always, picking up the refuse he makes wherever he goes, always excusing herself for the trouble he causes. Foley, the local politician, is a good fellow, believing sincerely that Tammany is a kind of philanthropic society, but despite his hearty manner, we understand from the way he treats his henchman, from his reaction to the slightest word of criticism, the brutality that goes with his "Democratic" kindness. Pearl, Leo's pianist daughter, is the type of romantic artist who from deep hurt tries to live in an ivory tower of "pure beauty": her loneliness, her frustration, her almost comic adjustment to everyday life is embodied in slightly distorted physical mannerisms.

It is impossible in the space of a short article to point out all the ramifications of the director's problem, the pitfalls and obstacles that may attend its solution or the errors that may be committed in its name. Suffice it to say, that the scene (designed by Boris Aronson), though adequate to the naturalistic demands of the play, is not quite in the tradition of the realistic box-set. It is abstracted to convey the sense of any middle-class room, to give some feeling of a "home" which is the actual milieu of the play without sacrificing the quality of a *stage* as a place where artists have a right to express something more than the "naked facts."

PAINTER TURNED DRAMA CRITIC

CHARMION VON WIEGAND'S main interest in the arts was as a painter and art critic. We met first when her husband, Joseph Freeman, whom I knew as both editor of the *New Masses* and as a distinguished literary critic, introduced Charmion as "the daughter of Karl Von Wiegand." I could hardly believe that William Randolph Hearst's famous foreign editor was the father of this brilliant and extreme-left radical young woman. At that time, the Hearst press was the symbol of yellow journalism, and Von Wiegand had won fame on the staff of rabble-rousing, warmongering journalists whose campaign over the sinking of the *Maine* had involved the United States in the Spanish-American War. Our meeting was just a few years before Orson Welles depicted these events in *Citizen Kane*.

Charmion avoided any discussion of her father and turned the conversation to her opinions of playwrights she admired, from John Howard Lawson to Eugene O'Neill. I thought her remarks were brilliant and asked Joe Freeman why he didn't have her write for the *New Masses*. He said that she wasn't that political but suggested that I try to add her criticisms to those of Gassner, whom both of them admired. Charmion enthused over the idea. She agreed to do a piece on Lawson for our next issue, but said she would need "more writing time and more space" to do justice to O'Neill. She went on to talk about her essays, and I got so excited by the potential of such major pieces that I asked her to write without a deadline for any particular issue. Just to do them in her own time. I had John Gassner read them in addition to Molly, George, Mark, and myself, and John said wistfully, "If only I could write such special pieces for you instead of trying to cover so much each month." However, adding Von Wiegand's writings to those of Gassner raised the stature of *New Theatre* in the eyes of theatre people like Lee Strasberg, Harold Clurman, and Cheryl Crawford, whom I considered far greater authorities than anyone else I knew.

I often wondered whether Karl Von Wiegand ever read the copies of *New Theatre* I sent to him. One thing for sure, neither he nor Papa Hearst ever imagined that when we were short of money for lithographs we got them done free of charge by Hearst art department workers who were secretly opposed to Hearst policies and sympathetic to our views and eager to help. When we confided how we got hundreds of dollars' worth of lithographs for *New Theatre* at Hearst's expense, Charmion said that would make her doubly pleased to contribute her articles without the payment we could not afford.

Her article on theatre comes first, those on Chaplin and Reinhardt in our later selections for the movie section from *New Theatre*.

The Quest of Eugene O'Neill

FROM THE MOON-DRENCHED CARIBBEES TO THE FOOT OF THE CROSS

BY CHARMION VON WIEGAND

WHEN *The Hairy Ape* was produced by the Provincetown Players in the spring of 1922, a number of radical literati jumped to the conclusion that Eugene O'Neill had written a revolutionary, even a proletarian play. Nothing could have been further from the truth. Because of this initial error, radicals in 1934 were astonished and disappointed to see *Days Without End*, a play in which O'Neill sought refuge in the bosom of the Catholic church. They felt as if he had betrayed not only them but himself.

Yet few playwrights of modern times have been more consistent. The journey from the moon-drenched Caribbees to the foot of the cross has been a steady and necessary progression. O'Neill himself has made no bones about the meaning of *The Hairy Ape*, although he never grasped the full implications of his own play. In 1924, he wrote:

"*The Hairy Ape* was propaganda in the sense that it was a symbol of man, who has lost his old harmony with nature, the harmony which he used to have as an animal and has not yet acquired in a spiritual way. Thus, not being able to find it on earth nor in heaven, he's in the middle, trying to make peace, taking the 'woist punches from bot' of 'em.' This idea was expressed in Yank's speech. The public saw just the stoker, not the symbol, and the symbol makes the play either important or just another play. Yank can't go forward, so he tries to go back. This is what his shaking hands with the gorilla meant. But he can't go back to belonging either. The gorilla kills him. The subject here is the same ancient one that always was and always will be the subject for drama, and that is man and his struggle with his own fate. The struggle used to be with the Gods, but is now with himself, his own past, his attempt to belong."

Here we have from the author himself the key not only to *The Hairy*

Ape but to his entire works. Hailed as a daring innovator in the drama, O'Neill was never a revolutionary writer—neither in content nor in technique. The rebellion which he dramatized was rooted in old moral presuppositions. It is true that in his early plays there appear proletarians: sailors, stokers, farmers, Negroes, poor whites, white-collar intellectuals. But these characters—seen through the eyes of their author, who never penetrates beneath the surface to their real psychology—embody merely the more lurid, romantic, exterior aspects of such people. When O'Neill develops a character internally, the character is always a middle-class intellectual seeking to escape into another class.

This type of escape resembles somewhat the annual excursion of the summer tourist to Europe: he deserts his native milieu for a foreign and exotic one; here, unhampered by home conventions, he temporarily enjoys a spurious freedom. But it would never occur to this tourist to take out citizenship papers and to settle down in a foreign country. It never occurs to O'Neill to desert his own class and to align himself with the working class.

In his first plays, O'Neill employed the sea or the farm as a backdrop for the romantic dissatisfaction with life. He portrayed sympathetically a series of poor, morbid, unhappy characters. In the Broadway theatre with its indoor drawing-room setting and its conventional bourgeois characters this was a startling novelty. But never once did O'Neill explore the depths of his characters; never did he indicate that their psychic disturbances had roots in social ills. The misery of the poor as of the rich was always ascribed to a malignant fate working havoc with man's life.

DRAMA AND WILL

From the beginning, O'Neill has been the dramatist of the petit bourgeois intelligentsia, lost between the heaven of the upper classes and the earth of the proletariat. Not yet fifty, he has written a score of full-length plays and half as many short ones. He is at an age when his most mature creative work might be expected to be ahead; yet his plays may already be viewed in retrospect, since, like his illustrious literary forebears, Chateaubriand and Huysmans, he has collapsed in the arms of the church. The dramatist who will emerge after such a religious conversion can never be quite the same as he who wrote *The Great God Brown* and *Desire Under the Elms*.

At bottom O'Neill's ideas are the ideas popularized by the French

Revolution. This is why his development so closely parallels the development of the famous romantics of the latter part of the nineteenth century.

The primary problem of Western drama has always been the problem of the will in action. In a period of cultural upsurge, the social will of the individual is healthy and functions normally toward a given goal, which may be reached by active striving. In a decadent period, on the other hand, when society is sick from ill-balance, the social will of the individual becomes weak, hesitant, atrophied, incapable of consciously striving toward a goal, and the goal itself becomes obliterated, obscure, or split into numerous goals. Of course a healthy society may contain individuals with sick wills. In the robust period portrayed by Shakespeare, we find a Hamlet, but it is interesting that, in spite of Hamlet's conflict and indecision, he achieves action in the end. Whereas in an ailing society, the will of a healthy individual may assume all the characteristics of the illness of the society. Both Hedda Gabler and Rebecca West were women of strong will without any outlet for their thwarted energy; both, in the society in which they lived, were doomed. Long ago in the nineteenth century dramatists in Europe had begun to feel the laming of the will which came with a slowing of the creative processes in bourgeois society and their plays reflected the conflicts which grow out of the dislocation of the will and the deed. The climax comes in the drama of Chekhov, where we are treated to a picture of a will-less intelligentsia throttled by censorship, deprived of political life, and sentenced to a goalless, aimless existence without even the hope or the desire for action. The favorite characters of O'Neill all exhibit a serious conflict of the will.

In order to grasp more fully the meaning of O'Neill's plays, it is necessary to examine the social roots of his development. The postwar period in the United States witnessed a revolt of the secure and increasingly prosperous middle-class intelligentsia from the conformity, ugliness, and standardization of Main Street, with its Babbitt concern for church socials, sports, movies, gin, and clandestine sex. In literature there were many spokesmen of this revolt, which spread like prairie fire throughout the country. An integral part of the new mood was the little theatre movement. The Carol Kennicotts of cultural adventure, who could not escape to the South Seas, Spain, or Greece, set up temples of art in the family barns, where they burned their orange candles at both ends in homemade Bohemias patterned after Greenwich Village and Provincetown. They demanded plays which voiced their inner discontent and which could be produced with two yards of theatrical gauze and a set of kitchen chairs and table. At this time, O'Neill, who had spent a year in Professor Baker's famous playwriting class Harvard 47, was turning out one-act plays simple enough for amateurs, yet embodying what seemed at the period a stark, relentless realism with a poetry of discontent profoundly nostalgic.

A HOSTILE COSMOS

O'Neill was at first above all a spokesman against Main Street—the drab conventional life of the "average" American. His revolt took the form of flight. Sailing on a Norwegian ship for Buenos Aires, he experienced the life of a sailor at firsthand. In all, he made four sea voyages and became an able seaman. Contact with crude reality, which remained in some respects his chief experience with the external world, left an indelible impression on his sensitive nature. The result was a series of one-act plays later produced under the name of *SS Glencairn*. All deal with the sea; the gorgeous moonlight nights of the Caribbean, its tropic islands, its sinuous brown women, are contrasted with the hard-drinking, hard-working lives of the sailors. These plays are in some respects the best things O'Neill ever wrote; their mixture of poetry and bad language was refreshing in the stale theatre of the period. Today their realism seems tinctured with romantic tradition and their bad language has become a convention in literature, a convention developed and handled with more mastery by Hemingway and other younger writers.

Seemingly formless both in technique and content, these early one-act plays contain the gist of O'Neill's major concern—the struggle of his own ego with the universe. He constructs a primitive, hostile cosmos pervaded by a blind fate hanging like the sword of Damocles over man's life—a fate in no wise affected by social forces or relationships. All his work mirrors a baffled quest for the long-lost innocence of happy childhood: his plays are never ends in themselves but stepping-stones toward his unreal goal. Fruitlessly the quest has led him away from reality to each of the traditional escapes of the romantics.

II

O'Neill's first really organized effort at drama was the long play *Beyond the Horizon*. Here he counterposed the romantic symbol of the earth as the mother of man and the sea as the symbol of freedom, dramatizing the conflict between the farm and the sea as if these two elements were the chief characters of the drama. The actual characters and the setting are naturalistic, yet there is a tremendous yearning to escape from the material and concrete in life. Robert and Andrew Mayo are brothers—already indicating the dual nature of O'Neill later fully developed in *The Great God Brown* and *Days Without End*. The former longs to go to sea to seek his dreams "beyond the horizon" and the latter longs to till the soil and create something from it. But fate intervenes in the person of Ruth, who promises love to Robert. The roles are reversed. Andrew, the practical man, goes to sea; Robert the dreamer remains to run the farm. Both suffer disillusionment and failure, for inherently both are the romantics, who cannot face reality. The plot of the play is developed like a novel, and this technique is used to spread the story over a long period of time. In this way the author evades bringing the characters together at a crisis, which would involve choice and a directive willpower. This evasion is not due to O'Neill's ignorance of the rules of the well-made play, for he was brought up in the Broadway theatre, and from the beginning understood its craft; it must therefore be attributed to a psychological aversion to a crucial choice! Time solves the problems of the characters in *Beyond the Horizon*; through the long years they remain passive instruments of an environmental fate. They scarcely ever act, and when they do they act to their own detriment; as in Act I when Robert, about to fulfill his desire of going to sea, changes his mind at the last moment and sends his brother instead. In fact the whole plot is evolved from this false choice, which proves an evil fate to everyone. Perhaps Robert was a victim of what the Freudians call *scheitern am Erfolg*, that catastrophe on the threshold of success, which comes from the fear of it. He did not dare to face the consequences of realizing his heart's desire, the voyage to sea. Hence his action in giving up the sea is not an act of will but an escape from the consequences which an act of will involves. His brother Andrew, while supposedly practical, is haunted by the same fate—a desire to escape from his heart's desire. Thwarted in love, he leaves the farm, his life work, and goes to sea, gaining prosperity and betraying his love of the soil by speculating in wheat.

O'Neill's repudiation of action and his emphasis on natural environment rather than on social background, have led him to depend on mood to carry his drama. Already in this first play, he is a master of mood. He is able to create atmosphere, an atmosphere that overhangs and sweeps through his later plays—the primitive sounds and colors of the jungle in *The Emperor Jones*, the macabre, sensual-puritan conflict in *Desire Under the Elms*, the morbid decaying lilacs of *Mourning Becomes Electra*. In this sense, his plays often achieve lyric poetry.

Compare O'Neill's last play, *Days Without End*, with his first long effort, *Beyond the Horizon*. The dialogue shows no inner development, no essential quality, that makes it inevitable, nor does it lend itself to quotation when torn from the context. When one remembers how the dialogue of Shakespeare has enriched the English language or even how Bernard Shaw's quips have enlivened the conversation of the present-day intelligentsia, one has an inkling of what creative dialogue may accomplish.

In *Beyond the Horizon* O'Neill's dialogue is cast in naturalistic form, but the speech misses the tang of spoken language. Only in ecstasy, madness, or drunkenness do his characters speak out of themselves as if from an imperative urge. Hence in later plays, where he shifts from naturalism to supernaturalism, the dialogue has a more sensitive quality. Like his master, Strindberg, O'Neill is most at home when he is dealing with neurotic, overstrained individuals. The theme of madness is ever recurrent in his plays. It occurs already in one-act plays *When the Cross Is Made* and *Ile*, and it is developed further in *All God's Chillun Got Wings*, *Strange Interlude*, *Dynamo*, and *Mourning Becomes Electra*.

It is O'Neill himself who has revealed that the sea, which is the romantic symbol of man's freedom in *Beyond the Horizon*, is a snare and delusion. In the one-acter, *Ile*, the wife of a whaling captain has dreamed of the free, noble life on shipboard, but taken on a voyage, she discovers that it is merely another form of captivity, enlivened by brutality, meanness, and monotony. When her husband insists on heading the ship northward away from port, and she is doomed to remain on board, she goes mad. Insanity may be an escape for some individuals but it solves no problems for the world as a whole. Hence O'Neill is compelled to seek some other romantic solution for human happiness.

Yet having portrayed life on the farm as drudgery, poverty, and monotony and life at sea as the same dull routine, O'Neill is still incapable of making the final judgment; that it is capitalist society which condemns the worker to slavery regardless of environment.

He continues the search for happiness in *The Emperor Jones*. Because of its use of expressionist technique and its choice of a Negro for hero, this play was the sensation of its time. Actually its basic idea is as old as Rousseau. We have the return to nature in the person of the simple, happy savage unhampered by the cares of civilization. The hero, an ex-Pullman porter, a civilized American Negro, with all the vices of the white man, has made himself king of a tropic island. Threatened by the natives, whom he has ruthlessly exploited, he plans escape back to civilization, where he may enjoy his stolen gains; but caught in the jungle, his progress becomes a backward journey into the racial memories of primitive existence and only the fatal legendary silver bullet stops his flight.

THE MEANING OF EXPRESSIONISM

The Emperor Jones departed from the conventional theatre of the time in two ways. It broke with the technique of the well-made play, with its solid three or four acts building to a climax. Instead it presented the scene succession of expressionist drama most successfully. The method was in keeping with Jones's flight through the forest and the fantasies he meets. Actually the play is a monologue with pantomime, for the other characters are either shadows of Jones's dream or else are introduced for local color and atmosphere. Jones is the sole protagonist.

O'Neill has been accused of borrowing this new stage technique from the Germans but he has denied the influence. There is no reason to doubt that he came to the method independently of the postwar German dramatists. But both the Germans and O'Neill have been profoundly influenced by Strindberg, who is actually the father of modern expressionism. It was Strindberg even more than Ibsen who reflected the breaking up of the organic relationships of bourgeois society and mirrored the resulting soul sickness of the intelligentsia. In Strindberg unconscious fantasy takes possession of the stage and drives out the everyday world. This was already apparent in the later Ibsen of *When We Dead Awaken*.

Expressionism represents not a beginning but an end. It celebrates the destruction of old forms in art and society and their dissolution into separate units. In expressionist art, the boundaries of form are loosened. Drama approaches painting and music, painting simulates music, and music painting. Likewise the boundary between the natural and the supernatural is obliterated. The dream assumes the vividness of reality and reality takes on the color of the dream life. Literature disintegrates into words and the words themselves lose meaning and become merely sound. Form in painting is dissolved into juxtaposed spectral colors. The disintegration of a social class sends its destructive vibrations into the most distant ivory towers of the intelligentsia, and the arts prophetically assume the sunset colors of the end. Expressionism in painting, poetry, drama, and music was perfected by the postwar Germans; it was a technique adapted to the petit bourgeois intelligentsia in pursuit of its own soul across the chaos of German society before that same intelligentsia had split into fascist and communist partisans. Eugene O'Neill, also a member of the petit bourgeois intelligentsia, unconsciously selected a method appropriate to a period of crisis in the halcyon days of the twenties in America and thus prophesied all unawares the coming economic and social crisis in a period of apparent prosperity and stability.

III

At the time of its first production, many people believed that in *The Emperor Jones* O'Neill had intended to champion the cause of the Negro. As a matter of fact, he was not at all interested in the Negro and his actual problems in the United States. Nor did he ever make any pretense of championing the Negro as a member of an oppressed race caught in the toils of imperialist exploitation. He used the Negro as a symbol of the lost paradise of the primitive world, a world as much a part of the white race as of the black. His interest in the Negro as a hero derived merely from his quest for happiness, and an unsuccessful attempt to solve it by a return to primitive nature. It is O'Neill himself who is hidden behind the black mask of Jones.

The story of the play may have been derived from some legend of the strange emperor Christophe in Haiti but O'Neill had no interest in the actual island of Haiti. He found there merely a jungle backdrop. Nor had he any interest in the history of the struggle of the Negroes of the islands. In a recent Soviet novel, *Black Consul*, the struggle of the islands for independence in the period of the French Revolution has been depicted. Against its social background, we see the full stature of that heroic Negro leader, Toussaint L'Ouverture. What a contrast to Emperor Brutus Jones, who is given all the vices and none of the virtues of the whites. Contrasted with him is Smithers, the white cockney, a thief and degenerate, who nevertheless feels himself the superior of Jones. O'Neill implies that white supremacy will always exist, that the human being is not capable of progress, that life does not change. The ex-Pullman porter who has acquired civilization, put back in his native environment, retrogresses to savagery and his aboriginal fears. With O'Neill, the Negro is always represented as a degenerate savage or ineffectual neurotic.

THE NEGRO AS SYMBOL

In the one-act play *The Dreamy Kid*, we see a young Negro gangster who has committed murder but who has a sentimental and superstitious fear of leaving his dying grandmother and this fear leads to his capture. In that play of miscegenation, *All God's Chillun Got Wings*, the hero is a studious and sensitive Negro, but the peevish and malevolent destiny which governs O'Neill's cosmos allows no way out for him, any more than for the Emperor Jones or the Dreamy Kid. This story of a mixed marriage raised a storm of protest at the time of its first production. But on examination, it is apparent that O'Neill only superficially departed from the prejudices of his class as regards the Negro. If he had intended to pose the problem whether there could be a happy marriage between a Negro and a white, he would have chosen two equals to mate; the conflict would thus have been all the more intensely dramatic. Instead O'Neill leaned over backward in his attempt at fairness and in this action reveals his prejudice. For the story sets forth how Jim Harris and Ella Downey are doomed to fail from the start, but the failure of their marriage is not due to a difference of races but to a difference of culture. Brought up together on the East Side pavements, Jim, the Negro boy, and Ella, the Irish girl, were childhood sweethearts. But when they meet years later and marry, life has dealt very differently with them. Ella has been a prostitute and has been deserted by her lover, the gangster Mickey, after she has borne their illegitimate child. Jim, on the other hand, is a sensitive, educated man, well off from the money his father earned trucking. Ella accepts Jim because he can give her security but grows to hate him because she feels inferior to him both in culture and character. This arouses her race antagonism and she tries to keep Jim down in order to keep her self-respect. She centers her neurotic conflict around making him fail at his law exams. She can maintain her white "superiority" only by making clear to him that he is too stupid to pass the white man's test.

O'Neill sends Jim and Ella to Europe, as if to demonstrate that even in France, where race prejudice is of a milder form, such a mating cannot be happy. But what are the facts? Jim's greatest weakness is a social one, for while he has educated himself, he has remained emotionally and sentimentally attached to the values which he acquired in the tough neighborhood on the East Side. Jim's education and money should have freed him from his old milieu and enabled him to find a place among the intelligentsia, but he himself believed that the Negro is actually inferior to the white man. He accepts Ella's prejudiced judgment as the truth. He allows her to keep him from social life in France, where they might have been accepted. The fact is that Ella is less ashamed of her Negro husband than afraid that, before people who do not accept racial prejudice, she will be shown up as his inferior—which she actually is. The play ends with Ella triumphant and secure in carrying out her neurotic pattern of receding back to childhood. Thus she solves the conflict between her desire for a child and her hatred of bearing a child whose father is black. And thus she also effectually keeps Jim from leaving her and escaping to an environment where he can succeed and be happy. The moral to be drawn from *All God's Chillun*

Got Wings is retrogressive and reactionary, and the apparent open-mindedness of the author makes it even more so.

That the Negro is used in the O'Neill plays as a symbol of the primitive nature of man becomes clearer in the *The Hairy Ape*. Here the hero is a white worker with a hairy chest who discovers that he has no place in the world as it is made today. Again O'Neill employs an expressionist method, a sequence of swiftly moving scenes, in place of the solid act which organically unfolds and develops an idea. Theatrically this is one of his most successful plays. The action moves with speed and inevitability, but it is a retrogressive and disintegrating action as in *The Emperor Jones*.

Yank, a stoker on a transatlantic liner, symbolizing the machine age, is insulted by a passenger, a girl of the upper classes. He discovers that he does not "belong." He sets out to get revenge on the girl's rich family, to find his place in the scheme of things. Violent and anarchic in his rebellion against society, Yank is repudiated by all—even by the IWW. He becomes an outcast everywhere. After a series of futile attempts to find a place, Yank lands at the zoo. The gorilla, symbol of the primitive past of man, repudiates him too. Yank is strangled to death in the gorilla's hairy arms.

On the surface *The Hairy Ape* may appear to be a proletarian play. It deals with a worker proletarian who is exploited and cheated. But actually the hairy chest of Yank is another mask disguising the petit bourgeois intellectual. The play voices the terror of that intelligentsia in a disintegrating bourgeois society; the proletariat is represented as brute force without intelligence and without culture; the upper classes are represented as shallow, cruel and cold. Unable to make a choice between the two classes, the petit bourgeois intellectual regresses to the old primitive world, but the path backward from organized bourgeois society to nature in the raw leads not to happiness but to death. The simple happy savage of Rousseau is a utopian dream in our modern industrialized world, and the intellectual who seeks that ideal of the past meets only with disaster.

FLIGHT TO THE PAST

But O'Neill is unwearied in his quest. If nature yields no satisfactory solution for human society, there is the flight backward to the romantic past of actual history. O'Neill has written two historical costume plays. The first of these, *The Fountain*, is a weak play, judged both as drama and as poetry. Yet because of its weaknesses, it conceals less and the symbols are easier to decipher. Ponce de León, Spanish conquistador, forsakes a life of conquest and governing to set out in search of the lost Fountain of Youth. The quest for his lost youth leads Ponce de León into an ambush prepared by the Indian chief he has tortured. Kneeling at the supposed fountain, Ponce de León sees his aged face reflected back and falls to the treacherous dagger. He loses his illusions along with his youth and finds a sorry consolation in the knowledge that the new generation will carry on.

In *Marco's Millions*, O'Neill essayed a satire on the American Babbitt who knows what he wants and gets it. But O'Neill's humor is saturated with sentimentality worthy of Babbitt himself. Marco sets out for the empire of Kublai Khan to enrich himself and his brothers. He comes, he sees, he conquers all the material riches of the emperor. But Marco has never had a soul, and when the greatest prize of all, the love of Princess Kukachin, symbol of beauty, is offered him, he passes by unaware and unmoved. The princess so slighted marries a potentate and dies slowly of disillusionment, and Marco, who has guided her to her new kingdom, returns home to Venice to wed his bride and to surfeit in riches. But the death of beauty makes Marco's triumph a hollow one, for a death of the spirit is worse than a death of the body, O'Neill seems to imply. Therefore happiness cannot lie in the material prosperity of the American bourgeoisie.

IV

Again O'Neill is undaunted by the failure of his historical quest. If the farm, the sea, the jungle, the romantic past offer no happy solution, there is one refuge praised by all the romantics—passionate love between man and woman. Early in his career, O'Neill chose this theme in a play which failed in production. Romantic love in *The Straw* keeps a sick girl alive and gives her hope in life. But that romantic passion is no more than a straw, O'Neill demonstrated later in another play which was never popular. *Welded* sets forth the conflict between passion and the individual ego. Michael, an oversensitive intellectual, and his wife, Eleanor, both demand that marriage allow them individual expression. When it does not, they try to separate but find that passion has welded them together. With or without personal happiness, they are doomed to remain together. *Welded* is in no wise as convincing as its great model *Totentanz*, and Strindberg has wrung deeper values from the sex struggle.

Desire Under the Elms is O'Neill's best play of romantic love, perhaps because other themes are interwoven with this leitmotiv. Two rivals, for the old New England farm of Ephraim, are his young son, Eben, and his newly married wife, Abby. Abby is a realist who wants her corner and security in the world and will wrest it at any cost. When her stepson Eben stands in her way, she determines to have a child by him and to pretend to Ephraim that it is his own. But an unexpected factor is the sudden passion which develops out of the relationship between Eben and Abby and sweeps them to destruction. To prove that she no longer has a desire for the property and that she genuinely loves Eben, Abby kills their child. Eben, overwhelmed with grief, summons the sheriff in revenge. But when he sees the law parting him from Abby, he relents and accepts his equal guilt. Victorious in their love, they go to accept justice. In its psychological pattern, we have a close analogy to Ibsen's *Rosmersholm*, where the stranger Rebecca West, having taken possession of Rosmer and his home, even to driving his wife to suicide, is overcome in the moment of success by Rosmer's ideas of guilt and expiation. So the girl Abby, who was unhampered by moral scruples, instead of killing old Ephraim kills her own love child and becomes a penitent sinner ready to suffer for her passionate love for her stepson. It is the old stern morality of New England which conquers the free spirit of Abby. *Desire Under the Elms* contains some of O'Neill's best poetical passages—rich in biblical imagery and scenes of rural beauty.

THE FAR LAND OF THE SOUL

Midway in his career, O'Neill's plays are divided into two kinds. The early plays dealt with the external world and its problems—the farm, the sea, the quest for gold, sexual passion, love of power, etc. In the later plays, the action shifts sharply from the world outside to "far land" of the soul.

In this internal country of the soul, secure from such pressing problems as the conquest of nature or of poverty, in a milieu increasingly prosperous and urban, the characters of O'Neill's later dramas devote themselves to contemplation of their inner lives. The unseen realm of the soul is mysterious and glamorous; it is a country which has already been skillfully charted by Chekhov and Schnitzler, European spokesmen of the petit bourgeois intelligentsia. O'Neill now sets off for it on a new expedition in search of his lost happy innocence. *The Great God Brown* and *Strange Interlude*, the most mature and complete products of his art, are the treasures brought back from this far journey into the invisible regions of the unconscious over which presides, as Pluto over the land of the shades, the great psychologist of the decaying bourgeois class, Sigmund Freud.

O'Neill's journey was not however a scientific expedition which brought new data of universal value to human conduct. Using Freud's charts to find his way in the land of the unconscious, O'Neill has actually explored only the outlines of a neurotic pattern common to the petit bourgeois intelligentsia in the United States.

O'Neill's use of symbols and of masks and other allegorical devices is often confusing; the meaning behind them has not been fused into a universal meaning which can arouse emotional response in multitudes of people; they are addressed to a small audience of bohemian intellectuals. O'Neill's invasion of the unconscious was a continuation of his old quest for happiness and love. But love has ceased to be, as in *Desire Under the Elms*, a physical presence containing subtle under- and overtones plucked painfully from the heartstrings. Love has been dissected into its constituent parts, in order to more minutely analyze its essence. There is sensual love, soul love, intellectual love, and the love of God, and each of these has its variations and gradations like the changing tints of a sunset. Man, in search of the lost harmony of prenatal bliss, gazes into the mirror and beholds his own image reflected, not merely one image, but multiple and varied images, as in the looking glasses of amusement park, each one distorted and different but never the essential soul of himself.

O'Neill's flight into the "far country" of the soul has its cause in the actual world. Is it not analogous to the escape of art in the same period into the world of the abstract? Profound social causes underlay this trend in America. It had occurred in Europe somewhat earlier. The fact is that the middle-class intelligentsia, chief creator of the bourgeois arts, had been deprived of a major economic and political role in society. Hence unable to function normally in the body politic, it was forced to create a world of its own, where in fantasy it could assume supreme power. It thus promulgated the theory of the freedom of the creative artist; it isolated that artist in an ivory tower far above the dust and tumult of the political arena. It jealously guarded his mythical freedom, which was in reality an exile, and pretended that it was *desired* when it was actually enforced by external circumstances. The sincere bourgeois artist was imprisoned in the tower to struggle there with his own internal conflicts; thereby he was prevented from discovering the social conflicts which were the primary cause of his own psychic disorders.

O'Neill, like all sensitively aware artists, has suffered greatly from the splitting of the world into two opposing planes—outside and inside.

His plays mirror the dualism of the position of the bourgeois artist perfectly. Because of this dualism, which he has sought to visualize by the use of devices such as the mask, the aside, or the actual splitting of a character into two roles, his dramas have never attained to the heights of great tragedy. Another playwright who has been obsessed with the same problem—a most acute problem for the petit bourgeois intelligentsia—is the Italian Luigi Pirandello. He has externalized it in terms of reality and unreality and used theatric devices with more adroitness and philosophical sleight of hand than O'Neill. That his sleight of hand should land him in the Fascist camp can be no surprise.

O'Neill's characters throughout remain two-dimensional. The problem of experiencing depth and space in the graphic arts is closely akin to the problem of the will in the drama. The heroes of Shakespeare's tragedies are men of power and action, their wills in conflict with real obstacles. The mad Lear on the heath in the storm evokes a scene of tremendous perspective both in the spiritual and in the actual world. Content and symbol are fused in one complete unit. In the whole theatre of O'Neill, we must search to find one character delineated with a strong will, striving to attain a specific end. Anna Christie, in some respects the most rounded portrait in all the plays, exhibits a seemingly definite will and a determination to gain her ends. But the last act is fumbled—actually the author wrote several endings for it—and it does not seem inevitable. Anna's marriage to the Irish sailor does not seem to solve her problem or fulfill her complete desire. Abby's strong will in *Desire Under the Elms* is broken by her discovery of love. Marco Polo alone seems to set out for a goal and to attain it; but it is a shallow and meaningless goal, which the author condemns and abhors.

V

In O'Neill's plays, life divides itself into two planes—the material world, which he represents as base, greedy for gold and power, shallow and dull; and the unseen world of the soul where he depicts man struggling for higher values and failing gloriously. Now the actual world's prizes of gold and power are sour grapes for the petit bourgeois intellectual, who must content himself with the shadowy realm of the soul. Here he is allowed untrammeled freedom to conquer "higher and better" values. Here he may assume the masks of power and nobility, but in his heart he is aware all the time that what he really desires lies across a forbidden wall. In the O'Neill theatre, the Babbitt, the successful bourgeois, is the fool and the villain; the dreamer who fails nobly is the hero. At bottom, the dreamer is actually the Babbitt too, albeit an unsuccessful one. And the hero-dreamer's revolt is doomed from the start to futility, for it is based on flight.

One of the most moving of O'Neill's plays, *The Great God Brown* contains passages of profound insight and poetic tenderness. Yet it contains no solution to O'Neill's quest. Therefore he takes revenge in depicting the Great God Brown or Babbitt as envious of the artist-dreamer, Dion Anthony. Dion, dying, wills to the Great God Brown his tragic mask—his noble aims and dreams. This mask poisons the life of the Great God Brown; he ceases to be content with his material, soulless existence and he craves to win the love of Margaret, the *Ewig-Weibliche* soul of woman.

Babbitt is defeated by the Bohemian artist; he is forced to accept the artist's values; he, too, develops a soul—and his soul becomes the source of Babbitt's bitter discontent with the cheap, material paradise of his worldly success. In the end, the soul of the artist Dion takes possession of the Great God Brown and destroys him. This modern miracle play externalizes the conflict in the soul of the petit bourgeois intelligentsia.

As a fable of the decay of present society, the play is truer than O'Neill perhaps intended; as theatre, it remains confused, the action will-less, emotionally unsatisfactory. The playwright is himself uncertain about the meaning of the dramatic symbols and the conflict which they present. All the O'Neill heroes are divided against themselves and are therefore incapable of absorbing the outside world in its depth and complexity; hence they never experience life in its fullest. Their eyes are always filled with undeciphered dreams. Yet they keep passionately affirming how they have loved, lusted, and lived. As a matter of fact, they have been so preoccupied with their internal problems that they have not even glimpsed the world of living reality.

As a foil to these hero-dreamers, these introvert knights of the nocturnal soul, O'Neill sets up a series of so-called "normal" people—Sam Evans, Marco Polo, Billy Brown, Peter Niles. Seen through the introvert eyes of their creator, they are nothing but clay figures, shallow, stupid, dull, immature. Yet, in order to be just, or perhaps for the sake of good theatre, he always portrays them as "good."

In *Strange Interlude*, O'Neill has attempted to come to grips with the unconscious. The *aside* is used to reveal the internal life of the character. Planes of existence assumed to be parallel and contradictory are externalized by the *aside*, just as they were externalized by the use of the mask in *The Great God Brown*. There are flashes of beauty and deep insight in this play, but during nine unwieldy acts, lengthened by the asides, which actually reveal nothing which could not have been dramatized in the action and conscious dialogue, the plot stagnates. O'Neill presents us with a beautiful neurotic heroine, Nina Leeds, whose passionate quest for fulfillment in love is the main theme of the drama. But this quest ends in a smug hanging onto comfort and contentment. Nina's life becomes shallow, worthless, meaningless; her only contribution to life is her illegitimate son, Gordon, palmed off on her husband by her lover and herself, in order to keep the husband "happy." He must be kept "happy" because he is so "good" and, above all, because he is "successful."

Nina's life is uncreative in every respect. Not one of the men with whom her life becomes entwined receives anything from her. Sam, her husband, makes money in spite of her. Darrell, the lover, neglects his work as a scientist and physician to hang onto her apron strings. Marsden, the old-maidish platonic lover, accepts her in place of his mother. Not one of these men is able to make a satisfactory and definite decision in any crisis. Whenever any character in the play acts, the action is usually one that would never be dictated by common sense or realistic aims. Nina's whole life is a series of decisions which complicate existence without helping anyone. They are supposed to be motivated by noble aims, but only because they deprive her of what she really wants. After her husband's death, when she might marry her lover, she prefers to drift into marriage with Marsden. This will enable her to spend the rest of her life doing nothing in a New England garden, while waiting for death to liberate her from a death of the spirit as complete as Marco Polo's, who never had a soul to worry over.

The emptiness and superficial character of the society portrayed in *Strange Interlude* becomes most clear in the boat race scene of the last act. Yet O'Neill does not look at his characters with a critical eye or analyze their threadbare ideals. If, like Ibsen in *Hedda Gabler*, he had laid bare the tragedy of a willful and beautiful woman whose only choice was in a barren marriage, the material might have been interesting. But in the twenties in the United States, there are many choices for a woman like Nina Leeds; we must assume that she *preferred* a loveless, secure marriage based on deception to facing the full implication of her passion for Darrell. We are therefore unmoved when all the characters are assembled for a grand climax to see Nina's son Gordon win a collegiate boat race! There is no action at all, for the characters have wavered so long that life offers them nothing but disillusionment as experienced by Darrell or the idiotic enthusiasm for puerile schoolboy matters that satisfies Sam.

Other playwrights have dealt with such aimless and actionless people and made drama out of their inertia and neurotic fears, but O'Neill does not step back far enough to see these people against their social background. Never are they as vigorous as the flesh and blood creatures of *The Cherry Orchard*. Never do they think beyond themselves of the problems of their fellowmen. The idealistic *Three Sisters* suffered more genuine pangs of soul in their provincial exile than do O'Neill's moderns on the decks of yachts, on top of penthouses in the metropolis, or wandering on the clipped lawns of Long Island estates. Of what use to visit the fantastic world of the unconscious when the secrets brought back are no more valuable than this dried seaweed of desire and these broken shells of lost hope? O'Neill has found no buried treasure in this Sargasso Sea of the soul. This is cheap dross like the treasure sought for so many years by the hero of *Gold*, who knew all the time that what he was seeking was brass.

VI

Perhaps O'Neill has surmised that for all his inimitable diving, he has brought up only brass; from now on, at least, he forsakes the invisible world of the unconscious and attempts to enter the real world of modern times, which has been made and molded by the industrial revolution.

O'Neill's quest led him to turn to the machine age. This may have been a reaction from the immediate postwar period, when the American intelligentsia, echoing a kindred mood in Europe, revolted against the machine. The too sensitive souls of Babbitt's sons fled to exotic countries and became expatriate. The stay-at-homes built their bohemian shelters against the standardized society made by the machine. But as prosperity increased and the petit bourgeois intelligentsia profited by it, they became more reconciled to the machine, which brought blessings to them as well as to the big bourgeoisie. Poets like Hart Crane were pioneers in building bridges from the world of traditional poetry, whose images stem from an agrarian world, to the new world of industry as yet uncharted in the poet's geography. Sensitive to these reactions, O'Neill essayed to write a play showing the machine as a Moloch. He dramatized the conflict in a series of abstractions. In *Dynamo*, the machine is presented as a monstrous god, jealous, relentless, demanding of his followers in return for services rendered absolute faith and the sacrifice of all instinctive desires including love. While employing modern symbols like hydrogenerators O'Neill actually speaks in accents of the preindustrial myth. If he had visualized the machine as life-destroying in the hands of exploiters, as useful in the hands of producers and workers in society, the myth might have had modern connotations. The story of Reuben Light—his conversion, atheism, his murder of his sweetheart, self-immolation on the machine—solved no problems for anyone. The story had no application; it was merely a study in psychopathology. Hence *Dynamo* remains a meaningless fable, unless one is supposed to deduce that chastity and atheism are fundamentally necessary to the control of the machine. *Dynamo* has no more real roots in the modern world of reality than has the pseudobiblical-classical drama *Lazarus Laughs*.

AWAY FROM REALITY

The plays now show an increasing inability to face reality altogether. They indicate desperate need of an escape; and carry the quest into another world of shadows, a world beloved by the romantic—the glory that was Greece and the grandeur that was Rome. This turning to the dream of the golden era enshrined in poetical tradition indicates an end to rebellion, a return to more conventional paths.

Although O'Neill has forsaken the unconscious depicted in *Strange Interlude*, he has not left behind Freud's prescriptions. He applies them now to interpreting the classical Hades, where dwell the pursuing furies of man's guilt. He choses the Electra myth made modern by Freud's famous complex to write a classic trilogy in the manner of Attic tragedy.

Mourning Becomes Electra sets forth the tragedy of a decaying New England family in the period following the Civil War. The trilogy, divided into three full-length plays—*The Home Coming, The Hunted, The Haunted*—closely follows the story of the doomed house of Atreus.

The classical legend recounts how Agamemnon, leader of the Greeks, returned from Troy and was murdered by his wife, Clytemnestra, and her paramour, Aegisthus. The killing was an act of revenge, for Agamemnon had sacrificed Iphigenia, Clytemnestra's younger daughter, to assure Greek victory over Troy. In return Electra and Orestes plot and carry out the murder of their mother and her paramour to avenge the murder of their father.

Attic tragedy based on this legendary history contains implications lost to modern audiences. For the Athenian spectator, the plays of Euripides and Sophocles had a meaning far beyond any single family tragedy of blood; they were ritual dramas whose choruses recounted the social history of the Greek race and celebrated a tremendous legendary event—the transition of Greek society from the matriarchal forms of the Orient to a newer society based on man's domination through the city-state. Greek drama encloses a whole world with a religion and ethic of its own, dominated by the idea of inevitable fate. In Attic tragedy, murder was not conditioned by mere personal pique or revenge but by far wider social issues. Clytemnestra killed because she did not accept the mores of Thebes and because she could not forgive her daughter's sacrifice for a cause she did not believe in. She personified an older form of society in which woman was not yet relegated to the family hearth alone. But her children, Orestes and Electra, belonged to the new order and they had been deprived of social position by the murder of their father, the king. Clytemnestra's crime was not the killing of her husband but the destruction of the head of the state. Electra's act was dictated by the need to obtain her portion of power and her brother's in the city-state. Here passion is inseparable from politics.

ATHENS AND BROADWAY

O'Neill has built his version of this tragedy on purely personal motives without any profound social significance. Despite its mastery of a brooding, decadent mood, his trilogy remains merely the chronicle of the crimes of a New England family. It could, perhaps, be interpreted as a study of the decay of the puritan mores in contact with pagan ideas, but it is so individual a tragedy that it has no general application to American life. Its inept chorus of New England small-town folk is merely an extraneous decoration in the archaistic fashion; it adds nothing to a tragedy which in itself is not inevitable. In the Reconstruction period, it was not necessary for Christine (Clytemnestra) to murder her husband, the returning general, in order to commit adultery, nor does Lavinia (Electra) need to murder her mother's lover and drive her mother to suicide in order to find her place in the sun. She could easily have gone away and married or, if she desired her mother's lover, there were other means of revenge. More normal alternative actions were open to all the characters than the ones they chose of murder and blood, or which their author chose for them in mechanical imitation of the Attic pattern. O'Neill's tour de force makes the characters too abnormal and different to awaken either pity or terror in a modern audience. Their demise occasions not regret but relief. The real purpose of tragedy is thus forfeited. *Mourning Becomes Electra* remains an archaistic nightmare of the golden age.

It is conceivable that a dramatist might achieve an effective tragedy of fate with a modern setting but O'Neill's trilogy does not achieve it.

The glory that was Greece becomes one more blind alley on the road to happy innocence. More elaborately constructed and technically more concentrated than his early plays, the trilogy has implications that are less realizable and less emotionally exciting.

VII

From pseudo-Attic tragedy O'Neill reacted by writing a successful Broadway comedy. This was scarcely his intention, but *Ah, Wilderness* is a play uncorroded by the bitter acid of pessimism. In it, O'Neill has succeeded, for the first time, in creating characters in three dimensions with the juice and savor of actual people. It is a boyhood comedy of happy youth placed in America in the halcyon days of 1905—long before the World War and the economic crisis—in another golden age now vanished forever.

But what does O'Neill choose to reveal as the "real life"? He depicts a Babbitt family in a small town; with approving good humor, untinged by criticism, he delineates the smug, conventional, everyday life of these people with rounds of church socials, Fourth of July picnics, movies, small gossip, drink, and repressed sex—a typical Grant Wood painting of American "national" life.

In this Main Street, from which at the beginning of the twenties all the Carol Kennicotts revolted, from which O'Neill's own rebellious dreamers fled to sea, the playwright settles down with a good-natured, middle-aged shrug of acceptance. Like Emperor Jones, he has gone around in a circle and has come out of the jungle at the same place he started from—the Main Street of Zenith with its Babbitts. Only a decade before, he had slammed the back door of respectable middle-class society and like Ibsen's Nora had gone forth to see the world. Now he has returned, a contrite prodigal in the well-pressed clothes of success to be admitted with honor into the front parlor, there to repent at leisure his associations with outcasts, sailors, workers, prostitutes, Negroes, free women, artists.

The dreamer O'Neill has capitulated to the Babbitt O'Neill, thereby reversing the story of the Great God Brown. Back in the fold of middle-class society, O'Neill embraces the most obvious, bigoted conventions of his class, and exhibits an intolerance which a cultured, bourgeois advocate of the status quo who has never questioned the fundamental postulates of capitalist society would blush to admit.

It now becomes quite clear that O'Neill's original revolt from middle-class standards *never involved a real break with bourgeois society.*

Rather it was an adolescent upheaval, a flight to bohemia common among the youth of the middle class, usually ending in a return to the conventional grooves of society. Every one of O'Neill's plays, read in the light of his total development, exhibits signs of a conflict never resolved. This was no other than the conflict of the petit bourgeois intelligentsia prior to the present economic crisis, when it had not yet found a political role, when it hated the big bourgeoisie and yet hated to be pushed down into the ranks of the proletariat. O'Neill was the spokesman for this tragic dilemma of the petit bourgeois intelligentsia which in the end will be compelled to choose between fascism and communism. It is for this reason that his characters exhibit the split will which destroys the unity of drama. The duality of his characters is forced on them by their position in society.

With *Ah, Wilderness*, O'Neill solved the conflict for himself by returning to the status quo. He thus regained the audience which he once forsook. But what effect has his capitulation had on his art? Exhausted in will by a sterile quest, he has become incapable of any action significant enough to create drama.

The plot of *Ah, Wilderness* is so petty that it scarcely sustains the burden of the action. For ever two hours we witness the spectacle of an old maid and her bachelor friend, engaged for years to marry, and again deciding *not* to marry; we witness the sorrows of an adolescent boy, who because of his "radical" ideas loses his childhood sweetheart and rebels against home restrictions, gets drunk, almost sleeps with a tart, and returns to the narrow path of duty and prospective conventional life and marriage.

There is no struggle, no action, no plot, and no ending. There is, however, homely humor and well-worn successful theatrical devices. Life has become so static that O'Neill's drama dies of sheer inertia. There is not even the suggestion that, beneath the shallows of this everyday life, a more significant drama exists which might be called forth in a crisis, as there is in the drama of Chekhov and Schnitzler. If "wilderness were paradise enow" it is a dull, vacuous paradise bought at the price of imagination, thought, and action—a hades worse than the medieval conception of hell. Now the tables have been turned: the Great God Brown has given *his* soul to Dion Anthony. Truly did Proust observe that, in the second half of his life, a man is often the opposite of what he was in the first.

Huysmans, on completing that bible of decadence, *A Rebours*, said: "After such a work, one of two things was open to me—either the muzzle of a pistol or the foot of the cross." This is the dilemma that now confronted O'Neill. Oversensitive, burdened with nostalgia, his color-loving, lyric soul could never submerge itself completely in the Babbitt ranks. He might put on the mask of Babbitt temporarily, but even the Babbitts would not be fooled. They would never accept him as one of themselves. O'Neill's quest has led him ever along a path of retrogression; now he has no other alternative but the church into which he was born. By returning to it, he returns to his mother and to that perfect love which could not be found elsewhere in the world. Hence it was inevitable that *Ah, Wilderness* should be followed by *Days Without End*, a miracle play of escape from the terrific dilemma of the middle-class intellectual in American society today.

FAREWELL TO LIFE

O'Neill is above all a sincere artist at the height of his maturity; he has felt the full impact of this dilemma, but he has evaded the responsibility thrust upon him in his role of spokesman and artist of the petit bourgeois intelligentsia.

Like so many others, including the distinguished author of *The Waste Land*, O'Neill has sought shelter in the violet shadows of Catholicism. *Days Without End* can scarcely be termed a play. Rather it is a public confession, a final melodramatic gesture of hopeless terror. The poet, discarding the mask of the Emperor Jones, Yank, Marco Polo, Ponce de León, the Great God Brown, Lazarus, Eben Cabot, Lavinia, Nina Leeds, and falling like a contrite child before the altar, cries out of a broken heart—"O son of man, I am Thou and Thou art I. Why hast Thou forsaken me?"

So sharp has become the conflict in O'Neill's soul that he has divided the hero of *Days Without End* into two people to be played by two actors. John and Loving are two halves of the same personality split apart—a modern Faust and his Mephisto. They are doomed to struggle against each other in a deadly duel, yet the plot chosen to set forth this internal combat is puerile and dull: it concerns itself with the material of all parlor drama, domestic adultery; the action has become even more static than in *Ah, Wilderness*. A frayed plot depicts how John Loving makes money for his adored wife while trying to satisfy his repressed creative urge by writing a novel of his problems. In this age of crisis, we are invited to the voluptuous soul writhings of a hero in a luxurious duplex apartment over the "enormous" offense of a casual and momentary adultery, from which even pleasure was absent. At that moment, there arrives a long-lost relative, a fatherly priest, who takes over all burdens. When John Loving has driven his wife to the verge of dying by indirectly revealing his great crime, he promises to be good and join the church, if she is saved by his prayers.

ART AND PROPAGANDA

There is something obscene in this hero's preoccupation with sex and soul, reminiscent of the Russian intelligentsia in the decadence following the defeat of the 1905 revolution. During that reaction, there occurred the same mystical vaporings and swoonings in the arms of the church which at the moment was helping to organize the gangs of Black Hundreds to terrorize and kill the Jews and the workers. So in 1930 in New York City, we observe John Loving, over after-dinner coffee impeccably served, politely give up his last gesture of revolt. In the word-duel between the priest Baird, who stands for the most obvious and reactionary elements in the Church, and Mephisto-Loving the play reaches its climax—a climax infected with the triteness and inaction of a bad propaganda tract. How odd that these authors who always demand the divorce of propaganda from their sacred art should be the first to commit the offense they decry, and without any subtlety whatsoever!

The split personality of John caught between the shafts of his alter ego, Loving, and his friend, the Priest Baird, delivers himself of this argument:

"Freedom demands initiative, courage, the need to decide what life must mean to oneself. To them [most people] that is terror. They explain away their spiritual cowardice by whining that the time for individualism is past, when it is their courage to possess their own soul which is dead—and stinking. Oo, they don't want to be free. Slavery means security—of a kind, the only kind they have the courage for. It means they need not think. They have only to obey orders from owners, who are, in turn, their slaves."

These are the ideas of Dostoyevsky's *Grand Inquisitor*, diluted and weakened. Here O'Neill pronounces verdict on himself, who has evaded the issue facing every intellectual in America today, whether he be a writer, painter, musician, or professional worker. The bourgeois intelligentsia, along with the workers, must face all the implications of the present crisis.

Europe's recent political history indicates the fate of the American petit bourgeois intellectual in the future. Until now, the intellectual had a choice: he might take a stand with the working class and their fight for freedom or he might retire into his ivory tower and hoist up the drawbridge in order to contemplate culture remote from the raging class conflicts. As the crisis deepens, the intellectual in order to live is compelled to abandon neutral territory. In the battle of the classes no-man's-land becomes untenable. To remain in the ivory tower demanding democracy and freedom, when these ideals are being destroyed all about us, is to take sides with decaying capitalism. To attempt to evade the issue is to tread the path of fascist sterility. Despite all pacifist and humanitarian principles, the liberal intellectual will have to orient himself in the coming struggle for power. Otherwise, if he does not perish physically, he will perish in the spirit.

O'Neill cannot evade the issue. Hiding in the church, he lies in the house of reaction. His hero John declares: "We need a new leader, who will teach us that ideal, who by his life will exemplify it and make it a living truth for us. A new savior must be born who will reveal to us how we can be saved from ourselves, so that we be free of the past and inherit the future and not perish by it."

John chooses the church and its security; his Mephisto twin, Loving, dies at the foot of the cross. But this cross is merely a way station for the petit bourgeois intellectual. The church is unable to solve the enormous economic problems of the world today. The choice can only lie between fascism and communism. Either society must be changed or it must go backward into chaos and reaction.

The split that is already occurring in the ranks of the petit bourgeois intelligentsia in America is fast losing O'Neill his audience. He was the leading dramatist of the twenties when the American bourgeoisie was the successful Marco Polo, economically prosperous, spiritually dead. Envious of the upper classes, contemptuous of the proletariat, and distrustful of itself, this class sought solace in sex, psychoanalysis, alcohol, and art—an art as remote from the reality of its own life as it was from the social reality as a whole. O'Neill was the poet of this class in the twenties. Today the petit bourgeoisie is making its choice between the capitalist mirages of the moment and the camp of the proletariat. There is a great, living, grateful, and thrilling audience awaiting those creative artists who choose to stake all for a new creative world. Out of the struggle for that world must necessarily stem a new and vital art, such as America has not yet dreamed of, but this art will move in a direction opposite to O'Neill's hopeless quest for mystical peace.

A PANORAMA
OF THEATRE ACTIVITIES

OF DOZENS of articles covering theatre in the 1934–37 period, I have made selections that give an overall view of the New Theatre movement's influence on and relation to established theatres. These groups include Eva Le Gallienne's Civic Repertory Theatre, Jasper Deeter's Hedgerow, the Theatre Guild, and the main newcomer, the Theatre Union. Because of its seminal importance, I treat the Group Theatre separately. There are articles too on the Yiddish Artef, the anti-Nazi German Neue Deutsche Theatre Gruppe in New York City, and the Hollywood New Theatre groups in order to give a coast-to-coast view.

I regret that we could not get publication rights at the time to the fine and funny musical *Pins and Needles*, but we do include a review of this Left comedy smash hit that proved "Theatre of Social Protest" could laugh at itself in the midst of more serious efforts dramatizing our social struggles and achievements.

Only space limitations prevent us from including more, in particular Paul Green's *Hymn to the Rising Sun*, Odets's *Silent Partner*, Albert Maltz's *Private Hicks*, Albert Bein's *Let Freedom Ring*, *Dimitroff* by Art Smith and Elia Kazan, *Parade* by George Sklar and Paul Peters, *Give All Thy Terrors to the Wind* by Paul and Clair Sifton, and A. B. Shiffrin's *Kids Learn Fast*.

Eva Le Gallienne–Ten Years

BY WALTER PELL

"Instead of producing rather dull plays by Ibsen because they are by Ibsen, it would be heartening if Miss Le Gallienne would join the theatre of 1935. It is rough and uncouth; the years have not polished or sanctified its plays. But it does matter to those of us who happen to be living now. And she is too important a person to be left out of it."
  RICHARD LOCKRIDGE, *New York Sun*

FIVE years ago Eva Le Gallienne's Civic Repertory Theatre loomed large in the theatrical picture. Today her old playhouse is the home of the

Theatre Union, and with the remnants of her company she drifts from half-successful road showings to two-week stands in New York.

Her last tour was short-lived, and her visit to Broadway was both a critical and financial failure. Why? It is time for a reevaluation of her ideal of the theatre, an analysis which may throw some light on her present situation and on the future course open to her.

In 1926 Miss LeGallienne founded her repertory theatre dedicated to "the great plays of the world," to use her own phrase. A careful consideration of what she believes to be "the great plays of the world" as indicated by her six years' repertory program and the plays which she has produced since she abandoned repertory, reveals great catholicity, but also certain very definite limitations.

Her repertory schedule at the Civic included Shakespeare, Goldoni, Molière, Ibsen, Chekhov, Tolstoy, the Sierras, the Quinteros, Heijermans, Bernard, Sutro, Barrie, Schnitzler, Andreyev, and Molnar. It is an impressive list. It includes many of the undoubted masterpieces of world drama. But more careful scrutiny reveals a startling fact. Leaving aside the two Shakespeare revivals, *Twelfth Night* and *Romeo and Juliet*, and the Russian plays, the whole list, with three exceptions, consists either of charming comedies or of plays dealing with the problems of the individual soul. Not one, with these few exceptions, dealt with the individual in relation to society, to the forces of *life today*. Passionate, tender, honest, and true they might be. Some, like the Ibsen dramas, were undoubtedly of supreme importance to the theatre and to the emancipation of the modern mind *when they were written*; today, in the light of a changed and arduous world, they are only historical and psychological documents, or effective stage vehicles.

The type of production which Miss Le Gallienne gave them did little to modernize, immediatize, or in any way regenerate them: often dramatic, scrupulous, and moving, her presentations never gave any hint of a creative reinterpretation or reevaluation of nineteenth-century enunciations of idealism and morality in the light of the twentieth century. *Camille* and *Hedda Gabler*, as seen on Fourteenth Street, were "great love stories"; *Liliom* and *The Master Builder* likewise. Of a definite point of view toward a parasitic society which forced one woman into prostitution, however glamorous, or allowed another to drive a creative writer into self-destruction and bore herself into suicide, not a trace.

The three plays whose subject matter was an exception to such disregard of social values were Heijermans's *The Good Hope*, Susan Glaspell's *Inheritors*, and Giraudoux's *Siegfried*.

The Good Hope dealt with the iniquitous conditions in the Dutch shipping business, where men were knowingly sent to sea in rotten-bottomed hulks so that their owners might collect the insurance accruing to them after a catastrophe. It is a powerful play, and its impact, when it was first written and produced three decades ago, is said to have been so terrific that it started a successful movement for the revision of the Dutch shipping laws. In the light of Miss Le Gallienne's record it is safe to assume, however, that she chose *The Good Hope* not for its social significance but because it was a magnificent dramatic vehicle for her and her company. The same is probably true of *Inheritors*, a fine play about the wide discrepancy between our so-called peculiarly American ideal of free speech and some actualities of life in a midwestern university town in the red-baiting years of 1919–20—a play, incidentally, which is too often forgotten today as one of the pioneers of our present theatre of social protest.

The Good Hope and *Inheritors* were both produced in 1927. Thereafter, with the exception of *Siegfried*, a vague and intellectual play about the temperamental and nationalistic differences between France and Germany today, the record is bare of anything even remotely savoring of contemporary social significance. Miss Le Gallienne might of course say that it was the fault of her audiences, that she could educate them (in the face of the unanimous opinion that she was attempting the impossible, when she founded her theatre) to appreciate Ibsen, Chekhov, and Goldoni, but not to swallow "social drama." She could point out that with all the good will in the world she could only afford (since her wealthy backers balked at *too* great an annual deficit) to produce *Inheritors* thirty-three times, *Siegfried* twenty-three times, and *The Good Hope* for around sixty performances in five years, as against a record of one hundred and sixty-four showings for *Cradle Song*, one hundred and twenty-nine for *Peter Pan*, and ninety-one for *Camille*.

The answer of course is that Miss Le Gallienne never *tried* to build up an audience for plays like *Inheritors*, as she did for plays like *Camille* or *Cradle Song*, because it was the latter type of play which she, as an artist and as a person, cared about. The degree of her personal bias is the more glaringly apparent when we consider the record of the Theatre Guild, an organization never distinguished for its preoccupation with social issues, which was nevertheless more eclectic in its choice of plays than Miss Le Gallienne. While the Guild revived *Faust* and *A Month in the Country* and *The Brothers Karamazov*, they also presented New York with Kaiser's *From Morn Till Midnight*, Capek's *R. U. R.*, Toller's *Man and the Masses*, Lawson's *Processional*, Kirchon's *Red Rust*.

Beyond any doubt Miss Le Gallienne performed a great service to the theatre when she proved that there existed an audience of people of small incomes who were hungry for the theatre, and this in an era when Broadway ticket brokers were demanding (and getting) ten, fifteen, and twenty dollars a pair for orchestra seats. It was Miss Le Gallienne's weakness, and inconsistency, however, that she never asked herself whether this audience, composed of white-collar workers, moderately circumstanced professionals, and students might not be interested in a different type of play from that to which she herself was addicted, and whether certain glaring inconsistencies in the world today did not demand expression in such plays, to such audiences.

Since 1926 she has presented only four American plays: *The First Stone* by Walter Ferris, *Dear Jane* by Eleanor Hinckley, and *Inheritors* and *Alison's House* by Susan Glaspell. In part this was no doubt due to the special conditions of repertory, which, by limiting the number of performances of any one play, also limited the royalties an author might expect. Most authors preferred the gamble of a Broadway production, a long run or a flop, to Miss Le Gallienne's policy of insuring her least successful play a certain number of performances by interspersing it with plays more popular at the box office.

The truth is that Miss Le Gallienne's preference in plays is but the reverse side of her personality, background, and method of revolt against the commercial theatre. Her background is that of a "cultured liberal"; and her approach to the problem of a worthwhile theatre is purely individualistic.

The Civic Repertory Theatre, in the days of its existence, was never anything but Miss Le Gallienne's theatre. She conceived it, raised the money which kept it going, chose its plays, staged them, and often played the leading roles. When she tried to play smaller roles, her public, essentially a personal one, protested.

An actress and director of undoubted ability and discrimination, who did not want to "star" at the expense of her fellow players, she was never able to assemble a more than second-rate company around her, or to hold the talented players who joined her company at one time or another: Nazimova, Ben Ami, and others. There were also promising young players who emerged from her Apprentice Group, such as Burgess Meredith and J. E. Bromberg, and then left her for Broadway. That she could not afford to pay good actors Broadway salaries was not a final answer, since she *was* able to offer them reasonable salaries for six and seven months of the year. The Group Theatre has been able to hold an astonishing proportion of its personnel on a moderate salary scale, because its artistic program has offered them opportunity for steady personal growth and participation in a genuine collective. These two things Miss Le Gallienne's theatre lacked.

She had a school, true enough, a free school for young beginners in the theatre, unique of its kind, and of great value, but of even greater potential value. Miss Le Gallienne herself was so harassed and overworked (again because of the individualistic setup of her theatre) that she had little time to devote to the students, or even to map out their work, which was entrusted for the most part to younger members of the company. Nor was her own conception of acting sufficiently articulated or systematized to be of service to students. The result was that the value of the Apprentice Group may be summed up in one word: inspirational. Of lasting training, there was very little. As for the company itself, though Miss Le Gallienne was able at times, particularly in the Chekhov's plays, by sheer force of her personality, and her own devotion and enthusiasm (a purely personal force, again) to spur them to ensemble playing far above their usual capacity, individual and collective, *as a whole* they were never more than a *supporting* company.

In summing up, although it contains much of both discrimination and devotion, Miss Le Gallienne's ideal of theatre is inevitably vitiated by certain traits of individualism, of vagueness, of isolation, which remove her from the living theatre. They have condemned her, if not to artistic sterility, at least to a more and more limited function in the theatre, in inescapable contrast to the ever-increasing social and artistic significance for which collective organizations like the Group Theatre, the Theatre Union, the Artef, the Theatre Collective, and the New Theatre groups all over the country are preparing themselves. They are rooted, through their plays and their audiences, in the living present.

By the very fact that she had the courage, the integrity, and the vision to turn her back on "stardom" and on the commercial theatre, Miss Le Gallienne has laid herself open to the demand that she go even farther, that she emerge from her ivory tower, that she throw in her efforts where they are so badly needed, not in embalming the theatre of the past, but in building the theatre of the future.

Memorandum on Hedgerow

BY MARY VIRGINIA FARMER

THE MOST interesting theatre in America today is housed in an old converted mill in Moylan-Rose Valley, Pennsylvania. From its unobtrusive beginnings in 1923—there was no "founding"; Jasper Deeter and others merely presented *Candida*—the Hedgerow Theatre has become a byword wherever theatre is envisaged in terms other than those of profit.

If it wished, it might become the most important theatre in this country as well as the most interesting. I do not know whether it cares about being important. In my opinion it ought to care. It is now so much of an entity that it has a distinctly social duty to perform toward its audiences; and toward the American theatre as a whole (or our hope of one), an artistic duty. At the present time neither of these responsibilities is being fulfilled as well as it should be, largely, it seems to me, because the organization does not exercise sufficient selectivity in its choice of plays, in the work of its artists, in the form of its productions, and in its social outlook. There is a hiatus between its keen understanding and high standards and the expression of these in theatrical terms.

Even as it stands today Hedgerow presents a tremendous accomplishment which should be encouraging and stimulating to every struggling new theatre. The first Hedgerow *play* was presented at the old mill in Rose Valley in April 1923 by Jasper Deeter, several people who were later to become members of the Hedgerow acting company, and others who were interested amateurs of the neighborhood. The *theatre*, and the company, began to take shape at the end of that summer, when three people were provided with board and lodging (in theory at least, and part of the time actually!) by weekend box-office receipts. The following summer saw the first theatre *house*, where ten or a dozen actors, members of the regular company and guest players, lived in attempted cooperation!

By the summer of 1926 the Hedgerow was carrying a debt of $11,000. Today, it is within a few hundred dollars of owning its own theatre outright. It is buying its own house with three acres of ground. It owns a truck, a bus, and a station wagon. It does its own printing and photography, its own laundry, raises its own vegetables, and grows the wool for its blankets on its own sheep. Members of the company take care of the housekeeping and marketing, and, in addition to these multifarious activities, keep a repertory of thirty-five plays going (playing six performances a week most of the year), including an average of eight new productions a season (new and old plays), with sets and costumes made entirely by the company! The theatre supports twenty-two people (its acting resources are larger, however, and include a special part-time group which appears in Irish plays and in other parts as well, and a number of Negro players who work with Hedgerow on a part-time basis when opportunity offers). Maintenance includes excellent food, every detail of personal *necessity*, any special health requirements, and $5.00 a week in cash, although this privilege is seldom used!

There are no debts other than the amortization on the theatre properties. There are no endowments on the books either, and few gifts of consequence. How has this growth in economic capacity been accomplished? Through the intake of a theatre seating 156 people, the highest priced seat being $1.65.

Twenty-two people run a theatre in a successful cooperation of living and artistry, with a saner interplay of energies and understanding, of leadership and group activity, than I have seen in any other place. More specifically, Hedgerow functions like this: There is an incorporation for business purposes, and the company. The separation between the two is purely technical. There is no departmentalization of personnel throughout the theatre. The two people who are responsible for the balance of income and expenditure also act, direct, build sets, and go to market. Everybody who is capable of giving correct change has charge of the box office at one time or another. One of the theatre's most valuable actresses, in association with one of the actors, recently reorganized the property department; another ran the costume department for years.

The theatre has a steady patronage from Philadelphia and its growing suburbs. This public, largely middle class, sees a wide variety of plays: tragedy, comedy, and melodrama by Shaw, O'Neill, Sherwood Anderson, Lynn Riggs, Ibsen, Shakespeare, Jean Jacques Bernard, Gantillon, Chekhov and many others old and new. On nights when *The American Tragedy* or Susan Glaspell's *Inheritors* or *The Emperor Jones* are on the bill, the audience becomes partly, sometimes predominantly, working class.

It is encouraging to hear in this connection that Deeter will direct two plays for the Philadelphia New Theatre, dividing his time equally between Hedgerow and Philadelphia, for the entire fall season. Hedgerow cannot fail to benefit from its director's close contact with the living labor theatre movement.

In thirteen years there have been one hundred and nineteen productions, of which thirty-one were world premieres and nine American firsts. The active season's repertory consists of thirty-five plays; in the winter there have been tours by bus and truck to almost every section of the country. In July this year the third annual Shaw festival took place—two weeks of Shavian plays.

There is an enormous variation, both in the level of acting and production and in the content of the plays. There is no better playing available—true, exciting, solidly related to the production and content of the play—than is to be seen in the Hedgerow production of *Saint Joan* and of Lynn Riggs's *The Lonesome West*. Almost as much may be said for *Liliom*. On the other hand, you may also see a good fast stock production—no better than that—of *The Devil's Disciple*, or a thoroughly bad production of one of Mr. Shaw's most outmoded plays, *The Doctor's Dilemma*, or a much better performance than it deserves of Shaw's *Misalliance*. The present repertory includes a version of *Alice in Wonderland* and other plays for children; in the past it has included Harry Wagstaffe Gribble's *March Hares*, and the mildest and most popular of A. A. Milne's romantic comedies.

The acting at its best is interesting, moving, satisfying; at its worst, although seldom false, and always sincere in intention, it is incomplete, undeveloped, and immature. The same unevenness is evident in the details of production. Lighting and scenery still err at times in taste or in interpreting the content of the play. It is not talent that is lacking so much as broad knowledge of the theatre, expertness, and care in detail.

I believe that Hedgerow should now train its artists more completely and more carefully, through special work as well as through rehearsals and performance. I believe that for the sake of the theatre the less developed and promising actors should be willing to step aside for a time from parts in which others could be more effective. The theatre must go into the next phase of growth for which, it seems to me, it is so obviously ready: that of an adult, world theatre, in which artistic callowness, sloppiness, and incompleteness have no place. If Hedgerow takes this step it will eventually be of far greater service to the beginner in the theatre, actor or producer, than it is now.

The Hedgerow repertory includes such social plays as Susan Glaspell's *Inheritors*, Andreyev's *King Hunger*, Ibsen's *Pillars of Society*, Sidney Howard's *Lucky Sam McCarver*, Bernhardi's *The Prisoner*, O'Neill's *Hairy Ape*, Giacosa's *Like Falling Leaves*, Faragoh's *Pinwheel*, Hallie Flanagan's *Can You Hear Their Voices?*, Shaw's *Heartbreak House*, the Dreiser-Piscator *An American Tragedy*, and O'Casey's *Plough and the Stars*. Such a record indicates profound human sensitivity, but little consistency in social point of view.

There is a growing desire in the Hedgerow Theatre for plays that speak decisively and to the point on the social, economic, and political issues of today, and I hope that this attitude will soon dictate the theatre's choice of plays and the productions it gives them.

Lastly, I hope that Hedgerow will turn its attention to the need for attaching playwrights to itself for training and creative work. The theatre's business and artistic relations with its writers are good, but it has no poets of its own. I once heard Deeter say that a theatre only reached its full dimensions when it could speak through its own poet. When will the collective theatres recognize that truth?

Idiot's Delight, Anatomy of a Success

BY DAVID SHEPPERD

Review of a Theatre Guild production written by Robert Sherwood

WHATEVER else may be said of *Idiot's Delight,* Robert Sherwood's latest play and the Theatre Guild's final production of the season, one thing is clear: it is a smash. It is also a good show. It has color: A hotel in the Alps bordering on four countries, a cast of characters which includes a German scientist, a French pacifist, a munitions magnate, a tantalizing Russian lady who is half mountebank, half soothsayer; an articulate and racy American hoofer, a bevy of night-club beauties. The play has literate lines and references that only readers of the better weeklies will properly appreciate: "Whoever wins (the war) Austria will lose," quotations from Thomas Mann, gibes at the stupidity of humankind, not-unsympathetic allusions to radical ideas, and a depreciation of jingoism. It is performed by a company of smart and engaging actors. With all this, and above all, there is the theme of war (the author is definitely against it), not any war but the specific brand that nowadays we chew every morning with our breakfast.

Such a play cannot and must not be dismissed. Its appeal is extremely broad. Its reflection of its fairly-well-to-do middle-class audience, our dominant audience for higher grade best-sellers and SRO successes, is almost perfect. Analyze and understand this play and you will have learned much about a great section of our cosmopolitan public.

Structurally *Idiot's Delight* is rather loose: there is not much plot and very little conflict in the sense of a struggle of wills. Most of the characters are *caught* in a situation over which they have no control and to which they do not see their own relation except as passive victims. The French "internationalist" is an exception, but at the outbreak of war the author shows that he loses his pacifist convictions and dies with a patriotic exclamation on his lips. (What is this "internationalist"? A synthetic figure without sharp definition. If he were a Radical-Socialist he would not call for "revolution," if he were a Socialist he would not speak of Lenin as his leader, if he were a Communist he would not hope to stave off war simply by an appeal to reason.) The German scientist is working on a cure for cancer, but when his fatherland is threatened he decides to give up his work, since humanity is not worth saving (although his country is apparently worth dying for). The Russian lady of doubtful origin hates war, but she has been the mistress of a big munitions manufacturer for some time. The hoofer apparently feels that if makers of armaments were put out of the way most of the trouble would be gone, but he never really encounters the villain (the munitions manufacturer) and the latter himself makes the presumably unanswerable point that he is fulfilling a task which was not set by himself alone. "Why are there no answers to my questions?" the hoofer asks despondently. The truth is (a) the questions are not properly put, (b) he doesn't ask the right people, (c) he isn't really a character, for a person as evolved as he is supposed to be might come closer at least to some theoretical answers!

Given these figures and circumstances there can be little drama. Instead there is conversation: bright, wistful, sexy, cultural, like an expensive steamship ad, and political in the intriguing manner of a *New Yorker* editorial. To lend punch and pathos to the situation we have the bing-bang and br-r-r-ing of an offstage war. However, the dish would lack intellectual piquancy if there were not some semblance of social comment; so we have a chorus number done cutely by Alfred Lunt and *les girls* which is interrupted by the sudden entrance of the internationalist, who screams that Paris has been bombarded, that they are all dancing in a world in ruins. But it is to be remarked that it is the dance number, with its lights, its bare thighs, its playfulness, and not the interruption, which is applauded and remembered by the audience.

Where does all this lead? At the end of the play the hoofer and the Russian lady alone in the hotel defy death that is being hurled down on the mountain by bombing war planes. He plays the piano and she clings to him. "We are the real people," she says, "and we know that the deadliest weapons are the most merciful"—and with that the curtain falls. In other words, these two (symbolical) artists who are the playboys and wantons of civilization express the idea that in this crazy, cruel, but rather nice world of ours it is really best to die. There is no consistent intelligence, there is no justice, there are no heroes, no valid fighters. If one dies then let it be at least with humor, music, a dash of romance and philosophy. It is the spirit of sorrowful acquiescence. You shake your head, sigh, and permit what you deplore.

Is it pessimism? Not at all: pessimism suggests pain, and the public in our theatre will not pay for that. Just as the play's action is loose and the characters only partly defined, so the tone of the play never mounts to anything like a dangerous tension. The quality is pleasant throughout without any palpable blood pressure. Art can arise from decadence, it can even arise from despair, hate, or mockery. But for art to arise from them they must be clear through a certain degree of force, of completeness, of experience. When ingredients of popular sentiment and prevalent notions are distilled and thinned down to fit the tastes of nearly everybody, you can really concern nobody and you get at best only entertainment.

A play of this kind might take on fresh meaning in a creative theatre. The Guild production is on the level of the play, in an undifferentiated way. It is a neat package. Mr. Lunt is an *actor* (there aren't so many) and he has a certain spicy sense of characterization, though he fails to convey any *complete person*. The last moment in the show reveals the nature of the whole production: positively and negatively. The air raid is raging and the two chief characters are at the piano. What is the relationship of these two elements? What impels the two people to go to the piano: fear, defiance, desire to drown out the hateful noise, bravado? Nothing is clear: the two characters simply sit there, a light shines up on their faces, a pretty picture is made.

Black Pit

BY HERBERT KLINE

Review of the Theatre Union production of a play by Albert Maltz

". . . t'ree 'clock come, I go wurk in pit . . . come out twelve 'clock night, take'm wash, eat leely bit, go sleep . . . come five 'clock morning, whistle blow, catch breakfast, smoke leely bit, rest leely bit . . . after while catch'm couple hour more sleep . . . den wurk again . . . live lak dis all my life . . ."
—Steve Kristoff, since dead from a fall of slate.

HERE, in the drama of a worker who betrays his class, is an important and highly original departure in working-class plays. Albert Maltz has to his credit our first revolutionary tragedy.

The *Black Pit* dramatizes the kind of life described above by Steve

Kristoff. Unlike *Peace on Earth* and *Stevedore*, this new Theatre Union play is not a thrilling stimulus to action, though the need for militant struggle is emphasized in a clear-cut revolutionary line throughout. Rather, it is a morality play of the proletariat, the moral tragedy of Joe Kovarsky, a militant young Slovak miner who weakens under the relentless, crushing, piling up of disaster after disaster, and ends by becoming a stool pigeon. The tragedy, centering upon the moral issues involved more than upon the fatal consequences of the stool pigeon's crime, is told with such understanding artistry that only a few sectarians, missing the point completely, mistake the human portrait of a man who is crushed by the system and by his own weakness for what they foolishly call "the glorification of a stool pigeon."

As the play opens Joe Kovarsky is taken from the arms of his young bride Iola to serve a term in prison on a trumped-up charge of having blown up a tipple during a strike. When he returns three years later, he finds that he has left one prison for another. His brother Tony has been crippled in a mine accident. Tony, his wife and children, and Iola have all been living on the $10.50 per week "compensation" awarded the paralyzed miner by the coal company. A company union controls the patch and conditions are worse than ever. Like every other miner with a strike record Joe is on the "blacklist."

After months of searching, Joe finally finds work under an assumed name. The miners are herded together in boarding houses that "stink like hell." They carouse and gamble on Saturday nights, throwing away their hard-earned pay to forget the loneliness and squalor of their lives in drunkenness and vice. One of the most exciting moments in the play comes when the miner Bakovchen leaps across the room to warn the newcomer against being drawn into conversation by a "stool pigeon." But Bakovchen's comradely warning does not matter, for a moment later the Super, having discovered Joe's real identity and record, fires him.

Upon his return home, Joe finds that Iola, as the wife of a blacklisted miner, cannot be attended to by the company doctor, even in childbirth. The Super offers to get the company doctor for Iola if Joe will accept a job as stool pigeon. Joe refuses contemptuously and Mr. Prescott leaves. And when his wife cries out her fear that, like her mother before her, she will die in childbirth for want of a doctor, Joe yells:

> "What you wan'——me be stool pigeon . . . tink I no wan' job——no wan' eat——no wan' have dochtor? Think I wan' you to have baby maybe die?"

Black Pit

In desperation, when his wife suggests that he fool the Super by "just pretending" to be a stool pigeon, Joe grasps at this straw and decides to take the job just long enough to get the doctor for Iola, and a few dollars to get away on afterward.

Although he is determined not to tell anything of importance, he is trapped by Prescott (in the one phony and wholly unnecessary scene in the show, the good old dictaphone is called upon to turn the trick—again!). He is forced to lie to his fellow workers when a strike is imminent as a result of the miners' suspicions that the mine is "hot" and liable to explode. Not only do his lies persuade the miners to return to the dangerous mine instead of striking, but worse still, on the very night that Iola is giving birth, the Super forces Joe to squeal on the new union that is being organized by Hansy McCulloh. Shortly afterward, at a picnic given by Joe to celebrate the birth of his son, it is discovered that McCulloh has been taken for a ride and beaten up by company thugs and that Joe lied about the mine not being "hot." Just then, it is heard that a miner has been seriously hurt in an explosion. Furious that they have been sent to work in a gas-laden mine, the men go out on strike. Joe denies his guilt at first but is forced to confess by Tony. Joe tells his brother that he was driven into taking his rat job, that he turned stool pigeon for all of them, for Tony too. The crippled miner cries out furiously.

> "No! Jesus Chris' you be lie. I no be like you. I go'n sleep on the groun' I go'n eat coal. I go'n die from starve 'fore I be cheat on odern miner. You wan' t be stool pigeon? You lak be stool pigeon. O.K. (He spits at Joe) I no gone stay in same howse wit' stool pigeon . . ."

And when Joe tries to tell Tony that he did it for Iola, because she would have died without a doctor, Tony answers:

> "Joe, Joe, bett'r be Iola die from baby—bett'r be you die from starve . . ."

Tony tells Joe to go away, the miners will never trust him again, and as his stool-pigeon brother departs, Tony wheels his cripple's chair to the window to watch the picket line outside. Then he turns to Iola, who is sobbing on the bed, and says:

> "Never mind . . . Lil fella gone grow up . . . he no crawn on belly to get pice bread . . . outside miners . . . by God, miners gone raise head oop in sun . . . holler out, Jesus Chris' . . . miner gone blow whistle . . . not boss blow . . . blow . . . Jesus Chris' I never gone die . . . I gone sit here wait for dat tahm." (The siren screams)

This recounting of the story of the *Black Pit* gives no idea of how effectively it was brought to life on the stage. The fine acting of Martin Wolfson, as Tony, brought home its revolutionary message. George Tobias, Harold Johnsrud, and Tony Ross made the boarding room scene unforgettable, and Clyde Franklin as the Super did nobly in an ignoble and rather heavily written part. Alan Baxter, as Joe Kovarsky, played the difficult role well except for that trace of a juvenile-lead quality which Brooks Atkinson pointed out justifiably in the *New York Times*. I wonder if the playwright, or the director, or Millicent Green was responsible for making Iola so cloyingly sweet?

The direction by Irving Gordon showed a real advance over that of *Sailors of Cattaro*. The handling of the scenes between Joe and the Super were excellent, but I was disappointed in the card-game strike meeting and the picnic scene. Here was a chance to play a rich script for all it was worth, to break completely with the somber, depressing tone of the play and thus to intensify the ensuing tragedy.

The lighting in the prologue, with the spot encircling Joe, Iola, and the minister, while the law stood back in the shadows (all this in a tiny room), made the scene look like a posed Hollywood close-up. Most of Tom Adrian Arcraft's sets were effective, however, and one, the exterior of Joe's house at night, was so fine that it brought spontaneous applause from the audience.

I believe that Albert Maltz missed two real opportunities to make his *Black Pit* an even finer play, and both result from his failure to give a proportionate representation to the lives of other miners besides Joe and Tony. If, instead of the tragic first scene, the playwright had shown the miners throwing a party for Joe's welcome home from prison, the betrayal of these men later would have been even more terrible. It is difficult to feel genuine sympathy over the reported deaths of characters whom we know only by name. Also, apart from our natural desire to see the miners at work sometime during the course of the play, the accident resulting from Joe's lies would have been far more dramatic if it had been seen instead of talked about.

Perhaps it is unfair to deal primarily with these few faults of *The Black Pit*. Its accomplishments are so high in quality of writing, in rich characterization, in sustained emotional intensity, that I urge every reader of NEW THEATRE not to miss this significant revolutionary tragedy.

The Artef

BY SAMUEL KREITER

THE ARTEF is one of the main stems in Yiddish proletarian culture. Going on its ninth year, it bids fair to survive the once lively art of the now decadent Yiddish histrionics.

In 1926, when the rank and file of American Jewish labor were junking bureaucratic leadership, a group of class-alert shop workers with a passion for the theatre formed a dramatic studio under the guidance of the actor-poet-regisseur, Jacob Mestel. For three years they rehearsed and studied the manifold subtleties of stage technique. Following the period of strenuous training, the studio matured into a compact artistic players ensemble under the more resourceful direction of Beno Schneider, a student for years under Vakhtangov. Besides the thirty-eight active players, the Artef maintains a studio for workers who desire dramatic training.

The Artef has successfully staged twelve productions which averaged thirty performances each, a good average considering that its playing time is confined to weekends and that the Artef operates without fat subsidies from big-hearted donors. Of the twelve productions three dealt with the American scene: *The Third Parade* by Paul Peters and Charles R. Walker, based on the bonus march to Washington; *In the Roar of the Machines*, an original play of American shop conditions by the Yiddish writer, F. Chernet; and *Drought*, adapted by N. Buchwald from Hallie Flanagan's *Can You Hear Their Voices*. The others were importations from Soviet repertory.

Though Jewish life is in a state of constant change, the Yiddish bourgeois theatre has not seen fit to change its threadbare pattern of inane mushy melodrama and Hasidic "romance" for a form of social art. As such it has failed to identify itself with the varied and multiple problems that face the masses today, an oversight which is fast becoming its downfall. The Artef, on the other hand, arrived as a robust instrument in the class conflict. It reflects mass struggle in place of mass suffering, which was a woebegone feature in the "social problem play" that served early radical immigrants as a means of registering passive protest.

Furthermore, the Yiddish bourgeois plays are wanting in creative and technical imagination, in live humor, in fresh acting talent, in good lines. Even the most simple-minded of playgoers are no longer entertained by the facial and vocal acrobatics of a Ludwig Satz, the good-natured crooning and spoofing of the elfish Molly Picon, the prostrate unreal dilemmas of a Jennie Goldstein. The better front of the trade, the Yiddish Art Theatre, fell upon evil days after sixteen years of near-heroic efforts on behalf of the finer play. Some of its disbanded troupers are now on the Coast doing earnest but ineffectual revivals. Others in New York have instituted themselves as the Yiddish Folk Troupe and premiered this season under Joseph Bulov in a Soviet melodrama, *The Verdict*, now playing at the Yiddish Folk Theatre. Meanwhile, their lost leader, Mr. Maurice Schwartz, is in Hollywood trying to ease into film work.

Defying the confusion in the Yiddish theatrical world, the Artef dramatizations of dominant revolutionary forces are fearless and uncompromising, and transcend the old smug conception of what constitutes dramatic effectiveness.

Nearly one hundred thousand people saw Artef productions in seven months last year. In the same time it provided workers' clubs with mass recitations, readings, and improvisations. The Artef is still in the stage of development. It has an ambitious schedule for this season and plans to go on "the road."

The artistic development of the Artef is evident in its current production of *Recruits*, which had its premiere at the new Artef Theatre on West 48th Street (the first workers' theatre on Broadway). The play creates, in nine impressive scenes, a stirring re-creation of life under the Czar. The method Beno Schneider employs in directing is a synthesis of Reinhardt's expressionism and Stanislavsky's naturalism. He had to undo the corrosive tradition of Second Avenue exhibitionism, to steer clear of sentimental realism, in order to get at the inner dramatic pathos and intense truth that underlies mass struggle, without deviating from character portrayal. This he achieved through remarkable restraint, through subtle coordination of line and movement reaching often into symbolism. *Recruits* is unforgettable in its picture of primitive conflict between the poverty-ridden workers of a Russian-Polish village and its handful of rich Jewish proprietors. The central theme, going back to 1828 under Czar Nicholas I, revolves around the bitter system whereby the children of the poor were impressed into long years of servitude in the army. The havoc created in the village by the arrival of the Czar's decree calling for Jewish conscripts, how the decree was met by the community elders who seek to shift the obligation of supplying the Czar with recruits upon the poor, how they finally trick Nachmen, leader of the happy-go-lucky artisans, into signing himself away for the army, the running thread of romance, superstition, and suffering, the vivid impersonations against the richly toned, slightly grotesque backdrops prepared by Mr. Solotaroff, make a moving, artistic comedy.

Anti-Nazi German Theatre in Yorkville, N.Y.

BY MOLLY DAY THACHER

IF the theatre should be dramatic of itself, Broadway for all its ballyhoo and lights is not. If you want to see a theatre that is, go to the anti-Nazi revue that is staged in the heart of Yorkville, New York's Nazi center, and see young German actors playing clearly and strongly and competently, to an audience of their neighbors, their satire of Hitlerism. These are shopkeepers and workers, people for years dispossessed from the theatre, who come to see a good musical show, and stay to be moved by strong laughter and shrewd ridicule against fascism.

The best production to come out of a workers' theatre since *Newsboy*, its revue form makes it amusing for an English-speaking audience as well as for Germans. It makes as craftsmanlike and effective a use as I have seen of the means at its command and the circumstances under which it works. The actors are not experienced and have great need of body and voice training as well as practice in many kinds of roles—therefore the revue form, with its short scenes and quick alternations of mood, of personalities, of songs and sketches, is used to relieve them of the burden of sustained performances. Sharp (and inexpensive) changes of costumes and properties maintain the interest and variety. The most serious sequences, the series of scenes showing the coming of fascism in Germany, is extraordinarily moving and pointed: in 1930, a girl persuading her boyfriend to go on a picnic with her instead of to a protest meeting against reaction—it's spring!; 1931, an old woman in a delicatessen store complaining of the high prices; a Social Democrat haranguing his listeners to keep in the middle of the road; then a file of prisoners singing the deep song of the concentration camps; the boy of the first scene saying good-bye to his girl as she prepares to escape across the border, telling her to carry the word of united front against fascism and war.

Limited by the narrow hall and small stage space, John Bonn shows in his settings the same craftsmanship that Rudolph Wittenberg put into writing and composing the revue for the company. The stage uses the full width of the room. Bonn makes two entrances on either side upstage, masked by flats parallel to the footlights, thus giving a variety of playing spaces: between the two flats, in front of each of them, the clear strip at the front of the stage, as well as full stage, the floor of the auditorium, and even the tops of the flats, across which one of the songs is sung. In this mastery of the limitations of the place and the company, as well as in the reaching of a real neighborhood audience, the Neue Deutsche Theatre Gruppe sets an example to the new theatres.

Footlights in Filmland

BY RICHARD SHERIDAN AMES

CONSIDERED theatrically, Hollywood is Southern California, although the film town is faintly suburban to the normal life of the nation's fifth city. Like Los Angeles, Hollywood has citizens who work and raise families, but its civic responsibility is toward thousands of curious pilgrims who come to witness the cinema and its folk, hoping wistfully to find them as outrageous as the fan magazines report. Hollywood itself is theatrical; so much so, in fact, that there is little dramatic energy left to function behind the proscenium.

The studios have their own top-heavy chores to perform, and they have enlisted most of the creative talent of the world's theatre at one time or another. One would think there might be an overflow, an informal and steady contribution of creative theatre into numerous, untenanted local playhouses, but that is not true. With but few exceptions all legitimate theatres in Southern California are feeders for the motion pictures.

Every first night is attended by a swarm of flesh peddlers intent upon selling the play or its actors to specially invited film potentates. Much of the audience is recruited from tourists who pay to see not the drama but the stars in the foyer.

Los Angeles does not possess an enlightened, loyal, legitimate theatre audience. It is too remote to be considered part of the "road," though its people rally to the occasional visiting star and are curiously spendthrift when offered almost any Shakespearean fare. Within the far-flung city are all kinds of audiences: sentimental midwesterners who remember John Drew; a group which liked the John Golden sort of play; Hollywood bohemians and transient worldings who can stomach anything from *The Green Bay Tree* to Shaw, and a handful of people who seek intelligent drama, though they have lost the theatre habit. Then there is an unfortunate younger generation which has never been in a theatre.

Any local producer has to consider these audience factors, and they are potent, no doubt, when he thinks of risking his money on a new production. Public apathy is so general that the professional theatre cannot really be said to exist in Southern California. Henry Duffy frequently supplies New York hits, nicely mounted, which succeed only when they boast star names. Civic enterprise brought Max Reinhardt's *A Midsummer Night's Dream*, which played to thousands in a natural setting. The advertising appropriation accounted for the phenomenon. This fall Reinhardt may offer *Twelfth Night*, and it is even hoped that Hollywood may be host to Gordon Craig next year, in which case lavish expenditure may be put to better purpose than in 1934. Reinhardt did put on a swell show, and his torchlight processions over the mountains have been exceeded only by Mt. Etna's last eruptions.

Most of the Los Angeles theatres are dark currently and even the picture palaces provide very little "flesh" entertainment. The capital of the motion picture is almost exclusively entertained by its homegrown film shadows. The situation would appear hopeless but for the largely unheralded efforts of sincere and ambitious laboratory theatres.

Whatever his faults, Gilmore Brown, managing director of the Pasadena Community Playhouse, fills a niche as the patron saint of drama in the Southwest. During difficult times he has allied his activities with Hollywood, effecting an interchange of players, directors, and props and leaving a taint of commercialism on a world-renowned organization housed in a completely equipped theatre plant.

The Playhouse was originally backed by Pasadena fortunes but Mr. Brown is eclectic in his own tastes. His dowager customers would withdraw their support if he went too far to the left or offered the hospitality of his stage to the Workers' Theatre. Yet he has dared his bourgeois audience with items such as Ivanov's *Armored Train*, Rolland's *Wolves*, Afinogenov's *Fear*, Flavin's *Sunday* and *Amaco*, and the first American production of Ibsen's *Love's Comedy*.

This summer the Playhouse offered all ten of Shakespeare's chronicle plays, presented consecutively for the first time in an English-speaking theatre. The undertaking was entirely successful since the performances were lusty and not overly reverent. Fashioned and performed by youth, the productions were the most invigorating treatment the Bard had received in these parts for years.

In sixteen years Brown's theatre has presented 700 different plays, the American record for one theatre. The Playhouse is kindly disposed toward new plays, even those concerned with social justice, but the lack of them hereabouts is only too evident.

Pasadena has erred badly in pretentious and clumsy tussles with claptrap *Cavalcade* and "prestige" productions like its world premiere of *Lazarus Laughed*. These very bad imitations of extravaganza were better left to Morris Gest or his like, when a suitable Maecenas can be found. They gave the Playhouse publicity but accomplished nothing. Better, by far, have been careful productions of most of the Shaw comedies, major O'Neill works, animated revivals of former American play hits beginning with the *Virginian*. The Playhouse followed Hoyt's *A Texas Steer* with Anderson's *Both Your Houses*, affording excellent contrast of two types of political play.

Paul Muni has graced its stage and Douglas Montgomery was brought up there. Its manifold activities, including a bustling school and tryouts on smaller stages, dilute the energies of its capable directorate, and it cannot be said that the Pasadena theatre has any definite direction. It is not preparing the way for the new social drama, and its standards in producing the old are constantly shifting. Pasadena harbors several hundred pre-Hoover millionaires whose bonds and currency fill its bank vaults. It's not exactly where you'd expect to find revolutionary theatre, yet its most publicized citizen is none other than ex-socialist Upton Sinclair! Sinclair's brand of utopian liberalism took a trouncing in California last November. Yet the response to his political crusade indicated that the state is not the sole preserve of the reactionaries. Nor are potential theatre audiences composed exclusively of those who can afford aisle seats.

Beginning as the Rebel Players, some years ago, what was later to become the Workers' Theatre in Los Angeles offered *The Belt* and *Squaring the Circle*. During 1934 *Stevedore* and *Peace on Earth* were offered with considerable response on the part of the public. Jascha Frank, who directed *Peace on Earth*, was given exactly $7 for his production, which managed to run four weeks, with an encouraging press. *Sailors of Cattaro* was given an enthusiastic production in a small theatre this spring, and Clifford Odets's one-acters, *Waiting for Lefty* and *Till the Day I Die*, dared Hollywood itself by appearing boldly in one of its major showhouses. The Odets plays were able to find only part of their rightful audience, but their director, Will Geer, learned to his dismay how powerful their content was. He was ambushed and brutally beaten by "Friends of New Germany."

Various attempts to develop a flourishing New Theatre in the Los Angeles metropolitan area have encountered obstacles. The city is the center of far-flung distances, without unity. It is no easy task to bring together diverse thousands who would eagerly rally to the support of a united front, revolutionary theatre. The material is here, but it needs welding. Perhaps vigorous leadership of the New Theatre League representatives will soon provide the necessary momentum.

While the film industry licks its chops after a highly satisfactory swill at the nation's box office during 1935, the literate citizens of the movie capital have to attend the theatre in books and periodicals. Despite eastern doubts, many Californians are mentally acquisitive, eager to see plays which grapple with realities and suggest social solutions. Superficially California's citizens may appear to be a quaint race of lotus-eaters, yet the ordeal of Tom Mooney, the Sacramento trials, San Francisco's general strike, and the bloody iniquities in Imperial Valley haven't inspired political docility.

They are, so it seems, ready and eager for plays which will enlighten and fortify them in their urgent quest for a rational social program, the deliverance of America from capitalistic self-interest and its political votaries. It is up to the new social theatres to supply them with such plays.

Pins and Needles

BY BEN IRWIN

Review of the Labor Stage production by
the Contemporary Theatre Company

WITH no fanfare but with a great deal of purpose, the first undertaking of Labor Stage, Inc., was launched Sunday evening, June 14, in the studios of the Princess Theatre in New York with the Contemporary Theatre Company. It was a satirical musical revue, *Pins and Needles*, which succeeded in being genuinely entertaining, if occasionally overambitious.

This revue was the initial tangible product of the decision of the American Federation of Labor at its last convention, when, for the first time in the history of the American labor movement, the concept of theatre as a means of education for workers was officially endorsed in the formation of Labor Stage. This first effort was watched critically by labor leaders and theatre people alike. Neither group had cause to be disappointed.

Presented in a tiny studio (because the Princess Theatre proper in which Labor Stage will ultimately place its productions will not be completely renovated for several weeks yet) and presented on a still tinier stage, *Pins and Needles* managed to project a charm and vitality that one often finds missing in Broadway revues whose production costs run several hundred times that of *Pins and Needles*.

An unusually good-looking and gifted cast of girls, among them particularly Peggy Craven and Elizabeth Timberman, a supporting cast of men with Lee Hillery and Louis Latzer deserving special mention, with Harold Rome and Earl Robinson supplying the music with two pianos, all contributed to the general success of the program.

Harold Rome, who supplied the major portion of the lyrics and music, displayed a fresh and engaging talent in his work. S. Syrjala, who was responsible for the production design, created some extraordinarily simple but effective settings for the various revue numbers.

Of the eighteen numbers in the show, several were outstanding, including "Pass at Me," "Not Cricket," "You Gotta Dance," and "Magic at Sea," the first three of which were contributed by Rome. The production, which now runs well over two hours, might be cut and tightened up to some advantage, although the timing, an important part of any revue, was splendidly handled, considering the limited playing area.

Emanuel Eisenberg's "Mother! Let Freedom Wrong," a good-humored if caustic bit of fun poking at the social theatre, got the least rise of any of the production material out of this reviewer, although the audience seemed to enjoy it. It was a particularly sophisticated piece of burlesque which apparently attempted to establish the fact that the labor theatre was healthy enough to laugh at itself.

In general, however, Labor Stage has made a valuable excursion into the field of the social revue and brought forth some really worthwhile material. The new theatres throughout this country, which are working closely with the Central Labor bodies in their communities, will do well to follow the example of Labor Stage and make further experiments with the vaudeville form, a native and important theatre technique.

The Contemporary Theatre Company, which intends to stay together as the permanent company of Labor Stage, has indeed made an auspicious beginning.

A "BACKSTAGE" RELATIONSHIP WITH HALLIE FLANAGAN

AFTER Elmer Rice resigned as head of the New York Federal Theatre Project over censorship of *Ethiopia,* Arthur Arent's play denouncing Mussolini's brutal attack on that small country, many people wondered how a relatively unknown young playwright, Philip Barber, could have been in a position to succeed the famous author.

Since the Project is long dead, I can reveal what happened without fear of damaging anyone's reputation. One night I received an anxious call from an actress friend in the Theatre Project. About a half hour later she came to the office in a nervous state. She confided her fears about an uncle she hated, the head of a large Democratic club, also an important, influential executive of a stage workers' union.

She said her uncle was a violent, vengeful man, so her name had to be kept out of her revelation that he was secretly a Mussolini admirer who favored the invasion of Ethiopia and was active secretly in a New York fascist underground society. He had enough political clout through the Democratic club and his union executive friends to bring pressure for his appointment to high office in the Theatre Project. If he got in, the liberal actors and directors with whom she sympathized and worked would have an enemy in a powerful position. And both Mrs. Flanagan, national coordinator of the Federal Theatre Project, and Elmer Rice would be stuck with a secret fascist pushing his friends and endangering the Project. My actress friend had read the letter exchange that I had with Hallie Flanagan in *New Theatre,* and urged me to see Mrs. Flanagan privately and try to forestall the uncle's plans. For family reasons, and her fears, I must give my word to never reveal her involvement.

I agreed and phoned Hallie Flanagan in Washington early the next morning. I asked for an appointment on an urgent matter I could not discuss over the phone. She reacted in a friendly manner and gave me a late-afternoon appointment. I remember I was nervous about my mission on the bus ride down. But not after her appreciative response as I explained the situation. She was shocked and said that she was expected to arrange for Elmer Rice's approval and announce the man's appointment within a few days. Unless she could decide on someone else immediately, and thus block the Democratic club's strong recommendation, there would be a political storm. A quick appointment she could ride out as a fait accompli. Then, to my surprise, Mrs. Flanagan asked if I knew anyone who was liberal but not politically Left for the post.

We discussed several writers and directors about whom Mrs. Flanagan expressed doubts. Then I suggested Philip Barber as a promising young playwright whose New Theatre League activities were liberal but not "too Left." Mrs. Flanagan remembered having met Philip at a college conference and agreed with my liking and respect for him. We also agreed that neither of us should reveal to anyone, including Philip and Elmer Rice, my role in this matter. The Federal Project was facing enough right-wing attacks without leaving her open to charges of *New Theatre* influencing her appointments. Mrs. Flanagan took down Philip's home number that I gave her, then made up her mind and said she'd call right away without mentioning I was with her. Luckily, she reached Philip immediately, told him about the position, and he was enthusiastic about coming to meet her in Washington the next day.

We were happy to hear this, and thankful to my anonymous actress friend. Then, having had a taste of using my influence, I decided to press my luck. I told Mrs. Flanagan that I'd just visited Hiram Motherwell, who was broke, sweating out the last of a publisher's advance on a book. He needed a job badly, so if there were any way . . . ? She reacted as I had hoped. Yes, she said she knew and admired Motherwell, who had encouraged and praised her work at Vassar with the Experimental Theatre, especially her play of social protest, *Can You Hear Their Voices?* Again, we agreed not to mention my "role" in her suggesting Motherwell to Rice and Barber. As things turned out, they gave Motherwell a good position a few days later. Both of my secret recommendations did fine, important work as long as the Federal Theatre Project lasted.

Here are selections reflecting direct *New Theatre* action in support of the Project that contributed so greatly to promoting many fine talents in the American theatre arts.

A Letter from Hallie Flanagan

Mr. Herbert Kline, Editor,
New Theatre,
156 West 44th St.
New York, N. Y.

Dear Herbert Kline:
You have asked me to tell you something of the new Federal Theatre Project. Your magazine is a friend of the theatre and of the un-

employed, and your question therefore deserves the most intelligent answer I can give it. I shall state the problem and the general plan under which we hope to operate. If you or the readers of *New Theatre* have suggestions to offer, I shall be glad to receive them.

The federal government allocated, as you know, $4,800,000,000 for relief under the Works Progress Administrator, Harry L. Hopkins. This appropriation included $27,000,000 for putting back to work musicians, writers, painters, sculptors, and theatre people. For each one of these fields there is a federal director; Mr. Nicolai Sokoloff for music; Mr. Holger Cahill for art; Mr. Henry Alsberg for writing; myself for the theatre. Each federal director plans to work through regional directors for some twelve areas throughout the United States, and because we are eager to work together in close cooperation, we are using, as far as possible, the same regional divisions. Responsible to the regional director, and through him to the federal director in Washington, there will be administrative directors of individual theatre projects.

Since this plan is for professionals, most of the projects will operate in New York, Chicago, or Los Angeles where unemployment is most acute. Such groups as Actors' Equity, the League of New York Theatres, the Dramatists' Guild, the National Theatre Conference, are sponsoring various units: playwrights' theatres for testing new scripts; Negro theatres in Harlem; a repertory of plays important in American theatrical history; a bureau of research and publication for dramatic material. Other projects are under way for vaudeville and specialty acts in connection with great recreation centers where dance orchestras of unemployed musicians will play for unemployed youth. The plan includes also the remodeling of the historic theatre in Charleston, South Carolina, where the oldest theatre in the United States will house a program reviving the plays done in the first theatrical season in America.

The CCC camp project is itself so vast in nature that one wishes for six years instead of six months to do it justice. Although some traveling companies will still provide entertainment for camps, the Federal project stresses a resident theatre director for each camp, such a director to plan amateur nights in which the camp members themselves write and perform plays. At present, 35 of the 200 camps in New York, New Jersey, and Delaware have such directors, and the requests have come to extend this activity to 2,000 CCC camps throughout the United States.

It will be seen that while our immediate aim in all these projects is to put to work thousands of theatre people, our more far-reaching purpose is to organize and support theatrical enterprises so excellent in nature, so low in cost, and so vital to the communities involved that they will be able to continue after federal support is withdrawn.

With this in mind we are encouraging, except for camp or educational projects, a low admission charge of 25¢ to $1.00, depending on geography of the unit involved. At the present time both theatre and cinema interests claim that free shows are hurting their trade; it is possible that they may also object to an admission charge on the ground of undercutting; but it seems the lesser of the two evils. We have consulted the representatives from the League of New York Theatres, Actors' Equity, the American Federation of Actors, the Scenic Artists' Union, the Stage Hands' Union; as rapidly as possible we wish to consult all theatrical unions involved. Obviously they would all prefer, as would the director of this project, a higher rate of pay than the security wage of $30 to $94 per month depending on skill and the geographic placement. However, we are confronted, not by theory, but by the condition that the same wage prevailing throughout the Works Progress Administration affects, necessarily, the art projects. Certainly the labor organizations can be assured that eighty percent of the entire allotment will be spent for labor costs; ten percent for small administrative salaries; and ten percent for production costs.

During the next few weeks of planning, and later, as the various projects start, we need the active interest and help of every person who cares about the theatre and about the problem of unemployment; we need the support of people who believe, as we do, that there is skill, experience, enthusiasm, and intelligence in the theatre people now on relief rolls and in the thousands of theatre people who will cooperate with them. We need the support of people who share our belief that the theatre horizon is not contracting but widening to include Santa Fe Desert, the Rocky Mountains, and the valley of the Mississippi; widening to include the arts of sculpture, music, architecture, the cinema; widening to include a consciousness of the social scene as well as the social register; widening in short, to include the impossible—that same impossible which has led our contemporaries to soar to the stars, whisper through space, and fling miles of steel and glass into the air.

We need the belief of all of you who care about the theatre in terms of the art and economics of 1935.

                    Sincerely,
                    HALLIE FLANAGAN,
                    Director,
                    Federal Theatre Project

HERBERT KLINE'S REPLY

Dear Mrs. Flanagan:

First, let me thank you for your prompt and friendly answer. The plans you outline for the Federal Theatre Project are of vital concern to NEW THEATRE. We see in the theatre project a welcome although shamefully belated effort to alleviate the distressing conditions prevailing among unemployed theatre workers. We see, also, an opportunity for the advancement of the drama throughout America as a medium for entertainment and education which will be within the reach even of the lowest-paid sectors of our population. We have no fear, since the appointments of such progressive talents as Frederic McConnell, Gilmore Brown, Elmer Rice, John McKee, and Professors Koch and Mabie, among others, that the project will be used as was the New York PWA under Colonel Boothe to further prowar propaganda.

Although you and your associates have our belief, interest, and support in terms of art, ability, and sincerity, *in terms of the economics of 1935*, there are several problems that we would like to bring to your attention.

First, there is the problem that you alone cannot settle—what kind of relief and how much? We believe that the sliding relief scales of the WPA are shamefully inadequate, that the American people who have created this country's wealth deserve better than a virtual starvation wage when they are forced to go on relief through no fault of their own. We ask with Alfred Kreymborg, "What has become of all your gold, America?" We believe in and support the efforts of all relief workers to gain more adequate relief. Furthermore, we support the stand of the unions that prevailing wages should be paid to all relief workers. For we fear that the relief projects will prove a menace to wage standards that the unions throughout American industry have established after long years of struggle.

The stage workers have had to fight hard for their prevailing standards. Everyone familiar with the abominable conditions that prevailed throughout the entire industry before the workers got together in their great victorious strike of 1919 realizes that the stage unions must be guarded against factors that tend to weaken them.

We, who represent labor in the theatre in our creative work, are as eager as you are to see the drama project get under way at once.

The stage unions and all other labor forces in the theatre will be able to cooperate to the fullest extent in carrying out the splendid plans you have outlined for the drama project.

Sincerely yours,
HERBERT KLINE

THE PUPPET MASTER
S. Bunin

A Statement by Elmer Rice

Given to the Press at the January 24 Showing of *Ethiopia*

THE IMPLIED charge that a carefully documented factual presentation of public events could conceivably affect our international relations is absurd on its face and doubly ludicrous to anyone who has read the script or seen a rehearsal of the production. Mr. Baker is merely trying to raise a smoke screen to conceal the real issue. That issue clearly is free speech. When I took this job last fall, I did so upon Mr. Harry Hopkins's emphatic and explicit assurance that Washington would not attempt in any way to censor the productions of the Federal Theatre Project. At my first interview in October, I informed the reporters that any attempt at censorship would be followed by immediate resignation. Washington has broken its word; I have kept mine.

The final decision to censor the Living Newspaper and thereby force my resignation did not come until after I had outlined for Mr. Baker some of the other productions which were being planned. These include a play called *Class of '29* which deals realistically with unemployment and the handling of relief; and a second issue of the Living Newspaper on the situation in the Southern states, touching on such vital subjects as lynching, discrimination against Negroes, and the plight of the sharecroppers (in other words, hitting the Democratic Party where it lives). Mr. Baker has already called off one Federal Theatre Project in Chicago, because in the opinion of Mayor Kelly it was uncomplimentary to the Administration and to the Democratic Party.

In short, we are confronted here not only with evidence of the growth of fascism, which always uses censorship as one of its most effective weapons, but with resolute determination of the Democratic Party to be reelected at all costs. In the face of that stern necessity, the fostering of the arts, the rehabilitation of unemployed professional men and women, and the constitutional guarantees of freedom of expression go by the boards.

I am sorry to be obliged to resign at a time when so many of the carefully laid plans of the Federal Theatre Project are nearing fruition. And it is difficult for me to sever my friendly association with Hallie Flanagan, Philip Barber, and the hundreds of fine earnest theatre workers who have given me their cooperation and support. But I am a member of the board of directors of the American Civil Liberties Union, the vice-chairman of the National Council on Freedom from Censorship, and the chairman of the Authors' League Censorship Committee. For fifteen years and more I have been actively engaged in fighting censorship in every form. The issue of free speech and the preservation of the Bill of Rights seem to me of greater moment today than they have ever been in the history of America. I cannot conscientiously remain the servant of a government which plays the shabby game of partisan politics at the expense of freedom and the principles of democracy.

A Scene from the Censored Play

BY ARTHUR ARENT

A news dramatization of the Living Newspaper Unit,
WPA (a Federal Theatre Project)

TELETYPE: "BETRAYED!" CRIES BRITISH PUBLIC.
TELETYPE: SHEFFIELD SHEFFIELD SHEFFIELD SHEFFIELD SHEFFIELD
(*Light up on street scene. Man, soap box, etc.*)

SPEAKER: ... and what do you think everybody else is going to say about this—all the little countries like Romania, Greece, Turkey, Jugoslavia, Poland, and the rest of them. What are they going to think of British diplomacy and the League of Nations now? ... I'll tell you what they're going to think! Suppose it was our country that was being invaded—Romania, Greece, or Turkey? Why, we'd be getting the same kind of raw deal that Ethiopia is getting now—that's what they'll say. And they'll wash their hands of the whole dirty business, and then you can throw the *WHOLE LEAGUE OF NATIONS INTO THE SCRAP HEAP, AND CIVILIZATION WILL BE PUT BACK ANOTHER TWENTY YEARS ... WE'VE BEEN BETRAYED!* (*Blackout*)

TELETYPE: LIVERPOOL LIVERPOOL LIVERPOOL LIVERPOOL

(*Light up on another street scene, another soap box, another agitator, a well-dressed, middle-aged woman.*)

WOMAN: (*Calmly, dispassionately—enumerating these successive steps on her fingers*) Look: the League decides that Italy is guilty of aggression of unprovoked assault on Ethiopia. They apply economic sanctions as a further emphasis of this guilt. So far so good. But what does Sir Samuel Hoare do? He decides to reward Italy for this aggression, for this unprovoked assault, by giving her practically everything she asks and more than she expected ... while Ethiopia, a nation that's hurting no one and just minding its own business, a nation that has been fairly judged to be the injured party, is stripped of almost everything it has that is worth taking! *AND THAT, MY FRIENDS, IS EXACTLY WHAT THE HOARE-LAVAL PEACE PLAN IS!* (*Blackout*)

TELETYPE: MANCHESTER MANCHESTER MANCHESTER MANCHESTER

(*Light up on another street scene.*)

GIRL: ... So Mister Baldwin says this is the only way a world war can be averted, does he? Well, what I say is this: What good is the League for anyhow? ... Didn't I read about some agreement in the Covenant which says that all the nations should support each other in outlawing an aggressor? And if this outlawing leads to a war of everybody concerned against this aggressor—well then, I say, didn't they think it meant that when they established the League, didn't they? ... *WE'VE BEEN BETRAYED!* (*Blackout*)

TELETYPE: LONDON LONDON LONDON LONDON LONDON

(*Light up on a Trafalgar Square scene.*)

SPEAKER: (*Cockney*) ... they comes before us and says, "Vote for Baldwin and the Conservative Party because the Conservative Party stands behind the League of Nations and the League will see that every nation gets a square deal," that's what they says. . . . And what do we do? We does what we're told like good little boys and girls and we votes them in with a majority of twelve million. *Twelve million!* . . . And *then* what happens? They proceed to forget every rotten plank in their platform and they get up a peace plan which is nice and sweet and fair and square for everybody . . . except Ethiopia . . . which has to give up half its territory so Italy won't make war on it anymore. . . . We've been betrayed. *BETRAYED!* (*Blackout*).

The Federal Theatre Presents

BY JOSEPH MANNING

THE FEDERAL THEATRE in New York, having emerged from an initial baptism of red tape, has now lifted four first-night curtains. One curtain—that of the Living Newspaper's *Ethiopia*—remains down.

Since Elmer Rice's resignation over the censorship issue there has been no further change in the production schedule. Philip Barber, the new regional director, is pushing through the original program. Thirty-six plays, ranging from Shakespeare to W. H. Auden, are in rehearsal; more than a dozen rehearsal halls, in addition to six theatres scattered throughout greater New York, resound with activity. The Lafayette Theatre in Harlem has been playing to good audiences since February 4.

Still, it cannot be said that the Federal Theatre is in full swing as yet. Several of the most important groups still await properties, costumes, and theatres. Because of delay and miscasting, several groups will not be able to show the best that they are capable of until their second or third productions.

In terms of accomplishment, the Negro Theatre up to now has outdistanced the other projects. Planned late last fall, this group was one of the first to begin rehearsal. Shortly after the new year the company moved into the Lafayette Theatre. Two shows were then under way: Frank Wilson's *Walk Together Chillun*, and the Orson Welles's adaptation of *Macbeth*. On February 4 the Wilson play opened to an enthusiastic audience. The performance was repeatedly stopped by outbursts of applause. Less than a fortnight later John Houseman, supervisor of the project, was called to a commercial engagement, and the Negro

Theatre, headed by Carlton Moss, has become established on a self-governing basis. It is planning an early March opening for the second show.

The Experimental Theatre, on the other hand, has met with interminable delays from the very first—delays not inherent in the organization of the unit. Under the expert guidance of James Light the company has been rehearsing *Chalk Dust* (a brittle comment upon modern educational methods) in the basement of the Daly Theatre. Under the supervision of Virgil Geddes the entire group has moved through the doldrums of interminable delay with notable fortitude and fine morale. Staff meetings are held regularly, the supervisors on this project having been the first to establish conferences for discussing personnel, plays, and the general progress of the work. Recently the directorial staff devoted a holiday to debating a script endorsed by several members of the group.

The character of the personnel mirrored in such incidents will be shown in the completed production. Against the background of a school room Light has built up a masterful interpretation, with eloquent moments reminiscent of the best achievements of the early Provincetown Theatre.

There are other companies doing a very special type of production which requires extensive rehearsal. The Kleist play, *Der Zerbrochene Krug*, is a good illustration. The German group with John E. Bonn directing has taken this eighteenth-century classic and given it a provocative modern treatment. Bonn, long familiar with advanced European technique, has forged a novelty which is likely to find admirers among those who look forward to the theatre of tomorrow.

A similar tendency to depart from beaten trails is evident in the production of W. H. Auden's *Dance of Death*. This "glorified satire with musical score" is being done by the Poetic Theatre, headed by Alfred Kreymborg. Emile Beilveau, formerly dramatic director for Briarcliff College, is directing. Excepting for a select Vassar audience (which requested a repeat performance) the play has not yet been seen in this country. The Poetic Theatre's second production will be Vachel Lindsay's *The Congo*, a mass recitation by Negroes.

The Popular Price Theatre, headed by Edward Goodman, who has been identified with the growth of the American theatre for twenty years, will follow *American Holiday* with T. S. Eliot's *Murder in the Cathedral*, and *Class of '29*, a compact and forceful statement of the economic crisis in terms of unemployed youth. The designs for *Murder in the Cathedral* have been made by Tom Adrian Cracraft, a leader in his profession; other members of the same group are Helen Arthur, Agnes Morgan, Halstead Welles, and Lucius Moore Cook.

The Federal Theatre, in New York as elsewhere, must not be regarded as one producing outfit dominated by a single dramatic theory. Rather must it be viewed as a small theatre world wherein there is vast diversity in talent, attitude, and in the scripts themselves. And each project in turn is a small world unto itself, involving countless variations in talent, ambition, and vision. A more polyglot institution can hardly be imagined. German, Yiddish, Russian, Hebrew, Polish, French, and at least one Nigerian dialect are all in evidence, not only among the actors but in the scripts. The old and the new are both to be found—playwrights long dust and boys just out of their teens— there is no discrimination, no arbitrary barrier. Courageous is the least that can be said of a program embracing such variety despite the non-theatrical limitations imposed upon it by the ever-ingenious WPA.

The often-repeated question, "Why is the Federal Theatre taking so long to get under way?" is difficult to answer simply.

The first few months have served as an apprenticeship for many, and the seemingly insurmountable obstacles have been overcome one by one. Supplies for running operations are now on hand: lumber, paint, tools; the theatres have been renovated and are ready for action. What is more important, the companies have in many instances developed group unity, and professional association has created a lasting spirit of confidence. Considering the size of the Federal Theatre and the numerous personalities, there is relatively little friction. The hardships and trials have served to weld rather than disintegrate. The prevalent attitude is determination to succeed even in the face of challenges which might have weakened or destroyed less conscientious craftsmen.

The Living Newspaper

BY MORRIS WATSON

THE CURRENT edition of the Living Newspaper at the Biltmore Theatre, *1935*, recounts various happenings of the year for which it is named and represents a deliberate experiment in the matter of presenting news visually.

The Living Newspaper's first offering, *Triple-A Plowed Under*, took a single theme and developed it along news lines and actually was more pamphlet than newspaper. In *1935* unrelated items are presented on the same program, and the temper of the year, rather than the history, is stressed.

The edition opens its story at 11:58 P.M. of the last day of 1934 with a crowd of merrymakers at Times Square. The commentator asks if they remember Hindenburg, John L. McGraw, and Marie Curie, who died in 1934. And do they remember the assassination of King Alexander and the burning of the *Morro Castle*? Midnight comes with a blast of noise.

"Make news!" the commentator pleads. Twelve representatives of the Great American Public get into a box to judge the events and the Voice of the Living Newspaper quickly announces January 2, the opening of the trial of Bruno Richard Hauptmann for the kidnapping and murder of Baby Charles A. Lindbergh, Jr. A Flemington, N.J., ballyhoo man proudly conducts a crowd of curious through the courtroom and tells them where Gloria Vanderbilt, Big Nick Cavarro, and other celebrities parked themselves for the trial. The trial goes on with the crowd rushing for seats, with reporters quarreling over the purchase of exclusive stories from the principals. Betty Gow is called. "I couldn't hear the baby breathe," Miss Gow testifies. As she speaks the courtroom blacks out, a spot comes up on a stylized witness stand in the center. The stand becomes a crib. She feels over the covers. Her expression becomes one of horror. She hesitates an instant. Then she screams: "Colonel Lindbergh! Colonel Lindbergh!" and rushes off. "Jafsie" Condon comes on to testify. But he does not testify. He acts out what he has to say and the mysterious "John" of Van Cortlandt Park and the cemetery helps him. The spotlight turns to an eerie green. Leaves rustle. "John" sits with the elderly Bronx pedagogue and asks: "Would I burn if the baby is dead?"

Thus the technique of reporting a trial visually without merely reproducing it on the stage in a word-for-word manner.

Next comes a scene that violates all the rules of dramatic writing. But the Living Newspaper is a combination of newspaper and topical revue. It is reporting the passage of the Wagner-Connery labor disputes bill in the terms of an actual case. A young lady appears to testify before an examiner for the board. Her words become reality. "They shut off the power and made us all go to a big room," she starts. She is talking about the Somerset Manufacturing Company of Sommerville, N.J. The curtain opens on a bunch of scared young girls and reveals the lengths to which small New Jersey towns will go to keep America safe for the exploited open shop. The episode ends with another piece of testimony acted out. One of the young ladies finds her pay is short. She goes to the office girl. She's right. Her pay is short. But wait—that's the book for the NRA code inspector. According to the book she gets *paid* by, the miserable wage she got is all she had coming. No climax. The critics call it anticlimax. The boys of the fourth estate who edit the Living Newspaper are just telling a story for what it is worth. The scene may lack the customary punch expected at the end of a dramatic sketch. Anyone viewing it, though, should be able to see why labor needs some legal protection.

That the scene should have a "wallop" at the end may be a valid criticism. I'm not saying that it isn't. The usual news story is written with the punch at the top. We newspapermen are newly wedded to the theatre. We have a lot to learn about each other. A dozen more editions should put us in step. The stride may surprise us.

A sop to humor follows the labor problem in *1935*. Bugsy Goldstein is sore as hell. Officials have rerated the public enemies—and he's only No. 6. Just a flash. The Great American Public plays a Giants-Dodgers ball game from its bunting-bedecked jury box. The scene means nothing to me because I never saw the Dodgers play. I can't take sides here. The fans laugh like hell, and that makes it a good item for the Living Newspaper's sports page.

Barbara Hutton gets married. This time to a count. The Living Newspaper falls back on the manner in which Miss Ruth McKenny handled the story for the *New York Post*: the manager of a Woolworth five-and-ten would be glad to let the *Post* photograph one of its workers who also was to be a bride that day—only Miss Hutton might not like it!

The next scene makes its own comment on the human race. William Deboe is hanged at Smithland, Ky. Folks turn out early to get good seats. Deboe was convicted of rape. He points to his accuser and says: "If I had five hundred dollars I wouldn't be here, she'd a taken it." What a thing to say! "Not if you offered me a thousand," she comes back. A preacher intones the Lord's Prayer. "Peanuts, popcorn, crackerjack," yells the candy butcher. So far as we could determine, the scene is staged exactly as it happened. Two minutes before the curtain went up on opening night the actor who plays the preacher became convinced the Living Newspaper was poking fun at the Lord's Prayer. He said he wouldn't go on! We had to explain the idea.

Under the general heading of "Trivia" comes the case of the prisoner who was forgotten, who served eighteen years of a five-year sentence, and the man who advertised that he found a lady's purse in the backseat of his automobile. He was willing to pay for the ad himself if the owner would explain the matter to his wife, who couldn't imagine how the purse got there. A laugh.

The Voice of the Living Newspaper sweeps through the mention of several other headlines of 1935 and then Dutch Schultz comes on the scene—to beat the law, to die at the hands of the mob. The Great American Public discusses matters, not too relevantly. Then Huey Long manipulates his legislators like puppets and swaggers on to his assassination. The legislative scene is stylized. It becomes a living cartoon and through it the Living Newspaper learns that it can pack potency into its editorial page.

The Great American Public again—to disagree on whether the assassination of Huey Long was a national crisis, and wind up by being indifferent to the whole matter.

In 1935 Jeremiah T. Mahoney and Avery Brundage argued about American participation in the Olympic games at Berlin. "Sport must confine itself to the affairs of sport and no other," says Brundage. The Living Newspaper reports the incident, and illustrates sport as it is practiced in the land of the Nazis. The best tennis player is removed from his team because he is a Jew. A Polish-Jewish soccer player is killed. A Catholic swimmer is stoned. The Living Newspaper doesn't say anything is right or wrong. The audience does pretty well in making its own decision on the matter. I know of no way to censor hisses.

John L. Lewis makes a plea for industrial unionism. President William Green of the American Federation of Labor is adequately quoted. The Living Newspaper tries to illustrate the argument. No kick there.

The China Clipper flies from Asia to America in 62 hours for the sake of commerce. A thriller, and another experiment. The Living Newspaper is feeling its way.

Angelo Herndon in jail with a "mercy" sentence of 18 to 20 years on the chain gang.

"That's sho' death," says another prisoner who spent six months on a Georgia chain gang. Here a test of visual reporting. The prisoner stands in the cell and describes the horrors of Georgia torture. The lights on him dim. The curtains open slowly and the audience gets a vivid glimpse of what he is saying. Silhouettes against a red light wield picks on a road. Over them hover the ominous, 20-foot-high shadows of guards, rifles and whips held in position of "ready."

"Ef yo' cain't stand it no mo' and drop in yo' tracks that ol' whip come crackin' down agin and somp'n make yo' get up and raise a pick and drop a pick agin," the prisoner says. The silhouetted whip cracks.

The crowd is in Times Square again. Horns are tooting. Bells are ringing.

Happy New Year! Welcome 1936.

It is difficult to compare this kaleidoscopic report of the year's events which lent themselves to staging with the Living Newspaper's first edition, *Triple-A Plowed Under*, which tied the plight of the farmer to the plight of the city man and disturbed the mental processes of those who saw it. In other words, it made people think. *1935* hasn't as much of that virtue, and it is open to a great deal more criticism. Each of its scenes is likely to be judged from a purely theatrical standpoint. They cannot, as did the scenes of *Triple-A Plowed Under*, flow into each other, contributing to another.

Many times likely I have been asked: "Whose idea is the Living Newspaper?" The answer is: "I don't know."

The business of presenting news on the stage has been tried before —in vaudeville, by workers' clubs, in the Workers' Laboratory Theatre of New York and elsewhere. I also have hearsay evidence that Ben Hecht and Charles MacArthur once toyed with the idea and that similar enterprises flourished for a time in Berlin and Moscow.

Whatever the idea behind the Living Newspaper in the beginning, circumstances and influences of one kind and another have modified it. A literally rough estimate of it at the moment would be: "Combine the newspaper and the theatre and to hell with the traditions of both."

My own connection with the enterprise was an accident. Last October the Newpaper Guild of New York was looking for some way to absorb a few of its unemployed in the newly formed Federal Theatre Project. The Guild's unemployment committee went to Elmer Rice, then the regional director for New York.

Rice suggested that a Project be formed to present news on the stage. The committee began looking for someone to head the project. The first I heard of it was when I was asked if I knew of anyone who would fit the job. I didn't. The heavy hand of coincidence entered the plot at this point and I found myself "at liberty." To cut the corners on this explanation, there was thrust upon my shoulders the task of organizing the project.

I was greatly excited by the idea. For many years I had been covering living drama and visualizing it in terms of the stage. The amazing thing about the Living Newspaper is that it was so late in coming. The explanation may be that newspaper men have been timid about barging into the theatre and theatre men have been bound by too many traditions. There has been plenty of friendly conflict between those of us in the Living Newspaper who are of the fourth estate and those who are of the theatre.

Elmer Rice lent a vigor to the Living Newspaper which still is apparent. In the beginning we thought we would dramatize current news, it never occurring to us at the moment that the current news at hand was likely to be very weak stuff. The Living Newspaper staff of dramatists began culling the papers and writing for all they were worth on such items as "Tart Shoots Lover" and "Robber Seizes Jewels of Movie Queen." Rice's criticisms resulted in a complete reorganization of my own news sense. Rice said things were going on in the world and he thought we ought to talk about them. I agreed. He thought of things that affected people's lives and happiness and he didn't care if we stepped on a few toes and made somebody mad.

Armed with this moral backing, we decided to dramatize that part of the news which was controversial, hence current when we reached the stage with it.

INVITATION TO A HARLEM PARTY

PUBLISHING the first issue of an American magazine to credit the great contributions Negroes made to the theatre arts came about through a visit to New York by a friend, Richard Wright, at that time an unknown writer. He had not yet won fame for his novel *Native Son* and the play based on it which Orson Welles directed. Dick had done his first writing in Chicago, during his John Reed Club days, when George Redfield, Mark, and I were editors of the literary quarterly *Left Front*.

Langston Hughes had invited Dick to a Harlem rent party, and he got us invited too. A whole group of us went: George, his wife Louise of the New Dance League, Mark and his wife Wanda, who worked for Musicians' Local 802, and Molly Day Thacher (without her husband, Elia Kazan, who was acting in a Group Theatre play that evening). So we were six whites and one black, together taking the subway to a Harlem artists' apartment near 125th Street.

When we arrived we found a grand party going on. Other guests, besides Langston, included Augustus Smith and Eugene Gordon among the writers; Rex Ingram, Leigh Whipper, and other actors of the *Stevedore* cast; also various artists, dancers, actors, and musicians.

We had a wonderful time—dancing, singing, gabbing, arguing, drinking wine, beer, some hard stuff, eating—there was plenty of soul food and Jewish delicatessen. During the lively discussions, an idea struck me for a special issue of *New Theatre*.

"Does anyone know of an American magazine publishing a whole issue on Negroes in the theatre arts with talents like the ones assembled in this room?"

Nobody did. But everyone in there responded to the idea, and right then individuals promised some of the articles and poems for our selections. Only Richard Wright didn't complete the one-act play he had pledged. He had to advise us at the last minute that his publisher was pressing him to deliver his novel or void the contract. I always regretted the loss of that play.

Our issue devoted to Negro theatre arts talents received highly favorable reviews, especially in the Negro press. Mark and his main New Theatre League aide, Ben Irwin, reported that, more than ever before, Negro groups were being formed and blacks were joining white groups.

Years later, Mark coproduced with Canada Lee a successful Broadway production, *On Whitman Avenue*, about the rights of Negro workers to live near munitions factories during World War II. Canada, who had won acclaim as both a very successful prizefighter and jockey, told us that reading our special issue on Negroes had stirred in him faith in his potential to turn from a professional life in sports to his third career as an actor in theatre and films, where he starred in productions of *Lifeboat, Body and Soul, Lost Boundaries,* and *Cry the Beloved Country*.

Many years later I had the honor of meeting Martin Luther King, Jr., and discussing with him our Negro arts issue. He knew of the plays that had been written about, such as *They Shall Not Die* and *Stevedore*, and credited them as having been important steps in the opening up of American minds to the concept of racial equality.

From *Uncle Tom's Cabin* to *Stevedore*

BY EUGENE GORDON

EVER since the night Uncle Tom first shuffled upon the stage, American drama has emphasized the ruling-class concept of the Negro's place in this social order. It makes no difference that Uncle Tom and other "Negroes" often were whites smirking under burnt cork and groveling under kinky wigs; the idea of the Negro's place was so emphatically implied that succeeding generations of colored actors have naturally assumed the stereotype.

The ruling class decreed the Negro's place to be down below, in the spheres both of economics and of art, and permitted none but white men to personate the ruling-class concept of the black man. Society cut the pattern for black-white relationship, slave-plantation mode of production, plotting the outline with blacks on the lowest level. Since men habituate themselves in all relationships according to their peculiar roles, enacting their parts automatically, the roles of master and slave bore a constant relation to each other.

Uncle Tom's Cabin reflected ruling-class opinion of the Negro's place in bourgeois American life, although neither Harriet Beecher Stowe, who wrote the novel, nor Charles Townsend, who adapted the play, purposed it. The points of view of the South and the North were fundamentally identical: the Negro was definitely a being *psychologically* doomed to slavery forever. *Uncle Tom's Cabin* reflected this viewpoint. For instance:

> ELIZA: Yes, down the river where they work you to death. Uncle Tom, I'm going to run away, and take Harry with me. Won't you come too? You have a pass to come and go at any time.
>
> TOM: No, no—I can't leave Mas'r Shelby dat way. But I won't say no to your goin'. But if sellin' me can get mas'r outer trouble, why den let me be sold. I s'pose I can bar it as well as any one. Mas'r always found me on the spot . . . he always will. I never have broken trust, nor used my pass no ways contrary to my word, and never will. It's better for me to go alone, than to break up the place and sell all. Mas'r ain't to blame, and he'll take care of my wife and little 'uns!

Harriet Beecher Stowe's plan of attack on slavery was gradually to destroy it so that the ensuing hardships to the master would not be too great: reduce his property by removing a slave here and there, now and then, until all are freed. Uncle Tom falls in with the plan: better for him to go alone "than to break up the place and sell all." "Mas'r ain't to blame," so be tender with him. It is the fault of the system. Mas'r is, in a way, as much a slave as Uncle Tom. This sentiment is implicit in that one passage. The whole play implies more.

Loyalty and devotion in general are the essence of nobility: a slave is noble if loyal and devoted. This is the lesson of Christianity. It is ruling-class ideology; it is the message of *Uncle Tom's Cabin*. The author commends Uncle Tom for remaining with Mas'r Shelby. Speaking through the playwright, the ruling class commends all Negroes who are loyal and devoted to the white master class.

Tom was neither loyal nor devoted to his last owner, Legree. Why? Because Legree was not of the master class. He was an upstart, villainous, poor white, deserving and receiving contempt. Slaves were taught loyalty and devotion to those God ordained to rule; this doctrine implied scorn for those hired to rule.

Uncle Tom's Cabin reflects ruling-class ideology from another angle. Tom's second owner, St. Clare, is speaking to Maria, St. Clare's wife: "I've brought you a coachman, at last, to order. I tell you he is a regular hearse for blackness and sobriety," and so on. The audience has already met George Harris and Eliza. Harris is a "pretty good-looking chap," for he is "kind of tall," has "brown hair" and "dark eyes"; in other words, George Harris is an octoroon. His wife, Eliza, is also "as white as you are," Shelby tells Haley, the slave trader.

Does all this detail about the physical appearance of Tom, Harris, and Eliza serve no purpose than to heighten dramatic interest? Hardly; but dramatic interest is heightened not only by showing that slavery's leprous hands often fell on "whites," but that "white" Negroes were given less than blacks to mumbling nonsense about loyalty and devotion. The "full-blooded" Negro, implies the author, is inferior to the Negro with "white" blood. Mixed bloods are portrayed as impatient of restraint, as if slave psychology is foreign to them alone.

Uncle Tom's Cabin was the artistic expression of the industrial bourgeoisie on slavery. It was also the expression of the ruling class as a whole: roughly, the capitalists in the North and slaveholders in the South. It was the conviction of this class that it had a God-ordained right to be. The fundamental "right," therefore, of one class to rule another was not the question at issue. The question was how to reconcile differences between the nonslaveholders and the slaveholders so as to unite the ruling class. Was Uncle Tom more effectively exploited by the wage slavery of the North or by the chattel slavery of the South? That was the question reconciliators must consider. The author of *Uncle Tom's Cabin*, however, was as unaware of her role of reconciliator as Paul Green or Eugene O'Neill is unaware today of assuming a traditional attitude toward, and repeating traditional slurs about, the Negro. The man who dramatized her novel similarly played his role.

Uncle Tom's Cabin was one of the first instances "where an attempt is made to present to the American public in a realistic manner the authentic life of the Negro," asserts Montgomery Gregory in his introduction to the plays in *The New Negro*. The other drama, he says, was Dion Boucicault's *Octoroon*. Gregory thinks these plays "served to rationalize somewhat the stage conception of the Negro," which, until now, had been the "darky" of minstrelsy, "and accustomed the theatre-going public of Negro characters in other than the conventional 'darky' roles."

Gregory's saying that *Uncle Tom's Cabin* "served to rationalize somewhat the stage conception of the Negro" is correct. It was "somewhat," in a most limited sense. *Uncle Tom's Cabin* and *Octoroon* no more presented "in a realistic manner the authentic life of the Negro" than the earlier minstrels had done. In minstrelsy, the slave was an irresponsible happy-go-lucky; in "serious" drama, he was a saint who had only to die to join the "authentic" angels. To the playwright whose interests were one with the rising bourgeoisie, the Negro was capable of development as a free man. These playwrights agreed that in neither case should the black man be a member of the ruling class.

"The minstrel tradition continued until the middle nineties, when John W. Isham organized a musical show, *The Octoroons*," declares Gregory. There followed a succession of musical comedies, the casts of which were completely Negro. The minstrel tradition did not end with the Negro's writing and producing musical comedy, but continued in a more refined form. When the Negro produced for the first time in his own theatre he recognized and adhered to the stereotype—with trifling variations—that the ruling-class tradition had cast on the psychology of Americans.

The dialectical development of American drama dealing with the Negro reveals itself clearly. *Uncle Tom's Cabin*, despite its capitalist bias, *was* antislave. To that extent it was an advance over all earlier plays concerning the Negro. Bringing the Negro on the stage with whites in *Uncle Tom's Cabin* and *Octoroon was* a part of the general sympathetic treatment Negroes were to expect from liberals.

We can appraise these various plays correctly only by taking each of them in relation both to its period and to American drama as a whole. When we look at American drama in this way we discover the significant position the Negro has held in it.

The tradition of Negro inferiority and white superiority penetrates even such recent "realistic" plays as Ridgley Torrence's *Granny Maumee, The Rider of Dreams,* and *Simon the Cyrenian*, Eugene O'Neill's *The Emperor Jones* and *All God's Chillun Got Wings*, Paul Green's *In Abraham's Bosom, The No 'Count Boy,* and *Roll, Sweet Chariot*, DuBose Heyward's *Porgy*, and Howard Culbertson's *Goat Alley*.

They Shall Not Die, quickly followed by *Stevedore*, were a clean break with tradition: the first presentations of straightforward realistic plays dealing with the continued economic enslavement of the American

Negroes. These plays have been discussed elsewhere in full, but the slavery which they describe will have to be destroyed before the Negro can take the place on the stage which his talents—displayed through two centuries of appalling obstacles—prove he is entitled to. The new theatres of social protest, as many Negro actors are beginning to find, offer them the only stages on which they can play without caricature the real stories and characters of their race.

On the White Man's Stage

BY AUGUSTUS SMITH

IN 1821, while Negroes enslaved on Southern plantations used the banjo and bones and created minstrelsy—the only distinctive American contribution to the theatre—a group of Negroes in New York performed Shakespeare and received a foretaste of the discrimination which was to handicap the progress of their race in the theatre. Before an enthusiastic audience, in a theatre in African Grove at the corner of Bleecker and Mercer Streets, they performed Shakespearean dramas popular at the time. A summons to magistrate's court interrupted their schedule, and upon a promise never again to act Shakespeare they were dismissed. But the players cleverly outwitted the authorities for at least two years. An 1823 playbill in G. C. D. Odell's *Annals of the New York Stage* shows that they circumvented the decision by interspersing scenes from *Othello* and *Richard III* with comic acts.

Colored minstrelsy developed and continued—until white actors, realizing its cash value, capitalized upon it by introducing blackface impersonations. *The Atlantic Monthly* of 1867 tells us that the first of these impersonators was Dan Rice. During 1830 he heard a Negro singing in the streets of Cincinnati, appropriated his songs and imitated his character, and ended with a successful countrywide tour doing "blackface impersonations." There followed a deluge of white actors in burnt cork —exaggerated caricatures of the Negro people. The vogue grew until it was only by blacking himself, and imitating his imitators, that the Negro could keep a place for himself in the theatre!

The entry of the Negro on the professional minstrel stage came in 1852 when Lew Johnson, Negro, organized a group of free Negroes near Richmond, Virginia, into "Lew Johnson's Plantation Georgia Minstrels." These performers introduced new features to the minstrel pattern of that day: the tantalizing stop-time dance, and developments of the jig and buck-and-wing. Billy Kersands, the most famous minstrel of the time, introduced the Virginia Essence. The Bohee Brothers brought in the soft-shoe dance, which they performed as they played their banjos.

To whom did they play? At first to empty orchestras—because—although whites did not attend, Negroes could sit only in the balconies. Later, when their vogue increased, to all-white audiences who excluded Negroes from the theatres entirely. Later still, colored theatres were set apart for Negro audiences.

Later came the Georgia Minstrels, the Hicks and Sawyer Minstrels, the Richard and Pringle, the McCabe and Young, and finally Callender's Minstrels, which gave Gustave, Charles, and Daniel Frohman their start in things theatrical.

A typical troupe were the Lucca family, father, mother, and four sons, all of them extraordinarily talented. Their first big recognition came at the Broadway Tabernacle in New York, where, on the anniversary of the Antislavery Society, in 1853, they were received "with the wildest enthusiasm." They later toured the country, giving concerts of Negro songs, sketches, and dances, playing in halls, plantation barns, tobacco sheds, and being paid in chickens, hams, honey, or whatever they could get.

The first successful departure of the Negro from the strict minstrel form did not come until 1890. Then Sam Jack, a white burlesque theatre owner, decided to "glorify" the colored girl. He assembled the pick of male Negro actors—Sam Lucas, Fred Piper, Billy Jackson—and a chorus of sixteen beautiful *light* colored girls. This selection of an all-light chorus was forced by the white man's prejudice and has militated against darker girls in show business to this day.

Oriental America was the first colored show to play Broadway proper. John W. Isham took it to Wallack's Theatre (then Palmer's Theatre) in 1895. He had had a success with *Octoroons*, which replaced the burlesque, specialties, cakewalk, hoedown, and walkaround finale with a medley of operatic selections.

The concert was another field in the Negro's struggle for a place in the theatre. Among the most popular of the women singers was Elizabeth Taylor Greenfield, "The Black Swan," who was known on two continents. Best known of all was "The Black Patti," Sisseiretta Jones, who returned from a triumphant European tour to join *Black Patti's Troubadours* and sing with them in a run of several years at Proctor's Fifty-eighth Street in New York.

Bob Cole, author and composer of her show, revolted against the miserable compensation he received for his work from the white managers, Voelckel and Nolan. Complaints gained him nothing, so he gathered up his music and walked out. The managers caused his arrest. In court Bob Cole fearlessly declared: "These men have amassed a fortune from the product of my brain, and now they call me a thief. I won't give them my music." But it was a ruling-class court, and Bob Cole lost. The loss of his courageous but futile one-man strike led Cole to another effort: he united other Negroes to produce a show under their own management. Their *A Trip to Coontown* was the first complete departure from the minstrel pattern. It had continuity and plot: it was the first Negro musical comedy. By the turn of the century many flourishing Negro theatricals gave promise of emancipation on the stage.

During the run of *The Sons of Ham* came the race riots of 1900 in New York, provoked by police brutality. Crazed mobs ran through the theatre district shouting "Get Ernest Hogan! Get Williams and Walker!" Hogan, who was playing at the Winter Garden, was kept for safety all night in the theatre. Walker had a narrow escape on the streets.

A recurring wave of Jim Crowism about 1906—the result of a new crop of white comedians in blackface—drove the Negro from the Broadway area again. Some productions took to the road, others retreated to Harlem, and a few individual actors found places in white musicals. At the same time, in Chicago, the Pekin Stock Company was being formed. They specialized in original Negro musical comedies, encouraging and developing Negro writers and composers, and performed versions of plays like *My Lady's Garter* and *Voice in the Dark*. Original scripts were *Captain Rufus, Who's Stealing,* and *The Mayor of Jimtown* (revived as *Shuffle Along*). Prominent in the company was Charles Gilpin. In 1909, Susie Sutton made a hit in *The Return of Eve*. In 1912, Evelyn Ellis was the lead in the production of *Goat's Alley* in Philadelphia.

In 1917, when the theatre as a whole was experiencing a revival, Anita Bush gathered some of the best Negro talent from all over the country to form a Harlem company. After a brilliant start dissension arose, and Charles Gilpin left to found the now famous Lafayette Players. From their ranks came many of those now famous in the acting profession: Abbie Mitchell, Laura Bowman, Hayes Pryor, Lionel Monogas, Clarence Muse, Cleo Desmond, Ida Anderson, Barrington Carter, Evelyn Ellis, Charles Olden, "Babe" Townsend, A. B. DeComatherie, Jack Carter, and Edna Carter. They produced such plays as *Madame X, The Love of Chu Chin, Within the Law*, and they sponsored performances of *Othello* with Sterling Wright, who had been acclaimed for his performance of the leading role in Boston.

At the same time a company of less known actors was assembled by Mrs. Emily Hapgood—with such compelling result that Robert Edmond

Jones staged three one-act plays by Ridgely Torrence for them at the Garrick. The plays were highly praised by the critics, and for his work in *Rider of Dreams*, Opal Cooper was given seventh place in the list of most distinguished acting performances of the season. Among actresses, Inez Clough was given ninth place for her work in *Simon the Cyrenian*.

There were four hundred Negro theatres in America at that time, most of them alternating between musical and dramatic stock. Eighty of them comprised a sort of vaudeville chain known as T.O.B.A., or "Toba" —Theatre Owners Booking Association. The Negro vaudevillians interpreted the initials as "Tough On Black Actors."

Now Negroes began to appear frequently in parts in white plays. The best-remembered performances are Gilpin in *Abraham Lincoln* and *Emperor Jones*; Abbie Mitchell in *Coquette* and *Porgy*; Rose McGlendon in *Porgy*, *In Abraham's Bosom*, *Earth*, and *Never No More*. Gilpin's *Emperor Jones* was the oustanding performance of the season and brought him the vote of the Drama League as one of the ten persons who had contributed most to the American theatre that year. The Drama League, as was its custom, gave a dinner for those selected—and the chauvinists of press and stage set up a howl to have Gilpin's invitation withdrawn. Failing in this, they tried to coerce him into staying away. He attended the dinner.

An ever more flagrant provocation against the Negro people occurred during the rehearsals of *All God's Chillun Got Wings*. This time it was those contemptible twins of reaction, Hearst and McFadden, who led the howl for blood. We quote an editorial in Hearst's *American*:

> The failure of the audience to scrap the play and mutilate the players would be regarded as a token of public anemia.

The Southern ruling-class feeling was neatly voiced by a founder of the Daughters of the Confederacy, Mrs. J. Arnold:

> The scene in which Miss Blair is called upon to kiss and fondle a Negro's hand is going too far even for the stage. The play may be produced above the Mason-Dixon Line, but Mr. O'Neill will not get the friendly reception he had when he sent *Emperor Jones*, his other colored play into the South.

That the Southern ruling class approved of *Emperor Jones* is significant commentary on Mr. O'Neill's most famous treatment of a Negro.

In recent years all-Negro musicals have grown common. *Shuffle Along*, whose music altered the American mode of popular music, launched the incomparable Florence Mills. *Dixie to Broadway* gave Paul Robeson his chance. *Chocolate Dandies*, by and with Sissle and Blake, introduced Josephine Baker, and was the most lavish Negro musical ever produced. *Africans* was a failure, but it introduced Ethel Waters.

The Ethiopian Art Players of Chicago, who included many of the old Lafayette company, came to New York with *Salome, The Comedy of Errors,* and *The Chip Woman's Fortune*. The critics approved of the last, but like their predecessors of 1821 they could not stand the idea of Negroes playing classics—no matter how well they performed them.

John Wexley's *They Shall Not Die* and Paul Peters and George Sklar's *Stevedore* are the first clean breaks from tradition. These authors bring the Negro upon the stage as a genuine human being, showing him in his actual relation both to the productive forces and to the whites of his class. Their portrayals mark the difference between distortion gleaned from without and perception gained from within.

Alliances once unthinkable, alliances between white workers and black workers, have evolved from the changed relationships as shown in these plays.

The interval between *Uncle Tom's Cabin* and *Stevedore* marks the difference between a Negro who servilely bowed himself into his place *beneath* the whites and the one who militantly takes his place *beside* his white fellow worker. Plays like *They Shall Not Die* and *Stevedore* are effective weapons against those innumerable economic and cultural differences which will persist for the black man until we destroy the last vestige of slavery.

Trouble with the Angels

BY LANGSTON HUGHES

AT EVERY performance lots of white people wept and almost every Sunday while they were on tour some white minister invited the Negro actor who played God to come and speak to his congregation of white Christians, and thus help improve race relations—because almost everywhere they needed improving. Although the play had been the hit of years in New York, the Negro actors and singers were paid much less than white actors and singers would have been paid for performing it. And although the dramatist and his backers made more than half a million dollars, the colored troupers, now on tour, lived in cheap hotels and slept often in beds that were full of bugs. Only the actor who played God would sometimes, by the hardest effort, achieve accommodations in a white hotel, or be put up by some nice white family, or be invited to the home of the best Negro family in town. And thus God began to think that everything was lovely in the world. As an actor he really got awfully good write-ups.

Then they were booked to play Washington, and that's where the trouble began. Washington, the capital of the United States, is, as every Negro knows, a town where no black man is allowed inside a theatre, not even in the gallery. Of course they have a few moving picture houses in their own African ghetto where they can go. But downtown in the legitimate playhouses, no accommodations are made for colored people. Washington is worse than the deep South in that respect.

But God wasn't at all worried about playing Washington. He thought sure his coming would improve race relations. He thought it would be fine for the good white people of the Capital to see him—a colored God —even if the Negroes couldn't. Not even those Negroes who worked for the government. Not even Congressman DePriest!

But several weeks before the Washington appearance of the famous "Negro" play about the charming darkies who drink eggnog and fry fish in heaven, and sing almost all the time, storm clouds began to rise. It seemed that the Negroes of Washington had decided, strangely enough, that they wanted to see this play. But when they approached the theatre management on the question, they got a cold shoulder in return. The theatre management said they didn't have any seats to sell to Negroes. They couldn't even allot a corner in the upper gallery—there was such a heavy demand from white folks.

Now this made the Negroes of Washington mad, especially those who worked for the government and constituted the best society. The colored singers got mad, too, and the teachers at Howard, and the ministers of the colored churches who wanted to see what a black heaven looked like on the stage.

But nothing doing, the theatre management was adamant. They really couldn't sell seats to Negroes. Although they had no scruples about making a large profit on the week's work of the Negro actors, they just couldn't permit Negroes to sit in their theatre.

So the Washington Negroes wrote to God, this colored God who had been such a hit on Broadway. They thought sure he would help them. (But Negroes have always been stupid about God, even when he is white, let alone colored. They still keep on expecting help.)

So the Ministerial Alliance wrote to him when he was playing in Philadelphia. What a shame, they said: White folks will not allow us to come to see you perform in Washington! We are getting up a protest. We want you to help us! Will you?

Now God knew that for many years white folks had not allowed Negroes in Washington to see any shows—not even in the churches, let alone in the theatres! Of late even the Catholic churches were barring them out of mass. So how come they suddenly thought they ought to be allowed to see Him in a white theatre?

Besides, God was getting paid pretty well, and pretty well-known. So he answered their letters and said that his ink was made of tears and his heart bled, but that he couldn't afford to get into trouble with Equity. Also, it wasn't his place to go around the country spreading dissension and hate, but love and beauty. And it would surely do the white folks of the District of Columbia a lot of good to see Him, and it would soften their hearts to hear the beautiful Negro spirituals, and see the lovely black angels.

And maybe the company would try to give one special show for the Race.

So the black drama lovers of Washington couldn't get any satisfaction out of God by mail—their colored God. When the company played Baltimore, a delegation of the "best" Washington Negroes went over to their neighboring city to interview God. In Baltimore, Negroes, at least, are allowed to sit in the galleries of the theatres. After the play, God received the delegation in his dressing room and wept about his inability to do anything concerning the Washington situation. He had, of course, spoken to his management about it and they thought it might be possible to arrange a special Sunday night performance for Negroes. God said it hurt him to his soul to think how his people were treated, but the play must go on.

The delegation left in a huff—but not before they had spread their indignation to other members of the cast of the big show. And among the angels there was a great discussion as to what they might do about the Washington situation. (Although God was the star, the angels, too, were a part of the play.)

Now, among the angels there was a young Negro named Johnny Logan, who had never really liked being an angel, but who, because of his baritone voice and his Negro features, had gotten the job during the first rehearsals of the play in New York. Now he was an old hand at being an angel, since the play had been running three years.

Logan was from the South—but he hadn't stayed there long after he grew up. The white folks wouldn't let him. He was the kind of a young Negro most Southern white people hate. He believed in fighting, in bucking against the traces of discrimination and Jim Crow, and in trying to knock down any white man who insulted him. So he was only about eighteen when the whites of Augusta ran him out of town.

He finally came to New York, married a waitress, got a job as a redcap, and would have settled down forever in a little flat in Harlem had not some of his friends discovered that he could sing and persuaded him to join a Redcap Quartet. And out of that had come this work as a black angel in what turned out to be a Broadway success.

Just before the show went on the road, his wife had their first kid, so he needed to hold his job as a singing angel, even if it meant going on tour. But the more he thought about their forthcoming appearance in a Washington theatre that wasn't even Jim Crow—but that barred Negroes altogether—the madder he got. And finally he got so mad that he caused the rest of the cast to get all worked up, too—except God. And the angels decided to organize a strike!

At that distance from Washington, the black angels—from tenors to basses, sopranos to blues singers—were up in arms, and practically everybody in the cast, except God, agreed to strike.

"The idea of a town where colored folks can't even sit in the gallery to see an all-colored show. I ain't gonna work there myself."

"We'll show them white folks we've got spunk for once. We'll pull off the biggest actor's strike you ever seen."

"We sho will."

That was in Philadelphia. In Baltimore, their ardor had cooled.

"Man, I got a wife to take care of. I can't lose no week's work!"

"I got a wife, too," said Logan, "and a kid besides, but I'm game."

"You ain't a trouper," said another.

"Naw, if you was you'd be used to playing all-white houses. In the old days . . . ," said the man who played Methuselah, powdering his gray wig.

"I know all about the old days," said Logan, "when black minstrels blacked up even blacker and made fun of themselves for the benefit of white folks. But who wants to go back to the old days?"

"Anyhow, let's let well enough alone," said Methuselah.

"You ain't got no guts," said Logan.

"You're just one of them radicals, son, that's all you is," put in the old tenor who played Saul. "We know when we wants to strike or don't."

"Listen, then," said Logan to the angels who were putting on their wings by now, as it was near curtain time, "if we can't make it a real strike, then let's make it a general walk-out on the opening night. Strike for one performance anyhow. At least show the white folks that we don't take it lying down. And show the Washington Negroes that we back them up—theoretically, at least."

"One day ain't so bad," said a skinny black angel. "I'm with you on that."

"Me, too," several others agreed as they crowded into the corridor at the curtain call, and went up on the stage. The actor who played God was standing in the wings in his frock coat.

"Shss-ss!" he said.

Monday in Washington. The opening of that famous white play of Negro life in heaven. Original New York cast. Songs as only darkies can sing them. Uncle Tom come back as God.

Negro Washington wanted to picket the theatre, but the police had an injunction against them. Cops were posted for blocks around the playhouse to prevent a riot. Nobody could see God. He was safely housed in the quiet home of a Negro professor, guarded by two detectives. The papers said black radicals had threatened to kidnap him, to kidnap God!

Logan spent the whole day rallying the flagging spirits of his fellow actors. They were solid for the strike when he was around, and weak when he wasn't. No telling what them Washington cops might do to them if they struck? They locked Negroes up for less than that in Washington. Besides they might get canned, they might lose their pay, they might never get no more jobs on the stage. It was all right to talk about being a man and standing up for your race and all that—but hell, even an actor had to eat. Besides, God was right. It was a great play, a famous play! They ought to go on, and hold up its reputation. It did white folks good just to see Negroes in such a play. That nigger Logan was crazy!

"Listen here, you might as well get wise. Ain't nobody gonna strike tonight," one of the boys told him about six o'clock in the lobby of the colored Whitelaw Hotel. "You just as well give up. We ain't got no guts."

"I won't give up," said Logan.

When the actors reached the theatre, they found it surrounded by cops and the stage full of detectives. In the lobby there was a long line of people—white, of course—waiting to buy standing room. God arrived with motorcycle cops in front of his car. He had come a little early to address the cast. With him was the white stage manager and a representative of the New York producing office.

They called everybody together on the stage. The Lord wept as he spoke of all his race had borne to get where they were today. Of how they had struggled. Of how they sang. Of how they must keep on struggling and singing—until white folks saw the light. The strike would do no good. The strike would only hurt their cause. With sorrow in his heart—but more noble because of it—he would go on with the play. And he was sure his actors—his angels—his children—would, too.

The white men accompanying God were very solemn, also, as though hurt to their souls to think what their Negro employees were suffering—but far more hurt to think that they wanted to jeopardize a week's box-office receipts by a strike! That would hurt everybody—*even white folks!*

Behind God and the white managers stood two big detectives.

All gave up but Logan. He went downstairs to fight, to drag them out by force, to make men of darkies just once, to carry through the strike. But he couldn't. Nobody really wanted to strike. Nobody really wanted to sacrifice anything for race pride, or decency, or elementary human rights. No, they only wanted to keep on appearing in a naive dialect play about a quaint funny heaven full of niggers.

The management sent two detectives downstairs to get Logan. They were taking no chances. Just as the curtain rose they dragged him off to jail—for disturbing the peace. All the other colored angels were massed in the wings for the opening spiritual when the police took the black boy out. They saw a line of tears running down his cheeks. Most of the actors thought he was crying because he was being arrested—and in their timid souls they were glad it wasn't them.

The Lord God Jehovah in his frock coat did not even turn his head. He was getting "in the mood" for his triumphant first appearance before the Washington white folks.

A NEW THEATRE GREETING FOR ADOLF HITLER'S FLAGSHIP, THE S.S. BREMEN

OFTEN real-life drama intruded on our magazine work. Our most dangerous experience came some months after our march through Yorkville that stopped Nazi Bundists from continuing attacks on *New Theatre* news vendors.

The flagship of the German fleet was to arrive in New York harbor. Fritz Kuhn of the German-American Bund, releasing a fanfare of Nazi propaganda worthy of Goebbels himself, proclaimed that the SS *Bremen*'s trip was to demonstrate Adolf Hitler's desire for "peace" and for "friendly relations," especially with the millions of German-Americans who felt loyalty to the Fatherland. Kuhn warned "radicals and Jews" not to make trouble and promised protection for all who wished to welcome the *Bremen*.

The New York Police Department issued a warning that demonstrators, hostile or friendly to the Germans, would not be allowed on the docks near the *Bremen*. At *New Theatre* we felt we had to do something dramatic to inform the public about the real purpose of the flagship's mission—to spread Nazi propaganda.

We realized the police, by keeping demonstrators at a distance, would make our protests ineffective.

"What if we board their ship," someone suggested, "and do as they did at the Boston Tea Party? Instead of throwing tea overboard, we could scatter leaflets and demonstrate on the decks."

The rest of us responded with enthusiasm mingled with fear. "It's a great idea," one of us said. "But they have Gestapo aboard every ship; their stewards and sailors include many tough party members who'd probably knock hell out of us, and they'd outnumber us badly."

I guess we were more scared than we would admit as we finally decided to take the risk. We would infiltrate in twos or threes, a dozen of us carrying fancy wrapped gift packages, as if for friends or relatives among the arrivals. In the packages would be folded banners, placards, and leaflets denouncing the Nazis. Energetically, we began preparing the printed slogans and leaflets we'd spring on the Nazis: Adolf Hitler Oppresses the German People; Condemn the Nazi Book Burners; Göring Threatens, "When I Hear the Word 'Culture' I Reach for My Gun"; Fritz Kuhn's Bund Betrays American Democracy.

We pledged to keep our plan secret and agreed on a zero hour timed for shortly after the announcement that visitors could board the *Bremen*.

Soon the day came and the time for action arrived. Our girlfriends and wives waited apprehensively on the dock, with first-aid kits hidden in their purses. My younger sister, Evelyn, was near to tears in fear for us as we moved past the mounted police, then mingled, unsuspected, with the genuine visitors. There were a few uneasy moments as we climbed the gangplank where burly men in plainclothes stood guard, apparently Gestapo protection against troublemakers. But they let us pass, assuming we were like the other friendly visitors, many of whom were also carrying gifts in brightly wrapped packages.

We had kept our oath of secrecy. But at the time, we didn't suspect that a similar idea had also occurred to some tough members of the Maritime Union. They had used the same strategy as we had, boarding a few at a time at a gangplank farther down from us. A few minutes before our planned zero hour, their boarding forces, about thirty to our dozen New Theatreites, surprised everyone—including us—by raising banners and placards and shouting their anti-Hitler slogans.

As the ship's Gestapo guards and crew rushed to surround the union members, we went into action: raising our banners and placards, scattering leaflets, shouting our denunciations of Nazism. We were fortunate most of the attack was concentrated on the Maritime Union group, who fought back as they were driven to the gangplank nearest them. We also were attacked, pushed, shoved, swung at, and forced toward the gangplank we had boarded. We struck back as best we could. Nearby, the Nazi toughs had knocked down a few Maritimers and were beating them savagely, until their comrades managed to rescue them and carry them off to safety. If not for that other, bigger group, we no doubt would have suffered more. Fortunately we had only a few bruises from partially parried blows as we beat our retreat, still shouting our anti-Hitler denunciations and acknowledging applause from cheering onlookers on the docks.

We felt proud that we had carried out our mission and that for a brief moment we had "occupied" Nazi German territory. Ours was a tiny victory in contrast to the major ones of Hitler's forces then occupying the Saar in Europe. Still we made sure Americans would know from the press and radio that fellow citizens had protested Nazism on the decks of the Nazi flagship. Afterward Kuhn and the Nazi propagandists screamed about "radical and Jew inhospitality to the friendly Germans" of the SS *Bremen* and their American fascist sympathizers and friends.

Some months later a young writer, who was being acclaimed for his first play, *Bury the Dead*, wrote a short story, "Sailor Off the *Bremen*." As Irwin Shaw told me when we met recently (several months before he died), what we did that day almost fifty years ago gave him the idea for a short story that ranks to this day as an American classic. With his imagination and talent, Irwin turned the Nazi beatings, which seriously maimed one of the Maritime demonstrators, into an unforgettable story of justified revenge. Thus our "invasion" of the Nazi flagship helped make literary as well as political history.

Shifting Scenes

IN ADDITION to dozens of requests for production rights to Irwin Shaw's *Bury the Dead* from new theatres and leading little theatres throughout the country, letters commending the play continue to come into the NEW THEATRE offices. Gus Goldstein, former sergeant, Reburial Unit, Graves Registration, Army Service Corps, writes:

"This letter is being written the morning after reading NEW THEATRE's *Bury the Dead*, by Irwin Shaw.

"During the year 1919 after eighteen months of warfare, I was assigned to the cemeteries at Romagne sous Montafaucon and Thiaucourt, France, where I handled 10,500 bodies of American soldiers. I am the sergeant of *Bury the Dead*.

"I am told that Irwin Shaw is only 23 years of age. He could not have been in the World War. There have been no wars of that nature since 1918.

"I am truly astounded at the perfect understanding that Shaw shows of the lack of reaction with which we operated our automatic bodies. His portrayal of the living corpses (the Soldiers, the Sergeant, the Captain and the Generals) could not be better if he had taken notes during the war.

"We, who went through the ordeal, would have shown no more excitement if the bodies we handled would have stood up and refused to be buried.

"Kindly convey my heartiest congratulations to Mr. Shaw."

A reader writes from Canada:

"With great interest I read the last issues of NEW THEATRE. With joy I welcomed the existence of such a big left theatre movement in America which was for me a big surprise.

"I am myself a man of the theatre, and I came to America from Poland where we try in very poor conditions to create a theatre of the struggling people. We have to contend with the persecution of the fascist dictatorship which combats fiercely any effort of development of the consciousness of the working class. But the response which every one of our performances called forth among the people made us go on with the fight.

"In the April issue of your magazine I read Irwin Shaw's *Bury the Dead*, and I felt that it is a play of special significance and value in the struggle which we are waging against war. I want to translate it into Polish in order to introduce it to members of our Experimental Theatre of Warsaw which perhaps will try to put it on the stage. Therefore, I apply to you for permission to make this translation. I cannot assure you of any compensation for it because our theatre is working under well-known illegal conditions supported by workers from their starvation wages. I will try also to put it in one of the workers' papers but they wouldn't be able to pay for it either. But I think, and I am sure that the same is the opinion of the New Theatre League and the author, that such a play should be a property of the whole working class, and the best and the only real reward for their work is the echo which this play will arouse in the minds of the Polish workers."

Bury the Dead

BY IRWIN SHAW

A Play about the War That Is to Begin Tomorrow Night

CHARACTERS

FIRST, SECOND, THIRD, and FOURTH SOLDIERS
SERGEANT
FIRST CORPSE (PRIVATE DRISCOLL)
SECOND CORPSE (PRIVATE SCHELLING)
THIRD CORPSE (PRIVATE MORGAN)
FOURTH CORPSE (PRIVATE WEBSTER)
FIFTH CORPSE (PRIVATE LEVY)
SIXTH CORPSE (PRIVATE DEAN)
CAPTAIN
FIRST, SECOND, and THIRD GENERALS
DOCTOR
CHARLEY and BEVINS, Privates
REPORTER
EDITOR
BESS SCHELLING, JOAN BURKE, JULIA BLAKE, KATHERINE DRISCOLL, MRS. DEAN, MARTHA WEBSTER
A Priest, A Rabbi, Two Whores, A Soldier Stenographer, A Radio Voice, Passerby, Three Businessmen, and Others.

SCENE: *The stage is bare except for a platform about seven feet high which runs along the back, parallel to the footlights. Across the back of it is an irregular entanglement of barbed wire.*
(The light comes up on the platform which represents a torn battlefield, now quiet, some miles behind the present front lines. A burial detail of four SOLDIERS stand in a shallow trench digging a common grave to accommodate six bodies. The bodies are piled near them wrapped in blankets. A SERGEANT stands on the edge of the grave, smoking. The SOLDIER nearest him stops digging.)

FIRST SOLDIER: Say, Sergeant, they stink. *(Waving his shovel toward the corpses.)* Let's bury them in a hurry.

SERGEANT: What the hell do you think you'd smell like after you'd been lyin' out for two days—a goddamn lily of the valley? They'll be buried soon enough. Keep digging.

SECOND SOLDIER: *(Scratching himself.)* Dig and scratch! Dig and scratch! What a war! When you're not diggin' trenches, you're diggin' graves...

THIRD SOLDIER: Who's got a cigarette? I'll take opium if nobody's got a cigarette.

SECOND SOLDIER: When you're not diggin' graves you're scratchin' at fleas. By God, there's more fleas in this army...

FIRST SOLDIER: That's what the war's made for—the fleas. Somebody's got to feed 'em.

FOURTH SOLDIER: I used to take a shower every day. Can you imagine?

SERGEANT: All right, Mr. Lifebuoy, we'll put your picture in the Saturday Evening Post—in color!

SECOND SOLDIER: When you're not scratchin' at fleas, you're being killed. That's a helluva life for a grown man.

THIRD SOLDIER: Who's got a cigarette? I'll trade my rifle—if I can find it—for a cigarette. For Christ's sake, don't they make cigarettes no more? *(Leaning, melancholy, on his shovel.)* This country's goin' to the dogs for real now.

SERGEANT: Lift dirt, soldier. Come on! This ain't no vacation.

THIRD SOLDIER: *(Disregarding him.)* I heard of guys packin' weeds and cowflop into cigarettes in this man's army. They say it has a tang. *(Reflectively.)* Got to try it some day.

SERGEANT: Hurry up! *(Blowing on his hands.)* I'm freezin' here. I don't want to hang around all night. I can't feel my feet no more.

FOURTH SOLDIER: I ain't felt my feet for two weeks. I ain't had my shoes off in two weeks. *(Leaning on his shovel.)* I wonder if the toes're still connected. I wear an 8A shoe. Aristocratic foot, the salesman always said. Funny—going around not even knowin' whether you still got toes or not. It's not hygienic really.

SERGEANT: All right, friend, we'll make sure the next war you're in is run hygienic.

FOURTH SOLDIER: In the Spanish-American War more men died of fever than—

FIRST SOLDIER: *(Beating viciously at something in the grave.)* Get him! Get him! Kill the bastard!

FOURTH SOLDIER: *(Savagely.)* He's coming this way! We got him cornered!

FIRST SOLDIER: Bash his brains out!

SECOND SOLDIER: You got him with that one! *(All the SOLDIERS in the grave beat it, yelling demoniacally, triumphantly.)*

SERGEANT: *(Remonstrating.)* Come on now, you're wasting time.

FIRST SOLDIER: *(Swinging savagely.)* There. That fixed him. The goddamn—

FOURTH SOLDIER: *(Sadly.)* You'd think the rats'd at least wait until the stiffs were underground.

FIRST SOLDIER: Did you ever see such a fat rat in your whole life? I bet he ate like a horse, this one.

SERGEANT: All right, all right. You're not fightin' the war against rats. Get back to your business.

FIRST SOLDIER: I get a lot more pleasure killin' rats than killin' *them*. *(Gesture toward the front lines.)*

SERGEANT: Rats got to live, too. They don't know no better.

FIRST SOLDIER: *(Suddenly scooping up rat on his shovel and presenting it to SERGEANT.)* Here you are, Sergeant. A little token of our regard from Company A.

SERGEANT: Stop the smart stuff! I don't like it.

FIRST SOLDIER: *(Still with rat upheld on shovel.)* Ah, Sergeant, I'm disappointed. This rat's a fine pedigreed animal—fed only on the choicest young men the United States turned out in the last twenty years.

SERGEANT: Come on, wise guy ...

FIRST SOLDIER: Notice the heavy, powerful shoulders to this rat, notice the well-covered flanks, notice the round belly—bank clerks, mechanics, society leaders, farmers—good feeding—*(Suddenly he throws the rat away.)* Ah—I'm gettin' awful tired of this. I didn't enlist in this bloody war to be no bloody grave digger.

SERGEANT: Tell that to the President. Keep diggin'.

SECOND SOLDIER: Say, this is deep enough. What're we supposed to do—dig right down to hell and deliver them over firsthand?

SERGEANT: A man's entitled to six feet o' dirt over his face. We gotta show respect to the dead. Keep diggin' ...

FOURTH SOLDIER: I hope they don't put me too far under when my turn comes. I want to be able to come up and get a smell of air every once in so often.

SERGEANT: Stow the gab, you guys! Keep diggin' ...

FIRST SOLDIER: They stink! Bury them!

SERGEANT: All right, Fanny. From now on we'll perfume 'em before we ask you to put them away. Will that please you?

FIRST SOLDIER: I don't like the way they smell, that's all. I don't have to like the way they smell, do I? That ain't in the regulations, is it? A man's got a right to use his nose, ain't he, even though he's in this goddamn army ...

SERGEANT: Talk respectful when you talk about the army, you!

FIRST SOLDIER: Oh, the lovely army ... *(He heaves up clod of dirt.)*

SECOND SOLDIER: Oh, the dear army ... *(He heaves up clod of dirt.)*

THIRD SOLDIER: Oh, the sweet army ... *(He heaves up clod of dirt.)*

FIRST SOLDIER: Oh, the scummy, stinking, goddamn army ... *(He heaves up three shovelfuls in rapid succession.)*

SERGEANT: That's a fine way to talk in the presence of death.

FIRST SOLDIER: What do you expect, Sergeant, we're just common soldiers.

SECOND SOLDIER: Come on. Let's put 'em away. I'm getting blisters big enough to use for balloons here. What's the difference? They'll just be turned up anyway, the next time the artillery wakes up.

SERGEANT: All right! All right! If you're in such a hurry—put 'em in ...

(Two SOLDIERS jump out of the grave and start carrying the bodies and passing them down into the trench where the other two SOLDIERS lay them down, out of sight of the audience.)

SERGEANT: Put 'em in neat, there.

FIRST SOLDIER: File 'em away alphabetically, boys. We may want to refer to them later. The general might want to look up some past cases.

FOURTH SOLDIER: This one's just a kid. I knew him a little. Nice kid. He used to write dirty poems. Funny as hell. He don't even look dead ...

FIRST SOLDIER: Bury him! He stinks!

SERGEANT: If you think *you* smell so sweet, yourself, Baby, you oughta wake up. You ain't exactly a perfume ad, soldier.

THIRD SOLDIER: Chalk one up for the sergeant.

FIRST SOLDIER: You ain't a combination of roses and wisteria, either, Sergeant, but I can stand you, especially when you don't talk. At least you're alive. There's something about the smell of dead ones that gives me the willies ... Come on, let's pile the dirt in on them. *(The SOLDIERS scramble out of the grave.)*

SERGEANT: Hold it.

THIRD SOLDIER: What's the matter now?

SERGEANT: We have to wait for the chaplains. They gotta say some prayers over them.

FIRST SOLDIER: Oh, for Christ's sake, ain't I *ever* going to get any sleep tonight?

SERGEANT: Don't begrudge a man his prayers, soldier. You'd want 'em, wouldn't you?

FIRST SOLDIER: God, no. I want to sleep peaceful when I go ... Well, where are they? Why don't they come? Do we have to stand here all night waiting for those guys to come and talk to God about these fellers?

THIRD SOLDIER: *(Plaintively)* Who's got a cigarette?

SERGEANT: 'Tenshun! Here they are!

(A Roman Catholic PRIEST and a RABBI come in.)

PRIEST: Is everything ready?

SERGEANT: Yes, Father.

FIRST SOLDIER: Make it snappy! I'm awful tired.

PRIEST: God must be served slowly, my son.

FIRST SOLDIER: He's gettin' plenty of service these days—and not so slow, either. He can stand a little rushin'.

SERGEANT: Shut up, soldier.

RABBI: Do you want to hold your services first, Father?

SERGEANT: There ain't no Jewish boys in there, Reverend. I don't think we'll need you.

RABBI: I understand one of them is named Levy.

SERGEANT: Yes. But he's no Jew.

RABBI: With that name we won't take any chances. Father, will you be first?

FIRST SOLDIER: I want to get it over with! Bury them! They stink!

PRIEST: Young man, that is not the way to talk about one of God's creatures.

FIRST SOLDIER: If *that's* one of God's creatures, all I can say is, He's slippin'.

PRIEST: My son, you seem so bitter . . .

FIRST SOLDIER: For Christ's sake, stop talking and get this over with. I want to throw dirt over them! I can't stand the smell of them! Sergeant, get 'em to do it fast. They ain't got no right to keep us up all night. We got work to do tomorrow. Let 'em say their prayers together! God'll be able to understand.

PRIEST: Yes. There is really no need to prolong it. We must think of the living as well as the dead. As he says, Reverend, God will be able to understand . . .

(He stands at the head of the grave, chants the Latin prayer for the dead. The RABBI goes around to the other end and recites the Hebrew prayer. In the middle of it, a groan is heard, low, but clear. The chants keep on. Another groan.)

FIRST SOLDIER: I heard a groan. *(The RABBI and PRIEST continue.)* I heard a groan.

SERGEANT: Shut up, soldier!

FIRST SOLDIER: *(Gets down on one knee by side of grave and another groan.)* Stop it! I heard a groan.

SERGEANT: What about it? Can you have war without groans? Keep quiet! *(The prayers go on. Another groan. The FIRST SOLDIER jumps into the grave.)*

FIRST SOLDIER: It's from here! Hold it! *(Screaming.)* Hold it! Stop those goddamn parrots! *(Throws a clod of dirt at end of trench.)* Hold it! Somebody down here groaned. *(A head appears slowly above the trench rim. A man stands up slowly, facing the rear.)*

FIRST SOLDIER: He's alive.

SERGEANT: Why the hell don't they get these things straight? Pull him out!

FIRST SOLDIER: Stop them! *(As the services go on.)* Get them out of here! Live men don't need them.

SERGEANT: Please, Father, this has nothing to do with you. There's been some mistake...

PRIEST: I see. All right, Sergeant. *(He and RABBI join hand in hand and leave. All the SOLDIERS are hypnotically watching the man in the trench, arisen from the dead. The CORPSE passes his hand over his eyes. The men sigh, horrible, dry sighs, another groan is heard from the trench.)*

FIRST SOLDIER: *(In trench.)* There! It came from there! I heard it! *(A head, then shoulders appear as the SECOND CORPSE stands up. He passes his hands over his eyes in the same gesture which drew sighs from the men before. There is absolute silence as they watch the arisen CORPSES. Then, silently, a THIRD CORPSE rises, next to the FIRST SOLDIER. The FIRST SOLDIER screams, scrambles out of the trench, and stands watching. There is no sound save the very light rumble of the guns. One by one the CORPSES arise and stand in their places, their backs to the audience. The SOLDIERS don't move, scarcely breathe. They stand there, a frozen tableau. Suddenly, the SERGEANT talks.)*

SERGEANT: What do you want?

FIRST CORPSE: Don't bury us.

THIRD SOLDIER: Let's get the hell out of here!

SERGEANT: Stay where you are! I'll shoot the first man that moves. *(Drawing pistol.)*

FIRST CORPSE: Don't bury us. We don't want to be buried.

SERGEANT: *Christ! (To men.)* Carry on! *(He rushes off, calling.)* Captain! Captain! Where in hell is the captain...? *(His voice fades, terror-stricken. The SOLDIERS watch the CORPSES, then slowly, all together, start to back off.)*

SIXTH CORPSE: Don't go away.

SECOND CORPSE: Stay with us.

THIRD CORPSE: We want to hear the sound of men talking.

SIXTH CORPSE: Don't be afraid of us.

FIRST CORPSE: We're not really different from you. We're dead.

SECOND CORPSE: That's all...

FOURTH CORPSE: All—all...

FIRST SOLDIER: That's all...

THIRD CORPSE: Are you afraid of six dead men? You, who've lived with the dead, the so-many dead, and eaten your bread by their side when there was no time to bury them and you were hungry?

SECOND CORPSE: Are we different from you? An ounce or so of lead in our hearts, and none in yours. A small difference between us.

THIRD CORPSE: Tomorrow or the next day, the lead will be yours, too. Talk as our equals.

FOURTH SOLDIER: It's the kid—the one who wrote the dirty poems.

FIRST CORPSE: Say something to us. Forget the grave, as we would forget it...

SECOND SOLDIER: Do you—do you want a cigarette...?

SERGEANT: *(Re-enters with CAPTAIN.)* I'm not drunk! I'm not crazy, either! They just got up, all together—looked at us. Look—look for yourself, Captain. *(The CAPTAIN stands off to one side, looking. The SOLDIERS stand at attention.)*

SERGEANT: See?

CAPTAIN: I see. *(He laughs sadly.)* I was expecting it to happen—some day. So many men each day. It's too bad it had to happen in my company. Gentlemen! At ease! *(The SOLDIERS stand at ease. He leaves. The guns roar suddenly. Fadeout.)*

(The spotlight is turned on another section of the stage. Discovered in its glare are three GENERALS, around a table. The CAPTAIN stands before them.)

CAPTAIN: I'm only telling you what I saw, gentlemen.

FIRST GENERAL: You're not making this up, Captain?

CAPTAIN: No, General.

SECOND GENERAL: Have you any proof, Captain?

CAPTAIN: The four men in the burial detail and the sergeant.

THIRD GENERAL: In time of war, Captain, men see strange things.

CAPTAIN: Yes, General.

SECOND GENERAL: You've been drinking, Captain, haven't you?

CAPTAIN: Yes, General.

SECOND GENERAL: When a man has been drinking, he is not responsible for what he sees.

CAPTAIN: No, sir. I am not responsible for what I saw. I am glad of that. I would not like to carry that burden, along with all the others.

FIRST GENERAL: Come, come, Captain, confess now. You were drinking and you walked out into the cold air over a field just lately won and what with the liquor and the air and the flush of victory...

SECOND GENERAL: Take another drink with us now and forget your ghosts.

CAPTAIN: They weren't ghosts. They were men—killed two days, standing in their graves and looking at me.

FIRST GENERAL: Captain, you're becoming trying...

CAPTAIN: I'm sorry, sir. It was a trying sight.

SECOND GENERAL: Forget it! A man is taken for dead and put in a grave. He wakes from his coma and stands up. It happens every day—you've got to expect such things in a war. Take him out and send him to a hospital!

CAPTAIN: Hospitals aren't for dead men. What are the generals going to do about it?

THIRD GENERAL: Don't stand there croaking, "What are the generals going to do about it?" Have 'em examined by a doctor. If they're alive send them to a hospital. If they're dead, bury them! It's very simple.

FIRST GENERAL: Take a doctor down with you. Have him make out an official report. And let's hear no more of it.

CAPTAIN: Yes, sir. Very good, sir. *(Wheels to go out):*

SECOND GENERAL: Oh, and Captain...

CAPTAIN: *(Stopping.)* Yes, sir.

SECOND GENERAL: Stay away from the bottle.

CAPTAIN: Yes, sir. Is that all, sir?

SECOND GENERAL: That's all.

CAPTAIN: Yes, sir.

(The light leaves the GENERALS. It follows the CAPTAIN as he walks across stage. He stops, takes out a bottle, takes two long swigs. Fade-out.)

(The guns rumble louder. They have been almost mute in the preceding scene. We see the burial scene again. The DOCTOR is examining the CORPSES. He is armed with a stethoscope, and is followed by a soldier STENOGRAPHER and the FIRST and THIRD SOLDIERS, impressed as witnesses. The CAPTAIN observes.)

DOCTOR: *(As he finishes examining the FIRST CORPSE.)* Number one. Evisceration of the lower intestine. Dead forty-eight hours.

STENOGRAPHER: Number one. Evisceration of the lower intestine. Dead forty-eight hours. *(To the SOLDIERS.)* Sign here. *(They sign.)*

DOCTOR: *(Examining SECOND CORPSE.)* Number two. Bullet penetrated the left ventricle. Dead forty-eight hours.

STENOGRAPHER: Number two. Bullet penetrated the left ventricle. Dead forty-eight hours. Sign here. *(The SOLDIERS sign.)*

DOCTOR: Number three. Bullets penetrated both lungs. Severe hemorrhages. Dead forty-eight hours.

STENOGRAPHER: Number three. Bullets penetrated both lungs. Severe hemorrhages. Dead forty-eight hours. Sign here. *(The SOLDIERS sign.)*

DOCTOR: Number four. Fracture of the skull and avulsion of the cerebellum. Dead forty-eight hours.

STENOGRAPHER: Number four. Fracture of the skull and avulsion of the cerebellum. Dead forty-eight hours. Sign here. *(The SOLDIERS sign.)*

DOCTOR: Number five. Destruction of the genitourinary system by shell splinters. Death from hemorrhages. Dead forty-eight hours. Ummn. *(He looks curiously at the CORPSE'S face.)* Hmm . . . *(Moves on.)*

STENOGRAPHER: Number five. Destruction of the genitourinary system by shell splinters. Death from hemorrhages. Dead forty-eight hours. Sign here. *(The SOLDIERS sign.)*

DOCTOR: Number six. Destruction of right side of head from superorbital ridges through jawbone. Hmm. You'd be a pretty sight for your mother, you would . . . Dead forty-eight hours.

STENOGRAPHER: Number six. Destruction of right side of head from superorbital ridges through jawbone. You'd be a pretty sight for your mother, you would. Dead forty-eight hours. Sign here.

DOCTOR: What are you doing there?

STENOGRAPHER: That's what you said, sir.

DOCTOR: I know. Leave out "You'd be a pretty sight for your mother." The generals wouldn't be interested in that.

STENOGRAPHER: Yes, sir. Sign here. *(The SOLDIERS sign.)*

DOCTOR: Six, is that all?

CAPTAIN: Yes, Doctor. They're all dead?

DOCTOR: All dead.

CAPTAIN: A drink, Doctor?

DOCTOR: Yes, thank you. *(He takes a long drink from the proffered bottle. Holds it, pockets stethoscope with the other hand. Stands looking at the CORPSES, lined up, facing rear. He nods, then takes another long drink. Silently hands bottle to the CAPTAIN, who looks from one CORPSE to another, then takes a long drink. The STENOGRAPHER follows them out of sight when they leave. The two SOLDIERS, left behind, edge nearer to the CORPSES.)*

FIRST CORPSE: *(To the THIRD SOLDIER.)* Do you want a cigarette?

THIRD SOLDIER: *(Accepting with an embarrassed half-grin.)* Thanks, Buddy. I-I-I'm awful sorry. I—thanks. *(He takes the cigarette and saves it carefully. Blackout.)*

(Spotlight on the GENERALS, facing the CAPTAIN and the DOCTOR.)

FIRST GENERAL: *(Holding the DOCTOR's reports.)* Doctor!

DOCTOR: Yes, sir.

FIRST GENERAL: In your reports here you say that each of these six men is dead.

DOCTOR: Yes, sir.

FIRST GENERAL: Then I don't see what all the fuss is about, Captain. They're dead—bury them.

CAPTAIN: They refuse to be buried.

THIRD GENERAL: Do we have to go into that again? They're dead. Aren't they, Doctor?

DOCTOR: Yes, sir.

THIRD GENERAL: Then they aren't standing in their graves, refusing to be buried, are they?

DOCTOR: Yes, sir.

SECOND GENERAL: Doctor, would you know a dead man if you saw one?

DOCTOR: The symptoms are easily recognized.

FIRST GENERAL: You've been drinking, too.

DOCTOR: Yes, sir.

FIRST GENERAL: The whole damned army is drunk! I want a regulation announced tomorrow morning in all regiments. No more liquor is to be allowed within twenty miles of the front line upon pain of death. Got it?

SECOND GENERAL: Yes, General. But then how'll we get the men to fight?

FIRST GENERAL: Damn the fighting! We can't have stories like this springing up. It's bad for the morale! Did you hear me, Doctor, it's bad for the morale and you ought to be ashamed of yourself!

DOCTOR: Yes, sir.

FIRST GENERAL: Thank you, sir!

THIRD GENERAL: This has gone far enough. If it goes any further, the men will get wind of it. We have witnessed certificates from a registered surgeon that these men are dead. Waste no more time on it. Bury them! Did you hear me, Captain?

CAPTAIN: Yes, sir. I'm afraid, sir, that I must refuse to bury these men.

THIRD GENERAL: That's insubordination, sir.

CAPTAIN: I'm sorry, sir. It is not within the line of my military duties to bury men against their will. If the general will only think for a moment he will see that this is impossible.

FIRST GENERAL: The captain's right. It might get back to Congress. God only knows what *they'd* make of it!

THIRD GENERAL: What are we going to do then?

FIRST GENERAL: Captain, what do you suggest?

CAPTAIN: Stop the war.

CHORUS OF GENERALS: Captain!

FIRST GENERAL: *(With great dignity.)* Captain, we beg of you to remember the gravity of the situation. It admits of no levity. Is that the best suggestion you can make, Captain?

CAPTAIN: Yes, but I have another—If the generals would come down to the grave themselves and attempt to influence these—ah—corpses—to lie down, perhaps that would prove effective. We're seven miles behind the line now and we could screen the roads all day to protect your arrival.

FIRST GENERAL: Umm—uh—usually, of course, that would be—uh ... We'll see. In the meantime it must be kept quiet! Remember that! Not a word! Nobody must know! God only knows what would happen if people began to suspect we couldn't even get our dead to lie down and be buried! This is the goddamnedest war! They never said anything about this sort of thing at West Point. Remember, not a word, nobody must know, quiet as the grave, mum! Ssssh!

SECOND AND THIRD GENERALS: Sssh!

(The light fades, but the hiss of the GENERALS hushing each other is still heard as it falls on another part of the stage, where two soldiers are on post in the front lines, behind a barricade of sandbags. The sound of guns is very strong. There are flashes of gunfire.)

BEVINS: *(A man past 40, fat, with a potbelly, graying hair showing under his helmet.)* Did you hear about those guys that won't let themselves be buried, Charley?

CHARLEY: I heard. You never know what's gonna happen next in this lousy war.

BEVINS: What do you think about it, Charley?

CHARLEY: What're they gettin' out of it, that's what I'd like to know. They're just makin' things harder. I heard all about 'em. They stink! Bury 'em. That's what I say.

BEVINS: I don't know, Charley. I kind of can see what they're aimin' at. Christ, I wouldn't like to be put six foot under now, I wouldn't. What the hell for?

CHARLEY: What's the difference?

BEVINS: There's a difference, all right. It's kinda good, bein' alive. It's kinda nice, bein' on top of the earth and seein' things and hearin' things and smellin' things.

CHARLEY: Yeah—smellin' stiffs that ain't had time to be buried. That sure is sweet.

BEVINS: Yeah, but it's better than havin' the dirt packed onto your face. I guess those guys felt sorta gypped when they started throwin' the dirt on 'em and they just couldn't stand it, dead or no dead.

CHARLEY: They're dead, ain't they? Nobody's puttin' them under while they're alive.

BEVINS: It amounts to the same thing, Charley. They should be alive now. What are they? A parcel of kids. Kids shouldn't be dead, Charley. That's what they musta figured when the dirt started fallin' in on 'em. What the hell are they doin' dead? Did they get anything out of it? Did anybody ask them? Did they want to be standin' there when the lead poured in? They're just kids, or guys with wives and young kids of their own. They wanted to be home readin' a book or teachin' their kid C-A-T spells cat or takin' a woman out into the country in an open car with the wind blowin' . . . That's the way it musta come to them, when the dirt smacked on their faces, dead or no dead . . .

CHARLEY: Bury them. That's what I say. *(There is the chatter of a machine gun off in the night. BEVINS is hit. He staggers.)*

BEVINS: *(Clutching his throat.)* Charley—Charley. *(His fingers bring down the top sandbag as he falls. The machine gun chatters again and CHARLEY is hit. He staggers.)*

CHARLEY: Oh, my God . . . *(The machine gun again. He falls over BEVINS. There is quiet for a moment. Then the eternal artillery again. A spotlight picks out the FIRST GENERAL, standing over the prone forms of the two soldiers.)*

FIRST GENERAL: *(In a hoarse whisper.)* Sssh! Keep it quiet. Nobody must know! Not a word! Sssh! *(Blackout.)* *(A spotlight picks out another part of the stage—a newspaper office. EDITOR at his desk, REPORTER before him, hat on head. The REPORTER has only one arm.)*

REPORTER: That's the story! It's as straight as a rifle barrel, so help me God.

EDITOR: *(Looking down at manuscript.)* This is a freak, all right. I never came across anything like it in all the years I've been putting out a newspaper.

REPORTER: There never was anything like it before. It's somethin' new. Somethin's happening. Somebody's waking up.

EDITOR: It didn't happen.

REPORTER: So help me God, I got it straight. Those guys just stood up in the grave and said, "The hell with it, you can't bury us!" God's honest truth.

EDITOR: It's an awful funny story. *(Into telephone.)* Get me Macready at the War Department.

REPORTER: What about it? It's the story of the year—the story of the century—the biggest story of all time—men gettin' up with bullets in their hearts and refusin' to be buried . . .

EDITOR: Who do they think they are—Jesus Christ?

REPORTER: What's the difference? That's the story! You can't miss it! You goin' to put it in? Lissen—are you goin' to put it in?

EDITOR: Hold it. *(Takes telephone.)* Macready!

REPORTER: What's he got to do with it?

EDITOR: I'll find out. What're you so hot about, anyway? Hello! Macready? Hansen from the New York . . . Yeah . . . yeah . . . Lissen, Macready, I got this story about the six guys who refuse to be . . . yeah . . .

REPORTER: What does he say?

EDITOR: O.K., Macready. Yeah. If that's the way the government feels about it. . . *(Hangs up.)*

REPORTER: Well?

EDITOR: No.

REPORTER: For Christ's sake, you've got to. People have a right to know.

EDITOR: In time of war people have a right to know nothing. If we put it in it'd be censored, anyway . . .

REPORTER: Ah, this is a lousy business.

EDITOR: Write another human-interest story about the boys at the front. That'll keep you busy. You know—that one about how the boys in the front line sing "I can't give you anything but love" before they go over the top.

REPORTER: But I wrote that last week.

EDITOR: It made a great hit. Write it again.

REPORTER: But—those guys in the grave, Boss. Lloyd's 're givin' three to one they won't go down. That's a story . . .

EDITOR: Save it. You can write a book of memoirs twenty years from now. Make that "I can't give you anything but love" story a thousand words. And make it snappy. The casualty lists run into two pages today and we got to balance them with something . . . *(Blackout.)*

(A rumble of guns. The burial trench again. At one side the three GENERALS with the CAPTAIN.)

CAPTAIN: There they are, gentlemen.

SECOND GENERAL: Who do they think they are . . . ?

THIRD GENERAL: It's against all regulations. I'd show 'em.

FIRST GENERAL: Quiet, please, quiet. Let's not have any scenes . . . This must be handled with authority—but tactfully. I'll talk to them! *(He goes over to brink of grave.)* Men! Listen to me! This is a strange situation in which we find ourselves. I have no doubt but that it is giving you as much embarrassment as it is us . . .

SECOND GENERAL: *(Confidentially to THIRD GENERAL.)* The wrong note. He's good on artillery, but when it comes to using his head, he's lost . . . He's been that way ever since I knew him.

FIRST GENERAL: We're all anxious to get this thing over with just as quickly and quietly as possible. I know that you men are with me on this. There's no reason why we can't get together and settle this in jig time. After all, there's no reason why you men would really want to stay above ground, is there? No. I grant, my friends, that it's unfortunate that you're dead . . . But being dead, why should you wish to make believe you're alive? In the final analysis, gentlemen, that is what you're doing. I'm sure that you'll all listen to reason. Listen, too, to the voice of duty, the voice that sent you here to die bravely for your country. Gentlemen, your country demands of you that you lie down and allow yourselves to be buried! Our flag must fly at half-mast and droop in the wind while you so far forget your duty to the lovely land that bore and nurtured you. Every voice that cries from America begs you to lie down. The voices of the pure women of America standing bravely beside their men in this war, mothers, sisters, wives, the voices of the little children of America who must be protected from the grim horror of this war, the voices that come from Maine, from Iowa, from Kentucky, from California, from the mountains and the plains of your native land, calling to you to lie down to be buried and honored as brave soldiers of the republic who have fought the good fight and have perished nobly in it. *(He wipes away a tear, overcome.)* I . . . I find it difficult to go on. I love America, gentlemen, its hills and valleys. If you loved America as I did, you would not . . . ah . . . *(He sniffles briskly, dabbing at himself with a large handkerchief.)* I have studied this matter and come to the conclusion that the best thing for all concerned would be for you men to lie down peaceably in your graves and allow yourselves to be buried. *He waits. (The CORPSES don't move.)*

THIRD GENERAL: It didn't work. He's not firm enough. You've got to be firm right from the beginning or you're lost.

FIRST GENERAL: *(To CORPSES.)* Men, perhaps you don't understand. I advise you to allow yourselves to be buried. *(They stand motionless.)* You're dead, men, don't you realize that? You can't be dead and stand there like that. Here—here—I'll prove it to you! *(He gets out the doctor's reports.)* Look! A doctor's reports. Witnessed! Witnessed by Privates McGurk and Butler. This ought to show you! *(He waves the reports, glaring at the CORPSES, shouting.)* You're dead, officially, all of you! I won't mince words! You heard! We're a civilized race, we bury our dead. Lie down! *(He reads from another paper.)* Private Webster! Private Schelling! Private Morgan! Private Driscoll! Private Levy! Private Dean! As Commander-in-Chief of the Army as appointed by the President of the United States in accordance with the Constitution of the United States, and as your superior officer, I command you to lie down and allow yourselves to be buried. Lie down! *(They stand, silent and motionless.)* Tell me—What is it going to get you? Answer me! I asked you a question, men. Answer me! If I were dead I wouldn't hesitate to be buried. Answer me . . . what do you want? *(As they remain silent.)* Tell me! Answer me! Why don't you talk? Explain it to me, make me understand . . .

SECOND GENERAL: *(Whispering to the THIRD GENERAL.)* He's licked. It was a mistake moving him off the artillery.

THIRD GENERAL: They ought to let me handle them.

FIRST GENERAL: *(Bursting out.)* Lie down! *(The CORPSES stand immobile. He rushes out, moaning.)* Oh, God, oh, my God . . . *(Blackout.)*

(Spotlight, red, picks out two WHORES on a street corner.)

FIRST WHORE: I'd lay 'em all right. They oughta call me in. I'd lay 'em. There wouldn't be any doubt in anybody's mind after I got through with 'em. Why don't they call me in instead of those generals? What do generals know about such things? *(Both WHORES go off into fits of laughter.)* Call the War Department, Mabel, tell 'em we'll come to their rescue at the prevailing rates. *(Laugh wildly again.)* We're willing to do our part, like the papers say—share the burden! Oh, my Gawd, I ain't laughed so much . . . *(Laugh again. A MAN crosses their path. Still laughing, but professional.)* Say, Johnny, Johnny, what'che doin' tonight? How'd ya like . . . ? *(The MAN passes on. The women laugh.)* Share the burden—Oh, my Gawd! *(They laugh and laugh and laugh, clinging to each other. Blackout, but the laughter goes on.)*

(The THIRD SOLDIER's voice is heard singing "Swing Low, Sweet Chariot" as the light comes upon the Burial Scene. The four SOLDIERS of the burial detail and the SERGEANT are seated some distance from the grave.)

THIRD SOLDIER: This is a funny war. It's rollin' downhill. Everybody's waitin'. Personally, I think it's those guys there that—*(He gestures to grave.)*

SERGEANT: Nobody asked you. You're not supposed to talk about it.

FIRST SOLDIER: Regulation 2035a.

SERGEANT: Well, I just told ya. *(The SERGEANT breaks in on the SECOND SOLDIER's song.)* Say, lissen, think about those guys there.

How do you think they feel with you howlin' like this? They got more important things to think about.

SECOND SOLDIER: I won't distract 'em. I got an easy-flowin' voice.

SERGEANT: They don't like it. I can tell.

FIRST SOLDIER: Well, *I* like to hear him sing. And I'll bet they do, too. I'm gonna ask 'em. *(He jumps up.)*

SERGEANT: Now, lissen! *(The FIRST SOLDIER slowly approaches the grave. He is embarrassed, a little frightened.)*

FIRST SOLDIER: Say, men, I—*(The CAPTAIN comes on. The FIRST SOLDIER stands at attention.)*

CAPTAIN: Sergeant . . .

SERGEANT: Yes, sir!

CAPTAIN: You know that none of the men is to talk to *them* . . .

SERGEANT: Yes, sir. Only, sir . . .

CAPTAIN: All right. *(To FIRST SOLDIER.)* Get back.

FIRST SOLDIER: Yes, sir! *(He salutes and goes back.)*

SERGEANT *(Under his breath to the FIRST SOLDIER)*: I warned ya.

FIRST SOLDIER: Shut up! I wanna lissen to what's goin' on there! *(The CAPTAIN has meanwhile seated himself on the edge of the grave and has brought out a pair of eyeglasses, which he plays with as he talks.)*

CAPTAIN: Gentlemen, I have been asked by the generals to talk to you. My work is not this. *(He indicates his uniform.)* I am a scientist, I might even say a philosopher, my uniform is a pair of eyeglasses, my usual weapons test tubes and books. At a time like this perhaps we need philosophy, need science. First I must say that your general has ordered you to lie down.

FIRST CORPSE: We used to have a general.

THIRD CORPSE: No more.

FOURTH CORPSE: They sold us.

CAPTAIN: What do you mean . . . sold you?

FIFTH CORPSE: Sold us for twenty-five yards of bloody mud.

SIXTH CORPSE: A life for your yards of bloody mud.

CAPTAIN: We had to take that hill. General's orders. You're soldiers. You understand.

FIRST CORPSE: We understand now. The real estate operations of generals are always carried on at boom prices.

SIXTH CORPSE: A life for four yards of bloody mud. Gold is cheaper.

THIRD CORPSE: I fell in the first yard.

SECOND CORPSE: I caught on the wire and hung there while the machine gun stitched me through the middle to it.

FOURTH CORPSE: I was there at the end and thought that I had life in my hands for another day, but a shell came and my life dripped into the mud.

SIXTH CORPSE: Ask the general how he'd like to be dead at twenty. *(Calling, as though to the generals.)* Twenty, General, twenty!

CAPTAIN: Other men are dead.

FIRST CORPSE: Too many.

CAPTAIN: Men must die for their country's sake, if not you, then others. This has always been. Men died for Pharaoh and Caesar and Rome two thousand years ago and more, and went into the earth with their wounds. Why not you?

FIRST CORPSE: Men, even the men who die for Pharaoh and Caesar and Rome, must, in the end, before all hope is gone, discover that a man can die happy and be contentedly buried only when he dies for himself or for a cause that is his own and not Pharaoh's or Caesar's or Rome's...

CAPTAIN: Still—what is this world, that you cling to it? A speck of dust, a flaw in the skies, a thumbprint on the margin of a page printed in an incomprehensible language.

SECOND CORPSE: It is our home.

FIRST CORPSE: We have been dispossessed by force, but we are reclaiming our home.

CAPTAIN: We have no home. We are strangers in the universe and cling, desperate and grimy, to the crust of our world, and if there is a God and this is his earth, we must be a terrible sight in his eyes.

FOURTH CORPSE: We are not disturbed by the notion of our appearance in the eyes of God.

CAPTAIN: The earth is an unpleasant place and when you are rid of it you are well rid of it. Man cheats man on this earth and the only sure things are death and despair. Of what use, then, to remain on it once you have permission to leave?

FIFTH CORPSE: It is the one thing we know.

SIXTH CORPSE: We did not ask permission to leave. Nobody asked us whether we wanted it or not. The generals pushed us out and closed the door on us. Who are the generals that they are to close doors on us?

CAPTAIN: The earth, I assure you, is a mean place, insignificantly miserable.

CHORUS OF CORPSES: We must find out for ourselves. That is our right.

CAPTAIN: Man has no rights.

FIRST CORPSE: Man can make rights for himself. It requires only determination and the goodwill of ordinary men. We have made ourselves the right to walk this earth, seeing it and judging it for ourselves.

CAPTAIN: There is peace in the grave.

THIRD CORPSE: Peace and the worms and the roots of grass. There is a deeper peace than that which comes with feeding the roots of the grass.

CAPTAIN: *(Looks slowly at them, in turn.)* Yes, gentlemen ... *(turns and walks off.)*

(The FIRST SOLDIER moves slowly up to the grave.)

FIRST SOLDIER: *(To the CORPSES)* I ... I'm glad you ... you didn't ... I'm glad. Say, is there anything we can do for you?

SERGEANT: Lissen, soldier!

FIRST SOLDIER *(Passionately ... harshly)*: Shut up, Sergeant! *(Then very softly and warmly to the FIRST CORPSE.)* Is there anything we can do for you, friend?

FIRST CORPSE: Yeah. You can sing ...

(There is a pause in which the FIRST SOLDIER turns around and looks at the SECOND SOLDIER, then back to the FIRST CORPSE. Then the silence is broken by the SECOND SOLDIER's voice, raised in song. It goes on for a few moments, then fades as the light dims.)

(Different colored spotlights pick out three businessmen on different parts of the stage.)

FIRST BUSINESSMAN: Ssh! Keep it quiet!

THIRD BUSINESSMAN: Sink 'em with lead ...

SECOND BUSINESSMAN: Bury them! Bury them six feet under!

FIRST BUSINESSMAN: What are we going to do?

SECOND BUSINESSMAN: We must keep up the morale.

THIRD BUSINESSMAN: Lead! Lead! A lot of lead!

SECOND BUSINESSMAN: What's the matter with the generals? What are we paying them for?

CHORUS: Ssssshhh! *(Blackout.)*

(Spotlight on the congregation of a church, kneeling, with a priest praying over them.)

PRIEST: O Jesus, our God and Christ, Who has redeemed us with Thy blood on the cross at Calvary, give us Thy blessing on this holy day, and cause it that our soldiers allow themselves to be buried in peace, and bring victory to our arms, enlisted in Thy cause and the cause of all righteousness on the field of battle. Amen. *(Blackout.)*

(Spotlight on newspaper office.)

REPORTER: Well? What are you going to do?

EDITOR: Do I have to do anything?

REPORTER: Goddamn right you do. They're still standing up. They're going to stand up from now till Doomsday. They're not going to be able to bury soldiers anymore. It's in the stars. You got to say something about it.

EDITOR: All right. Put this in. "It is alleged that certain members of an infantry regiment refuse to allow themselves to be buried."

REPORTER: Well?

EDITOR: That's all.

REPORTER: *(Incredulous.)* That's all?

EDITOR: Yes, Christ, isn't that enough? *(Blackout.)*

(A baby spotlight on the loudspeaker.)

VOICE: It has been reported that certain American soldiers, killed on the field of battle, have refused to allow themselves to be buried. Whether this is true or not, the Coast-to-Coast Broadcasting System feels that this must give the American public an idea of the indomitable spirit of the American doughboy in this war. We cannot rest until this war is won—not even our brave dead boys . . .

(The headquarters again.)

FIRST GENERAL: Have you got any suggestions?

CAPTAIN: I think so. Get their women.

FIRST GENERAL: What good'll their women do?

CAPTAIN: Women are always conservative. It's a conservative notion—this one of lying down and allowing yourself to be buried when you're dead. The women'll fight your battle for you—in the best possible way—through their emotions. It's your best bet. *(Mocking.)* Always at your service.

FIRST GENERAL: Women—Of course! You've got it there, Captain! Get out their women! We'll have these boys underground in a jiffy. Women! By God, I never thought of it . . . Send out the call. Women! *(Fadeout.)*

VOICE: *(Mellow, persuasive.)* We have been asked by the War Department to broadcast an appeal to the women of Privates Webster, Schelling, Morgan, Driscoll, Levy, and Dean, reported dead. The War Department requests that the women of these men present themselves at the War Department office immediately. It is within their power to do a great service to their country. *(Blackout.)*

(The spotlight illuminates the FIRST GENERAL, where he stands, addressing six women.)

FIRST GENERAL: Go to your men. Talk to them. Make them see the error of their ways, ladies. You women represent what is dearest in our civilization—the sacred foundations of the home. We are fighting this war to protect the foundations of the homes of America! Those foundations will crumble utterly if these men of yours come back from the dead. I shudder to think of the consequences of such an act. Our entire system will be mortally struck. Our banks will close, our buildings collapse—our army will desert the field and leave our fair land open to be overrun by the enemy. Ladies, you are all gold star mothers and wives and sweethearts. You want to win this war. I know it. I know the high fire of patriotism that burns in women's breasts. That is why I have called upon you. Ladies, let me make this clear to you. If you do not get your men to lie down and allow themselves to be buried, I fear that our cause is lost. The burden of the war is upon your shoulders now. Wars are not fought with guns and powder alone, ladies. Go ladies, do your duty. Your country waits upon you. Here is your chance to do your part, a glorious part . . . You are fighting for your homes, your children, your sisters' lives, your country's honor. You are fighting for religion, for love, for all decent human life. Wars can be fought and won only when the dead are buried and forgotten. How can we forget the dead who refuse to be buried? And we *must* forget them! There is no room in this world for dead men. They will lead only to the bitterest unhappiness . . . for you, for them, for everybody. *(Blackout.)*

(Spotlight illuminates the trench where PRIVATE SCHELLING, the SECOND CORPSE, is talking to his wife. BESS SCHELLING is a spare, taciturn woman, a farmer's wife, who might be twenty or forty or anything in between.)

BESS SCHELLING: Did it hurt much, John?

SCHELLING: How's the kid, Bess?

BESS: He's fine. He talks now. He weighs twenty-eight pounds. He'll be a big boy. Did it hurt much, John?

SCHELLING: Is the farm going all right, Bess?

BESS: It's going. The rye was heavy this year. Did it hurt much, John?

SCHELLING: Who did the reapin' for you, Bess?

BESS: Schmidt took care of it—and his boys. Schmidt's too old for the war and his boys are too young. Took 'em nearly two weeks. The wheat's not bad this year. Schmidt's oldest boy expects to be called in a month or two. He practices behind the barn with that old shotgun Schmidt uses for duck.

SCHELLING: The Schmidts were always fools. When the kid grows up, Bess, you make sure you pump some sense into his head. What color's his hair?

BESS: Blond. Like you . . . What are you going to do, John?

SCHELLING: I would like to see the kid—and the farm—and . . .

BESS: They say you're dead, John . . .

SCHELLING: I'm dead, all right.

BESS: Then how is it . . . ?

SCHELLING: I don't know. Maybe there's too many of us under the ground now. Maybe the earth can't stand it no more. You got to change crops sometime. What are you doing here, Bess?

BESS: They asked me to get you to let yourself be buried.

SCHELLING: What do you think?

BESS: You're dead, John . . .

SCHELLING: Well . . . ?

BESS: What's the good . . . ?

SCHELLING: I don't know. Only there's something in me, dead or not dead, that won't let me be buried.

BESS: You were a queer man, John. I never did understand what you were about. But what's the good . . . ?

SCHELLING: Bess, I never talked so that I could get you to understand just what I wanted while I—while I—before . . . Maybe now . . . There're a couple of things, Bess, that I ain't had enough of. Easy things, the things you see when you look outa your window at night, after supper, or when you wake up in the mornin'. Things you hear when you're busy with the horses or pitchin' the hay and you don't really notice them and yet they come back to you. Things like lookin' at rows of corn scrapin' in the breeze, tall and green, with the silk flyin' off the ears in the wind. Things like seeing the sweat come out all over on your horse's fat flank and seein' it shine like silk in front of you, smelling horsey and strong. Things like seein' the loam turn back all fat and deep brown on both sides as the plough turns it over so that it gets to be awful hard walkin' behind it. Things like takin' a cold drink of water outa the well after you've boiled in the sun all afternoon, and feelin' the water go down and down into you coolin' you off all through from the inside out. Things like seein' a blond kid, all busy and serious, playin' with a dog on the shady side of a house. There ain't nothin' like that here, Bess.

BESS: Everything has its place, John. Dead men have theirs.

SCHELLING: My place is on the earth, Bess. My business is with the top of the earth, not the underside. It was a trap that yanked me down. I'm not smart, Bess, and I'm easy trapped—but I can tell now. I got some stories to tell farmers before I'm through—I'm going to tell 'em . . .

BESS: We could bury you home, John, near the creek—it's cool there and quiet and there's always a breeze in the trees.

SCHELLING: Later, Bess, when I've had my fill of lookin' and smellin' and talkin'. A man should be able to walk into his grave, not be dragged into it.

BESS: How'll I feel—and the kid—with you walkin' around—like—like—that?

SCHELLING: I won't bother you . . . I won't come near you.

BESS: Even so. Just knowin'—

SCHELLING: I can't help it. This is somethin' bigger'n you . . . bigger'n me. It's somethin' I ain't had nothin' to do with startin'. It's somethin' that just grew up outa the earth—like—like a weed—a flower. Cut it down now and it'll jump up in a dozen new places. You can't stop it. The earth's ready for it.

BESS: You were a good husband, John. For the kid . . . and me . . . won't you?

SCHELLING: *(Quietly)* Go home, Bess. Go home! *(Blackout.)*

(The spotlight picks out the FIFTH CORPSE, PRIVATE LEVY, where he stands in the grave, with his back to the audience. His woman, a pert, attractive young lady, is facing him.)

JOAN: You loved me best, didn't you, Henry—of all of them—all those women—you loved me the best, didn't you?

LEVY: What's the difference, now, Joan?

JOAN: I want to know it.

LEVY: It's not important.

JOAN: It's important to me. Henry, you're not a live man, are you, Henry?

LEVY: No, I'm all shot away inside.

JOAN: *(Looking around fearfully.)* I don't like this place.

LEVY: I'm sorry they dragged you all through this to get you here, Joan.

JOAN: Must wars always be fought in the mud like this? I never expected it to look like this. It doesn't look like this in the pictures. It—it looks like a dump heap . . .

LEVY: You've gotten your shoes muddy. They're pretty shoes, Joan.

JOAN: *(Forgetting, at the familiar tone of compliment, the place and the man from which it came.)* Do you think so, Henry? They're lizard. I like them too. It's so hard to get a good pair of shoes nowadays. You're so nice about such things, Henry.

LEVY: Do you still dance, Joan?

JOAN: Oh, I'm really much better than I used to be. There're so many dances back home nowadays. Dances for orphan relief and convalescent hospitals and Victory Loans. I'm busy seven nights a week. I sold more Victory Loans than any other girl in the League. I got a helmet—one of their helmets . . . *(With a kind of shudder for the enemy.)* One with a bullet hole in it, for selling eleven thousand dollars worth.

LEVY: Out here we get them for nothing—by the million—bullet holes and all.

JOAN: That sounds bitter. You shouldn't sound bitter.

LEVY: I'm sorry.

JOAN: I heard Colonel Elwell the other day. You know Colonel Elwell, old Anthony who owns the mill. He made a speech at the Red Cross banquet and he said that was the nice thing about this war, it wasn't being fought bitterly by our boys. He said it was just patriotism that kept us going. He's a wonderful speaker, Colonel Elwell, I cried and cried.

LEVY: I remember him.

JOAN: Henry, do you think we're going to win the war?

LEVY: What's the difference?

JOAN: *(Shocked.)* Henry! What a way to talk! I don't know what's come over you, really I don't. You used to be such a charming man.

LEVY: *(Laughing a little.)* Poor little Joan. I won't talk anymore.

JOAN: Why the papers say that if *they* win the war they'll burn our churches and tear down our museums and . . . and rape our women! *(LEVY laughs.)* Why are you laughing, Henry?

LEVY: I'm dead, Joan.

JOAN: Then why don't you let them bury you?

LEVY: There are a lot of reasons. There were a lot of things I loved on this earth.

JOAN: A dead man can't touch a woman.

LEVY: The women, yes—but more than the women, more than touching them. I got a great joy just from listening to women, hearing them laugh, watching their skirts blow in the wind, noticing the way their breasts bounced up and down inside their dresses when they walked. It had nothing to do with touching them. I liked to hear the sound of their high heels on pavements at night and the tenderness in their voices when they walked past me arm in arm with a young man. You were so lovely, Joan, with your pale hair and long hands.

JOAN: *(Touching it.)* You always liked my hair. No woman will walk arm in arm with you, Henry Levy, while you cheat the grave. Not Doris, or that shifty-eyed Janet, or . . .

LEVY: No. But there will be the eyes of women to look at and the bright color of their hair and the soft way they swing their hips when they walk before men. These are the things the earth still owes me, now when I am only thirty. A full seventy years, to be ended by an unhurried fate, not by a colored pin on a general's map.

JOAN: They're not only pins. They mean something more.

LEVY: More? To whom? To the generals—not to me. To me they are colored pins. It is not a fair bargain—this exchange of my life for a small part of a colored pin.

JOAN: Henry, how can you talk like that? You know why this war's being fought—

LEVY: No, do you?

JOAN: Of course. Everybody knows. We *must* win. We must be prepared to sacrifice our last drop of blood.

LEVY: Do you remember last summer, Joan? My last leave. We went to Maine. I would like to remember that—the sun and the beach and your soft hands—for a long time.

JOAN: What are you going to do?

LEVY: Walk the world looking at the fine, long-legged, girls, listening to the sound of their light voices with ears that the generals would have stopped with the grave's solid mud.

JOAN: Henry; Henry! Once you said you loved me. For love of me, Henry, go into the grave. For love of me!

LEVY: *(Lightly.)* Poor Joan! *(He lifts his hand toward her protectively. She recoils.)*

JOAN: Don't touch me!

LEVY: Go home, Joan. Go home. *(Blackout.)*

(The spotlight picks out the THIRD CORPSE, PRIVATE MORGAN, and JULIA BLAKE. She sobs.)

MORGAN: Stop crying, Julia. What's the sense in crying?

JULIA: No sense. Only I can't stop crying.

MORGAN: You shouldn't have come.

JULIA: They asked me to come. They said you wouldn't let them bury you—dead and all.

MORGAN: Yes.

JULIA: *(Crying)* Why don't they kill me too? I'd let them bury me. I'd be glad to be buried—to get away from all this. I—I haven't stopped crying for two weeks now. I used to think I was tough. I never cried. Even when I was a kid. It's a wonder where all the tears can come from. Though I guess there's always room for more tears. I thought I was all cried out when I heard about the way they killed Fred. My kid brother. I used to comb his hair in the morning when he went to school. Then they killed you. They did, didn't they?

MORGAN: Yes.

JULIA: It's hard to know like this. I—I know, though. It—it makes it harder, this way, with you like this. I could forget easier if you—but I wasn't going to say that. I was going to listen to you. Oh, my darling, it's been so rotten. I get drunk. I hate it and I get drunk. I sing out loud and everybody laughs. I was going through your things the other day— I'm crazy. I go through all your things three times a week, touching your clothes and reading your books. You have the nicest clothes. There was that quatrain you wrote to me that time you were in Boston and . . . First I laughed, then I cried—it's a lovely poem—you would have been a fine writer, I think you would have been the greatest writer that ever . . . I . . . Did they shoot your hands away, darling?

MORGAN: No.

JULIA: That's good. I couldn't bear it if anything happened to your hands. Was it bad, darling?

MORGAN: Bad enough.

JULIA: But they *didn't* shoot your hands away. That's *something*. You learn how to be grateful for the craziest things nowadays. People have to be grateful for something and it's so hard, with the war and all. Oh, darling, I never could think of you dead. Somehow you didn't seem to be *made* to be dead. I would feel better if you were buried in a fine green field and there were those funny little flowers jumping up around the stone that said Walter Morgan, Born 1913, Died 1936. I could stop getting drunk at night and singing out loud so that people laugh at me. The worst thing is looking at all the books you piled up home that you didn't read. They wait there, waiting for your hands to come and open them. Oh, let them bury you, let them bury you—There's nothing left, only crazy people and clothes that'll never be used hanging in the closets. Why not?

MORGAN: There are too many books I haven't read, too many places I haven't seen, too many memories I haven't kept long enough . . . I won't be cheated of them . . .

JULIA: And me, darling, me? I hate getting drunk. Your name would look so well on a nice simple chunk of marble in a green field. Walter Morgan, Beloved of Julia Blake . . . With poppies and daisies and those little purple flowers all around the bottom, and—*(She is bent over, almost wailing. There is the flash of a gun in her hand, and she totters, falls.)* Now they can put my name on the casualty lists, too—What do they call those purple flowers, darling? *(Blackout.)*

(The spotlight follows KATHERINE DRISCOLL, as she makes her way from corpse to corpse, looking at their faces. She looks first at the SIXTH CORPSE, shudders, covers her eyes and moves on. She stops at the FIFTH CORPSE.)

KATHERINE: I'm Katherine Driscoll. I—I'm looking for my brother. He's dead. Are you my brother?

FIFTH CORPSE: No.

(KATHERINE goes on to the FOURTH CORPSE, stops, looks, moves on to the THIRD CORPSE.)

KATHERINE: I'm looking for my brother. My name is Katherine Driscoll. His name—

THIRD CORPSE: No. *(KATHERINE goes on, stands irresolutely before the SECOND CORPSE.)*

KATHERINE: Are you—? *(Realizing it isn't her brother, goes on to the FIRST CORPSE.)* I'm looking for my brother. My name is Katherine Driscoll. His name—

DRISCOLL: I'm Tom Driscoll.

KATHERINE: Hel—Hello. I don't know you. After fifteen years—And—

DRISCOLL: What do you want, Katherine?

KATHERINE: You don't know me either, do you?

DRISCOLL: No.

KATHERINE: It's funny—my coming here to talk to a dead man—to try to get him to do something because once long ago he was my brother. They talked me into it. I don't know how to begin—

DRISCOLL: You'll be wasting your words, Katherine—

KATHERINE: They should have asked someone nearer to you—someone who loved you—only they couldn't find anybody. I was the nearest they said—

DRISCOLL: That's so. You were the nearest—

KATHERINE: And I was fifteen years away. Poor Tom—It couldn't have been a sweet life you led these fifteen years.

DRISCOLL: It wasn't.

KATHERINE: You were poor, too?

DRISCOLL: Sometimes I begged for meals. I wasn't lucky—

KATHERINE: And yet you want to go back. Is there no more sense in the dead, Tom, than in the living?

DRISCOLL: Maybe not. Maybe there's no sense in either living or dying, but we can't believe that. I traveled to a lot of places and I saw a lot of things, always from the black side of them, always workin' hard to keep from starvin' and turnin' my collar up to keep the wind out, and they were mean and rotten and sad, but always I saw that they could be better and some day they were going to be better, and that the guys like me who knew that they were rotten and knew that they could be better had to get out and fight to make it that way.

KATHERINE: You're dead. Your fight's over.

DRISCOLL: The fight's never over. I got things to say to people *now*—to the people who nurse big machines and the people who swing shovels and the people whose babies die with big bellies and rotten bones. I got things to say to the people who leave their lives behind them and pick up guns to fight in somebody else's war. Important things. Big things. Big enough to lift me out of the grave right back onto the earth into the middle of men just because I got the voice to say to them. If God could lift Jesus—

KATHERINE: Tom! Have you lost religion, too?

DRISCOLL: I got another religion. I got a religion that wants to take heaven out of the clouds and plant it right here on the earth where most of us can get a slice of it. It isn't as pretty a heaven, there aren't any streets of gold and there aren't any angels, and we'd have to worry about sewerage and railroad schedules in it, and we don't guarantee everybody'd love it, but it'd be right here, stuck in the mud of this earth, and there wouldn't be any entrance requirement, like dying, to get into it. Dead or alive, I see that, and it won't let me rest. I was the first one to get up in this black grave of ours, because that idea wouldn't let me rest. I pulled the others with me—that's my job, pulling the others. They only know what they *want*—I know how they can get it.

KATHERINE: There's still the edge of arrogance on you.

DRISCOLL: I have heaven in my two hands to give to men. There's reason for arrogance.

KATHERINE: I came to ask you to lie down and let them bury you. It seems foolish now, but—

DRISCOLL: *(Tenderly.)* It's foolish, Katherine. I didn't get up from the dead to go back to the dead. I'm going to the living now.

KATHERINE: Fifteen years. It's a good thing your mother isn't alive. How can you say good-bye to a dead brother, Tom?

DRISCOLL: Wish him an easy grave, Katherine.

KATHERINE: A green and pleasant grave to you, Tom, when, finally—finally—green and pleasant. *(Blackout.)*

(The light shows PRIVATE DEAN, the SIXTH CORPSE, where he stands in shadow listening to his mother, a thin, shabby, red-eyed woman of about forty-five. She is in the full light.)

MRS. DEAN: Let me see your face, Son.

DEAN: You don't want to see it, Mom.

MRS. DEAN: My baby's face—Once before you . . .

DEAN: You don't want to see it, Mom. I know. Didn't they tell you what happened to me?

MRS. DEAN: I asked the doctor. He said a piece of shell hit the side of your head—but even so . . .

DEAN: Don't ask to see it, Mom.

MRS. DEAN: How are you, Son? *(Dean laughs a little bitterly.)* Oh, I forgot. I asked you that question so many times while you were growing up, Jimmy.

DEAN: How did Alice take it when she heard?

MRS. DEAN: She put a gold star in her window. She tells everybody you were going to be married. Is that so?

DEAN: Maybe. I liked Alice.

MRS. DEAN: She came over on your birthday. That was before this—this happened. She brought flowers. Big chrysanthemums. Yellow. A lot of them. We had to put them in two vases. I baked a cake. I don't know why. It's hard to get eggs and fine flour nowadays. My baby, twenty years old... Let me see your face, Jimmy, boy.

DEAN: Go home, Mom. It's not doing you any good staying here.

MRS. DEAN: I want you to let them bury you, Baby. It's done now and over and it would be better for you that way...

DEAN: There's no better to it—and no worse. It happened that way.

MRS. DEAN: You had such a fine face. Like a good baby's. It hurt me when you started to shave. Somehow, I almost forget what you looked like, Baby. I remember what you looked like when you were five, when you were ten—you were chubby and fair and your cheeks felt like little silk cushions when I put my hand on them. But I don't remember how you looked when you went away with that uniform on you and that helmet over your face. Baby, let me see your face, once.

DEAN: Don't ask me. You don't want to see. You'll feel worse—forever—if you see.

MRS. DEAN: I'm not afraid. I can look at my baby's face. Do you think mothers can be frightened by their children's...?

DEAN: No, Mom.

MRS. DEAN: Baby, listen to me, I'm your mother. Let them bury you. For your sake and mine and your father's, Baby.

DEAN: I was only twenty, Mom. I hadn't done anything. I hadn't seen anything. I never even had a girl. I spent twenty years practicing to be a man and then they killed me. Being a kid's no good, Mom. You try to get it over as soon as you can. You don't really live while you're a kid. You mark time, waiting. I waited, Mom—but then I got cheated. They made a speech and played a trumpet and dressed me in a uniform and then they killed me.

MRS. DEAN: Oh, Baby, Baby, there's no peace this way. Please, let them...

DEAN: No, Mom.

MRS. DEAN: Then once, now, so that I can remember you, let me see your face, my baby's face...

DEAN: Mom, the shell hit close to me. You don't want to look at a man when a shell hits close to him.

MRS. DEAN: Let me see your face, Jimmy...

DEAN: All right, Mom. Look! *(He turns his face to her. The audience can't see his face, but immediately a spotlight, white and sharp, shoots down from directly above and hits his head. MRS. DEAN leans forward, staring. Another spotlight shoots down immediately after from the extreme right, then one from the left, then two more, from above. They hit with the impact of blows and MRS. DEAN shudders a little as they come, as though she were watching her son being beaten. There is absolute silence for a moment; then she starts to moan, low, painfully. The moan rises to a wail. She leans back, covering her eyes with her hands, screaming. Blackout. The scream persists, fading, like a siren fading in the distance, until it is finally stilled.)*

(The spotlight on the FOURTH CORPSE, PRIVATE WEBSTER, and his WIFE, a dumpy, sad little woman.)

MARTHA WEBSTER: Say something.

PRIVATE WEBSTER: What do you want me to say?

MARTHA: Something—anything. Only talk. You give me the shivers standing there like that—looking like that . . .

WEBSTER: There's nothing that we can talk to each other about.

MARTHA: Don't talk like that. You talked like that enough when you were alive—always seemin' to blame me because—well, because we didn't get along. It's not my fault that you're dead . . .

WEBSTER: No.

MARTHA: It was bad enough when you were alive—and you didn't talk to me and you looked at me as though I was always in your way and always went out when you wanted to have a good time.

WEBSTER: Martha, Martha, what's the difference now?

MARTHA: I just wanted to let you know. Now I suppose you're going to come back and sit around and ruin my life altogether?

WEBSTER: No. I'm not going to come back.

MARTHA: Then what . . . ?

WEBSTER: I couldn't explain it to you, Martha . . .

MARTHA: No! Oh, no—you couldn't explain it to your wife. But you could explain it to that dirty bunch of loafers down at that damned garage of yours and you could explain it to those bums in the saloon on F Street!

WEBSTER: I guess I could. *(Musing.)* Things seemed to be clearer when I was talking to the boys while I worked over a job with grease on my hands and a wrench in my pocket. And I managed to talk so people could get to understand what I meant down at the saloon on F Street. It was nice, standing there of a Saturday night, with a beer in front of you and a man or two that understood your own language next to you, talking about big things or little things, about Babe Ruth or the new oiling system Ford was putting out or the chances of us gettin' into the war . . .

MARTHA: It's different if you were rich and had a fine beautiful life you wanted to go back to. Then I could understand. But you were poor, you always had dirt under your fingernails, you never ate enough, you hated me, your wife, you couldn't stand being in the same room with me . . . don't shake your head, I know. Out of your whole life all you could remember that's good is a beer on Saturday night that you drank in company with a couple of bums.

WEBSTER: That's enough. I didn't think about it then . . . but I guess I was happy those times.

MARTHA: You were happy those times, but you weren't happy in your own home! I know, even if you don't say it! Well, I wasn't happy either! Living in three damned rooms that the sun didn't hit five times a year! Watching the roaches make picnics on the walls! Buying food that a real human being would've stuffed into the garbage pail!

WEBSTER: I did my best.

MARTHA: Eighteen-fifty a week! Your best! Eighteen-fifty, condensed milk, a two-dollar pair of shoes once a year, five hundred dollars insurance, chopped meat. God, how I hate chopped meat! Eighteen-fifty, being afraid of everything, of the landlord, the gas company, scared stiff every month that I was goin' to have a baby! Why shouldn't I have a baby? Who says I shouldn't have a baby? Eighteen-fifty, no baby!

WEBSTER: I woulda liked a kid.

MARTHA: *(Caught up short.)* Would you? You never said anything.

WEBSTER: No. But it's good to have a kid. A kid's somebody to talk to.

MARTHA: *(Almost tenderly.)* At first . . . in the beginning . . . I thought we'd have a kid, someday . . .

WEBSTER: Yeah. Me too. I used to go out on Sundays and watch men wheel their kids through the park.

MARTHA: There were so many things you didn't tell me . . . Why did you keep quiet?

WEBSTER: We were talking through walls, after the first year.

MARTHA: You should have told me.

WEBSTER: I was ashamed to talk to you. I couldn't give you anything.

MARTHA: I'm sorry.

WEBSTER: In the beginning, it looked so fine. I used to smile to myself when I walked beside you in the street, Martha, and other men looked at you.

MARTHA: That was a long time ago.

WEBSTER: Things were good then. What happened to us, Martha?

MARTHA: Maybe I know.

WEBSTER: A kid would've helped.

MARTHA: *(Getting sharper.)* No, it wouldn't. Don't fool yourself, Webster. The Clarks downstairs from us have four kids and it didn't help them. The kids're dirty and they're sick all winter and they yell their blasted heads off. Old man Clark comes home drunk every Saturday night and beats 'em all with his shaving strap and throws plates at the old lady. Kids don't help the poor. Nothing helps the poor. I'm too smart to have sick, dirty kids on eighteen-fifty . . .

WEBSTER: That's it . . .

MARTHA: A baby in the house. A house should have a baby. But it should be a clean house, with a full icebox. *(Pause.)* Why shouldn't I have a baby? Other people have babies. Even now, with the war, other people have babies. They don't have to feel their skin crawl every time they tear a page off the calendar. They go off to beautiful hospitals in lovely ambulances and have babies between colored sheets! What's there about them that God likes, that he makes it so easy for them to have babies?

WEBSTER: They're not married to mechanics.

MARTHA: No! It's not eighteen-fifty for them. And now . . . now it's worse. Your fifteen dollars a month. You hire yourself out to be killed and I get fifteen dollars a month. I wait on lines all day to get a loaf of bread. I've forgotten what butter tastes like. I wait on line with the rain soaking through my shoes for a pound of rotten meat once a week. At night I go home and watch the roaches. Nobody to talk to, just sitting, watching the bugs, with one little light because the government's got to save electricity. You had to go off and leave me to that! What's the war to me that I have to sit at night with nobody to talk to? What's the war to you that you had to go off and . . .

WEBSTER: That's why I'm standing up now, Martha.

MARTHA: What took you so long, then? Why not a month ago, a year ago, ten years ago? Why didn't you stand up then? Why wait until you're dead! You live on eighteen-fifty a week, with the roaches, not saying a word, and then when they kill you, you stand up! You fool!

WEBSTER: I didn't see it before.

MARTHA: Just like you! Wait until it's too late! There's plenty for live men to stand up for! Eggs you can eat and butter and sunlight in your bedroom. A baby and lights at night and somebody to talk to! They're there, waiting. People have them! All right, stand up! It's about time you talked back. It's about time all you poor miserable eighteen-fifty bastards, stood up for themselves and their wives and their dirty,

Bury the Dead

rickety children! Tell 'em *all* to stand up! Tell 'em! Tell 'em! *(Blackout.)*

(VOICES call. Speakers are sometimes spotted individually, sometimes in groups. Occasional VOICES call in the dark. The VOICES start low, almost in a whisper, not very fast, and grow in speed, intensity and volume as the scene progresses. They overlap each other often. The NEWSBOY's VOICE, for example, is heard under the other voices, never by itself.)

FIRST GENERAL: *(His hands to his lips.)* It didn't work. But keep it quiet. For God's sake, keep it quiet...

REPORTER: *(In harsh triumph.)* It didn't work! Now, you've got to put it in! I knew it wouldn't work! Smear it over the headlines!

EDITOR: Put it in the headlines—They won't be buried!

NEWSBOY: It didn't work! Extra! It didn't work!

BUSINESSMAN: *(Hoarse whisper.)* It didn't work! They're still standing...

DOWAGER'S VOICE: Somebody do something.

NEWSBOY: Extra! They're still standing!

DOWAGER: *(Frightened.)* Don't let them back into the country.

REPORTER: *(Triumphantly.)* They're standing. From now on they'll always stand! You can't bury soldiers anymore!

FIRST SOLDIER: They stink. Bury them!

DOWAGER: What are we going to do about them?

BUSINESSMAN: What'll happen to our war? We can't let anything happen to our war...

PRIEST: Pray! Pray! God must help us! Down on your knees, all of you, and pray with your hearts and your guts and the marrow of your bones.

REPORTER: It will take more than prayers. What are prayers to a dead man? They're standing! Mankind is standing up and climbing out of its grave!

ANOTHER WOMAN: Have you heard? It didn't work.

NEWSBOY: Extra! Extra! They're still standing!

MRS. DEAN: My baby...

BESS SCHELLING: My husband...

JULIA MORGAN: My lover...

CHARLEY: Bury them! They stink!

CAPTAIN: Plant a new crop! The old crop has worn out the earth! Plant something beside lives in the old and weary earth...

NEWSBOY: Extra! It didn't work!

BUSINESSMAN: Somebody do something. DuPont's passed a dividend!

PRIEST: The Day of Judgment is at hand...
FIRST WHORE: Where is Christ?
FIRST SOLDIER: File 'em away in alphabetical order...
DOCTOR: We don't believe it. It is against the dictates of science.
FIRST WOMAN: Keep it quiet!
BESS SCHELLING: My husband...
JULIA MORGAN: My lover...
MRS. DEAN: My baby...
A CHILD'S VOICE: What have they done with my father?
DOWAGER: Somebody do something. Call up the War Department!
BUSINESSMAN: Call up Congress! Call up the President!
DOWAGER: Somebody do something.
FIVE VOICES: Put them down!
REPORTER: Never! Never! Never! You can't put them down. Put one down and ten will spring up like weeds in an old garden.
THIRD GENERAL: Use lead on them, lead! Lead put 'em down once, lead'll do it again! Lead!
A YOUNG CLERGYMAN: *(Spotted.)* Put down the sword and hang the armor on the wall to rust with the years. The killed have arisen.
PRIEST: The old demons have come back to possess the earth. We are lost...
A YOUNG WOMAN'S VOICE: *(Very strong.)* The dead have arisen, now let the living rise, singing!
BUSINESSMAN: Do something, for the love of God, do something...
PRIEST: We will do something.
A YOUNG MAN: *(Insolent.)* Who are you?
PRIEST: We are the church and the voice of God. Those corpses are possessed by the devil, who plagues the lives of men. The church will exorcise the devil from these men, according to its ancient rite, and they will lie down in their graves like children to a pleasant sleep, rising no more to trouble the world of living men. The church which is the voice of God upon this earth, Amen. *(A chorus of "Amen's" blends with the reading.)* I exorcise thee, unclean spirit, in the name of Jesus Christ; tremble, O Satan, thou enemy of the faith, thou foe of mankind, who hast brought death into the world, who hast deprived men of life, and hast rebelled against justice, thou seducer of mankind, thou root of evil, thou source of avarice, discord, and envy. *(Silence. Then the CORPSES begin to laugh, lightly, horribly.)*
YOUNG WOMAN: *(Triumphantly.)* No...
CHORUS: No!
NEWSBOY: They're licked!
A MAN'S VOICE: This isn't 1918—This is today!

YOUNG WOMAN: See what happens tomorrow!
THE YOUNG MINISTER: The old order changeth, yielding place to new.
MAN'S VOICE: *(Triumphantly.)* Anything can happen now! Anything!
DOWAGER: *(Frantic.)* They're coming! We must stop them!
REPORTER: *(Sardonically.)* How?
BUSINESSMAN: We must find ways, find means . . .
REPORTER: *(Exulting.)* They're coming! There will be no ways, no means!
CHORUS: *(Strong mocking.)* What are you going to do? What are you going to do? *(They laugh.)*
THIRD GENERAL: Let me have a machine gun! Sergeant! A machine gun! *(The light comes up on the trench. A machine gun is set to the left of it. The GENERALS are clustered around it.)* I'll show them! This is what they've needed!
FIRST GENERAL: All right, all right. Get it over with! Hurry! But keep it quiet!
THIRD GENERAL: I want a crew to man this gun. *(Pointing to FIRST SOLDIER.)* You! Come over here! And you! You know what to do. I'll give the command to fire.
FIRST SOLDIER: Not to me you won't. This is over [for] me. I won't touch that gun. None of us will. We didn't hire out to be no butcher of dead men. Do your own chopping.
THIRD GENERAL: You'll be court-martialed! You'll be dead by tomorrow morning . . .
FIRST SOLDIER: Be careful, General! I may take a notion to come up like these guys. That's the smartest thing I've seen in this army. I like it. *(To DRISCOLL.)* What d'ye say, Buddy?
DRISCOLL: It's about time. *(The THIRD GENERAL draws his gun, but the other GENERALS hold his arm.)*
FIRST GENERAL: Do it yourself.
THIRD GENERAL: Do it myself? Why should I?
SECOND GENERAL: It was your idea.
THIRD GENERAL: No, let somebody else do it.
FIRST GENERAL: Who?
ALL GENERALS: *(To each other.)* You!
THIRD GENERAL: Let's draw lots. The short straw . . . *(He puts out his hand, from which rise four straws. The GENERALS draw, the THIRD drawing last.)*
FIRST and SECOND GENERALS: You! It's you! Go ahead!
THIRD GENERAL: *(Stupidly.)* Me? Why me? Oh, my God! *(He looks down horrified at gun then slowly gets down on one knee beside it, the*

other GENERALS behind him. They sneak offstage. The CORPSES move together, facing the gun. VOICES call as the GENERAL fumbles with the gun.)

YOUNG MAN: Never, never, never . . .

JULIA: Walter Morgan, Beloved of Julia Blake, Born 1913, died 1936.

MRS. DEAN: Let me see your face, Baby . . .

MRS. WEBSTER: All you remember is a glass of beer with a couple of bums on Saturday night.

KATHERINE: A green and pleasant grave . . .

BESS: Did it hurt much, John? His hair is blond and he weighs twenty-eight pounds . . .

JOAN: You loved me best, didn't you—best?

CAPTAIN: Four yards of bloody mud . . .

BEVINS: I understand how they feel, Charley. I wouldn't like to be under the ground now . . .

YOUNG WOMAN: Never! Never!

CHORUS: Never!

MRS. WEBSTER: Tell 'em all to stand up! Tell 'em! Tell 'em!

(The CORPSES start to walk toward the left, not marching, but walking together, silently. The GENERAL stiffens, then starts to laugh hysterically. As the CORPSES reach the edge of the grave he starts firing, the gun shaking his shoulders. Calmly, in the face of the chattering gun, the CORPSES walk soberly toward the GENERAL. For a moment, they obscure him as they pass. In that moment the gun stops. The CORPSES pass on, off the stage, like men who have business that must be attended to in the not-too-pressing future. The GENERAL is seen slumped forward over the gun. There is no movement on the stage for a fraction of a second. Then, slowly, the four SOLDIERS of the burial detail break rank. Slowly they walk, exactly as the CORPSES have walked, past the GENERAL. The last soldier, as he passes the GENERAL, deliberately, but without malice, flicks a cigarette butt at him, then follows the other SOLDIERS off the stage. The GENERAL is the last thing we see, humped over his quiet gun, which points at the empty grave as the light dims, in the silence.)

CURTAIN

Copyright applied for February, 1936.

Bury the Dead was first performed for the benefit of NEW THEATRE and the New Theatre League at the 46th Street Theatre in New York on March 14th and 15th [1936] by the *Let Freedom Ring* acting company, directed by Worthington Minor and Walter Hart. As we go to press, negotiations are under way for an extended run, with the probability that the play will open with the original cast at a Broadway theatre early in April.

A THEATRE TOUR TO EUROPE DURING THE TIME OF HITLER'S GROWING POWER

THE MOST exciting and valuable experience of my editing years began when the Intourist Russian-American Travel Bureau promoted a *New Theatre* Tour in 1936 to Moscow's Theatre Festival, with stops en route in Paris, Prague, Berlin, Warsaw, and London. At a hasty editors' conference, we agreed that I should take the six weeks tour and use it to strengthen ties with foreign writers and theatre, film, and dance groups.

Fourteen people signed up, some of whom would join the tour at various stops along the way. Those going from the New York area included Edward Maltz, brother of playwright Albert, who volunteered to handle our tour's travel, hotel, and business details so I would have time to make the magazine contacts. Hollywood author Sanora Babb, who was in London with her husband, cameraman James Wong Howe, planned to join the tour in Paris. And Dudley Nichols and his wife, Esta, arranged to meet us in Moscow. Dudley, with whom I had become friends during the *Bury the Dead* period in Hollywood, had written the screenplay for John Ford's film, *The Informer*.

Soon we were on our way, not realizing fully we were heading into the heightening of conflicts that would eventually end the uneasy sort of "peace" Germany's von Clausewitz (in an earlier century) had referred to as "an interval between wars."

In those days international trips were made mostly by ships, not planes. I hadn't been to sea since I left home in Davenport, Iowa, in 1931, seeking a life of adventure in order to emulate my writer-hero, Jack London. That earlier voyage from New York to Cuba, Panama, and the West Coast was via freighter, the SS *Colorado*, where I had signed aboard as a member of the black gang, the seamen who worked in the engine room, doing the rough, dangerous job of tending the engines or working high above them on swaying crosswalks. Now on a luxury liner, the *Aquitania*, my only "problem" was adjusting from a *New Theatre* diet of Nedicks and Horn and Hardart Cafeteria food to the rich cooking of a three-star French chef.

I was anticipating my first visit to the famous capital of France, the country whose great literature had influenced my teenage years.

In our few days in Paris, we visited all the tourist highlights, including the Eiffel Tower and the Louvre. But we met many literary lights as well. I met the famous surrealist poet, Louis Aragon, the most prominent spokesman for the French Left and the Popular Front, who had helped Popular Front leader Henri Barbusse organize the League Against War and Fascism. Aragon arranged for us to meet Louis Jouvet, the director-star whose *School for Brides* by Molière was among the finest productions I have ever experienced. We also met stage and film critic Leon Moussignac, who later contributed to *New Theatre*, and film director Jean Renoir, who years later would become a good friend in Hollywood. And two German antifascists who had escaped arrest by Hitler's SS, the UFA Studio film directors G. W. Pabst and Max Ophuls, who also contributed to *New Theatre* later on. Our visit to Paris was short, but we did as much as we could to promote the magazine before going on to our next destination, Prague.

In that lovely old city, we saw a performance by Czech comedy stars Voskovec and Werrich, who were staging a marvelous musical satire that ridiculed Nazi threats to overthrow Czechoslovakia and annex the Sudetenland. Made up as clowns, they exchanged barbed witticisms, commedia dell'arte style, which convulsed the audience. Many men in the audience were in uniform, for at this time the democratic Beneš government was proclaiming Czech determination to resist the German enemy if war came.

Backstage after the play, "V. & W." welcomed us with patter from American song titles and movie subtitles, as if the two spoke and understood English. Whatever "translation" was needed was done by a contributor to *New Theatre*, a talented young Prague director, Hans Burger. The four of us could hardly imagine then that I and my fiancée, Rosa Harvan, would return in April 1938, on the eve of Hitler's threatened May 1 invasion, to film with their aid the first anti-Nazi documentary, *Crisis*. (Two others helped me with *Crisis*, American foreign correspondent Vincent Sheehan and a brilliant Czech cameraman, Alexander Hackenschmied, with whom I also later filmed *Lights Out in Europe*, showing the Nazi invasion of Poland.) This backstage visit, which had seemed just an amusing, enjoyable part of our tour, affected all our lives, since these Czechs were able to use my "connections" to help them escape death in 1938 after the Munich appeasement betrayal, when the

Nazis took over. Fortunately, all our Czech theatre friends that we had made on the 1936 tour found refuge in America. And a few years later, during World War II, one of them, Hans Burger, returned to Prague as an American soldier.

The tour moved on to Germany where our USSR passport visas were scrutinized warily by the Nazis checking arrivals at our Berlin hotel. They had to be polite, for it was a time of Olympic hospitality toward foreigners, ordered by Hitler to present a peaceful Third Reich to a fearful world. We entered our third-floor rooms and discovered an amazing view. On the street below a huge parade was moving by, a veritable sea of swastika emblems and thousands of cheering, heiling Germans. The timing of our arrival was perfect: it was like arriving at a drama as the curtain was rising while strident music clamored in the background.

We could hardly believe our eyes. There below, fifty yards away, was not a "stage Hitler" as in anti-Nazi plays but, as if specially arranged for our viewing, Adolf Hitler himself! Standing in a long, black, open car, with Goebbels and Göring seated behind him, he waved his hand, then raised his arm in a fascist salute to the cheering crowds shouting "Heil Hitler! Heil der Führer!" The procession stopped momentarily as some teenage girls in Hitler Youth uniforms prostrated themselves on the pavement in worship of "Der Schöner Adolf." Guards lifted the girls up, pulled them back, and Hitler was gone from our sight.

Our visit coincided with Hitler's unhappiness over Germany's success in the Olympic games being shattered by a slim, graceful, incredibly superior American Negro youth, Jesse Owens, who showed his heels to the best the German Nordic champions could offer. Owens's victories infuriated Hitler, who avoided congratulating him. We Americans were joyful over this defeat of the "master race" on the international sports stage. But the mass idolatry the crowds of Germans directed toward Hitler was a frightening sign that Germany was heading toward a military confrontation. (Unknown to us at the time, it would indeed begin in a few days with General Franco's fascist invasion of republican Spain.) Our tour plans did not include patronizing the German theatre or the Olympics, so we were glad to leave.

Warsaw, the beautiful, historic capital of the reborn Poland, was a quiet, joyful relief after the noisy, ominous Nazi spectacle in Berlin. Poland's independence had been reestablished after World War I at a conference in America, in Pittsburgh, led by the great patriot-pianist, Ignacy Paderewski. Americans were popular and welcome in Warsaw, and newspapers featured Jesse Owens's victories and Hitler's Olympic defeats.

We saw a play on a patriotic theme, traditionally presented and well performed. Our most dramatic view of life in Poland, however, was off-stage, on a visit to the Warsaw ghetto, where the streets were alive with colorful activities, almost as if staged from a story by Sholem Aleichem. Despite some well-dressed people and prosperous shops, we saw poverty everywhere. Sanora, Ed, and I started taking photographs of little, ragged Jewish children who enjoyed mugging for our cameras.

Suddenly a Jewish worker in overalls, his hands grimy from factory labors, interrupted us. He invited us to see where he worked, and said no more except that his name was Jacob and that he had learned some English fighting in the Polish-American Legion during the World War.

With curiosity, we went along with him as he led us to an apartment-house entrance, then down some rickety stairs. He opened a door to a small, windowless room where about fifteen men, women, and teenagers were grinding forks, spoons, and knives for a living. They smiled, welcoming us, as Jacob picked up a knife, hefted it, and said they also made longer ones, dagger length, for the "Haganah," their self-defense groups patterned on the Palestine Zionist underground. Jacob told us that he and the people we saw were not Zionists but socialists striving to unite Jewish and Polish workers against Nazis and anti-Semitic Poles. The daggers would serve as weapons, along with the pistols and rifles they had hidden, onto which they would attach long knives and bayonets.

We asked Jacob why he risked confiding this to strangers. He answered candidly. They knew of us from a hotel desk clerk, a Jew who had taken a Polish name. He had sent word that Americans with Russian visas were coming. Jacob and his group wanted Americans and Russians to know the Polish underground was planning to resist even if, as was being rumored, reactionaries were to influence the Polish government to make a deal allowing Hitler's forces to cross through Poland to attack the Soviet Union. We could hardly believe we were hearing such thoughts at a chance encounter. Soon a young boy entered, warning us that Polish police summoned by a janitor informer were on the way. Jacob hurriedly led us out through a back entrance. It was like a nineteenth-century scene from a movie chase as Jacob hailed a Jewish drosky driver, who pulled up his horse, cursed the police, and took us safely to our hotel. In a while we were packed, ready for the train and eager to reach our main destination, the USSR.

A new international crisis marked our arrival in Russia. Huge signs were being hastily erected in the Ukrainian city of Kiev, not far from the border where we had been welcomed as *Americansky tovarischi*. The signs and radio news, blasting from loudspeakers, reported General Franco's fascist invasion of republican Spain. Everywhere on our tour—Kharkov, Odessa of the famous steps shown in Eisenstein's film *Potemkin*,

Leningrad, and especially Moscow—wide publicity was given La Passionaria's fervent outcry from Madrid, "No pasarán!" with translations They Shall Not Pass on huge signs and on flags in Russian, English, French, Italian, Greek, and Chinese.

For Soviet contacts and *New Theatre* articles, our editorial staff had relied on Jay Leyda, a brilliant scholar, translator, and fine writer. An American studying at Eisenstein's film school, Jay was a talented editor who could deliver foreign material in a manner comprehensible to American readers, as could his talented wife, Chen I-Wan, on dance.

My joy in meeting the major talents of the Soviet theatre was tempered by nights brooding about Spain. Victory in Spain would enable Hitler and Mussolini to outflank the democracies and cripple our hopes to defeat the fascist dictators. It was a drama greater than any on our Left stages, for it was the beginning of a frontal attack on our hopes for a Popular Front that would defeat fascism.

Nevertheless, we were in Moscow to see the festival, and my main objective was to meet the great creator of the Stanislavsky system, the author of *My Life in Art* and *An Actor Prepares*.

Brooks Atkinson was attending the festival for the *New York Times*, and I was glad to meet him there and hear his high praise of the work of the Moscow Art Theatre and the Tairov, Meyerhold, and Jewish State theatres. It was a thrill also for me to be received warmly by my Russian counterpart, the editor of *Soviet Theatre*, the famous playwright Afinogenov, whose plays *Fear* and *Distant Point* I had read in translation and admired. He was pleased when I handed him an article I had written on the ship about the highly favorable reception of Russian plays and films in America. And like many other Soviet writers, film directors, and dancers that we met, he promised to write an article on contemporary Soviet dramatists and send it to me in New York. Others who promised were the playwright Korneichuk, film director Ermler, and dancer Ulanova. Perhaps Soviet censors intervened, for not even one promised article reached us. And the only personal thing I ever heard of Afinogenov again was the tragic news of his death during the defense of Moscow.

At that time in Russia, we saw no evidence of fear of Germany, only confidence in the Red Army, Navy, and Air Force. Playwrights, directors, actors, and dancers we spoke with were angered by Charles Lindbergh's highly publicized praise of Göring's Luftwaffe as superior to the Soviet flyers. They scorned Western opinions that the Wehrmacht was superior to the Red Army, and cited the fate of Napoleon if Hitler dared to attack Russia. The dangers from fascism seemed remote at times as we became involved with the tremendous vitality and spectacle of Moscow's theatre companies, some of which—the Moscow Art Theatre, the Bolshoi—

dated back to czarist times. We saw festival performances every night and some daytime rehearsals—brilliant productions of Russian classics and also masterpieces of the Western world.

One day we were received at a backstage reading by Konstantin Stanislavsky himself. He was a tall, strikingly handsome, aristocratic type who had come from a wealthy family background. From what Stanislavsky said during our conversations (via Afinogenov as interpreter), he seemed well adapted to the revolutionary, proletarian stage. So too did his distinguished cofounder of the Moscow Art Theatre, Nemirovich-Danchenko, and their great actors, Moskvin, Tarkhanov, Kachalov, and Olga Knipper Chekhova (the widow of Anton Chekhov). Jay Leyda, our mutual friend and editor, had kept them informed about *New Theatre*'s published articles on the Stanislavsky system and its influence on New York's Group Theatre.

On a different occasion, we had another warm welcome from another great director, Vsevolod Meyerhold, also backstage, after seeing his production of *The Inspector General*. Meyerhold's associate director, Seki Sano, a Japanese antifascist exile, translated our conversation. In his directing, Meyerhold used innovative, nontraditional techniques, and I admired his staging of Gogol's masterpiece. It was the greatest production of the twenty plays I saw in Moscow and Leningrad. Years later, while I was filming *Acting*, Lee Strasberg confirmed my reaction to Meyerhold's production. Strasberg also expressed his admiration for Meyerhold in his article in *New Theatre*, "The Magic of Meyerhold."

Our most exciting evening was a special performance of *Princess Turandot* arranged in honor of our *New Theatre* group. We saw the pages of *New Theatre* on Russian theatre, opera, and dance come to life before us in superb staging. After the performance, a curtain call speech asked the audience to welcome the American *tovarischi*, and we were thrilled by the enthusiastic, standing ovation.

Offstage an incredible drama of public trials and confessions was taking place in Moscow. Revolutionary heroes like Zinovyev, Radek, and Marshal Tukhachevsky were being condemned, then executed by firing squads for alleged, undocumented, secret negotiations with Hitler's Nazis. I remember Dudley Nichols, a former journalist, doubting the confessions and being deeply disturbed, as I was, by news of these tragic events. We thought of Benedict Arnold and his betrayal of our American Revolution. But here so many betrayals seemed highly questionable. Somehow these reports of treachery and executions of former patriots refuted Lincoln Steffens's influential statement, made after his USSR tour, "I have seen the future and it works." It seemed to us that the execution squads were firing in great haste. But these were mysterious matters. Behind the high, forbidding Kremlin walls, Stalin-ordered executions were taking place, which the Russians we met were reluctant to discuss. Evidently they were so fearful of reprisals they always changed the subject.

Our tour continued to Leningrad, where we saw more theatres and ballets of comparable excellence. As in Moscow, there were no Western newspapers in Leningrad to tell us what was really going on at the trials; and of course, an English-language Russian newsletter gave only the official version. Most Russian writers, directors, and actors to whom we spoke seemed evasive; others justified these trials and executions as part of Russia's preparation to resist betrayers aiding fascism. However, my belief in "plots" that had been exposed and punished by Soviet "justice" was shaken. Not even Maxim Gorky, "the conscience of the Russian Revolution," had dared to question the trials publicly. In truth, the only conspiracy that seemed certain was a conspiracy of silence—not a single Soviet intellectual or artist made a public protest.

Whatever troubles we had in America with censorship and reactionary acts against us, we could fight back in the press and in courts of law, relying upon our constitutional rights. Our doubts about Soviet democracy began in late summer 1936, nearly twenty years before Nikita Khrushchev confirmed that Stalin had perpetrated unjust trials and forced false confessions to destroy competition for power from his revolutionary comrades and justify their executions. But in 1936, for all our doubts, Stalin's leadership seemed to us a main hope for joining Western leaders in a democratic coalition against fascism.

After we left Leningrad and reached London, the newspapers were headlining the Russian trials and seemed as mystified by them as we were. The war in Spain was on the back pages.

Our theatre tour had arranged for us to see productions of Shakespeare and Shaw in the British acting style, so very different from the ensemble staging of the Stanislavsky system—yet equally impressive. The English theatre was glamorous and free of political pressures. But our most memorable theatre experience in London was one that I delighted in telling Clifford Odets about on my return. It was an East London workers' theatre production of *Waiting for Lefty*, in which the taxi drivers used cockney pronunciations for Odets's oh-so-American dialogue. Otherwise it was a fine performance and moved the English audience, which reacted emotionally and enthusiastically, just as audiences were reacting in America and many foreign lands.

We returned to New York. The news from Loyalist Spain was worse: Franco's forces were advancing against poorly armed defenders. In New York, too, the Moscow trials and executions were being publicized much more than in London, with many details that made them seem even more a terrible, inexplicable crisis in Soviet life. But in the *New York Times*, Brooks Atkinson wrote, for the most part, favorably about the positive achievements of Soviet theatre arts. And so did we in *New Theatre*, increasing foreign theatre arts coverage and leaving issues raised by the trials to political publications. We were also deeply affected by our concern for Spain and took part in benefits to raise money for medical aid to the Loyalists, who were sacrificing so much to stop Franco. But above all, our main problem was how to keep *New Theatre* going despite almost overwhelming financial pressures.

The following selections reflect our emphasis on international theatre, film, and dance as part of a United Front effort to support the democratic West and our potential socialist ally, the USSR.

Reinhardt Hails a Popular Front Play

BY ELIZABETH MEYER

MAX REINHARDT returned to Hollywood to begin intensive preparations for his forthcoming film, *Danton*. His present preoccupation with the French Revolution led him to stop in Paris on his way to the Salzburg Festival to see the presentation of Romain Rolland's play, *Fourteenth of July*. Anticipating nothing more than a routine performance of one of his favorite plays, Professor Reinhardt was not prepared for what he now glowingly calls "one of my greatest experiences in the theatre!" It was not the performance of the actors Professor Reinhardt referred to, it was that of the audience!

"Those people had probably never been to a theatre in their lives," he exclaimed. Celebrating the first Independence Day under the Popular Front, they followed every line of the historic revolutionary document with tremendous intensity, applying its meaning to situations today. Every other sentence drew salvos of applause. Through the increasingly close contact between actors and audience, the whole theatre rose to such a pitch of excitement that at the end of the performance actors and audience burst spontaneously into the "Internationale," sung at the top of their lungs. The atmosphere was revolutionary, but shot through with joy, with delight; not with bitterness or hate. One could imagine, from the spirit of these people, the atmosphere in the folded-arms strikes where the protesters spent the period of occupation dancing, singing, playing games. Enthusiasm, ebullience, and control were paramount. A most heartening experience in a war-obsessed world.

As the audience was filing out, a man stood up on a seat and started to make an antirevolutionary speech. The people listened quietly to the man, a fascist, for some moments. Then, as he got more and more violent, they all started chanting: "Discipline! Discipline!"; not, as might be thought, in the sense of "Beat him up! Discipline him!" but to themselves, in the sense of "Control yourselves! Let's keep discipline!" The chant progressed good-naturedly; the audience filed out laughing; the fascist was left talking with furious vehemence—to an empty house!

The whole enterprise was engineered by a group of young artists, who had organized what was to be one evening's performance of Rolland's play. The response had been immediate. Actors for the crowd scenes were recruited from men off the streets who volunteered of their own accord to play for nothing. Several actors from the Comédie Française offered their services; Picasso painted a curtain for them; Honegger and several of the leading modern composers offered new music which was played during the intermissions. The one night's performance turned into a theatre packed to capacity week after week.

This popularity was due not only to the contemporaneousness of the subject matter, but also to the fact that the play is based on the idea of a revolutionary impulse which springs directly from the people. All other works on the Revolution slight the role of the people and stress that of the leaders. "A crowd," Professor Reinhardt elucidated, "can be like a woman: fall in love with a man, a leader, who attracts, who sways it. On the other hand, a crowd can get an idea from the air: from literature which it cannot read; from talk which it does not hear; from necessities created within its own consciousness. The idea lurks in the unconscious, from where, in an instant, it may emerge as an irresistible impulse. To represent the unconscious, Romain Rolland, in the *Fourteenth of July*, uses the character of a child. This child it is who summons the people to storm the Bastille; the impulse emerging from the unconscious carries them, not to break into a bakery, where hunger would be immediately satisfied, but to the Bastille, the symbol of oppression. The child leads them to a real, a deep revolt. It is because Rolland's play deals with this leadership of the people by themselves that audiences in France today responded to it as an expression of the present."

This audience was to Professor Reinhardt a wonderful sign: the sign of a new receptive, a new critical force. This is what Reinhardt feels is necessary to the theatre today. The small coterie of "first-nighters," the circumscribed group of habitual big-city theatregoers, is too small, too limited, to have in its hands the destiny of an art. He feels, too, that haphazard control of a medium reaching a vast new public is not enough. Governments must realize the importance of this means of talking to the people, of having contact with the people. Some governments do realize it, and this, in one or two cases today, happens to be unfortunate. But the principle is right. The government needs the people; the people need the theatre; and the theatre needs the support of the government. A small group who control production of plays, a small group who form an audience: these are not enough today. Art cannot flourish, cannot function when confined to a minor place in the feverish life of a few large cities.

In France the right conditions seem to be forming. The government has taken its first step toward a national theatre by reorganizing the three state-subsidized theatres. Under new management, the Comédie Française will present the best modern authors; the Opera will employ the talent of the best modern composers. New works will be commissioned from every source of talent available—a possibility unheard of in these erstwhile tradition-ridden institutions. The possibilities in the French theatre are enhanced, according to Professor Reinhardt, by the happy accident of the present golden age of French actors. All at the same time, the stage can offer, to name a few: Boyer, Bauer, Fresnay, Blanchard, Remue, Berry, Clarion. Such an assemblage is almost unheard of in the history of the drama. These actors, in the past, have almost always starred in separate vehicles, but may now be united in through-and-through beautifully cast productions. If the new conditions in France continue, bringing impulse from all sides, putting people in charge who have the ability, the taste, the talent, the state backing, that enables them to unite actors, painters, musicians, writers, one may hope that there will be, in France, a Golden Age of the Theatre!

Impressions of Nazi Drama

BY H. W. L. DANA

"HEIL HITLER!" muttered the Minnesingers with their harps and long medieval robes as, on the way from their dressing rooms to the stage, they filed past the official with whom I was standing. It was a gala performance of Wagner's *Tannhäuser* at the Berlin Opera House this year,

Impressions of Nazi Drama

DRAMA UNDER THE SWASTIKA
Phil Wolfe

and to show me how much alive the German theatre was under the Nazis (which I had ventured to question) the authorities had invited me to view the performance from backstage. They pointed out to me with pride the eighty-four squares on the huge stage which could be shifted to right or left and raised or lowered and they rubbed their hands with delight at the marvelous mechanism of their stage. I began to feel that they gloated also on the marvelous mechanism of their actors. The Pilgrims with their cowls and gowns and staffs marched by to the strains of Wagner's "Pilgrim's Chorus" but, instead of making the sign of the cross, gave the same greeting, "Heil Hitler!", before going on the stage. It all seemed one further indication of the subordination of the theatre to the Führer. Wagner is the one German genius of the past who is allowed to blaze out in full blast. Yet Wagner's renewed life seemed only a renewed death. Most incongruous of all, the scantily clad Venus, as she went by us in her greasepaint on her way to the Venusberg, greeted us with a "Heil Hitler!" though she seemed so bored by having had to repeat this ritual so often that she seemed to be mumbling merely the vowels "A-I-A."

Another evening the proud present director of the Berlin Opera House, an enormous man named Klein, insisted on taking me to the State

Theatre where they were putting on a first performance of a much-advertised new version of Shakespeare's *Hamlet*. He took me under the enormous circular stage which he had just invented with no less than six different elevators in it of different shapes, now raised to form the parapets of Elsinore or now lowered for a grave. From under this strange contraption we could hear through the cracks over our heads the voices of Gustaf Gründgens, the Nazi-appointed director of the theatre, mouthing the lines of his strangely neurotic and Hitler-like Hamlet. When the actor playing the ghost of Hamlet's father came under the stage where he was to utter his underground admonition "Swear!", I was quite prepared by this time to have him give instead the greeting "Heil Hitler!" When from understage we heard poor Ophelia going mad above us, I felt that I could not blame her.

For six weeks this year I went practically every night to the theatres in Berlin. Each year since Hitler came into power I have stopped to see something of the Nazi theatres on my way to or from my visits to the Soviet theatres. Each year the contrast has become stronger. I found the Moscow theatres expanding and broadening their scope in response to the ever-widening culture of the people. In Berlin, on the contrary, in spite of all effort to pump up enthusiasm for the theatre, to increase the subsidies threefold, to honor the first performances with the august presence in what had been the Kaiser's box of Hitler, flanked on one side by Goebbels and on the other side by Göring, I felt that the range of the theatre was contracting and that the life had gone out of it.

There are those who still insist that the Dictatorship of the Proletariat and the Dictatorship of Fascism come to the same thing. Yet, if in no other way, the essential difference can be tested by the widening of culture in the Soviet Union and by the narrowing of culture in Nazi Germany. Of all forms of culture the theatre is the one that best shows the reaction of the public and here is the acid test which shows the renewed vitality of the Soviet stage and the stagnation if not the actual death of the Nazi stage.

"The German stage is dead!" So said the great German actor Bassermann a year ago when he stood at the grave of the banished Moissi and threw into the grave the ring of Iffland—the ring which had been handed down generation by generation from the celebrated actor of Goethe's time. It may be you feel that there was something theatrical in his gesture and that there was some exaggeration in the statement. Yet in a very real sense: "The German stage is dead!"

It was not the brunt of the World War nor yet the humiliation of the Versailles Treaty which killed German drama. On the contrary, in the years immediately after the war it was the German expressionists—Ernst

Toller, Georg Kaiser, Fritz von Unruh, Walter Hasenclever, and the rest —who were introducing into defeated Germany a drama of revolt far more vigorous than anything that was to be found at that time in victorious England, France, or Italy. At the beginning of 1933, German drama, in spite of the efforts at suppression by the Nazis, was still very much alive and kicking. Frederich Wolf and Bert Brecht were bringing a new courage and a new bitterness on the stage, and workers' theatres were springing up everywhere. Once when storm troopers tried to break up one of these performances, the actors and audience moved the scenery and all to a nearby beer hall, and when the police raided them there the actors mingled with the audience so that the police had to content themselves with arresting the scenery.

But with the coming into power of the Nazis, all these plays have been completely *verboten* and all these playwrights have been driven out or have left in voluntary exile. The great theatre directors, Reinhardt, Jessner, Barnowsky, Piscator, have one by one been banished; and the only director of genius left, Jürgen Fehling, I found hampered in every way and forced to work on worthless material. Independent dramatic critics, such as Alfred Kerr, are exiles in Paris and those who remain are ordered to have "reverence" for all Nazi plays. The great actors, like Moissi or Bassermann, have gone into compulsory or voluntary exile, and the actor, Hans Otto, who tried to resist the Hitler regime, was murdered by the Nazis.

What, then, remains? The living actors whom I saw seemed strangely dead-alive. As has been said: "Every German actor must be a storm trooper on stage." They seem to go through their acting with the same mechanical motions that they use in the Nazi salute or in the greeting "Heil Hitler!" When I asked some actors why they were willing to put up with these conditions, one of them gave a significant answer: "The Germans *must* do everything willingly." He implied that if the Germans were to give their real opinions of Hitler, it would be a very different matter and to illustrate this he told me an anecdote of Hitler at the barber's: how Hitler asked the barber what could be done to prevent his forelock from falling down on his forehead and how the barber, after getting immunity for what he might say from the Führer, told him that if he would give the people complete freedom to say what they really thought about him, then his hair would stand on end all right.

During the six weeks of my stay this year in Berlin, the control of the theatres was significantly transferred from the Ministry of Culture to the Ministry of Propaganda. This brings the stage as well as the screen, the radio, and the press directly under Goebbels, who likes to play upon them, in his own words, "as upon a vast keyboard." A bad play written years ago by Goebbels called *The Wanderer*, which had been rejected everywhere, is now ordered to be produced. This means not merely the presence everywhere of Nazi propaganda but the absence of culture. To plead today in the name of culture is to bring the Nazi retort: "When I heard the word 'culture,' I reach for my revolver." "Don't think with the brain," Germans are told, "that is a Jewish attitude —think with the blood!"

Even German culture of the past is under suspicion. Lessing is too full of the brotherhood of man. His Nathan the Wise is a Jew and utters the unutterable sentiment "that all countries have good people." Schiller is too much a lover of liberty and his heroines, Maria Stuart and the Main of Orleans, too often non-Germans. Goethe the Nazis dare not prohibit, and I saw a good many of Goethe's plays that had an almost embarrassing greatness. *Iphigenia* breathed a lofty spirit of reconciliation and tolerance that made one blush for Hitlerland, and in *Egmont*, when Clara stirs up the crowd crying "Free Egmont," one almost expected to hear her cry "Free Thälmann!"

The very dearth of "safe" German plays forced the Ministry of Propaganda to give its approval to a host of foreign plays. "Unser Shakespeare" the Germans, to be sure, hardly look upon as a foreigner, and I saw half a dozen of his plays, ranging from a very poor production of a very great play such as *King Lear* (surely far inferior to the performance by the Jewish Theatre in Moscow) to a very poor play such as *Two Gentlemen of Verona* in a very brilliant and very free adaptation by Hans Rothe. But recently these "Ur-Shakespeare" versions by the author of *The Battle About Shakespeare* have been forbidden. A good Spanish Catholic and monarchist such as Calderón seemed safe. So was Oscar Wilde's *Ideal Husband* and Shaw after he had praised Hitler.

Having seen Jacques Deval's *Tovarish* in the original French version and in the English adaptation by Robert Sherwood, I was very curious to see the Nazi version by Curt Götz. I found that the visiting Soviet Commissar, upon whom the Czarist Prince and Princess are forced to wait at table in Paris, instead of being made the most brilliant of all the guests, here gets his face slapped to the satisfaction of the orthodox Nazi element in the audience. The whole last act of the Bolshevik's triumph is omitted as embarrassing to the Great H. and the two great G.'s who sat in the imperial box. On the two occasions when I saw Hitler this year, it seemed to me that in spite of all the playing of bands, there was less spontaneous enthusiasm than before and I got a sense that in the theatres the audiences did not like these foreign plays done over to suit *his* taste.

What was there in the German theatres besides the carefully hand-picked German classics and innocuous foreign plays? How about new German plays? Contemporary social problems were too risky. Either they might be taken to show that all was not well in the totalitarian state or else the plays would be such an obvious whitewashing of conditions that there might be embarrassing groans from the audience at the wrong moment. The two safest subjects seemed to be either loud and empty farces on the one hand or plays based on past history.

The most popular of the loud and supposedly "wholesome" farces was one called *The Rumpus About Iolanthe*, in which the audience seems to have got its chief delight in live animals in the poultry yard and in which the central character, Iolanthe, proved to be a very large and very German pig. Each program was provided with a candy pig, tied on by a pink ribbon, for the audience to eat in the entr'acte.

The new plays safely based on past history were all special pleading for the National Socialist Party and its policy. One of January of this year, von Zwehl's *Uprising in Flanders*, and another of March of this year, Klucke's *The Devil's Concert*, both deal with the same time and period, the revolt of the Spanish Netherlands, as Goethe's *Egmont*, but carefully avoid the generous implications of Goethe's work and are merely carefully prepared foretastes of the present narrow nationalism of the Nazis.

Shortly before the Nazis came into power, Ferdinand Bruckner, by origin a Romanian Jew, had written a very successful play, *Queen Elizabeth*, which Nazi rowdies had tried to break up. Now they had set up their dictatorship, they not only completely forbade this play, but tried to replace it by another play about Queen Elizabeth, Hans Schwarz's *Rebel in England*. The "rebel," the Earl of Essex, is a sort of prototype of Hitler, whom the blond-haired youths salute with a Nazi salute and a "Heil Essex!" and who utters the typical Hitlerian threat: "Heads must roll!" Ambassadors from Russia, resembling German caricatures of Bolsheviks, come with a modest proposal that the Virgin Queen should become the wife of Ivan the Terrible, who had already gone Henry VIII one better by having seven wives. Elizabeth parries by proposing that Ivan should marry the lady whom Essex secretly loves.

Hanns Johst, now the Nazi head of repertoire, made his fame by his play *Schlageter* about the Nazi martyr during the French invasion of the Ruhr who dies crying "Deutschland erwache!" I saw another play of Johst's produced this winter, *Thomas Paine*, in which it is Tom Paine who is the prototype of Hitler and at Valley Forge beats on the drum as he sings his patriotic song. The fact that Washington came in smoking a corncob pipe, that the American Revolutionary soldiers march to the goosestep, and that Valley Forge was said to be in "Western Pennsylvania" and that from there across the "White Mounts" lay—not the state of Maine—but the Great West, was all a little disconcerting to Americans. The fact that Thomas Paine was put in the same prison cell with King Louis XVI and that he came out sixteen years later to find the Directory still in power must have been equally disconcerting to the French. Hans Johst modestly explained to me that Shakespeare and Shaw had taken equal liberties with history. Why should not he?

In May of this year, Alfred Mühr's *White Eagle* gives us a good fascist picture of the revolt of the Poles under Pilsudski against the Russians. In June of this year, another ultrapatriotic play, *Fighters and Dreamers*, represented in the Germany of 1849 Nazi ideals triumphant over the liberals of that period, who are represented as Jews.

Since June, the latest and most spectacular of Nazi dramas has been, of course, the Olympic games. Here, of course, the 100-percent Nordics were supposed to be the heroes of the performance and those of darker skin the villains. But something seems to have gone wrong with the performance and we find some of the Negroes running away with the show. The actors apparently did not stick to their lines. As is often the case with Nazi drama, the final effect is quite different from what the Ministry of Propaganda had intended.

François Villon in Prague
Drawings by John Groth

François Villon in Prague

BY CHARLES RECHT

CZECHOSLOVAKIA is a Slavonic island in a Teutonic sea. Czechoslovakia has unemployment and a severe economic crisis, and she is in constant imminent danger of fascist invasion. Within the country the Sudeten movement, led by Henlein, is a plain fascist Hitler-inspired plot, aiming to disrupt and destroy the republic. But Czechoslovakia has an awakened group of Left intellectuals who are aware of the menace within and without and are trying to rouse the people to a sense of their danger. Among them are George Voskovec and Jan Werrich, who run the Prague Theatre Liberated. In Prague you will see their billboards and their theatre simply designated as V. & W. The theatre was formerly called Spoutane (*Enchaîné*) but the literary friends and colleagues of the two talented founders objected and in the second year of its existence the title was changed to Theatre Liberated.

They have taken Prague by storm. Their present bill, called *The Ballad of Rags*, has been playing to crowded houses for six months, and will soon be replaced by their new bill, *The Local Patriot*. I am sorry indeed that I'll miss the *Patriot*. He will probably bear a close resemblance to some people I know in the States.

Think of a theatre of the Left, unabashedly so, being frequented by high government officials! Masaryk, known now as the Father of His Country, not only visited the V. & W. but permitted a photograph of the incident to be used in the program.

Of the show, or the revue, *The Ballad of Rags*, it should be said that it is not the plot which is the thing but the courage of the theme and the acting of Messrs. V. & W. The play begins with a scene in the "lower depths." An old actor carrying a bundle on a walking stick wanders into a group of poor wretches. The group chide and jeer him about the treasures he has in his bag. He answers that they are mere tatters, the clothes of actors who used to play Shakespeare and the classics. The group fall on the bundle and pull out these tattered costumes. What kind of a play can they give in such rags? François Villon, the poet! They all dress on the stage and the play begins. Lines from Villon's poems are mingled with songs and ribaldry, and there are choruses and some dancing. The ballad of the old whore is recited exactly as Villon wrote it, by one of the women playing the part of an old beggar. Werrich, who is more portly than his colleague, plays the part of a curfew ringer of Paris, while Voskovec, the more slender, is a town wag, a rogue, and acts most of the time as a stooge for W. As this talented pair, who are not only playwrights but excellent actors and singers, have really no part in even the meager plot, they have great liberty in commenting on contemporary matters—and how well they do it!

The scene where W. explains to V. how they smashed the atom in America is unforgettable. Local humor is difficult to translate—perhaps one line will give the cue: Werrich, looking very intense and holding the atom between the thumb and forefinger, is showing Voskovec how to hold the atom.—By its end? asks Voskovec.—No, simpleton, did not I just explain that the theory shows its endlessness? So they agree to grasp the atom by its *endlessness*.

One of the topics they discuss is Bolshevik propaganda. Of course, they agree, there is starvation in Russia. But these Bolsheviks are masters at propaganda. They stuff the people with food. The working people all look as though they had had a course in eating at the best restaurant in Prague—but naturally it's all done for show, for sake of the tourist. And do you know what happened to an editor (naming a conservative paper in Prague) when he was in Moscow? He was on to this trick of stuffing 'em as propaganda. He was walking in a park. He saw a very buxom girl, and just for scientific reasons, you understand, wanted to see if it was real fat or pneumatic tires and decided to pinch the legs of the girl. And what do you know, she turned around and hit him on the nose. Which shows the Bolsheviks will never submit to an impartial investigation of the facts. Propaganda, all propaganda, says V. That's what I've been telling you, says W.

The curfew ringer and his friend catch the Mayor of Paris prowling the streets in his nightshirt. They refuse to recognize his identity and jail him. But during the dialogue W. tells how he had to take courses from the city authorities on how to ring the curfew. He goes through the lessons. His demonstration of the component parts of a spear, and how to handle it, is a biting satire on militarism.

None of this is buffoonery. Back of it lies the desire to reflect the rottenness of our world and change it. Clowns though they are on the stage, appearing in the habiliments of clowns, the author-actors are dedicated to a serious task.

"Our repertoire," they write in the program of the theatre, "will consist of satire aimed against cultural fascism and for democracy. In the carnival heyday of dictators which prevails today in our fantastic capitalist regime, in the disintegration of bourgeois morality, the imbecility of economic chaos, the grotesque disproportion between the miracles achieved by the scientific mind and the twilight of political fanaticism, in this labyrinth of the twentieth century, there appears to us the hope for a new social order, which promises economic justice to reward humanity for the suffering of our day."

Why did they select the period of François Villon? It seems very distant from the struggles waged today. But an analysis of the period reveals many striking parallels between that time and the present. "Try to place yourselves in the France of the beginning of the fifteenth century, when the so-called Hundred Years' War had uprooted the economic life of the land, when the weak and cowardly Charles VII could do nothing to remedy conditions. Add to that the deep dissension within the church and the unrest of the common people, who were obliged to carry the burden of the criminal irresponsibility of their rulers. At the very time when Western Europe was at the close of the medieval mystical-gothic civilization, a breach was being made in the stagnating cult of Christian resignation, and in its place a new spirit was being ushered in: the renaissance of man. Into this background steps François Villon, a poet, the true proletarian of his day. He typifies the dawning of the idea that poverty need not wait until death releases it but that it can rise up and fight. That was a novel thought for that time. His poet contemporaries were occupying themselves with formalism and empty phrasemongering. Villon's verses were the revolutionary cries of his day. Five hundred years later they retain their vigor and remind us of the fighting rhymes of Arthur Rimbaud.

"It is the fate of the poet who dares to proclaim a new world order, to live on the extreme periphery of society. He becomes a part of the circle of social outcasts and felons made by man's law. Such was the fate of Villon. We have used such facts as we had of Villon's life, against a background of the poverty of the masses, the worthlessness of social parasites, and the struggle of the poet against the bourgeoisie, who were fearful of his poetry lest it provoke the common people.

"If you will compare our satire with the reported life of Villon, you will see that we deal rather freely with the subject. In order to be able to do so, we selected an episode which is even more obscure than most of the data obtainable on the life of the poet, the episode of the love affair of Master François with Katherine de Vauxelles. We also took the liberty of coupling this love affair with the brawl which ended with the killing of Philip Sermoise. Our conscience is clear, however. We have not engaged in historical reportage but in satire based on historical analogy. Not documentary exactness, but dramatic effect, was our concern.

"We have used two or three of Villon's poems as recitations in the

play, while our main theme song is based on this quotation from his works:
> 'For food the wolf will leave its lair,
> And want will drive goodman to treason.' "

In the manner of the Russians, V. & W. have strung a narrow banner across the proscenium which bears the couplet just cited. In addition, they have incorporated it into their own "Song of Villon," set to music and sung first by themselves and later by the small chorus of the revue. It follows the spirit of the Villon ballad. Villon was probably the popularizer, if not the real creator, of the ballad form. In the translation of his poetry into other languages much is lost. In the original the crude form is well suited to the primitive language and the theme. In quoting V. & W.'s "Song of Villon," this writer is faced with a greater difficulty than was Mark Twain with the translation of his own story of the "Jumping Frog." The original poem was in old French; it was then translated into poetic Czech by a leading Czech poet, later adapted by V. & W. into a form to suit their theatrical purpose—and is now translated into English with the aim of recreating it in the style of the Villon period. After so thorough a metamorphosis the song now appears as follows:

Voskovec and Werrich:
"The Song of Villon"
(Also called "Hey, Mr. King!")

We sent a questioning to the baccalaurii,
Et item doctor, et item rector,
Why only poor wretches are jailed sine privilegii?
The rich thief the Cardinal has as benefactor!
If all this the King would just yearn
There'd be a turn—
We—the chaff—would be the kern!
  Refrain
    Oh, Mr. King, do please awake—
    Come among us dressed in rags.
    Learn how we starve and ache—
    Mr. King, for Mercy's sake—
    Dine on crust and sleep on bags.
    You, mighty Lords, whose foul was fair,
    We too shall have harvest season,
    Then thunder will be in the air—
    For food the wolf will leave its lair

And want will drive goodman to treason.
Some day out of den and basement
We, the unfeared, run in unison
Dark'ning your gate and basement.
With lusty shout from gaol and prison
The birds we'll set free of snare.
To fear us now you have good reason
For want does drive goodman to treason
And hunger has been our fare."

Soviet Diary

BY HAROLD CLURMAN

Excerpt from an informal diary kept by the author during a five-week visit to the Soviet Union devoted chiefly to a study of the Soviet theatre.

Saw *The Sorceress* at the Jewish Theatre. I wanted to see this production that was first presented in 1922 because it represents a certain extreme in stylization, which at a certain time in America was considered the norm of stylization. It also marks the first big production of Gronovski, who in those days was a leading figure in the Soviet theatre. In general, it was impossible for me to consider this production as a work of art: I looked at it more as a document in theatrical history. Unless one regards it in this light it is difficult to understand why it should have assumed so much importance in its day. There is almost no story left of the original material, and what story there is is absurd and dramatically without function. What we see is a grotesque harlequinade —angular, distorted, abstract, garish, noisy. It is full of gestures, leaps, somersaults, nonsensical rhymes, bewildering props, heterogeneous songs, dances, and a kind of crazy choral comment conveyed through strange sounds, stranger bits of mimicry, and all sorts of corkscrew contortions.

This production was worked on for two years and is relatively short: two and one-half hours. The first minute I looked at the stage I said to myself "All this is stuff and nonsense," the next minute I thought "Why shouldn't it be?" and as the scenes progressed I felt myself thinking "How much charm and life there is in it!" The fact is that it is all very clear, simple, even concrete, when one relates it to the period with which it was concerned. It is a folk picture or ballet of the old Jewish ghetto.

But this ghetto is crazy and fantastic because the Bolsheviks are going to clear it out; build anew so that it will become an unbelievable memory of the past, an impossible dream, half nightmare, half joke. The Jew of the new Socialist society is roaring his mockery of the cramped, dislocated life of the old ghetto. He is sweeping it away with energy and laughter. He buries it by making of it a topsy-turvy masque. And with the old ghetto, the actors of the new Soviet Jewish Theatre were breaking the shackles of theatrical convention inherited from the old Jewish Theatre. At one moment a character cries out in a comic wail, "They are dead! they are dead! they are dead!" "Who is dead?" the chorus clamors. "The old Jewish theatres" is the reply. So the sentimental intonations of the provincial Jewish stage, the little comedy tricks, the fake pathos, the childish heroics, the professional Jewish theatre sweetness are all satirically exaggerated and caricatured.

Even the set, which at first sight looks like a perfectly arbitrary arrangement of surfaces, is based on the definite reality of a Russian Jewish village before the revolution with its poverty-stricken wooden materials, its ramshackle architecture, its cockeyed, helter-skelter, tattered effect. Though it is essentially a stage construction which permits the varied acrobatics of all the strange characters, the set gives the feeling of the kind of place the old ghetto was. Understood in this light the production is a real Bolshevik product. And the actors at the time— themselves liberated from diverse Russian, Polish, and Romanian ghettos—must have felt it and acted it with all the enthusiasm of their young, vigorous bodies (no doubt the two years were used to train themselves to perform all the acrobatic stunts of the show), acted it with the joy of victory, with the hopefulness of pioneers amid the ruins of an old world, with the iconoclasm of revolutionaries. And the audience likewise must have understood it quite clearly. . . . So once again we see that what appeared in pictures and hasty interpretations like mere left-wing artiness was actually an expression of reality. From this again we learn that the outer aspect of art can be understood only in relation to an inner content, and that for art to function it must be organic with a people at a certain definite time under certain definite conditions. When such stylizations were merely imitated as they came to be in some of our "experimental" theatres, they represented at best nothing but the Freudian writhings of arrested adolescents. Not that this production is without its blemishes of flatness, of "modernistic" sophistication, and of mere bizarrerie. Today the actors play it coldly, without much inner urge, youthful plasticity, or sense of fun. They have no emotion, and it is all a little like a bad reproduction of a bright painting. Gronovski never did work emotionally with his actors, but they had emotion at first that came from their personal relation to the period and to the situation. Now only the form remains, but as an actor of the company explained, it remains technically accurate because Gronovski worked it out so that if the actor turned the wrong way he was likely to get a crack on the nose, or if he made a badly timed cross he might have one of his colleagues crash down on his head. "Gronovski did this on purpose," the actor said, "he wanted every movement to be as strictly coordinated as a machine." Indeed the production has something of the precise nature of a cuckoo clock.

After the performance I go backstage to talk to Goldblatt. He plays the leading part and he is at the same time the founder and chief director of the Gypsy Theatre. Our conversation leads to some interesting, though familiar facts. The company plays in Moscow till May 18. Then it goes to Leningrad till the first of July and after that it tours the Union till September. Following this the actors take a six-week vacation. The regular Soviet vacation is four weeks, but the actor is allowed these extra two weeks because as a worker he is supposed to be on the job only five days a week but since this is not always possible even with a large company playing repertory (there are forty-one in this group) the two weeks are added to compensate for the extra days he has worked during the season. Vacation in the Soviet Union is "with pay." Goldblatt informed me that a doctor had been to the theatre that very day to examine the actors and advise them where it would be best for them to spend this vacation. The mountains were recommended for some, the sea for others, etc.

"I wonder if you realize how lucky you are," I said. "The Jewish actors in New York are having a hard time and the American actors are no better off." Goldblatt answered, "I do understand our good fortune. I was born in Romania and our only dramatic school was in Bucharest. If I wanted to study there I had to be baptized, as no Jew was permitted to enter. Second, the tuition was so high that I could not have afforded to pay even for one month. But now I teach in our own dramatic school. The students are young people from the provinces, eighteen or nineteen years old. They are given free board and lodging in Moscow. During the day for about five hours they are instructed in all the branches of theatrical craft. At night as part of their training they are asked to see all the productions, and of course they do not pay for their tickets. Added to this they are given fifty or sixty rubles for pocket money. This goes on for four years and only then is it decided whether or not they may join the theatre. They imagine that life for the actor is this way everywhere."

In talking to Goldblatt about Gronovski, who is now a successful and wealthy director of bourgeois films in Paris, I asked him why he had left the theatre. "Because he is an impressionable fool," was the answer.

When we came out of the dressing room onto the stage-landing I saw a big call-board all plastered with typewritten material. "What is that?" I inquired. "That is the theatre newspaper. It is used as a means of mutual criticism. Actors may write their criticisms of one another, of the director, the organization, anything they feel strongly or clearly about. The directors can do the same, as well as any members of the collective—including stagehands." "What is the main paper now?" I asked pointing at the center of the board. "That is a comment by our electrician. He says that the criticisms directed against the theatre lighting are justified but for the lighting to be improved more time must be devoted to light rehearsals." I asked further, "Why don't the actors write letters to one another if they want to criticize each other. Why do they put the criticism on the board?" "That is the most impersonal and at the same time the friendliest way—this open criticism by means of the newspaper. The actors learn from one another, help one another this way. There is no desire to hurt or to find fault for its own sake. This system benefits everybody. All the actors learn and discipline themselves because of this, whereas personal discussions cause bad feelings and do great mischief." I go away quite impressed.

It Makes You Weep

AN INTERVIEW WITH STELLA ADLER ON SOVIET ACTORS

BY JANET THORNE

THERE is a theatrical legend to the effect that a curtain never rises without an Adler behind it, so when Stella Adler reports on the life of the actors whom she saw in the Soviet Union, there is behind her a long knowledge of how actors exist in most other countries.

"It makes you weep, when you think—an actor in Russia as a matter of course has at least forty weeks of *work* a year. And he has a vacation with pay besides. That is, he is paid fifty-two weeks a year. And the bigger theatres all have vacation quarters where they take the actors and their families for summer work."

How do the actors get into the companies?

"Nearly every important theatre has connected with it a technicum—a theatre school. But each theatre is so different from every other in its style that when a pupil selects a technicum he is attaching himself to a particular technique."

Can they just pick a school like that?

"They apply for admission. But the basis for selecting them is so different from anywhere else. In the Comédie Française, for instance, a girl is admitted to the school because she has a nice body. But in Russia she doesn't have to look like Joan Crawford. (If she does, she'll probably play character parts and old women.) So long as she has two arms and a brain and her teeth—if she has talent she can be admitted. If there is one particular fault, a bad voice, that needn't exclude her. They have three years to work with her, and they concentrate on this.

"The courses they have! I've never seen anything like it: three or four forms of acting work, dancing, acrobatics, plastique, gymnastics, and in the Meyerhold technicum, biomechanics. Their voice work is marvelous, really related to the theatre. I've never seen it done before. In the Meyerhold classes I saw feats of diction performed by boys and girls eighteen and twenty, such as *no* actor I've heard could do. They actually stylize the voice production. They juggle with sounds. It is theatrically efficient speech. There are classes in the history of the theatre, of music, of the other arts; in the Left theatres they also study Marxism, dialectic materialism, social problems, all those things.

"All the time they're in the technicum they're paid. They do the technical work in the theatre's productions. They're the stage managers and stage hands, and build the sets, especially those who are training to direct —but the directors act, too. In their last year they prepare productions of their own, and under the direction of the theatre's regisseurs they take out plays into the provinces, to accustom them to playing before audiences in bigger parts. They're used in the theatre's productions in mobs and small parts. Their teachers are the older actors and the directors."

Does Meyerhold, for instance, teach?

"No. His other directors do."

What happens when they graduate?

"They go into the company of the theatre, or if there's no room for them, they go into the provinces and start to work in other theatres in the tradition of the one where they studied. There's practically no unemployment."

But an actor doesn't wander into a town and decide to start a theatre there?

"No, no, no. They're sent out in units, by the Department of Education or Art or whatever it is. It's all planned. But they have a chance to show what they can do. For instance, there are two theatrical clubs in Moscow where the actors go after performances or on their free nights—they work in repertory and there are sometimes several actors trained for one part so they have nights off—and the student actors and directors show their productions there. Goldblatt, when he was a student director, won some sort of competition for the best propaganda play there, and as a result of that production he was given a theatre of his own. It's now the Gypsy Theatre, one of the most exciting in the city. Their costumes...!"

What about the costume bills?

"They get what they want. The theatres are self-supporting. They're always full. And if they need a particular thing for a production, they get it. When they need fine costumes—they're finer than anything I've seen by the Paris couturiers. At the Moscow Art Theatre for instance. Because the best artists work on them. But their equipment! In almost every theatre, two revolving stages or three, and elevator stages. Lee Strasberg and I nearly died."

Spain Says "Salud!"

BY ANGNA ENTERS

IF YOU are a Spanish village fisherman (who backbreakingly works night and day to earn about forty cents a day—maybe) and you and your fellows self-protectingly break into your village church and find fascist machine guns and ammunition, you are a Red terrorist seeking to destroy "Civilization." If, however, you are a Moor (Mohammedan) or Spanish Legionnaire (hired thugs of the hated *Tercio*) fighting for fascist money to maintain the most criminal peonage in Western Europe, you are defending "Civilization."

This irony—not the facts, as I saw the guns brought out, and it wasn't pleasant for an "Aryan" to witness Christ's church used as an arsenal for Mohammedan mercenaries against Christians—is perhaps too broad; but it is born of the shock when, reaching Gibraltar in a British destroyer from Málaga, I realized the "decent" outside world was "misunderstanding" a tragic struggle against the meanest economic servitude as a stock civil war between "law-and-order" and "Red terrorists"—i.e., the Spanish people, an inadequately (pathetically, in fact) armed mass of gallant men and women who, for the first time in a thousand years, have a chance—unless destroyed by the Nazi-Fascist itch to intervene— to overthrow feudalism. Hitherto my activities centered in theatre and graphic arts, and I sought to communicate my sentiments in those forms —but this "misunderstanding" is so remote from truth that verbal testimony in press and radio became obligatory. Interest, however, seemed to be concerned primarily with my personal adventures; hence I gladly avail myself of NEW THEATRE's apparently intuitive invitation for "impressions"—with the defensive warning that deadline haste makes them scattered.

I cannot report that one side is all Pure and the other wholly Evil— only theologians can do that. Nor am I condoning violence because it is People's Front violence. Yet to say that, in this instance, it is kill or be killed—unavoidable answer to ruthless provocative violence by fascists (always remember that the present bloodshed was begun by them) feverish with terror that the Spanish people will eradicate peonage— you do not have to be a Liberal, Republican, Socialist, Communist, Syndicalist, or Anarchist—merely a human being. Spain today says "Salud!"—literally translated "health" and "general welfare" and means it.

Arriving in Spain in late May one sensed immediately a spirit of dramatic tension. Spanish life always seems somehow theatrical, and the impression was as if one had come during the interval following a first-act curtain. The atmosphere was vibrant with ominous calm, the lull-before-the-storm kind, as if all Spain suspensefully awaited the second act. (The first act having been the People's Front election of February 1936, and the subsequent strike repercussions.) On the surface Spanish life pulsated with familiar intoxicating vivacity. In hard bright sunlight the *plazas de toros* (bullrings) celebrated the (sometimes) magnificent dance of death. Under velvety sapphire skies southern Spain, sitting in the same bullrings at *operas flamenca*, heard the exalting *cante jondo* songs quavering and soaring ecstatically. Sincerely pious religious processions gorgeously reverenced saints and sacred images.

But there were significant signs of change!

Sunday mornings the walls of the bullring echoed to the voices of the Social Revolution. The workers were using the bullrings as meeting places.

A Workers' Theatre had rented a Málaga theatre for a week—an equally extraordinary innovation in pleasure-loving southern Spain. In this Workers' Theatre one saw little scenes dramatizing the strikes and labor union activities interspersed with Spanish dance and music. (No social change will affect Spanish dance or music. In that sense, the

Spanish people are as inflexibly traditional-classic as the Chinese. And why not? It is *their* dance and music.) The audience, so lean and poorly clad, was touching to watch. The theatre, the spoken word, is the only way most of them could be reached—for, as to reading and writing (they rarely have to add their wages), the majority are illiterate. The "civilizers" who have hired the mercenaries have seen to that.

In the villages one saw (and heard not far from my own house) *centros* or meeting places where the workers, each evening at eight, and they came right from their work, sometimes walking distances of two and three miles, were lectured as to the advantages of solidarity. Sometimes, especially on Saturday evenings, the voices exhorted the fishermen and men from the *campos* (fields) could be heard into early hours—so much so that, being ill and kept awake, my sentiments, unsoftened by the garden's fragrance and its white walls which seemed to float in the glistening Mediterranean, were fascist.

These Workers' Theatres and *centros* were symptomatic of the change since I had left Spain the preceding September. These were little things —seen with the eyes of industrialized Europe and America with their trade union history—but startingly symbolical in the Spain I had known for five years each spring or summer since the 1931 political revolution. I had seen the joy attendant upon that revolution deflated as the people slowly realized they were merely rid of a political king. The real kings, the fascists in the army, industry, and agriculture, still ruled—and how! They ruled so that Spanish workers would remain serfs who worked, dressed, and lived like coolies. Extremes of poverty and plenty are laceratingly ghastly in Spain. The smug meanness of Spain's *ricos* has to be seen to be believed. Through the stone walls of dogmatically nourished ignorance light began to seep. That is why you read of unrest, pillage, and church wrecking.

The struggle which followed the 1931 republican revolution culminated inevitably in the People's Front of February 1936—a defense against fascism. A tide of victorious strikes began to buffet Spain's economic structure with Dempseylike blows. Late in June I wrote to my concert managers that over my garden's walls near Málaga I could see and hear the revolution brewing.

These were some of the signs during June:

In my village I had seen almost all the men march past the church in a massed demonstration of silent anger.

I had been through a grim general strike, lasting a week, when nothing—nothing—moved, because the *Jefe* (chief) of the Málaga Fishermen's Union had been shot down in an encounter with the Guardia Civil—who are always loyal to the winning side.

I had seen his funeral cortege up the Calle Larios, while almost half of Málaga nervously watched while men with faces which were masks of terrifying vengeance followed their leader borne in a coffin draped in red. No priests were permitted to participate in this cortege.

Strike after strike—like a relay race.

The rich, one knew, were frenetic and panicky.

The people were calm and extraordinarily confident.

These signs pointed to "Something"—an upheaval, volcanic in intensity—but I expected no explosion until October, a personal guess, as in July tension seemed to ease.

On Saturday morning, July 18, Málaga was almost its old gay self. Even the trams (after two weeks of strike silence) ground out their screeching iron music in the sunshine's glare. The cafés of the Calle Larios—Málaga's opulent commercial avenue—were crowded with their usual male habitués. You heard the typical strident appeals to buy lottery tickets, latest Madrid papers, *canarias* (bananas) and shine your shoes. In the luxe *ultramarinos* (glorified grocery shops) baskets were being filled for the first time in a week. True, the steel shutters on the store windows were down, and police guarded their doors—but all were agreed the strike of the *dependientes* (clerks) soon would be over. It was as if all in Málaga simultaneously were breathing one gargantuan sigh of relief. Málaga now could settle down to the proper celebration of the *verano* (summer). Málaga now could look forward to a real *corrida de toros*, the annual August fiesta. Málaga was at peace.

Yet late that afternoon, a third of Málaga, including the whole of Calle Larios, was in flames; dead and wounded strewn in the streets; bullets crackled and shells burst, as civilians, armed by the government, wearing red arm bands, swept through the blazing town in confiscated motors, carrying vengeance and death to the *ricos* and fascists, who sniped at them from rooftops and high windows.

Who or what could have caused this frightful bloodshed within the space of a few hours?

There is only one answer—the *ricos* and their monumental stupidity, plus the additional blunder of using Moors. Spanish hatred of the Moors is traditional, and the fascists in using the Moors united liberals and Communists alike in a common cause, irrespective of political-economic beliefs.

I was not present during the initial outbreak. Early that afternoon I had returned to my house in the outskirts of Málaga—about half an hour by motor. The countryside was positively bucolic. The first sign of trouble in our village was a little after eight o'clock that night. There was a sudden rush of men, with old-fashioned guns and short meaningless daggers, down the village's steep hill yelling "La luz"—"La luz"—"Put out the lights." Suddenly the village was plunged in medieval blackness. Then there was some shooting. I didn't know what had happened, but when I went to the window facing Málaga I could see it was in flames. All night the rushing up and down the hill went on—but now only whispering could be heard. I sat all through the night, not knowing exactly what was going on.

The next and following days were revelatory. On reaching Málaga, solicitously escorted to the American Consul's house by four armed guards generously provided by the local Popular Front committee in control of the village, I learned that about four o'clock Saturday afternoon (July 18), at the Calle Larios, a group of military officers and a few soldiers (who didn't know what they were to be used for) read, or tried to read, a proclamation declaring martial law. One of the *Gardes d'Asaltes*—who correspond to New York policemen as to uniform but not as to political sympathies—objected, and a Captain Julin (the name may be spelled incorrectly) of the military group shot him down. Shooting between these military and the police then followed instantaneously. Though the fascist "revolt" was planned to begin simultaneously in North and South that July 18 day—the flare-up in Málaga was an accidental anticipation. The People's Front groups did not know of this "revolt" plan. When news reached Málaga several hours later that the *Tercio* (Foreign Legion) had crossed the Straits from Spanish Morocco and had landed in Algeciras, hoping to march up the road—about five hours by motor—to Málaga, bridges were bombed and defense precautions were taken, such as putting out the lights of my village, which was in the line of march.

Málaga itself was an amazing spectacle. It was as though June's threatening atmosphere had cleared. The faces of the people somehow were different—fresh, with an "up" expression. Here were the same poorly clad men of the Workers' Theatre with guns slung over their shoulders patrolling the streets. Houses all were decked with protecting red flags. This did not mean that all in the houses were "red"—on the contrary, it indicated only that they were for the republic. All motors on the streets were in the hands of People's Front committees or the police. They too had red gauze covering one of the headlights. After the first three days of fighting, the trams began to run, crowded with citizens, armed and unarmed, some taking the ride to see a destroyed Málaga, others going to work. On the trams, groups of young men and women joyously sang the "Marseillaise" (taught in Spain's republican schools since 1931) and the "Internationale." Everyone was feeling good! The attitude toward foreigners—like myself—was friendly. While I was in

Málaga I did not hear of one act of violence against a foreigner or his property. There was destruction, confiscations—as of food for the poor, or motors, in many instances returned each evening—but no looting. When I told the Málaga Committee my work for the theatre and in painting was in my villa half an hour from the town, I was escorted personally by the president of Málaga's Socialist Party with four armed guards, one being the president of the *Bomberos*—no—no, it's just Spanish for plumbers—along a road still unclear of fascist snipers. I made the mistake of trying to pay them—and they needed all the money they could get for the defense of Málaga—yet they would take nothing. And they had more important things to do!

This is a last-ditch war to the death—for life—by the Spanish people. They will win.

DANCE

NEW THEATRE
AND THE MODERN DANCE WORLD

EDNA OCKO, our highly articulate and dedicated dance editor and critic, was the principal figure in *New Theatre*'s involvement with modern dance. Unlike John Gassner and Robert Stebbins, who were brought in after I became editor, Edna had begun writing for the magazine before I arrived, after giving up her career as a dancer in a New Dance League group. Edna had felt, and quite rightly, that her work at *New Theatre* would prove an important contribution to the revolutionary dance movement.

As I remember, Edna at first looked askance at having to deal with me, a newcomer to the city, who had grown up in Iowa, so far from America's dance culture centered in New York City. And, I confess, I felt somewhat intimidated at that time by Edna's encyclopedic knowledge of the art of dance, past and present. I was also a bit apprehensive about "acting like an editor" in a field so foreign to my experience.

NEW DANCE GROUP IN NEW THEATRE SKIT
Norris

However, Edna soon proved quite tolerant of my naïveté and helped me understand her special field. I also had help and encouragement from Leo Hurwitz, who was well informed about the dance world and involved in it through his wife, dancer Jane Dudley, and his sister, who danced and wrote under the stage name Sophia Delza. Both Jane and Sophia were associated with other talented young dancers whom I knew and admired: Anna Sokolow, Miriam Blecher, Lily Mehlman, Sophie Maslow, Nadia Chinowsky, Edith Segal, Lillian Tarnower (a shy girl who later became famous as editor of *Dance Magazine*); and Bill Matons and José Limón, two of the relatively few male dancers at that time. The performances of these young dancers and their company gave me attractive reasons to become intrigued by this exciting art form. I was also determined to acquire enough knowledge about dance to do my job as editor in chief, and for that Edna's help was invaluable.

Edna commented with insight and perception about the major figures of modern dance, especially Martha Graham, Charles Weidman, and Doris Humphrey, and the rising younger star, Helen Tamiris. As a result of Edna's tutelage, I acquired enough understanding to help her raise the *New Theatre* dance section to become as prominent in the dance world as our theatre section was in drama.

The main problem for us in writing about dance was having to depict in words what the majority of our readers had not seen—and what might not be repeated again. Additionally, dance criticism is difficult to do well, since unlike theatre or film, there is no dialogue to talk about, usually there is no real plot or story, and rarely are there repeat performances or showings for readers of the reviews to see and evaluate for themselves. Edna, however, managed, in her own reviews and in those she edited, to communicate clearly and coherently the artistic spirit, purpose, and meaning of modern dance and the dance performances reviewed in *New Theatre*.

Edna also promoted and guided *New Theatre*'s support for dance groups and its sponsorship of benefit performances, where the energetic young dancers, with revolutionary fervor, were not above handing out *New Theatre* subscription leaflets to the audience or selling the magazine in the lobby or outside on a street corner. Benefit dance recitals that had at first been performed before small audiences in dimly lit Greenwich Village halls and small, decrepit theatres moved uptown into larger quarters. They became so important and well attended that one major benefit recital drew over five thousand people and helped establish *New Theatre* as a major voice in dance, which reached beyond the limited circle of the budding revolutionary dance movement.

Often recitals were preceded by benefit dinners. I recall one such dinner when Martha Graham was our guest of honor. I was seated next to her at the head table, with Edna Ocko and Edna's husband, Sidney Meyers (who wrote under the name of Robert Stebbins), sitting nearby. Miss Graham praised our magazine and spoke with appreciation of the dance reviews, which had expressed the highest admiration for her performances but had also urged her to take a political stance comparable to the stance Clifford Odets and Irwin Shaw were taking in their theatre of social protest. Very graciously, Miss Graham said we should understand that her aim was not to present overtly revolutionary dance. She explained that her work did try to express growing social significance, but the growth was expressed gradually, without direct, political commentary. I didn't press the point. I changed the subject to two mutual friends she had worked with, the sculptor Isamu Noguchi, who had so brilliantly designed the sets for her performances, and Archibald MacLeish, for whom she had choreographed the dance sequences of *Panic*.

Throughout the subsequent decades, whenever I had the opportunity, I went to see Graham's work, and I am glad our *New Theatre* reviews added to the public's awareness of her greatness. Martha Graham's contributions to dance have continued into the present decade. On May 11, 1984, Martha Graham turned ninety, and a year-long celebration of her birthday was inaugurated in January at a gala performance of the Paris Opera Ballet. For the first time, the Martha Graham Dancers appeared on that historic stage, and Rudolph Nureyev appeared as guest artist in Miss Graham's *Phaedra's Dream* prior to its New York premiere. It seems fitting that the selections from *New Theatre*'s dance sections begin with Edna Ocko's appreciative commentary on Martha Graham's pioneering achievements for the modern dance during the mid-1930s.

Whither Martha Graham

BY EDNA OCKO

MARTHA GRAHAM is an artist who consistently turns away from the depiction of the life around her. One does not doubt that a person of her sensitivity and perception can be moved by the exciting and profound implications, artistic and social, of the world in which she lives. Yet, perhaps out of sheer terror for the contemporary scene, perhaps out of an artistic inability to cope with so turbulent and brutal a present-day existence, her research and her endeavors, her movement and her thinking, fly from this palpable, the real, aching-to-be-interpreted world to past periods, lost civilizations, and ancient or medieval art forms. Her interests zigzag unpredictably across the centuries with a virtuosity and a brilliance that leave her audience gasping in an attempt to keep up with her, or even go back with her. She will be, on one night, medieval, pre-Aeschylean, pre-white man Indian, and more recently, preclassic.

A review of her recent solo recital not only presents her in this panoramic light but suggests, to my mind, a searching for *psychic integration* (apart from the technical integration of her movement) that becomes almost tragic in its frustration. Her path is a passionate pilgrimage to find substance on which to build. So we see her, in her eagerness to take root, and in her fear lest she choose too hastily, "painting a large and suggestive social canvas," performing historic cycles, and seeking, paradoxically, to find herself by losing herself in the ages.

Her single dances in this recital, while complete units, serve as prelude and interlude for these more expansive creations. *Prelude*, with which she opens her program, is that—no more, no less; *Lamentation*, a revival by popular request, and *Satiric Festival Song*, a scintillating and witty parody, I suspect, of herself. All the other numbers are part of these cycles, and we shall deal with them chronologically.

Ekstasis was created at a time when she sought severe simplicity and purity of line. These "lyric fragments" are Greek; recreations in the pure simplified style of this early period; it draws us from this world into the land of nectar and ambrosia and high Olympus. The dance fragments are lyric, lovely, pure—and of another day.

Frenetic Rhythms is a cycle of three dances called "dances of possession." Despite Miss Graham's disavowal of literal content in her dances, her naming of them demands of the audience a consideration of each title in relation to the dance. Not being of the inner circle who confer with Miss Graham on the "meaning" of her dances, I feel my interpretation as good as any. It seems to me, then, that she goes through the ages, depicting the current obsession of that time; the first—primitive, the possession of the body through rhythms of terror at the unexplained and unanticipated; the second—medieval, the possession of the spirit and flesh by the rhythms set up through religion and mysticism; the third—modern (a distinct achievement for Miss Graham), possession of the mind and soul by the rhythms of contemporary decadent living with its vice, its abandon, its gripping and sinister cruelty, its jazz and mechanical intimations.

When this third dance was first performed, one had hopes that Miss Graham had at last remarked the stirring qualities extant in the rhythms of contemporary activity. Surely, the enthusiasm this dance evoked in her audience was not altogether due to the emotional excitement her sheer virtuosity always exacts from these onlookers. Here the applause was more lusty, more sympathetic; she struck responsive chords in the hearts and understanding of her followers because this dance expressed *them* and their lives, expressed the milieu in which they lived and in which they moved, the rhythm and the madness were their own.

But Miss Graham withdrew from this field hurriedly. Her two new cycles seek to recreate another time, another place, and still not in complete identification with that time and place. Although these cycles are sincere as creations, they show a peculiar lack of faith, in that they both contain elements of satire and parody for the subject matter she chooses to deal with. They sketch the dance expression of another century, that century of court dance, of dance in the reign of the royal aristocrat, with its superb and unperturbed hypocrisy. *Phantasy*, three short dances, choose titles from this early classic period: Prelude, Musette, Gavotte. Though they move as dances on the stage, they fail to contain the strength and power usually found in the work of Miss Graham.

Transitions as a new direction of Martha Graham was the *pièce de résistance* of the evening. The four dances are called: "Prologue," "Theatre Piece No. 1–Sarabande," "Theatre Piece No. 2–Pantomime," and "Epilogue."

These dances (again I hasten to add, I imagine) outline the majestic, hollow grandeur of that period of the court. "Prologue," preceding the court dances proper, opens with tambour and flute sounding attention to what follows—as if a page were to announce the beginnings of the entertainment. Then comes "Sarabande," classic and horrible, with the exaggeration reminiscent of "Pavane" by Angna Enters in which she recreates the murderous Medici court. The third dance is "Pantomime," with, I quote John Martin, "the impersonal voice of the child furnishing the main part of the accompaniment. Now he is spelling out words W-a-r, M-a-r-c-h, D-e-a-t-h, B-r-e-a-d." Finally, the epilogue, a dance that, in its shifting and wavering design, seems to pose the question, "Whither?"

Why all this fervor and passion for the seventeenth century? Is it that Miss Graham, by presenting that period in history, really means us to make a transition to this one? Then why not dance this period? Why masquerade the intention of the work in the trappings of another age? Two answers suggest themselves. Either the creator finds herself artistically unable to detach herself from the world in which she functions, view it with impersonal, farseeing, prophetic eyes, and rebuild it into an artistic crystallization for the audience to view in all its vice and virtue and prophecy of change. Or else the creator misguidedly believes that by combining a criticism of present society with a re-creation of the past, she plans a more important artistic unity, a sort of portmanteau masterpiece, a killing of two birds with one stone. Or perhaps we attribute too much to the artist's intention. Perhaps Miss Graham merely wants, at this time, to do "Sarabandes" and "Gavottes" and "Musettes"? Perhaps in her next recital, or in the one following, having peregrinated through the ages, she will come to the present by a process of elimination.

But that is not sufficient. If she is artist enough to mold exciting choreographic dances from subject matter that needs this kind of historical documentation, why not let the world of today be the document from which to be inspired? Can she not see its tumultuousness, its terrific, directed activity, its portents of revolution and change, its prophecy of a new and brighter society, its vast masses of people, of workers, whose struggles, heroisms, joys, aspirations, and very movement form the lifeblood of inspiration? The audience of Miss Graham is rapt and admiring, her leadership in the field of American dance as yet unchallenged. Yet if she must always turn away from the quick and the living, if the world of today is too much with her, how then can the temporal onlooker really be one with the artist and grow through her growth? Let her explore the social canvas of today. We want *our* world to be presented to us. And a dancer like Martha Graham could do it well—if she wished.

Texts for Dancers

BY EDNA OCKO

THE BENNINGTON SCHOOL of the Dance, a branch of the college of the same name in Vermont, concluded its sessions with the presentation of two new works by Doris Humphrey and Charles Weidman. Appearing under their direction were members of their New York concert groups and approximately forty dancers from the Bennington Workshop. *With My Red Fires*, music by Wallingford Riegger, is the third section of the trilogy by Miss Humphrey, of which *Theatre Piece* and *New Dance*, presented this past season, are parts. Mr. Weidman's new work, *Quest*, is a "choreographic pantomime" with music by Norman Lloyd.

With My Red Fires is a narrowing rather than an extension of its predecessors. Because of the peculiar limitations of its theme, it has sacrificed all of the brilliant contemporaneity of *Theatre Piece* and most of the thrilling symphonic structure of *New Dance*. The Young Man and Young Woman, sentitively portrayed by Charles Weidman and Katherine Litz, are threatened by the malevolent influence of the Matriarch (Doris Humphrey), who seeks, through her influence on the girl, and failing there, through the incited fury of the group, to shatter the romance of the young lovers. In the course of this theme's development, two group dances stand out: the betrothal of the couple in the first section of the work and the pursuit of these same two in the finale. The former is vaguely reminiscent of the primitive *Glorification of the Chosen One* in *Le Sacre du Printemps* and the latter of an animated fragment of a Greek frieze. Miss Humphrey's dramatic portrait of the Evil One carries emotional conviction but, at the same time, a certain amount of ambiguity. She is summoned to her disruptive duties by the Choric Figures, two imperturbable characters in red, whose relationship either to the lovers or the Matriarch is never satisfactorily defined.

While we make no urgent plea for literalness in a dance, we do expect a minimum of consistency and clarity in a portrait once the director has taken the initial step of establishing a specific characterization. This clarity is lacking in the conception as presented at Bennington, and it contributes to a general feeling of puzzlement as to why and wherefore on the part of the onlooker.

There is no doubt that poignant and gentle understanding went into the creation of this opus, but it is a moot question whether the theme of frustrated romantic love was worth the superior talents of the artist. Miss Humphrey has amazing choreographic skill, amounting almost to genius; she has a keen and vital understanding of the artist's problems today; she has at her disposal, finally, an excellent group of dancers, men and women. As a mixed company, it is all the more capable of realizing any material conceived by the directors. Bearing in mind the exceptional talents of Miss Humphrey and Mr. Weidman, therefore, the potentialities of such a combination are limitless—given, of course, the intelligent selection of subject matter. Perhaps, in this instance, the reason for *With My Red Fires* being a minor work must be frankly attributed to the text. William Blake, whose obscure mystical poem, "Jerusalem II," supplied the program notes, is scarcely the poet-prophet of the twentieth century. His hierarchical cosmology is as defiant of modern interpretation as Swedenborg's, and as tangential.

Miss Humphrey is too fine and too modern a talent to dissipate her important energies among mystics and cultists. She must continue along new paths in the modern dance, paths which she herself has blazed in *Theatre Piece* and *New Dance*. There may be temporary setbacks and hesitations, but there cannot be any retracing of steps.

It is to Mr. Weidman's credit that he presented *Quest* to the select audience of Bennington as well as the student dancers from all over the country. In this work, they were brought face to face with a courageously conceived survey of the artist's dilemma in society today. Here was a fine example of an artist whose social convictions permeated his creations as well as his conversations, and did honor to the rapidly growing stature of his choreographic works.

In *Quest*, the Artist (Charles Weidman), guided by an inner strength to which he sometimes pays little heed, encounters the bludgeon of stupid criticism and the false front of patronage characteristic of any country. He next endures the *Kulturreinigung* of one nation (to remain unnamed), where first he is beguiled, by promises of fame and fortune, to create there, and then minutely measured and practically quartered when he is found "impure." Next he escapes desperately from participation in war, but his inner vision (personalized by Doris Humphrey) compels him to recognize the futile destruction and betrayal of his fellowmen. He finally leaps into contact with the world, and grasps hands with the weak, who, in an exciting conclusion, support and strengthen not only each other but their fellows.

The dance is a series of episodes: *Anthropometry* and *Patronage* are amusing skits; *Kulturreinigung*, *Pro Patria*, and *Affirmation* stirring and serious group compositions, and the *Allegories*, between Miss Humphrey and Mr. Weidman, delicate lyrical passages. It is in this abundance of varying material, although excellent in its own right, that we find our only objection. The transition from whimsy to social indignation is not an easy one and cannot, we feel, be successfully compassed in one continuous dance. While we know we should laugh at the spectacle of the artist quaking before patronizing females, we are not so certain how to react to the disillusionment of the artist under fascism; and because our picture of the artist is of a half-comic, easily tempted creature, we find ourselves fearful to chuckle at his vagaries because in that way we might be inadvertently led into like amusement at the unfunny spectacle of fascism and war which confronts him.

The root of the trouble lies in the difficulty of procuring an organized dance libretto or script containing a consistent and logical argument.

The modern dance is rapidly approaching a stage when dramatic continuity and climax will be necessary requisites for the complete unfolding of the theme. Miss Humphrey and Mr. Weidman are seemingly pioneering in this field, and it is inevitable that there be trial and error. Mr. Weidman's intention was a good and commendable one. Happily, in this case, most of his conception was transferred to the audience without confusion and misunderstanding. He runs a great risk, however, without a well-thought-out libretto, of lessening the genuine effectiveness of his serious projections, by juxtaposing them with his airily witty pieces. But that as it may, *Quest* is a retainable contribution to Mr. Weidman's repertoire, and it is hoped that many more people will be given occasion to see this work.

In praising the entire ensemble for its excellent cooperation and presentation, special mention must go to José Limón and William Matons, who not only contributed creative support to their director but also emerged as superb dancers in their own right.

The Fokine Ballets

BY BLANCHE EVAN

I WENT eagerly to the Stadium this summer in search of the "miracle" of choreography of which John Martin spoke in his review of *Scheherazade*. During the progress of the performance my eagerness was very quickly transformed into disappointment. The "tired businessman" has as his weekly fare, in almost any movie house presentation, this kind of pseudochoreographic miracle. The handling of ensemble was weak in comparison with any one of the Jooss ballets, and painfully weak in comparison with the least interesting of Humphrey's or Graham's group compositions. How monotonous the repeated use of cliché poses—Maxfield Parrish equally in evidence in the Oriental setting of *Scheherazade* and in what the program notes termed "pure dancing," the presentation *Elves*.

It is true that ballets like *Scheherazade*, created in 1910, were considered extremely radical from the point of view of dance form. It is true they were of immense importance in the development of the art of the dance and as a vehicle for the best musicians and stage designers of the time. But that is no reason why they in themselves could not have been integral pieces of choreographic form able to stand the test of revival. By analogy, the paintings of Picasso and Braque, who also were the insurgents of their time, have already become classic. Again one must disagree with John Martin when he says that only the passage of time will give these ballets "sufficient mellowness of perspective to assume a place in any permanent repertoire." Ballets like *Scheherazade* do not hold within them a single germ to make them worthy of resurrection as great works of choreographic art in the present or in the future.

The reason for this consummate failure of so widely heralded a ballet as *Scheherazade* embraces the historical, technical, and social phases of ballet in general.

The Degeneracy of Ballet—The Perugini definition of the art of ballet is "a series of solo and concerted dances with mimetic actions, accompanied by music and scenic accessories telling a story." Any balletomane in the world will tell you that without the complete harmony of all these elements, a ballet performance must be a failure. The ballet school which is the nucleus of ballet theatre production has followed in America a direct line of degeneracy. The Russian ballet masters who emigrated to America forced ballet into this degeneracy by commercializing their schools, by eliminating all study of the expressive medium of ballet, which is pantomime, by allowing mere children to work in toe slippers before any muscular development had taken place, and finally by emasculating the artistic forces of ballet until only the skeleton of technique was left. Without the combination of great pantomime artistry with technical skill, the art of ballet cannot exist. The performance of Fokine's pupils at the Stadium proved this. Even if Fokine's choreography for *Scheherazade* were great, his dancers who today are prepared to execute only the correct *number* of "steps" (and this is being generous to the cast) cheapen and vulgarize the work by their utter ignorance of mime and by their complete lack of sensitive interpretation. The love scenes of Zobeide, the heroine of *Scheherazade*, executed in the manner of the Folies Bergère, are a good example. The same choreography handled by Karsavina and Nijinsky must certainly have shone to better advantage. Stripped of the assistance of great expressive artists, the Fokine choreography does not stand as exciting, pure formal design. It becomes in this case decidedly barren and banal.

Motivation in Creation—It is not *chiefly* that there is "unemployment and social upheaval" today, as John Martin says, that we cannot be "seriously carried away" by the revival of *Scheherazade*. It is rather that at the time of its creation, in 1910, the motivation for creation had no attachment to reality. Not only was it detached from the contemporary scene. Fokine did not even *interpret* the atmosphere in which it was placed, but merely presented a conventional viewpoint in a stereotyped setting. Isadora Duncan also went to a foreign source for her material. But in her case, she strove to capture the spirit of the Greeks rather than merely to reproduce a Greek scene.

Sunk in the subsidies of the Imperial Court of Russia and in the capitalists' court that followed Diaghilev, Fokine believed he could shut his eyes to the burning realities of the world in which he lived. In 1910, there were the same preparations for war as there are today; the same savage persecution of racial and religious minorities as occur in Hitler Germany. Five years before, the Russian masses returning from the Russo-Japanese War had fought a bloody civil war. Such was not the material that the Russian choreographers chose. Unlike the great Russian writers of the same period, such as Gorky, Fokine worked with themes arbitrarily and depended for their vitality on the gorgeous decor of Bakst in which they were dressed.

There was nothing real in the motivation and nothing enduring in the results.

Ballet *can* have a wide appeal because it is the most inclusive of the theatre arts, embracing as it does dancing, mime, music, scenic accessories. But it will never achieve a mass audience, it will never be great, until it finds its themes in reality, either in the present world of events, or, if it chooses to work with historical material, in the field of keen interpretative history, or in the rich traditional folk material of the world. The reaction of the audience to the ballets presented at the Stadium is proof of this. The ballets were received very unenthusiastically. The general apathy was only slightly disturbed by weak applause for occasional technical feats. (It is a compliment to the modern dance that the sequence of a number is never broken by the intrusion of applause rendered for mere acrobatics.) The theatre may be the legitimate home of fantasy, but only that fantasy deeply rooted in the earth can make an audience part of it.

Despite the new activities of ballet, the Monte Carlo Ballet Russe, the Fokine Ballets, the American Ballet Company, despite the backing of wealthy patrons, ballet will not live unless its directors and its choreographers are willing to forgo their courtly dreams of the nineteenth century. The *Alma Mater* work presented by the American Ballet, a careful satire on college life, caught a vibrant reaction from the audience that none of the *Reminiscence* ballets were able to do. Both choreographed by Balanchine, the former spoke to the audience in contemporary terms, whereas the latter tried unavailingly to carry it back to an atmosphere of gilded halls and purple-clad page boys—an atmosphere with which it could feel no bond whatsoever.

Moreover, the ballet organizations will have to wake up intellectually before they can develop further. The following quotation from Molière actually appears in the American Ballet Program sold at the Stadium (25c and worth it for the laugh). It is inconceivable that Molière's satire should be cited as a serious credo in the year 1935:

> All the ills of mankind, all the tragic misfortunes that fill the history books, all political blunders, all the failures of great commanders, have arisen merely from lack of skill in *dancing*....
> When a man has been guilty of a mistake, either in ordering his own affairs, or in directing those of the State, or in commanding an army, do we not always say: So-and-so has made a false step in this affair?...
> And can making a false step derive from anything but lack of skill in *dancing?* (*Le Bourgeois Gentilhomme*)

Wouldn't it have been wonderful to have prevented the tragic misfortune of fascism by teaching Hitler to delicately point his toes, or Mussolini to change his military stride to the flowing walk of Duncan? Of course, we might try to teach them to leap backward from Ethiopia!

Fokine, Balanchine, Massine—you must forget the past that served its formal purpose. Give America new ballets of its time. Discard the loves of Zobeide and dance the love and desire and struggle for a new life and a better world in which to create and live.

LINCOLN KIRSTEIN: FIFTY YEARS AGO IN *NEW THEATRE*

IN 1984 American ballet celebrated fifty years of achievement thanks largely to the efforts in 1934 of two rich young intellectuals from Harvard, Edward Warburg and Lincoln Kirstein. Warburg did not remain active in the dance world, but Kirstein is as active today in ballet and theatre as he was then.

During 1933 and early 1934, the Ballet Russe de Monte Carlo toured the United States. For the first time, many Americans saw Russian-trained dancers perform in the works of the great Russian choreographers, including works by the young maestro, George Balanchine. The performances received great acclaim, and John Martin's enthusiastic reviews in the *New York Times* made the entertainment world aware that

America had no ballet company of any real importance. After the tour ended, Lincoln Kirstein, who had become obsessed by ballet, persuaded his classmate, Edward Warburg, to contribute from his family resources to bring Balanchine back, not just for a dance tour but to create a ballet company in America with potential for international distinction. Balanchine was responsive to the ballet aspirations of the two young Americans and returned to America with an associate, Vladimir Dimitriev. Both Russians were disciples of the legendary Diaghilev. Balanchine began planning ballet productions, and Kirstein and Warburg founded the School of American Ballet in January 1934 with Dimitriev as its first director—just about the time *New Theatre* began stimulating the revolutionary renaissance in the theatre.

I met Lincoln Kirstein shortly after I became editor of *New Theatre*, through mutual friends, who had suggested he write for the magazine. Lincoln was a very tall young man with a striking presence, about my own age, and we hit it off well from the start. I enjoyed Lincoln's flair for wit, satire, and sometimes ribald humor—although I should admit I showed some doubts, initially, about this scion of the enormously wealthy Filenes of Boston and the social circles he traveled in. Several of our staff wondered if Kirstein was slumming at our crummy (but clean) 14th Street office, using *New Theatre* to get left-of-center publicity for his ballet aims, in addition to promoting ballet on the right among the rich, those most likely to support it. However, Lincoln's charisma and friendly warmth soon put us at ease. He offered to write not only on dance but also on theatre and film, which resulted in his articles "Dance in Films" and "James Cagney."

I recall that after our first magazine meeting ended Lincoln invited me to dinner at a better restaurant than I was accustomed to. I found him an entertaining raconteur who told irreverent stories about the high and mighty of that other world he frequented, so far from *New Theatre*. One amusing anecdote concerned the Prince of Wales and how Lincoln had guided England's future king from the revelry of Greenwich Village to the gaiety of Harlem's night spots, with his royal companion gamely trying to prove he could mingle happily with the common people. But mostly in our conversation that night Lincoln spoke seriously and eloquently about his principal aim in life (one that has been realized)—the creation of an American ballet company equal to any in the world that could present ballets in the classical tradition as well as develop ballets on American themes and concepts.

Lincoln was so articulate describing what he intended to write that, when his articles came in, they seemed as if they had been recorded as he spoke. In all he did and said he had style, and I enjoyed his friendliness whenever we came into contact. I hope Lincoln will enjoy rereading what he wrote for us so long ago.

Revolutionary Ballet Forms

BY LINCOLN KIRSTEIN

USED in connection with a spectacle, "ballet" has hitherto meant a series of theatrical dances more or less closely connected by pantomime based upon a story slight enough to be a pretext for the presence of a troupe of dancers, but in no way to interfere with the technical display involved. There have been notable exceptions to this, but only as exceptions. Used in connection with the vocabulary of the dance, "ballet" means a grammar of gesture and movement based on five positions of hands and feet, originating in Italy, spreading to France, flowering in Russia. In the course of its four-hundred-year history it has absorbed from its successive homes local, national, and social dances, occupational gestures, and innovations from individuals all along the line. As differentiated from ritual, folk, or social dancing, it is preeminently theatrical. Its limits are imposed for the sake of greatest legibility to the greatest number of people seeing it.

The word "ballet" has enjoyed a wide unpopularity in America for the last ten years. Most of the work which could, with an indulgent stretch of the imagination, be called "ballet" here on view was a dilute or corrupted form of the thing. "Ballet" meant girls in white tarlatans derived from Degas or high-class movie prologues. Recently when a popular ballet company displayed itself in New York, it aroused considerable intellectual distrust by its financial success, its opposition to the (to us) familiar exhibitions of our own "group" or "modern" dancers, and because few of its productions had anything more than a fragmentary or accidental interest. In spite of this, the word "ballet" is a good one and can still be used for the purposes of discussion.

The ballet was preeminently a post-Renaissance product. It flowered in the baroque ornament of Versailles and not until the nineteenth century was it entirely divested of a verbal accompaniment, which final separation did much to accelerate its decline as a dramatic instrument. The grammar, the idiom of ballet developed independent of its uses. The forms and combinations of its steps in the ore, as it were, are one of the great contributions of Western culture, comparable to the use of polyphony in music or aerial perspective in painting. Unfortunately, the uses to which this language was put, to a far too large extent, were mainly rhetorical. Expressiveness was sacrificed to brilliance, and difficult execution well achieved was canonized for its acrobatics. Ballet awaits a *Don Giovanni* or a *Hamlet*. Its succession is so elusive, depending as it does on difficult systems of notation or human memory, that what seemed great tragedy to the balletomanes of 1850 seems preposterous to us, and we are perhaps inclined to underestimate the intensity of ballets like *Giselle* or *Sleeping Beauty*. Perhaps they provided a satisfaction equal to great tragedy. Gautier and Pushkin thought so. But they have not survived for us, whatever the reason, like Mozart or Shakespeare. We still can be moved by individual dancers performing the magnificent arias in movement, *The Blue Bird* variation, or the pas de quatre from *Swan Lake*; but these in fragments.

The best of ballet has come to us by way of Russia. Italy and France had their dominance, with the attendant glories of Sweden and Denmark. But Russia lavished her full attention and her imperial thoroughness on the Western form, combined Italian acrobatics with French grace, and added an immortality of Slav consciousness and abandon. The Russian schools, state endowed, commanded the pick of European masters. The Russian theatres gave a possibility of perfection in production unknown anywhere else in the world. Their sense of the dramatic, of the-word-made-gesture plus the bodies molded to elastic steel, make the names of Karsavina, Nijinsky, and Pavlova living standards.

Yet before the war the Russian ballet became international. After the Paris season of 1909, and the subsequent Diaghilev period, Russia was content merely to provide great dancers. The ideas, the direction, were still Russian, but the Russians of a cosmopolitan society, the Russian made a citizen of the world, or more accurately a Parisian. In Russia the ballet schools were protected by the Revolution. Lunacharsky saw to that. Except in the winter, due to the lack of food and heat, the schools and theatres were continuously open. The Russians of today are probably the greatest technicians in the world. But the ballet productions in no way compare to the vitality of their cinema or dramatic theatre. The state of choreography in Russia today is not prewar. It is late nineteenth century. The ballet is extremely popular in both the great State Theatres, but the popular successes are the same successes that delighted audiences of 1894, 1904, and 1914. This is no fault of the Revolution. The Diaghilev ballet, carrying with it the greatest creative talent, left Russia for good in 1911. What was left after the war, except for Gorski, who in Moscow was the great composer of ballets and already an old man, and

Golizovsky, a real revolutionary but a special case, were merely middle-aged memories of the stock repertory. Golizovsky is still in Moscow. But due to the extent of the general torpidity of choreography he seems an extremist. It is forgotten that already in 1910 he created innovations surpassing Wigman, and structurally far stronger than Duncan. Now he seems an eccentric. His *Football Player* was a notable success.

In spite of this, the tone of ballet in western Europe has been predominantly Russian. The five choreographers of the International Diaghilev troupe were all trained in the Imperial School at Petrograd, with the exception of the last, who graduated from the State School of Leningrad. When Diaghilev died, his remnants and various brilliant White Russian children in Paris were formed into the Monte Carlo Ballet, which scored such a signal success in New York last season and which now returns. The Monte Carlo Ballet, creatively speaking, has little to recommend it, although as irrelevant amusement and delight for the sake of unique performers, it can be superb. The ballet dances are, largely speaking, from the Diaghilev repertory (1909–29). The few new ballets are an offshoot of his school: the ultimate of the snob Parisian chic of 1930–33. Its future life is questionable. It has few lively sources from any field on which to draw. Its unscrupulous direction, its overworked dancers, its secondhand repertory and intense commercialism, and the lack of any youthful creative descent makes it an historic echo, but still an echo. It should be seen by all for reference and comparison.

It might be useful to review the great composers of theatrical dances during the last thirty years to determine the future direction of the medium. Michel Fokine as a young man literally revolutionized the principles of ballet when at the turn of the century, in a famous letter to the directors of the Imperial Theatres, he proposed reforms which have determined the whole direction of dancing and which we now accept as commonplaces. He precipitated a romantic revolution, drawing heavily on Oriental exoticism, on Hellenistic Greece, on the great decadent imperial periods for a decorative and violent subject matter. He also utilized a Francophile storybook version of Russia itself, and his immortal *Petrouchka* is still danced in the Soviet Union, where it can be explained that the Charlatan is the imperial bureaucracy, the Moor is the old aristocracy, and Petrouchka is the eternal, unconquerable soul of the common Russian man. And in every sense, *Petrouchka* is a masterpiece, a milestone in the development of dance drama. Since the war, Fokine has lived in suspension in New York City. It is hard to believe that the composer of *Fire Bird*, of *Daphnis*, or *Spectre*, *Igor*, and *Sylphides*, is extant at the start of Riverside Drive. This summer, almost as an ironic specter, his old successes triumphed again, at least from the point of view of big audiences. But there is little else left.

Nijinsky was the immediate and given cause of Fokine's resignation from the Russian ballet, and in spite of his tragic, unachieved career, it is difficult not to consider him as the single greatest genius of dancing in modern times. Superlative as a classic dancer, before he was twenty-five he reversed classic dancing and established a new species of synthesized movement which has been the virtual source of modernisms ever since. Nijinsky could not support dancing as mere divertissement or attractive amusement for its own sake. In *Faun*, he composed a complete lyric incident in fluid movement, at one blow destroying the atrophied idea of Greece as Phidian Greece, and, with the re-creation of the monumental archaic, suggested the creation of a simple, direct, and profoundly felt modernism which was articulated in greater elaboration in the nationalist, prearcheological *Rites of Spring* and realized, in small, in *Jeux*—never to be realized largely in the unproduced but magnificently indicated formal dances for the music of Bach's preludes and fugues. Nijinsky hoped for dancing as an expression of human action as intense and direct as possible, unhampered by precedent, the legible objectification in terms of kinetic essences of the whole nature of human activity. Toward ritual, he proposed a mass dance drama, more important in scope and intention than any spectacle since the Greek ritual tragedy of the Bacchae. Nijinsky's great contributions to dance composition have not yet been realized, in the excess of emphasis on his own hideous personal disaster. Some inkling of his ideas may be gained from his wife's biography, but only by inference.

Léonide Massine was destined by a not very selective destiny to fill Nijinsky's place as choreographer for the Russian ballet. The only one of its composers not to receive the benefit of the rigid discipline of the State School, his education was really based on the classic Spanish dance. The company found themselves in Spain for the duration of the war. Hence, one easily notices a preponderance of abrupt positions in his work, nervous and comic, stemming from the instruction of the great Felix, who grounded him in the initial *Three-Cornered Hat*. Massine is an intellectual rather than a spontaneous or musical composer. His *shazki* or Russian fairy stories are ingenious and charming, but the preponderance of his work has been a repetition of his early pantomimic dances or, lately, a visualization of the symphonies of Tchaikovsky or Brahms. This direction can hardly be considered fortunate. A competition is immediately set up with the music, which is preeminently unsuitable for dancing. The greatest success possible is almost a literary tour de force. Very conscious of what is good theatre, he often misses what is good dancing and is inclined to repeat a sure-fire hit until it misses. He has become the solitary composer of the Monte Carlo Company, and his creation is centrifugal. Fokine unkindly referred to his Brahms *Choreartium* as "Wigman sur les pointes."

Bronia Nijinska, Vaslav's sister, composed a few ballets for Diaghilev, notably the *Village Wedding* of Stravinsky and *The House Party*. Both stemmed strongly from Nijinsky. A fine dancer herself, she has an unfortunate masculinity which, since she is not a man, is often her undoing. Lately she has attempted a choreographic *Hamlet*.

George Balanchine was Diaghilev's last composer. He is the son of the first musician of the Georgian Republic, Milaton Balanchivadze, who was signally honored this spring by a jubilee voted to him by the Soviet Union. Balanchine graduated from the State School in 1922. Under the strong influence of Kasian Golizovsky, he risked expulsion from the Academic Theatre by founding his own Young Ballet, among whose number were Tamara Geva and Alexandra Danilova, both now well known to New York. He was dissatisfied with the atrophy of the leftovers of the Imperial Theatres. Practicing in a disused factory, he presented finally an evening of dancing, *From Fokine to Balanchivadze*: the history of contemporary dancing. He took a poem of Alexander Blok's and in the forum of the deserted Dveranskyi Sobrani, the old House of Peers, his schoolmates danced the Blok verses while others recited them. It was the first step in an attempt to integrate dancing with the old, invaluable elements of poetry and music, the human voice and the melodic, instrumental line.

Balanchine served Diaghilev from 1924 to his death in 1929. It was the period of the disintegration of the ballet. The painters of the School of Paris were considered more important than either dancers or musicians. Novelty was at a premium. Titillation of the supersophisticated worldly society of Paris and London was the single effect of these few years. Diaghilev himself seemed disinterested. Nevertheless, Balanchine produced ten ballets, two of unusual strength, Stravinsky's *Apollo*, and the *Prodigal Son*, a drama of some religious feeling, based on episodes from a poem by Pushkin, with remarkable scenery by Rouault. On the one side Balanchine revived the crystal classicism of the pre-Fokine era, which he also had endangered in the recent insistence on the unsuspected. In the other he hinted at a curious sincerity, a desire to realize the full possibilities of dance drama.

Since 1929 his history has been vivid, from London, to Copenhagen, to Paris, to New York. At the age of thirty he is the head of the School of American Ballet. Work done he finds is old as death. The direction of dancing is entirely ahead, and at a different angle from anything previously accomplished. Except—there was the Blok in 1922, and the *Seven Capital Sins* in 1933. Few people who saw it took the *Seven Capital Sins* at anything but its face value. Nevertheless this baffling work by two superb young German Communist artists, Bert Brecht, the poet, and Kurt Weill, the musician, was an important landmark in dancing history. On a bare stage, the classical ballet steps abandoned, under glaring lamps, with no scenic illusion, the chapters in the adventures of one girl in search of food for her family was intoned by her sister and double, Anna-Anna. As each sin was committed, another paper door was smashed. The music, acrid and tuneful, was the equivalent but never the description of the dancing. An atmosphere of homely tension, desperation, and personal anguish was invoked, in combination with the monotonous, aching familiarity of the melodies that was both uncomfortable and splendid. Balanchine left Europe, splitting with the Monte Carlo Company, of which he had been cofounder, because he considered their direction retrograde and retardative.

At present the School of the American Ballet is in a state of gestation. It is attempting on the basis of the Russian State Schools, adapted to American needs, to create an excellent troupe of dancers. This takes time and patience. Balanchine luckily has both. But in the meanwhile he has experimented. He knows ballet as "ballet" is dead. The very word seems mortified. He has found an old word which may have a revivified meaning. Vigano, the Italian innovator of a century ago, composed ballets which he called *Choreodrame*: literally danced dramas. The idea of three ballet-divertissements in an evening is through, however persistent. Ballet as innocent amusement is far too little to demand of it. Dancing can be the equivalent of any of the other lyric or dramatic forms. Words, spoken by dancers or by an independent choir in unison, without music or with it; the greater participation of the audience as a contributory factor in heightening the spectacular tension, the destruction of the proscenium arch as an obstructive fallacy, the use of Negroes in conjunction with white dancers, the replacement of an audience of snobs by a wide popular support are all part of Balanchine's articulate program. In the rehearsal classes at the School, these ideas are becoming crystallized and closer to production. In his first choreodrame, *Tom*, based on the Stowe novel of slavery in the South, E. E. Cummings has heroically theatricalized that serious historic situation. The spectacle as realized will be more pantomime than dancing, more speech than song, more myth than ritual—but on its way to a closer realization of an enlarged drama, popular in its deep sense.

To understand ballet enough to be able to dance it requires at least a similar attitude of patience and application on the part of a student as learning how to play the piano. It is a highly technical and specialized form. Its exercises provide equilibrium to the body under unusual circumstances, speed in transitions, a constant fluidity, a capacity for moving in and through the air. There are those who are more fitted to be dancers than others, and some people naturally have an instinctive talent for theatrical dancing. Due to the half-considered reforms by Isadora Duncan, where with her characteristic fine indignation she insisted that everyone could dance, and to the exceeding dilettantism fostered by the central European system, many young people feel that all they need is the will to do it. In one sense, everyone can dance. Over the next ten or fifteen years an excellent weapon for social solidarity would be the revival or creation of group dances practiced only for fun at occasions when people meet. But these dances, dependent for their effect on a spontaneous ease and simplicity in execution, have nothing to do with theatrical dancing. One reason that dancing has not been taken seriously by the majority of people interested in films and the theatre is that the performances of "groups" or "concert soloists," however intensely well-intentioned, seem thin and only in occasional spots impressive as display. The dance audience in New York and in America is potentially enormous. But they have learned over the last two years to demand a presupposed technique, as efficient as a good musician's or a good actor's.

Ballet is an amalgam. In its purity it is rigid, backbreaking, and ridiculous. Even the standard of purity for our century, Fokine's *Sylphides*, is a romantic pastiche, based on lithographs of the mid-nineteenth century, embroidered with all sorts of sudden invention. For every decade, ballet changes. Massine has taken much from Wigman's arsenal. Balanchine's plastic stems from Golizovsky. But the skeleton underneath is strong enough, flexible and resilient enough to support any addition. Naturally a school is as necessary for theatrical dancing in America as it is in Russia. More so, for hitherto we have had none. Just as there are civic symphony orchestras supported by subscription in many cities, with allied conservatories, so can we have ballet schools and companies. The racial amalgam of America provides wonderful material for dancers. Many unusual indigenous combinations can enrich the stream. As for subject matter—the woods are full of it.

The school founded last year in New York is naturally experimental and in a large sense transitional. It is supported by a few individuals until a large group can be interested. It would be at the present moment disastrous to ally such an undertaking to government funds, even if some appropriation were conceivably handy. The school is occupied in constructing a technical apparatus which will not be the property of any one choreographer. Any instructed or even any convinced person may have a hand at employing the troupe when it reaches a decent stage of perfection. Classes will be given in composition to encourage as many choreographers as can be developed. But ballet is primarily a form against self-expression. It is a controlled design by a designer who has immolated himself in the general pattern, thinking of himself only as each separate dancer in relation to every other dancer.

To consider ballet as necessarily always the toy of rich men or the private pleasure of czars is unwise. So, for some centuries, were orchestras and paintings. When a state is achieved that recognizes its obligation to its members as something more than a stopgap distraction, American dancers can afford to learn at state-endowed schools, but not till then.

The last paragraph of a suggestive article by Harry Elion in the September number of NEW THEATRE embodies a major fallacy:

> The workers' dance took over a great deal of the bourgeois technique. In fact most of the leaders in the dance were trained to be bourgeois performers. The workers' dance must free itself from this influence and create a dance form that is expressive of the workers' needs. This form will come as a result of the revolutionary content, providing the dancers free themselves from the idea that all that has to be done is to give the bourgeois dance working-class content.

Somewhere Marx has said that revolutions are caused by the profoundest conservatives, those people who wish to conserve the best of those human properties which they have gained and which they are in extreme peril of losing. The government established by these revolutionaries, as in the case of the Soviet Union, is the most conservative, in the best sense, that exists in the world. The form of theatrical dancing, hitherto aristocratic and bourgeois, will change less than it will be amplified. Its most important part, its base, will not be discarded any more than Shostakovich discarded the form of opera. The workers need a demonstrated subject matter, a dramatized, legible spectacle, far more than they need a new *form* for its expression. A form is only a frame and a medium, call it feudal, bourgeois, or proletarian. It will be a signal service to the revolution if choreographers can give working-class content to the preceding form. If that is done, it will no longer be bourgeois but revolutionary.

A NOTE IN REPLY
by Harry Elion

"A form," writes Lincoln Kirstein, "is only a frame and a medium, call it feudal, bourgeois, or proletarian." However, neither a frame nor a medium can be used indiscriminately. It is not sufficient to leave the question of form at this point. There are quite a variety of dance forms. These are used by dancers according to the particular school of dancing a group happens to adopt.

Revolutionary dance content implies the use of class-conflict themes. To express the full meaning of such themes and to allow for its full development as is implied in the presence of conflict presupposes a form that is *structurally* dramatic. I quite agree that the history of the dance furnishes sufficient examples of dramatic forms. But these must be selected and developed to a higher level while static forms must be discarded. The ballet in its early stages was highly dramatic. It later degenerated along with other forms, during the period of bourgeois decline, and salvaged its static features only. Revolutionary content can again revitalize its dramatic or dynamic features. This principle of selection must be applied to all dance forms.

Men Must Dance
by Gene Martel

MEN have danced since the beginning. We all know that primitive man used movement as a means of making himself understood and of establishing a close communication with his gods, the forces that controlled the life around him. Throughout early civilization, the dance was an integral part of existence and celebrated almost every action of life. There were dances at the birth of a child, dances of courtship, of marriage, funeral dances, dances before and after battles. In many cases we find that men performed the most solemn dances, and there were those which no women were allowed even to witness, such as the initiation of a young boy into manhood.

Dancing was not a feminine pastime. Dancing was a man's art—at least until the advent of the ballet. The ballet was born and flourished during the era of doublet and hose, lace cuffs, perukes, and snuff. These furnishings parallel its superficiality, its lack of wholesomeness and strength—a reflection of the court life of the period. Decidedly a feminine art, tending only toward prettiness, it robbed man of his essential quality of virile movement and expression.

After a long period of stagnation, a great force appeared in the person of Isadora Duncan. Her first appearance in St. Petersburg in 1905 was all that was necessary to set off the spark to the powder keg of the modern dance. Fokine, the great ballet master, believing thoroughly in her theories of freedom but deploring her lack of sound technique, proceeded to inject her ideas into the established technique of the ballet. He broke away from the old academic form, with its rigidity of movement, and freed the whole body: making use of the hands, arms, and the torso where before only legs had moved.

Nijinsky continued the work of revolutionizing the ballet. We find him enlarging upon the vocabulary of foot positions by adding movements in a straight line, composing even more exercises for parts of the body ignored by the traditional form, and advocating a point which is a stronghold of the modern dance—namely, that "any imaginable movement is good in dancing if it suits the idea which is its subject." In other words, a decided trend toward the masculine, since all qualities of movement became acceptable, and men could use movements which showed them off to better advantage. The emergence of this new force is not yet sufficiently recognized in relation to men.

The strangest and most amusing fact in connection with the modern dance is that, excluding Fokine and Nijinsky, women have been the leaders, with an art which is singularly masculine—infinitely more so than that of the majority of male dancers. We expect all our young female dancers to display great physical strength and we are likely to get it. Our men, however, fall short.

Ted Shawn is credited with pioneer work in the field of male dancing in this country. His contribution was truly great. In addition, he developed a form which directly preceded our modern understanding of significant movement. Using the ballet technique as a foundation, he added a new freedom resulting in the "barefoot ballet" of the Denishawn School.

If we examine Shawn's work today, we find that his Oriental characterizations served and still serve to introduce strong dramatic movement; but in those dances not in a foreign style, the movement is altogether decorative and personal in the sense of making the audience conscious of performer rather than composition. We see his movement in the extremities, but the torso remains dead. Being such a large portion of the body mass, the torso, if used fully, obviously creates a form of expression far superior to one in which only arms, legs, and head are employed.

The modern dance has as its male leader in this country Charles Weidman, who has done more for the use of masculine strength and dramatic movement in dancing than anyone heretofore. It is difficult for many people to get any kind of perspective on his contribution, inasmuch as he is still pioneering in the modern dance.

Man's interest in modern dancing comes as a result of many things. For one, he desires strength and flexibility, which the modern dance offers to a greater degree than a gymnasium and with less consciousness of military drill. Then, he feels the need of mental and bodily coordination and rhythm. And thirdly, there is an emotional outlet which he sometimes will not admit or perhaps has never been conscious of.

Because of the dance's return to virility, men in all walks of life are turning to it. Businessmen, factory workers, and men in professions outside the field of art are learning to dance. Men, in their everyday activities, are in reality on the borderline of the dance. Acknowledged as the stronger sex, they have been more closely allied with those activities requiring greater scope of strength and movement. Even now, when woman is accepted as man's equal, when she is recognized in the fields of business and art, there are still the large-movement activities—operating the bigger machines, building, fighting wars, etc.—in which she has very little or no part to play.

Since man has gone this far, he needs only to take one small step to understanding that his dancing can grow from these very movements he ordinarily employs. If he were to realize this fact, dancing would not strike him as a woman's pastime any more than a ball game does. Inhibitions must be broken down; technique and the coordination of his experiences with dance symbolism acquired.

Our greatest problem is the lack of proper teachers for men. All artists are expected to build up a perfect balance of both masculine and feminine qualities in their work which eventually leads to a character described as neither masculine nor feminine but a synthesis of both. The intensity of a movement often determines its sex. There is the common ground whose movements refer to either and there are extremes which are either male or female. Most men are working with women teachers only so that they are overbalanced on the female side. Very few have had an intensely masculine influence. I believe it is important to their development as men dancers.

Work has been devoted to developing technique suitable for men. But this does not necessarily mean that women are excluded from the possibility of executing it. Women and men, in doing the same exercises, naturally adapt the movements to their own requirements and physical capabilities. This brings us to a subject of vital importance.

So many people, including dancers, have a notion that there exist radical differences in the various schools of the modern dance, and allegiance is sworn to one or another of these schools. It is true that differences exist; but what exactly are they? They are not, as many imagine, inherent in the technique of body movement itself, for despite the fact that we have no standard system such as the ballet has, we are all speaking the same language. Each school, emphasizing its particular characteristics, can be likened to separate dialects of this language. The differences lie only in the approach to the subject, the personality of the teacher, and the peculiar specialization of certain movements.

Each dancer chooses his own method of attack, but in the final analysis is working along the same lines as every other dancer who recognizes the fundamental principles of movement—which are universal. Our modern schools have grown directly out of personalities. Wigman, Graham, Humphrey-Weidman, to cite the pioneers, have all established their schools and their concert companies in their own image. They have given the younger dancers the materials with which to work; and it is our job to use these materials in our own way, eliminating the personal characteristics of those who handed them down. Concerning specialization—personalities have developed to a high degree certain movements or principles of movement which they consider important. For example, one school has dramatized the very act of breathing to a point where the body acts in exaggerated movement of contraction and release; another school has stressed swing, vibration, and so on. We have come to recognize the school a dancer has been the product of by these specialized movements.

Eventually there must be a dance which has an impersonal technique based on the general principles we all understand and adapted to our own needs. No one should be branded as a Graham dancer or a Humphrey-Weidman dancer but merely as a dancer, with a background of all the training necessary to one who uses the body as his medium of expression.

The language of movement is universal, establishing the closest kind of communication among people who are otherwise estranged from each other. This contact must grow, carried on by a large portion of society, rather than by a few scattered individuals who die out and carry their art with them. Man has the harder fight, having grown away from using the body as a medium of artistic expression. The confidence, understanding, and support of men must be gained. Men *must* dance; it is their natural heritage.

Nazi censorship of the arts and Charlie Chaplin's ironic satire in *Modern Times* were graphically depicted by Miguel Covarrubias on the March 1936 cover of *New Theatre*.

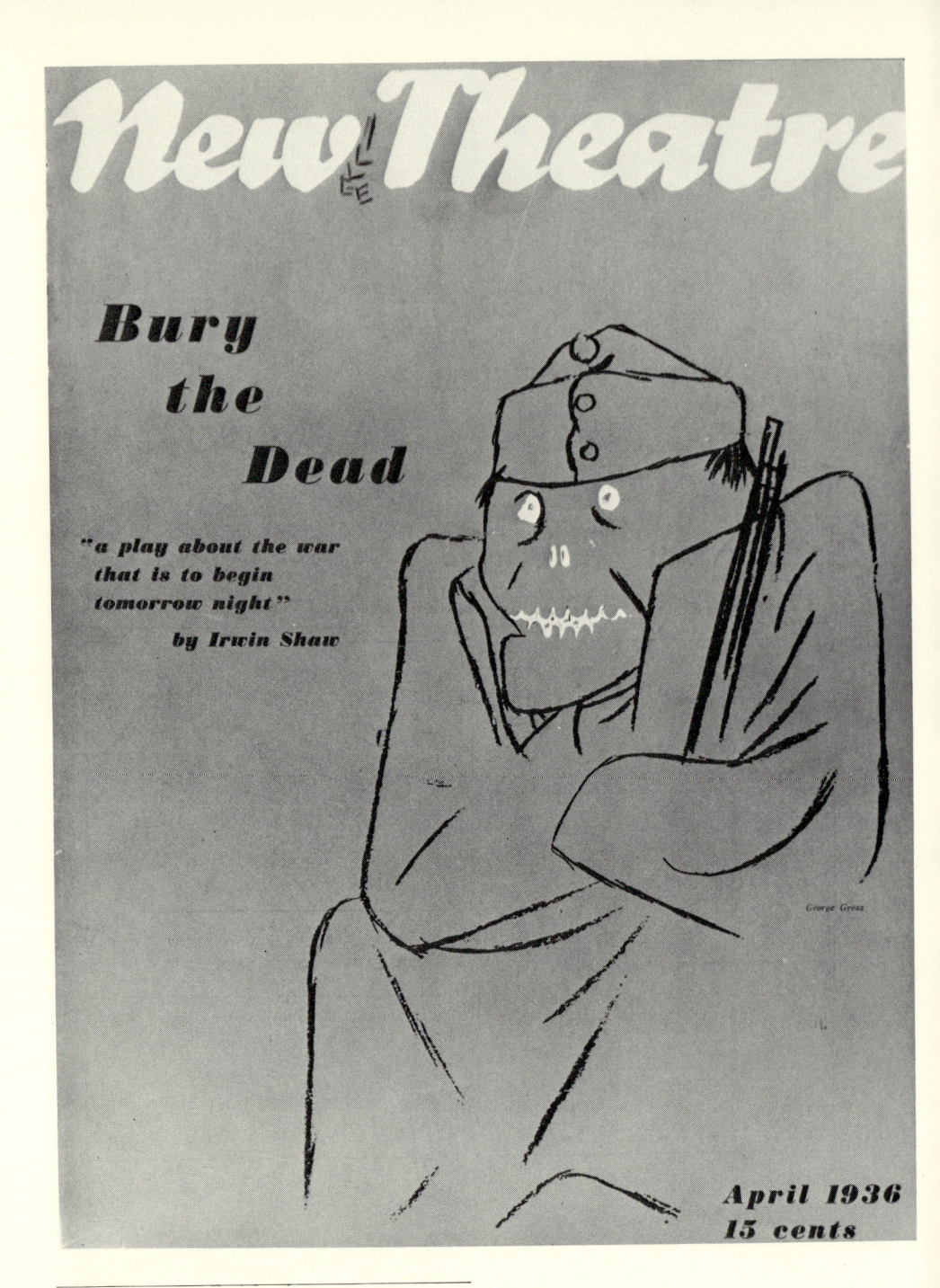

George Grosz designed this grim cover for the April 1936 issue, which featured the text of *Bury the Dead*.

Hitler's image dominates the June 1936 cover as his policies dominated and stifled creativity in the German film industry. The artist is William Gropper.

SAN FRANCISC
DOLLAR LINE
WESTERN WORKER
AMERICA
TODAY
MENACE OF FACISM
LENIN
MARINE WORKERS INDUSTRIAL UNION
WE DEMAND
MARINE

Hosen created this montage for an article in the September 1934 issue. Pictured are scenes from the Living Theatre production in San Francisco.

The WPA generated a veritable circus of theatrical activities that included festivals, marionette shows, and plays. The July 1936 cover is by Augustus Peck.

So You Want to Go Into the Theatre?

"The boss says you ain't the type."

"The producer just left for China. Want to leave a message?"

"Oh, why didn't I stay in the clothing business?"

"Wadda ya mean, more finesse? MGM likes me as I am, see?"

Portrait of a press-agent denying he started a scandal.

Drama critics ready to welcome new talent.

William Gropper's cartoons appeared in the April 1937 issue.

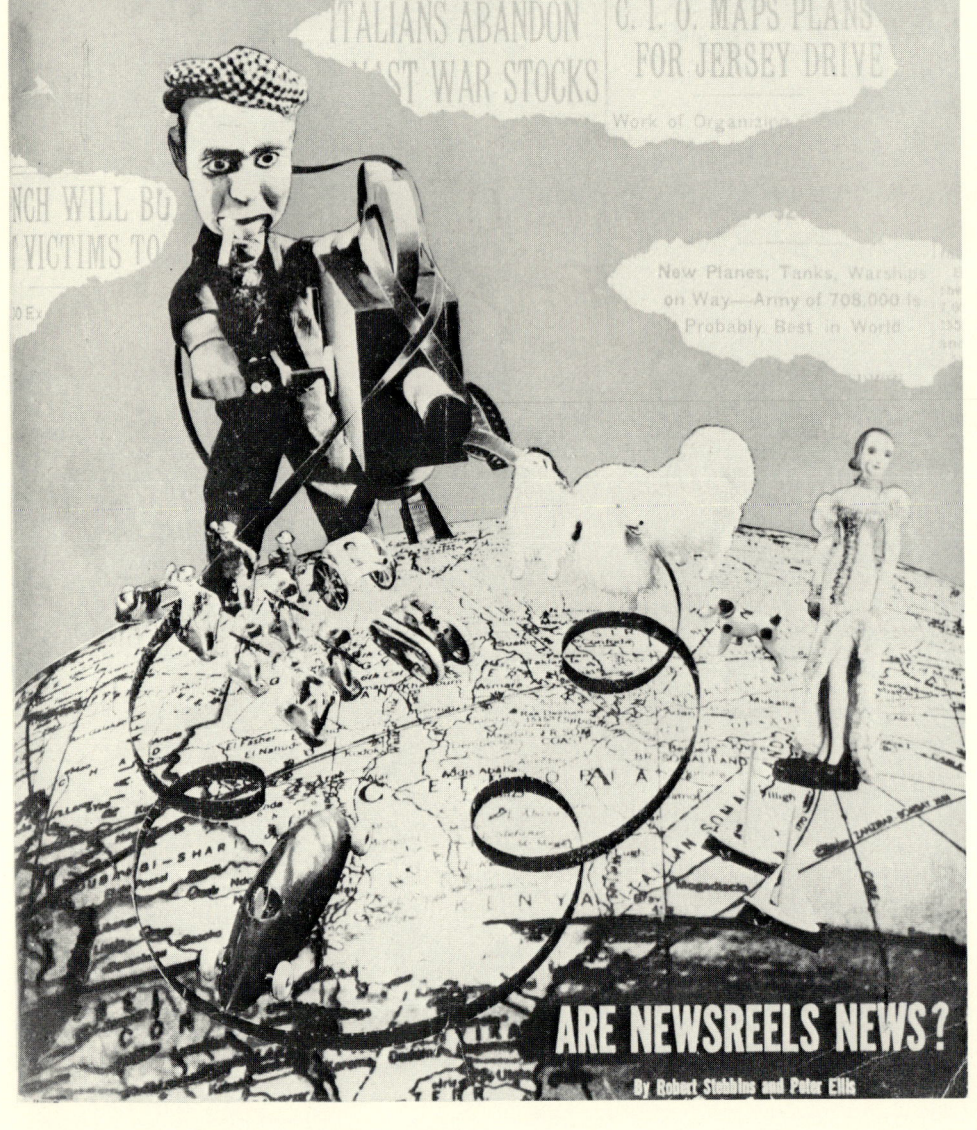

Lewis Jacobs designed the cover for the final issue of the magazine.

FILM

Gorky on the Films, 1896

In 1896 Maxim Gorky was in Paris. There he happened to be present at an exhibition of the first moving pictures produced by the great pioneer Lumière. He wrote two reviews of the occasion, which are among the first moving picture reviews on record. Reprinted by the Soviet film magazine *Kino Art*, they are not to be found in any of the editions of Gorky's collected works. The English translation is by Leonard Mins.
—The Editors

I AM AFRAID I am an undependable correspondent—without finishing the description of the factory department, I am writing about the cinematograph. But possibly I will be excused for wanting to give you my fresh impressions.

The cinematograph is a moving photograph. A beam of electric light is projected on a large screen, mounted in a dark room. And a photograph appears on the cloth screen, about two and a half yards high and a yard and a half high. We see a street in Paris. The picture shows carriages, children, pedestrians, frozen into immobility, trees covered with leaves. All of these are still. The general background is the gray tone of an engraving; all objects and figures seem to be 1/10th of their natural size.

And suddenly there is a sound somewhere, the picture shivers, you don't believe your own eyes.

The carriages are moving straight at you, the pedestrians are walking, children are playing with a dog, the leaves are fluttering on the trees, and bicyclists roll along . . . and all this, coming from somewhere in the perspective of the picture, moves swiftly along, approaching the edge of the screen, and vanishes beyond it. It appears from outside the screen, moves to the background, grows smaller, and vanishes around the corner of the building, behind the line of carriages. . . . In front of you a strange life is stirring, the real, living, feverish life of a main street of France, life which speeds past between two lines of many-storied buildings, like the Terek at Daryal, and nevertheless it is tiny, gray, monotonous, inexpressibly strange.

And suddenly it disappears. Your eyes see a plain piece of white cloth in a wide black frame, and it seems as if nothing had been there. You feel that you have imagined something that you had just seen with your own eyes—and that's all. You feel indefinably awestruck.

And again another picture. A gardener is watering flowers. The stream of water issuing from the hose falls upon the leaves of the trees, on flower beds, on the grass, the flowerpots, and the leaves quiver under the spray.

A little boy, poorly dressed, his face in a mischievous smile, enters the garden and steps on the hose behind the gardener's back. The stream of water becomes thinner and thinner. The gardener is perplexed; the boy can hardly keep from breaking into laughter—his cheeks are puffed out with the effort. And at the very moment that the gardener brings the nozzle close to his nose to see what's the matter, the boy takes his foot off the hose! The stream of water hits the gardener in the face—you think the spray is going to hit you, too, and instinctively shrink back. . . . But on the screen the wet gardener chases the mischievous boy; they run far away, growing smaller, and finally at the very edge of the picture, almost ready to fall to the floor, they grapple with each other. Having caught the boy, the gardener pulls him by the ear and spanks him. . . . They disappear. You are impressed by this lively scene, full of motion, taking place in deepest silence.

Another new picture on the screen. Three respectable men are playing whist. One of them is a clean-shaven gentleman, with the visage of a high government official, laughing with what must be a deep, bass laugh. Opposite him a nervous, wiry partner restlessly picks the cards from the table, cupidity in his gray face. The third person is pouring beer that the waiter had brought to the table; the waiter, stopping behind the nervous player, looks at his cards with tense curiosity. The players deal the cards and . . . the shadows break into soundless laughter. All of them laugh, even the waiter with his hands on hips, quite disrespectful in the presence of these respectable bourgeois. And this soundless laughter, the laughter of gray muscles in gray faces, quivering with excitement, is so fantastic. From it there blows upon you something that is cold, something too unlike a living thing.

Laughing like shadows, they disappear like shadows. . . .

From far off an express train is rushing at you—look out! It speeds along just as if shot out of a giant gun. It speeds straight at you, threatening to run you over. The stationmaster hurriedly runs alongside it. The silent, soundless locomotive is at the very edge of the picture. . . . The public nervously shifts in its chairs—this huge machine of iron and steel will rush into the dark room and crush everybody in it. . . . But, appearing on the gray wall, the locomotive disappears beyond the frame of the screen, and the string of cars comes to a stop. The usual scene of crowding throngs when a train reaches a station. The gray people soundlessly cry out, soundlessly laugh, silently walk, kiss each other without a sound.

Your nerves are strained; imagination carries you to some unnaturally monotonous life, a life without color and without sound, but full of movement, the life of ghosts, or of people, *damned* to the damnation of eternal silence, people who have been deprived of all the colors of life, all its sounds, and they are almost all the better for it. . . .

It is terrifying to see this gray movement of gray shadows, noiseless and silent. Mayn't this already be an intimation of life in the future? Say what you will—but this is a strain on the nerves. A wide use can be predicted, without fear of making a mistake, for this invention, in view of its tremendous originality. How great is its productivity, compared with the expenditure of nervous energy? Is it possible for it to attain such useful application as to compensate for the nervous strain it produces in the spectator? This is an important question, a still more important question in that our nerves are getting weaker and weaker, are growing more and more unstrung, are reacting less and less forcefully to the simple "impressions of daily life" and thirst more and more eagerly for new, strong, unusual, burning, and strange impressions. The cinematograph gives you them—and the nerves will grow cultivated on the one hand, and dulled on the other! The thirst for such strange, fantastic impressions as it gives will grow ever greater, and we will be increasingly less able and less desirous of grasping the everyday impressions of ordinary life. This thirst for the strange and the new can lead us far, very far, and "The Saloon of Death" may be shifted from the Paris of the end of the nineteenth century to the Moscow of the beginning of the twentieth.

I forgot to say that the cinematograph is shown at Aumond's, the well-known Charles Aumond's, the former stableman for General Boisdefre, they say.

Up to now our charming Charles Aumond has brought with him only 120 French women "stars" and ten men; his cinematograph exhibits so far very nice pictures, as you see. But, of course, this is not for long, and it is to be expected that the cinematograph will show "piquant" scenes of the life of the Paris demimonde. "Piquant" here means debauched, and nothing else.

In addition to the pictures mentioned above, there are two others. Lyons: women workers leave a factory. A crowd of lively, moving, gay, laughing women leave the wide gates, run across the screen and vanish. All of them are so nice, with such modest, lively faces, ennobled by toil. And in the dark room they are gazed at by their fellow countrywomen, intensively gay, unnaturally noisy, extravagantly dressed, with some makeup on their faces, and incapable of understanding their Lyons compatriots.

The other picture is *The Family Breakfast*. A modest couple with a chubby firstborn, "baby," is sitting at the table.

"She" is making coffee over an alcohol lamp, and with a loving smile looks on while her handsome young husband feeds his son with a spoon, feeds and smiles with the laughter of a happy man. Outside the window the leaves flutter, noiselessly flutter; the baby smiles at his father with all his chubby chin; everything bears the stamp of such a healthy, hearty, simple atmosphere.

And this picture is looked at by women deprived of the happiness of having a husband and children, the gay women "from Aumond's," stirred by the astonishment and envy of respectable women for their knowing how to dress, and the contempt, the disgusted feeling produced by their profession. They look on and laugh . . . but it is quite possible that their hearts ache with anguish. And it is possible that this gray picture of happiness, this soundless picture of the life of shadows is for them the shadow of the past, the shadow of their past thoughts and dreams of the possibility of such a life as this, but a life with bright, sounding laughter, a colorful life. And possibly many of them, looking at this picture, would like to cry, but cannot; they must laugh, for that is their sorrowful profession. . . .

At Aumond's these two pictures are something in the nature of hard, biting irony for the women of his hall, and will doubtless be removed. I am convinced that they will soon, very soon, be replaced by pictures in a genre more suited to the "Concert Parisien" and the demands of the fair. And the cinematograph, the scientific importance of which is as yet incomprehensible to me, will cater to the tastes of the fair and the debauchery of its hangers-on.

It will show illustrations to the works of De Sade and to the adventures of the Chevalier Fauxblas; it can provide the fair with pictures of the countless falls of Mlle. Nana, the protégée of the Parisian bourgeoisie, the beloved child of Emile Zola. Rather than serve science and aid in the perfection of man, it will serve the Nizhni Novgorod Fair and help to popularize debauchery. Lumière borrowed the idea of moving photography from Edison, borrowed, developed, and completed it, and probably did not foresee where and for whom his invention would be demonstrated.

It is surprising that the fair has not examined the possibilities of X rays, and why Aumond, Toulon, Lomache and Co. have not yet utilized them for amusement and diversion. And this omission is a very serious one!

Besides. Possibly tomorrow X rays will also appear on the screen at Aumond's, used in some way or other for "belly dances."

There is nothing in the world so great and beautiful but that man can vulgarize and dishonor it. And even in the clouds, where formerly ideals and dreams dwelt, they now want to print advertisements—for improved toilets, I suppose.

Hasn't this been mentioned in print yet?

Never mind—you'll soon see it.

THE GROWING ROLE OF *NEW THEATRE* IN THE WORLD OF FILM

WHEN I joined *New Theatre* in March 1934, the magazine concentrated mainly on the theatre. The film and dance sections were relatively small. Like Ben Blake's, my mind then was concerned mostly with theatre and playwriting. But after Ben left, I determined to bone up on film, the better to support our knowledgeable but part-time film editor, Irving Lerner.

In retrospect I wish I had known more about film—my main interests had been literature and drama. But before coming to New York, I had edited, together with Mark Marvin and George Redfield, film articles for *Left Front*, the publication of the John Reed Club in Chicago. And I also had some contact with the intellectual approach to film criticism, having read the one major Left critic, Harry Alan Potamkin, who had written perceptively in *Hound and Horn* on G. W. Pabst, René Clair, V. I. Pudovkin, and Sergei Eisenstein. However, I was most influenced by *Experimental Cinema*, a handsomely printed and illustrated left-wing film magazine, edited by Seymour Stern, an authority on Sergei Eisenstein as well as his friend. Stern's coeditors were Lewis Jacobs and David Platt, both important contributors to *New Theatre* and, in Platt's case, a coeditor with filmmaker Samuel Brody on several early issues. (Platt and Brody also helped publish *Film Front*, a journal of the Film and Photo League.)

By the time I joined *New Theatre* some of my midwest naïveté about cinema had changed to New York know-how. My newly acquired film knowledge came mainly with the encouragement of a new, close friend,

Leo T. Hurwitz (the *T.* standing for Tolstoy, for whom Leo had been named by a literature-loving father). I shared literary interests with Leo, a Harvard graduate, and I regarded him as a sophisticated New York intellectual whose warm welcome made me feel less of an Iowa outsider. I think my close friendship with such authors as James T. Farrell, Edward Dahlberg, Mike Gold, and Joseph Freeman gave me some status in Leo's eyes, as well as the self-confidence I needed as editor in chief to work with major talents in the theatre arts.

When Irving became so pressured by his job in commercial editing that he couldn't give his time to *New Theatre,* Leo proved a godsend as Irving's replacement. Although unpaid and part-time, Leo devoted every hour he could spare from earning his living in photography and film jobs. He was a good companion and a joy to work with in reorganizing the film section and giving it greater weight to balance the drama section. During the earlier months of Leo's work with me, we attracted writers who would later make their marks as film critics of great stature—although we did not guess it at the time. There was Lewis Jacobs, who would be heading for fame as the author of *The Rise of the American Film,* rightly regarded after its appearance in 1939 as a major work of film criticism. And Arthur Knight, the future film critic (along with Hollis Alpert) for the *Saturday Review of Literature* and author of an admirable book, *The Liveliest Art.*

I am glad for this opportunity to express my gratitude and credit Leo's creative contributions until he resigned the following year to help found Nykino, a film production company, with Ralph Steiner, another new friend, whom I remember for his good-natured kidding about my midwest accent. Ralph was a first-rate artist in both still and moving photography, and a successful fashion photographer who could make enough on a few of his photographs to help support his filmmaking interests. Ralph made two important films as cameraman-director during this period, the first taking its title from the Wobbly (IWW) song, "You'll Get Pie in the Sky By and By." A comic satire on organized religion, *Pie in the Sky* was made in 1934 with the aid of Irving Lerner and Molly Day Thacher and starred Elia Kazan in his first film role as a wily priest. It reflected Ralph's own flair for humor and was a welcome, if brief, change from the overwhelmingly serious subject matter of the Left. Five years later, *The City* received critical acclaim for its contrast of planned and unplanned environments. It was codirected with Willard Van Dyke, a newly arrived talent from San Francisco, who later won renown both for his creative work and as head of the Museum of Modern Art Department of Film. *The City* had some light, marvelously entertaining sequences, particularly one memorable one of New York types stuffing their faces at lunch counters. Such comic scenes helped *The City* secure a much wider distribution than other films from leftist sources.

We were lucky as well to have the aid of a major studio executive, who did his part-time film editor's work for us under the pseudonym "Louis Norden." His real name is a well-kept secret to this day, and we still meet occasionally as friends. And there were other part-timers, among them Lionel Berman, who also did important editing work for the magazine on time off from his public-relations job, and Jay Leyda, our former Moscow editor, who had returned from his studies with Eisenstein and worked in the Film Library of the Museum of Modern Art.

These many young talents I have mentioned figured in *New Theatre's* growing importance, not only to leftist filmmakers but also to Hollywood filmmakers, who were giving it greater recognition.

Our main problem, though, was that we did not have a regular monthly film reviewer of stature, and we needed to find one comparable to John Gassner in drama and Edna Ocko in dance. So we began searching, none of us realizing that the critic we needed was often right in our office—Sidney Meyers, Edna Ocko's husband, by profession a violist with an orchestra that provided him a regular income none of the rest of the staff could count on. Sidney, a dedicated film buff, often stopped by our magazine meetings to take his wife home and would kibitz with sardonic humor. His comic wisecracks about "movies" of the Left and the Right would break us up, but after the jokes would come penetrating analysis thrown off in effortless asides. Finally Leo, George, Molly, and I, with Edna's encouragement, persuaded Sidney to put his witticisms and analyses into writing every month as our main movie critic.

He proved a gifted writer of reviews and articles that delighted our staff and brought praise from Hollywood's professional filmmakers as well as from general readers throughout America and abroad. His brilliant contributions were a major factor in building the magazine's circulation, especially in Hollywood, as Gassner's articles had widened our influence in the Broadway theatre. Although music was Sidney's first love, we didn't learn until after his tenure as *New Theatre* critic was over that he had concealed a filmmaking talent, which led him years later to direct *The Quiet One*, one of the finest social documentaries of the 1940s, about a young Negro boy incarcerated in the Willowbrook institution.

Like other courageous contributors who risked their jobs and incomes by writing for a radical magazine like *New Theatre,* Sidney had to use a pseudonym to protect his orchestra position and earnings. He chose the name Robert Stebbins. It seems appropriate years after his death to begin our film section selections with his articles on the Museum of Modern Art historic showings of the early film classics he loved.

The Movie: 1902-1917

BY ROBERT STEBBINS

THE FIRST two showings of early films by the Museum of Modern Art Film Library provided one of the most stimulating movie sessions of recent years. Quite apart from the interest that the sources and first manifestations of an art have for us, the remarkable thing about these films was their indubitable validity.

Why there has existed such a degree of condescension toward the beginning of the industry is hard to say. Perhaps it was inevitable that most of us should feel little reverence for an art, the lifetime of which coincides almost completely with ours. In any event, the audiences which attended the Museum exhibitions obviously came prepared to howl at the crudities of the first flickers. It may be that the series of shorts called *Screen Souvenirs*, in which a presumably witty commentator jibes at the dismembered clips from the pioneer films and indulges in spurious sound effects, was in large degree responsible for this frame of mind. Fortunately, the Museum films were projected without benefit of commentator, and many of the audience left with more than respect for what they had seen.

I must confess to a growing feeling of astonishment as the creative vigor of these films became apparent. Georges Méliès's *A Trip to the Moon*, made in 1902, displaying extraordinary technical adroitness and daring, using at that early date close-ups, stop-motion, animation, and lap-dissolves, proved especially provocative. Here were many of the effects that modern cinematography prides itself upon, used with incisiveness and cinematic propriety. Where, therefore, was the vaunted technical superiority of the modern Hollywood film? True, Hollywood is infinitely capable *mechanically*, but her efforts bear little creative relation to the *technical* requirements of the material at hand.

All the innovations of the early filmmakers came directly out of conflict with the material which the director had to embody in cinematic form. Mrs. Griffith, in her book of reminiscences, *When the Movies Were Young*, tells how D.W., her husband, evolved the close-up. He had the problem of depicting a particularly deep-dyed variety of villain. Heretofore, the camera, which has a very narrow angle of vision, had always been kept well away from the scene and actors so that every shot included a large foreground of floor or sidewalk. Griffith wondered how he could convey the proper impression of Satanism with all that rug in the way. Suddenly he got the notion of bringing the camera close to the actor's face. At first his cameraman refused. No one to his knowledge had ever done so before. The public wouldn't stand for larger-than-life-size detail. But Griffith persisted. There was little studio supervision in those days and so the close-up was included in the repertoire of distinctive movie devices.

D. W. Griffith was represented on the Museum program by *The New York Hat* (1912), a story by Anita Loos, cast—Mary Pickford and Lionel Barrymore as principals. Among the extras were Lillian Gish, Mack Sennett, Jack Pickford, and Mae Marsh. This slender item was certainly not major Griffith, but there was already evidence of his consummate grasp of cinematic principles in the imaginative cutting. Mary Pickford was especially astonishing for one who had forgotten how really ingratiating and wholesome an actress she had been in the years before she turned author.

The technical brio and realistic wit of Mack Sennett's *The Clever Dummy* (1917), with Ben Turpin, Chester Conklin, and Wallace Beery, was absolutely unanticipated. That overwhelming moment when Ben Turpin, who is being pursued by Beery whose pocketbook he has picked, whizzes out of the frame on his incredible motorcycle brought our sense of complacency with the modern film to a full stop and provoked the question, "What's happened to the movies?"

We do not wish to appear professorial or snobbish. We have never shown sympathy with certain gentlemen of pedantic tendencies who cry, "After the Greeks—nothing!" or who affirm that after the early miracle plays and the Elizabethans, literature perished in the English-speaking world. Such contentions are obviously untenable, because wherever and in whatever age men come to grips with the material of life and craft, art is the miraculous result. The innovations of the postwar German film artists, namely dramatic lighting and new angles of vision, came about as a direct consequence of a new outlook on life. Life had become a complicated matter. Psychoanalysis, for instance, had revealed the existence of multiple layers of consciousness. The German contributions were the cinematic realization of these new concepts. Similarly, the Russian system of montage, with its brilliant crosscutting and richness of comment, resulted from the attempt to incorporate the dialectic philosophy of Marx and the new revolutionary fervor into the film. Meanwhile, Hollywood, which symbolizes eclecticism, sat back and contentedly used these cinematic advances to acquaint the American public with the talents of Rin Tin Tin, Jr.

Even such films as *The Fugitive*, produced in 1916 by Thomas H. Ince with William S. Hart, and *A Fool There Was*, with Theda Bara, directed in 1914 by Frank Powell, both of which appeared on the second Museum program, displayed distinct creative merit. Ince's superb direction of the crowd of cowboys and entertainers at the bar puts to shame such recent attempts in the same genre as *Rose of the Rancho*, for example. It was amazing to see how varied and yet well coordinated were the actions of each individual in the bar scenes. *A Fool There Was* was chiefly distinguished by the strange intensity it achieved through its lighting effects. In this film, the director, Frank Powell, had the task of presenting a moral concept—the struggle between good and evil. As a consequence, the film resolved itself into a series of contrasts. We are shown a decrepit Edward Jose lying in the ripe arms of Theda Bara and immediately we are taken back to the innocence of his child saying her prayers for Daddy, who is away with that bad woman. The lighting of the film serves the moral purpose with brilliant contrasts of almost complete shadow and startling whiteness. The last scene of the dying Jose is a remarkable example of this type of dramatic illumination.

So that my insistence on merit in so universally derided a film as *A Fool There Was* will not appear sheer willfulness, let me point out that in Hollywod today, in the vast majority of cases, lighting bears no relationship whatsoever to the content of a film. Bedroom farce, mutiny on the high seas, animal romances—all are bathed in that peculiar pearly luminescence that is everywhere accepted as good photography but which adds nothing dramatically to the narrative.

One last film in the Museum repertoire demands comment—*Queen Elizabeth*, made in France in 1911 and featuring Sarah Bernhardt and Lou Tellegen. The value of this film is chiefly historical, being largely a straight photographed play of no cinematic significance. At that, it is probably the prototype of similar efforts in pure play transcription, such as *Accent on Youth*, *Petrified Forest*, and Sacha Guitry's *Louis Pasteur*. Only last month, Mr. Guitry informed the press that in his estimation the motion picture should be nothing more than a film play, that the camera should be placed in a rigid position where it can include the stage and then never move. We trust that in Mr. Guitry's next film he will display the logical consistency of Sarah Bernhardt, who, after passing out on a fantastic mound of embroidered pillows, gets up to take her bows.

The Museum of Modern Art Film Library deserves the gratitude of film devotees for this unexpected opportunity to take stock of the present state of the film by comparison with past achievements. Perhaps if a wide enough public will be admitted to the showings, American audiences will be shocked from their complacent acceptance of Hollywood's 1936 claim to movie preeminence. After all, the superiority of *Riffraff* or *Black Fury* to *The Goddess* (of which the *New York Times* on January 24, 1916, said, "In the chapter of *The Goddess* released this week, the strikers attack the stockade of the coal barons") is problematical.

D. W. Griffith

BY RICHARD WATTS, JR.

DAVID WARK GRIFFITH is not only the father of every technical device known to cinema direction but is also the pioneer in the conception of the screen as a medium for social ideas. It is not that he was invariably the inventor of these directorial methods. For example, he is set down in film history as the introducer of the close-up, but the classic pre-Griffith photoplay, *The Great Train Robbery*, closes with a scene in which a bandit shown from the waist up aims his pistol at the audience and fires. It is distinctly a close-up and it is not the work of Griffith. Nevertheless he is the man who was responsible for the use of that celebrated device as a method for dramatizing an emotion and concentrating on the reaction of a character to a situation. In a word, he took the close-up, which had been used merely as a new way of photographing a scene, and gave it some psychological point.

In the same way, you are likely to find that every other method of camera manipulation now employed in Hollywood or any other photoplay manufacturing center was either devised or was developed along its proper dramatic channels by D. W. Griffith. His status as a social crusader, however, is certainly at least equally important and it has not been as frequently contemplated.

The Griffith crusades have been many and they have been of varying degrees of intellectual value. On the whole, I should say that the trouble with them has been that they were based on a sympathetic and easily aroused emotionalism that had much to do with sentimentality and not always a great deal with any hardheaded sense of reality. In a word, it was a kind heart, rather than a keen intelligence, that guided him in his soul-searching among ideas. But whatever the validity of his ideas, he has always been on the side of a cause that he has regarded with burning-eyed zealousness as a cause of justice. He has never been smart or clever or brittle. Always he has been in earnest, and he has proved that a frank earnestness of viewpoint can be of tremendous dramatic effectiveness. He is the father of many things in the cinema and not the least of them is this conception of the screen as the vehicle for a viewpoint.

His most famous film is, of course, *The Birth of a Nation*, and even after all of these years it remains a powerful and impressive photoplay. The scene of the little Colonel's return to his ruined home remains to this day touching and poignant, one of the great episodes among motion picture episodes. His hysterical picture of the horrors of Reconstruction and his ecstatic cheering for the glories of the Ku Klux Klan unfortunately reveal the extent to which his emotionalism could carry him, but there is no disputing the enormous, if decidedly overwrought, dramatic effectiveness of this section of the work. As a completely partisan account of a particularly ugly chapter in American history *The Birth of a Nation* still possesses a certain stunning power. But its cruel unfairness to the Negro is an inescapable blot upon it.

Being an essentially fair, if hysterical man, Griffith was not altogether oblivious to that fact, and it worried him. I do not think it is fair to say that he was merely worried because he felt that he had alienated an entire national group of paying filmgoers. What he did was to include in a happily forgotten war picture called *Hearts of the World* a scene in which a dying Negro soldier cried for his mother and a white comrade in arms kissed him as he perished. It was a shamelessly sentimental scene—Griffith has always loved the shamelessly sentimental—and it was a pretty shoddy and futile effort to make up for what he had done in *The Birth of a Nation*. In all of its intellectual implications it is far from being to Griffith's credit, and to this extent it is indefensible.

The Birth of a Nation was a great financial success and *Intolerance* was not, but I still think that *Intolerance* remains the greatest monument to the directorial genius of D. W. Griffith. In it the director told four parallel stories at once; one taking place in Babylon at the time of the fall, a second in Palestine during the crucifixion of Christ, a third in Paris during the St. Bartholomew's Day massacre, and the fourth in modern America. Instead of narrating these episodes one after another, Griffith presented them all at once, leaping from one century to another, from scene to scene, until all of the climaxes arrived at one time and you were kept busy darting between an automobile racing to Sing Sing with a reprieve from the governor and the escape of a Huguenot girl from the swords of the Guises. It was, I must say, all just a trifle confusing.

It is the Babylonian episode that is the magnificent achievement of the work. There still is nothing as superbly beautiful and exciting in film spectacle as the pictorial account of the greatness of Babylon and the tragedy of its fall. To this day film directors with much larger sums of money to spend strive without avail to equal its cinematic excellence. Mr. DeMille's vain efforts to equal its visual grandeur in such things as *The Sign of the Cross* and *The Crusades* have seemed embarrassingly puny beside it, not because the Babylonian chapter had more lavishness and a greater number of extras, but because Griffith had a far greater talent for superb visual effects and the dramatic power of cinematic movement.

Intolerance, however, is not notable merely because of its spectacle. It is deservedly famous because it was a pioneer effort to dramatize, not merely another story of young love and its trials, but a social theme. As the title suggests, Griffith was concerned with preaching the evils of intolerance and the fatal effect on both people and nations of widespread national or religious bigotry. It can hardly be said that such a theme is even outmoded at the present day. But the remarkable thing about the film's editorial viewpoint was that intolerance in modern America was shown in the framing of labor leaders and in the persecution of workers. Griffith was preaching social justice in the modern episode, and even though he preached in a conventional and overly melodramatic narrative—in story the American episode is the weakest of the four—there could be no doubt of his earnestness and his integrity.

As I have said, *Intolerance* was not a financial success. In fact, monetary difficulties have long dogged Mr. Griffith's footsteps, interfering with his plans and keeping him from carrying out all of his conceptions. A mind more emotional than searching and stalwart has not always been of help to him, although it provided him with the romantic zealousness that was so important in both *Intolerance* and *The Birth of a Nation*. A certain lack of taste, a frank excess of sentimentality and a curiously sadistic urge have been, I think, the chief causes of his troubles.

As proof of this, there is the case of one of the most famous of his pictures, *Broken Blossoms*. In that dramatization of one of Thomas Burke's Limehouse stories, all of the defects of the director, as well as some of his greatest virtues, are to be found. The tale of the girl whose father tortured her to make her commit a murder and of the young Chinese who loved her possessed all of the pictorial skill and sense of melodramatic effectiveness that have gone into Griffith's best works. At the same time it was overwrought in its amorous romanticism, given to scenes so extravagant in their sentimentality as to suggest that the man who made them was curiously lacking in critical sense, and filled with episodes of torture that were almost pathological in their joy in sadism. It was over the scenes in which the heroine was being whipped by her brutal father that there was the suggestion that a certain relish for contemplating cruelty was not lacking. The result is that *Broken Blossoms* was a sadistic spree, as well as a beautiful and poignant motion picture.

There was also to be found in that picture a tendency that has never been one of Mr. Griffith's most admirable traits. That was his propensity for making his heroines seem slightly half-witted in their passion for fluttering about. Giggling sweetly, running around in pretty little circles and merrily chasing birds about a field were the chief occupations of the Griffith heroines, when they were not being pursued by lecherous monsters. In *Broken Blossoms* Miss Lillian Gish was forced to be so fluttery that it has taken many years and performances in such stage works as *Hamlet* and *Within the Gates* to make people forget it.

The other Griffith films have seemed to me less important. *America*, a chronicle of the Revolutionary War, dramatized Paul Revere's ride with unequalled effectiveness but was only a good, average historical picture the rest of the time. *Isn't Life Wonderful?* dramatized the immediate postwar days in Germany with sensitivity but without the great Griffith dramatic sense in its best form. *Orphans of the Storm* again showed the director's genius for spectacle, but revealed his defects as clearly as it did his virtues. *Sally of the Sawdust* and *That Royle Girl* were hokum melodramas even though *Sally* introduced the incomparable W. C. Fields to the cinema. With the coming of sound Mr. Griffith has offered us but two works. His *Abraham Lincoln* was an interesting romantic chronicle of the most popular American hero, demonstrating that Lincoln never recovered from the death of Ann Rutledge, and *The Struggle* was a simply terrible drama about the evils of drink.

It is undeniably true that in his later days Mr. Griffith, who seems to have retired permanently from filmmaking, saw the procession pass him by. He saw directors with no fraction of his talents sweep on to success, while the course of social and aesthetic ideas rushed on beyond him. Yet it can never be forgotten that it was he who first made motion picture direction an art; that, for better or for worse, he is the father of the motion picture as it exists today. In any possible record of the cinema, he must stand at the head, as the man who molded the photoplay quite surprisingly into his own image and likeness. With all of his defects, he remains the outstanding figure in the development of the screen.

Billy Bitzer, Ace Cameraman

BY PHILIP STERLING

T HE ALLOCATION of honors for creative contributions to the motion picture is a difficult task. But if a medal is ever stamped with the face of David Wark Griffith, its obverse side will have to bear the likeness of Billy Bitzer, Griffith's cameraman.

The association of these two artists from the time Griffith stepped into the old Biograph studio in 1908 to the time he made *Broken Blossoms* is an historic example of the interdependence of the arts in the creation of motion pictures.

None can detract from the stature of Griffith as the single greatest force in the American film. Griffith did more than make great pictures. He brought into being the basic elements of the motion picture's inherent idiom. He developed mere tricks of photography into a method of creative expression. But he didn't do it alone. The collective nature of film art made it inevitable that he should share his efforts and his glory with others, and most of all with Billy Bitzer.

All too rapidly the illusion is growing up among a second generation of film lovers that the visual idiom now commonly employed with skillful variation by all directors sprang full-grown and armor-clad from the foreheads of one or two individuals. Even Griffith himself, in a recent radio broadcast, intimated that pure celebration and not the groping trial and error of a new and undeveloped art were responsible for the flashback, the close-up, the fade-out, the dissolve.

A talk with Bitzer, who is now past sixty and struggling in obscurity to keep his little family together on a WPA security wage, produces a new appreciation of the movie cameraman's role as a creative agent.

Bitzer's views on camera art need recording, but even more does his present personal relationship to the movie industry need to be told. Bitzer last worked in Hollywood in 1929, when he photographed *Drums of Love*. Having lost a fortune in the easy-come-easy-go days of Coolidge prosperity, he was working in New York filming screen tests and doing other photographic odd jobs when he asked for a chance to go back to Hollywood. Arriving in Hollywood, Bitzer worked the usual two weeks before approaching the pay window. The clerk had never heard of him. Bitzer repeated his name. The clerk looked through his records and came back saying, "I'm sorry, we have no one by the name of *Mitchell* on the payroll." A conference with the production manager revealed that no provision had ever been made to put Bitzer on the payroll at the $500 a week which was the common salary of the other top cameramen on the lot. Broke, and without much choice, Bitzer remained to work at a much lower salary than he had been led to expect. But Bitzer sought a recourse which has become increasingly popular on the West Coast since 1929. He set about organizing a union. In New York, it is not commonly known, Bitzer had been one of the founders of the International Photographers of the Motion Picture Industries, which embraced all of the lower-rank cameramen and assistants who could not get into the exclusive and expensive American Society of Cinematographers.

On the West Coast the industry was in a dither because of the coming of sound. Cameramen and assistants saw a danger in the low salaries which were being paid to many lesser sound technicians.

When Bitzer pointed out to his fellow photographers that they stood in danger of being reduced to similar levels, they were quick to respond, and Local 656 of the International Photographers of the Motion Picture Industries was set up in Hollywood. The producers were alarmed and Billy Bitzer, ace cameraman, the creative eye through which the great Griffith captured his visions of beauty and grandeur, was blacklisted.

Bitzer tells the story of an attempt to bribe him. An offer of $50,000 to retire from the union was made to him by a cameraman who had served his apprenticeship under him.

"Suppose I did quit now," Bitzer said. "I couldn't stop the union. Once these things get started no one man is big enough to call a halt. Besides, what will I be able to say when people ask where the great ace cameraman was during the struggle of his fellow photographers to organize? What will I be able to answer when people ask why Billy Bitzer wasn't in the fight? It isn't worth $50,000. I've had far more than that and a man who knows the value of money also knows how worthless money can be."

Thus Bitzer left Hollywood and found his way by painful stages to the Objective Reading Project maintained by WPA for the Board of Education in New York City. He has done motion picture work for the WPA administration, but his present job is to prepare film strips and recorded lectures used in visual education.

For all Hollywood's ingratitude, Bitzer is not embittered.

"When I see a movie," Bitzer said, "I grow smaller and smaller in my seat as I realize what they're doing in Hollywood today. Today's photography brings to life what I once dreamed of achieving in the era of slow film, inadequate illuminants, and unimproved cameras. With better equipment the boys have learned more. They know how to use their new tools."

Bitzer feels that while the average standard of Hollywood photography is high, unusual photography is achieved only when there is the proper kind of collaboration between cameraman and director. If the director has clear ideas of the visual effects he wants to achieve, if he is certain of the composition, the emphasis, and the dramatic quality he wants, his cameraman can become a pliant creative agent, Bitzer feels.

Lighting is something Bitzer seems to take for granted. A man can't take pictures unless he knows how to light up, he feels, but his ideas on lighting-up seem to hew closely to the line of the nonrealistic Hollywood tradition. He speaks of it largely in terms of keeping unflattering shadows off the faces of feminine stars. Despite this, it must be remembered that the battle scenes which swept over a vast plain in *The Birth of a Nation* are still among the most realistic ever filmed.

In the first decade of the century, screen stories were extremely simple and the methods of visualizing them were even simpler. Falling into a formula, moviemakers discovered all too quickly that the easiest pictures to make and the most salable were those in which love interest predominated. In this connection they were constantly troubled by one fact—the big love scenes appeared and disappeared too abruptly. This was because cutting was then elementary. It consisted simply of splicing sequence to sequence and hoping for the best. To compensate for their inadequate knowledge of cutting, everything was tried: soft focusing, gauze screens, whatnot. The first forward step was backlighting, which meant placing the subject between the lens and the source of light. This had always been avoided by cameramen because it meant that the faces of the actors were in shadow and either bad photographs or mere silhouettes would result.

Bitzer relates that on location in Fort Lee one day, while the actors were resting between sequences, Owen Moore and Mary Pickford, who were later married, used the recess for some mild lovemaking of their own. They happened to be sitting within range of Bitzer's camera, and the playful Billy thought it would be amusing if some scenes of Moore's and Pickford's tender interlude found their way to the screen of the projection room when the day's shooting was done. The blissful couple was between the camera and the sun. There was only one thing for Bitzer to do, turn the crank and shade the lens with his hand.

The little company that sat in the projection room that night got a thrill. Bitzer's trick gave far better results than he expected because the white gravel road at the edge of which Moore and Pickford were sitting reflected sufficient light to give effective illumination to the faces.

Elated by his accidental achievement, he took care to prevent others from thinking it accidental and studied the lighting conditions which made his little stroke possible until he knew how to reproduce them at will. Here was one method of visualizing a love scene different from the drab methods in use. On a second attempt, Bitzer shaded the lens with his cap and part of the cap appeared on the film. H. N. Marvin told Bitzer to "stop fooling around."

Undaunted, Bitzer cut the bottom out of a glue can and made a shade for the lens. When the film was projected it was discovered that the corners of the film frames were cut off by the curves of the glue can. The result of the glue can incident was the development of the iris, which made possible the fade-in and fade-out. Irises for fading didn't exist then. It was necessary to describe the nonexistent device and ask a manufacturer to produce one.

Griffith had long recognized the need for broadening and improving methods of camera expression, and Bitzer, proceeding from accident to conscious experiment, had produced the means.

Like the iris, the close-up and the flashback came into use as devices by which the director increased the expressiveness of his medium. Griffith often used to complain to Bitzer that there was no way of centering attention on a single individual in the highly dramatic moments of a picture. One early attempt to approximate the close-up consisted of photographing through a gauze screen with a circular opening. The effect was to throw the minor characters into a shadowy haze while the principal actor's face was seen sharply through the opening in the screen. This was quickly abandoned. Filters with clear centers were also tried and found wanting. Finally the fade combined with the close-up gave an effective means of centering attention on the emotions and actions of a single individual in a film.

Even Mary Pickford, who makes no claims in this field, contributed her bit to movie photography, according to Bitzer.

She complained repeatedly that when she went to the movies with her mother to see her pictures, she was discomfited to find that her screen images gave her a ghostly pallor. He told her she had seen a bad copy of the film. When she persisted, saying that all the copies gave the same ghostlike effect, Bitzer gave the matter some thought, but Mary herself solved the problem by suggesting that she use darker makeup. Tests proved Mary was right and makeup finally began to receive the detailed attention needed for its development into the highly specialized art which it is today.

"We took our work seriously in those days," Bitzer declares. "We were always experimenting, fooling around, playing with lenses and lights, not because we had any clear idea of what we were after but because we had a vague hope that we would hit on something." Ingenuity in the use of the camera was the measure of film art. It was not merely unschooled taste that led people to regard as art those things which are now dismissed as mere trick photography.

Bitzer, it has been pointed out, hasn't been embittered by his last Hollywood experience. He still hopes to get back into the industry, for he is as good a cameraman today as he ever was. But whether his name ever appears on the credit frames of another Hollywood movie or not, the camera will still be Bitzer's great and abiding passion. As long as he can lay hands on a box and a few feet of film he will continue to make pictures.

Little Charlie, What Now?

BY CHARMION VON WIEGAND

"THIS IS the saddest picture I have seen in America," said a Russian girl to me after the premiere of *Modern Times*. I also came away feeling that the pathos of the picture outweighed its humor, that in spite of many amusing situations the underlying theme was tragedy more than comedy.

I saw *Modern Times* twice. The first time I was part of a sophisticated New York audience which attends premieres. The laughter that greeted Charlie's appearance on the belt as a worker rippled on with scarcely an interruption to the end of the film. It was uproarious at those moments when Charlie was most cruelly walloped by fate—for instance in the scene when the automatic feeder goes berserk and splashes soup and whipped cream in Charlie's face, feeds him steel nuts, and buffets him with a wiper; again when he is pardoned from jail and put out of his cozy-corner cell into the cold world; or in the cabaret, when he loses his cuff with the words of his song scribbled on it and faces his audience blankly. It was plain that the audience in the theatre that night did not too closely identify itself with Charlie in his painful situations.

The second time I saw the film was on a holiday forenoon when the house was crowded with people anxious to take advantage of the cheaper morning prices. This time the laughter was louder in some scenes—for instance, when Charlie picks up the red flag from a truck and unwittingly finds himself leading a demonstration of unemployed (there were even cheers in the audience at this point); again when Charlie, penniless, consumes a gargantuan meal in a cafeteria and then summons the policeman from outside to come in and arrest him; or when, in the midst of a strike, he steps on a board which hurls a brick in the face of a policeman. But in contrast to the first night, there were pauses of tension and uncertainty. The audience seemed puzzled by certain situations and did not know how to respond. I am most anxious to see the film when it is released in the second-run houses and observe the reactions of an audience even less economically secure. But the first two reactions are sufficient to indicate the complexity of Chaplin's new masterpiece—as great a piece of work as he has ever turned out, but no longer in the style of pure comedy.

Modern Times is a mélange of satire, comedy, fantasy, and tragedy. It is not a unified work of art. Nevertheless, the creative level of this film is far beyond what Hollywood has hitherto produced. Supported by an excellent company, which includes his comely new leading lady, Paulette Goddard, and that lavishly mustached comedian, Chester Conklin, the whole film bears the distinctive stamp of Chaplin's personality. Idea, scenario, production, and chief role are all by Chaplin himself. Thus if ever a film had an opportunity to become a unified work of art, it is this one. Yet it fails to do so. It is interesting to pose the question: Is this failure due to Chaplin (in any one of his capacities as scenarist, producer, or actor) or is it due to something far more fundamental?

The critics, in reviewing *Modern Times*, have expressed mixed feelings about it. For the most part the reviewers of the daily press have loudly denied that the film has any social significance and they have insisted that it is merely a piece of uproarious slapstick, with Charlie at his best in the time-honored situations and gags. Again other critics, particularly of the weekly and liberal press, have credited Chaplin with a film of social criticism displaying a distinctly leftish approach. Much of the advance publicity emphasized this viewpoint. There is no doubt that the first caption of the film supports this latter theory, for it reads: "*Modern Times* is a story of industry, of individual enterprise—of humanity crusading in pursuit of happiness." This is followed by a shot of a herd of sheep in a runway and then by a parallel shot of a mass of workers coming out of the subway and passing through the factory gates. But this opening theme is not consistently upheld throughout the action—it appears for a moment, then is lost in situations not at all relevant to it, and reappears in ever fainter echoes until the end. Thus the meaning of the film remains *confused*.

On the technical side, *Modern Times* seems slightly archaic. It is true that the photography is beautiful, crystal clear, and as realistic as a Soviet film. But Chaplin persists in using a silent screen; the mode is that prior to the talkies. None of the characters speak. There is, however, incidental music and some sound devices. For the first time in a Chaplin film, there are spoken words, but they come from mechanical contrivances such as the loudspeaker attached to the television screen in the factory or the phonograph which explains the automatic feeding machine. And once Chaplin sings—for the first time we hear his voice and it is a pleasant, resonant voice which I, for one, would gladly hear again. Hence we know now that it is not due to any vocal difficulty that Chaplin refrains from accepting the advance of the talkie, but because he believes his art is dependent on a particular aesthetic, which permits only pantomime.

At times, it is true, the incidental music which underscores and sustains that pantomime is sufficient. But there are scenes which demand dialogue and to refuse it weakens the emotional effect. For instance, in the realistic scene when the gamine's father is killed in a food riot and she discovers the body in the street, we actually see Paulette Goddard's lips frame the words: "My father is dead." At the second performance, I caught several people around me spontaneously repeating the words out loud. Abstention from dialogue at this point, and other similar ones, definitely deprived the audience of pleasure. In such a moment, one film style collided head-on with another film style: an old convention of a particular theatre was used to straitjacket a new and more realistic convention of the film. Thus, in addition to a confusion in its theme, we have in *Modern Times* a distinct confusion of two styles in film technique.

What is the meaning of this confusion both in the content and in the form of the film? Does it signify that Chaplin is reactionary in his film technique and radical in his thematic material? Does it signify that he is a bad director unable to control that material? He has been accused of both faults. But I venture to say that it means neither.

Chaplin is the greatest comic artist of our era. As a creative genius, he is so sensitive to his environment that he has acutely felt the impact of the changes which are occurring in the body of our society. He has registered with the accuracy of a seismograph the confusion in the world today and particularly the confusion in the minds of the middle classes. Moreover, he has had the courage to break the old art mold in which his comic genius has always functioned. He has struck out as a pioneer on a new road in search of a new form in film. The confusion in his theme is thus the direct product of our times. The confusion in his style is due to the fact that his old style, in which he conceived the character

Charlie, has become antiquated and inadequate; it cannot be further developed to include the present pressing problems which confront contemporary society.

This confusion nevertheless marks Chaplin as ahead of the game and not behind it. *Modern Times* is the first *expressionist* film of contemporary American life. It is not, however, a perfect example of it. Expressionism is a style in art which always occurs historically in a period of social breakup. (It had its most recent flowering in postwar Germany.) The *structure* of *Modern Times* is expressionist; there is no organic plot, no actual development of action involving a set of characters. It consists of a series of scenes loosely bound together by two characters, Charlie, the hero, and his female companion, the *gamine*. Their mutual adventures are played against a shifting background of modern life, which includes the factory, the street, the jail, the waterfront, the hospital, the Hooverville shack, the department store, and the cabaret. Charlie is the little forgotten man wandering in quest of happiness across the chaos of our civilization. Each adventure robs him of one more cherished illusion. At the end, empty-handed and footsore, alone with his girl, he faces the open road, still debonair but secretly uncertain about the unknown future.

It is the scenario which keeps *Modern Times* from being a unified, expressionistic work. Its most serious weakness is the lack of any character development at all. Charlie remains fundamentally what he was at the beginning of his pilgrimage. He has learned nothing from his unfortunate adventures, experiences from which the most obdurate and thickheaded individual would conceivably have gained some knowledge or common sense. The reason why Chaplin has not allowed his creation, Charlie, to develop and change with experience is consistent. But to understand it, we must know what the essence of Charlie is, what he has symbolized in the old films prior to 1929. The early Chaplin films, particularly the slapstick reelers, were conceived within a small given framework. Within it, the world was basically taken for granted. The director, the character, the audience all accepted certain basic concepts about the world they lived in. It did not occur to them to challenge the presuppositions. Hence all three were included within a given framework and the work of art produced by them collectively—although of smaller scope than *Modern Times*—could be a unified production.

Chaplin created a fixed character, Charlie, for this old, supposedly stable world. His audience was the great middle class of America (which included a large portion of the working class too). The United States has always been the country of middle class *ideals*. In the days before the economic crisis, the worker also felt himself part of this class. He accepted the democratic illusions taught in public school, he shared some of the prosperity of the upper classes, and he emulated the manners of those above him. His believed the doctrine that honesty is the best policy and that hard work will be rewarded. In short he did not feel bound to his class as the worker did in Europe. In that past era so many self-made men attained wealth and position that the legend seemed true. Lincoln, the rail-splitter who became president, was the ideal hero of our democratic republic. Charlie, the beloved universal character of the film, was conceived out of this legend and he played for this audience. (It is interesting to note that Charlie in *Modern Times*, when he makes his jail cell cozy, tacks up a picture of Lincoln.)

Charlie, when he first made his debut on the shadow screen, won immediate favor. He *was* the common man, always incurably romantic, in that he saw through the hypocrisies and cruelties of the upper classes, yet aped their costume and fine manners and accepted their mask of chivalry as bona fide. Because of this, in all his early adventures of failure he continued to cherish the illusion that someday he would find the pot of gold at the end of the rainbow. He would escape out of poverty and humiliation into the glittering social heaven above him. His was an eternal quest for that miraculous moment when he would change his battered suit, emblem of shabby respectability, for a new one; when he would cease to pretend and become what he imagined the most wonderful thing in the world—*a gentleman.*

This same Charlie was an incorrigible optimist, as befits a citizen of a country of vast unexploited resources and the highest technique in the world. He thumbed his nose at fate, which always knocked him down on the threshold of paradise—when he thought he had stepped out of his class into the one above it. What made him so funny, so wistful, so mocking, was that he reflected the aspirations and the failures of millions of people like him. They saw him fail but they believed that *they* might succeed. They too had a hankering to thumb their noses at their superiors, to plant the custard pie full in the face of their enemies, and to climb over the backs of their fellowmen to individual success. Charlie might fail, but they could laugh from their vantage place of seeming security; for there was always the hope that they might be different. Charlie fulfilled their wishes on the *plane of fantasy.*

This early art of Chaplin was thus built entirely on illusion and fantasy. The character Charlie was fixed, the conditions were stable. The milieu was the eternal *now* of fantasy. For no matter how seemingly real —and the early film did not have sufficient development to treat anything realistically—the background of the city against which Charlie performed was actually nothing more than the painted scenic drop bodily transferred from vaudeville to the screen. All those absurd slapstick adventures never took place in the real world but in an imitation of it. In this world of escape which Charlie proffered his audience, everyone might enjoy the most painful failures, the most vulgar gags, the cruelest jokes, and achieve a release of their hidden desires. But if these same things had been acted on the plane of reality, they would have been too painful even for that hopeful and seemingly secure audience of early days.

The rules of the game in this world of fantasy were the same rules which were used in the classic theatres of the seventeenth and eighteenth centuries—particularly the commedia dell'arte. Chaplin, brought up in the English music hall and the American vaudeville, was in the direct line of that tradition, which has given us the ballet, the pantomime, and much of vaudeville. This old classic theatre, which may be traced, if you will, as far back as classic times, was a theatre of improvisation and of pantomime. It specialized in a set of stock types of characters. The actors improvised the action on a given theme without any text. The character remained fixed, unchanging; the situation always changed, thereby furnishing the element of novelty. The action took place on the plane of fantasy.

Chaplin is the only actor of modern times to create such a successful universal character. Adhering to the strict classic rules, he made Charlie. He preserved the eternal mask of a fixed set of characteristics and a fixed costume—the little man with the derby, the cane, and the broken-down shoes, striving in the midst of poverty to retain the gentility and courtesy which he believes are superior attributes; searching with a romantic heart for beauty in the most sordid and unlikely spots on earth. Charlie belongs with Scaramouche and Harlequin, characters of an earlier age who outgrew their creators and assumed reality as symbols of their time.

The movie in the period when Chaplin first began to act was silent. It was unrealistic. It employed theatrical sets as backgrounds. It provided the ideal conditions for this classic art. The human voice achieves stylization best in song; it would have shattered the illusion if the fantastic person Charlie had spoken. Chaplin wearing the mask of Charlie became the greatest pantomime artist of our epoch. The plastic quality of his face permitted him the most delicate nuances of feeling visually. His infinite grace of movement and the precision of his gesture placed him beside the oustanding dancers of our time.

The last years have seen a revolution in our film technique. The silent movie has been displaced by the talkie. Photography has become so supple a medium that it rivals the texture and the plastic form of painting. The result has been a great advance in cinema art, and this new art has been built on *realism*. The Soviet film was the first to include a much larger segment of reality within the conventions of the film. It founded a new school of producers, added a much wider field in thematic material, and posed a demand for a realistic school of acting far beyond any achieved so far in the Western European or American theatres. Thus the restrictions of the medium which Chaplin employed in his early films have been abolished.

Chaplin's last film, *City Lights*, already presaged change and posited the necessity for his leaving the old form and striking out for a new one. *City Lights*, however, was conceived and made before the economic crisis.

The year 1931 marked a historic turning point in the fortunes of the vast majority of people in the United States. The depression, which so largely affected the middle classes, has changed the audience which loved and followed Charlie. A deep rift has occurred. Those who still have a stake in the system and believe they can salvage their security will amalgamate with the classes above them. The others—the vast majority—have had their economic basis wiped out; their standard of living has dropped. They have had to give up their dream of rising in the social scale; instead they are being pushed down. There are millions of unemployed. There are millions on government relief. A new generation is growing up which has not been able to find a place for itself and for whom the old illusions are meaningless.

Therefore in making *Modern Times* Chaplin faced a serious dilemma. He had to deal with a changed technique in the cinema and a changed audience. As a result he had to choose a new theme. But he had on his hands a fixed character—Charlie—who belonged and existed within the limits of a given art. In short, Chaplin has had the same difficulty in turning a corner in his art as little Charlie has in turning a street corner in the film.

Modern Times thus represents Chaplin's crisis in art. It is a film, done on a large canvas, which grapples with the fundamental problems of our times. Its hero, however, is still the optimistic, lovable Charlie—a clown.

But against the background of modern times a hero cannot be the pure clown. Poverty, unemployment, hunger are serious themes—they are the stuff of tragedy. Only from the vantage ground of security can they appear comical. Chaplin is acutely aware of the tragic implications of his theme. He knows that you can no more have pure comedy than pure poetry today. We live in an age of transition and the world is passing through a crisis which will involve a struggle between two totally different concepts of society.

This is the reason for the confusion in theme and in style in *Modern Times*. Aesthetically the film moves in two planes—that of reality and fantasy. Sometimes they run parallel but more often there is a headlong collision between them. Chaplin has endeavored to preserve Charlie intact. He has tried to preserve the classic form. But he has also had to admit a new world of reality, and the two are inimical. One must destroy the other.

The first sequence of *Modern Times*, in the fantastic factory, is delightful satire with a social sting. Words are unnecessary here. The humor is light and gay and for this reason many things like the speed-up, the regimentation, the prying boss, the feeding machine, which in reality would be painful, are simply amusing. A worker going mad from the speed-up is a sad subject, but kept strictly within the old formula it becomes delightful pantomime.

But in the next sequence, we are dropped onto the plane of reality. We see the inside of a jail. We are taken out of doors on the waterfront. This is a picture of a real background. We meet the hungry little gamine stealing bananas. She is a real child and a pathetic one—not a stock character whom we know. In a way, the fact that Charlie meets this gamine symbolizes Chaplin's desire to come in contact with reality in his art. Throughout the following scenes of mutual adventure, we feel the difference between them as characters. The gamine is a real girl who has waked in a dream and met a dream character—Charlie. She might have met Santa Claus just the same way. She is practical—she finds a home even if it is a hut in Hooverville; she has a few romantic illusions; she doesn't think it wrong to steal bananas and bread. She is a proletarian of the city streets. She is delighted with Charlie—his fantastic chivalry, his fairy tales of a dream cottage. But as a real character she demands to speak, to tell her story. Her pantomime is never convincing since it is a convention of fantasy applied to a realistic character.

When Charlie leaves the jail, where he has been sent for inadvertently picking up a red flag and leading an unemployment demonstration, he puts on his old garments of gentility. He is again the gentlemanly bum. After we have seen him as a factory worker, this shabby fellow seems ridiculous, particularly in the scene with the policeman. Hence the scenes of demonstrations and strike are not excessively funny. (These shots included newsreel pictures and a part of Charlie's audience took them seriously. They enjoyed it most when he got the better of the cops, but they wished him to do this on purpose, while as a matter of fact

Charlie participated in the demonstration and the strike only by accident. In a critical and real situation, an audience demands of its hero purposeful action.)

But as the action progresses on the plane of reality, Charlie's situation becomes too serious for his gentlemanly pretense, for his costume. We do not believe in this costume, for the illusion which created it is not shared by all the audience anymore. Just as the film juggles two planes of action and thus creates an emotional confusion in the reactions of the audience, so Charlie juggles his costume. Halfway through the picture, there occurs a break. The plane of reality recedes. Charlie reverts to his old self. The action slows but the funny business is increased. The old slapstick becomes dominant. There are many more laughs, but there is no doubt that the most comic sequences in the film are for the most part repetitions of his early works—*The Skating Rink, The Nightwatchman, The Floorwalker, The Singing Waiter*, etc. These sequences bear the same relation to the film as the autobiography of literary men to their work. It is a necessary résumé at a critical turning point.

Throughout the film, Charlie remains the same wistful, romantic, lonely individual and this in spite of his experience in a factory as a worker. Here Chaplin misses one of the most progressive elements of the machine—the discipline it imposes and the collective spirit it awakens in the workers. We do get suggestions of this collective spirit in the demonstration and the strike but we do not participate emotionally because the character Charlie never does.

Moreover, if Charlie had experienced these new emotions, he would be changed by his experience. But he is a fixed character. Hence the dilemma of the director. In the film, if Charlie had stayed long with the gamine, he would have changed in spite of himself. But the director, believing he must keep faith with his audience, insists that he hold to the familiar character with its fixed characteristics, ignoring the fact that the audience is not the same old audience.

To the end, Charlie remains the same lonely little *individual*. We leave him at the crossroads, in his old suit, with a bromidic optimistic caption. But we too have been through his adventures and we don't believe that things will be better for him, that he will ever become a gentleman or improve his fortunes. If he learns nothing from experience, he will only run into more troubles and we will lose patience with him. At best, it is a sad ending.

What is Charlie going to do next time? Get rid of his antiquated costume and the things it stands for, join with his fellowmen in distress, with whom he so deeply sympathizes? (But if he should do the latter, he would no longer be the Charlie we have known in the past—the little knight-errant of the shabby derby.) His wistful but optimistic romanticism is as out of date in the world today as was Don Quixote's tilting at the windmills. His audience for the most part has had to give up their optimistic illusions. He faces an aesthetic crisis. To follow his audience, now so sharply divided, he will have to choose which half of it he wishes to reach—the secure upper minority, or the vast majority of common folk from whom he has always drawn his strength. If the latter, he will be forced to leave his respectable shabby suit behind or deed it as a farewell gift to the secure minority. I for one believe that as a character he has enough vitality to live on without it. I would like to see him change and grow in the realistic new film world, and to hear his voice speak for him. *Little Charlie, what now?*

(*Several days after the above article had been set up in print, the author's point of view received unlooked-for substantiation from the words of Mr. Chaplin himself, who declared in a press interview held on February 19:* "I shall probably veer away from my tramp role some day. I just can't make him talk. He is a vestige of the silent days."—The Editors.)

Louella Parsons: Hearst's Hollywood Stooge

BY JOEL FAITH

MENTION the name of Louella Parsons within the confines of any select group of Hollywood's trulls, bawds, panderers, and chiselers and you will hear a flutter of jealous but respectful conversation.

For Louella Parsons, movie editor of William Randolph Heart's Universal Service, is subject to the awe and envy of every Hollywood highbinder. She is feared and admired by filmland's leading executives, men well versed in the arts of throat slitting. From them and from a fringe of cheap hangers-on, Louella is given her due as a past master at tactics which require apt use of the claw and the fang.

Louella's chief function is to ballyhoo Marion Davies, the blond girlfriend of her boss. Willie's greatest sorrow is that with all his money and power he has not been able to convince the American people that his bosom friend is an actress. Year after year the senile Sultan of San Simeon pours out his gold in more and more lavish streams trying to buy popularity for Marion. His chief aide in that attempted fraud is Louella. Thus Willie, Marion, and Louella constitute the most powerful triumvirate in Hollywood.

Louella was one of the first to write motion picture news for Willie. She wasn't so much in those days until, through her, Willie, then a comparatively young blade when you figure he is still going pretty strong at 70, made the acquaintance of numerous young actresses. Then one day Louella, who knew the kind of man Willie was, introduced Marion Davies to him. It must have been love at first sight, for the little blond girl graduate of the Convent of the Sacred Heart in New York—wiser than most convent graduates—from that meeting on became the object of the great man's attentions.

Dated from that time, too, is the long, warm friendship between Louella and Marion. That friendship is compounded not alone of sentiment, because Marion and Louella need each other. In Louella, Willie's girlfriend has an ardent champion who will stoop to anything to delude her readers that Marion is an actress. In Marion, Louella has a powerful friend at court. On her dressing table Louella keeps a photograph of Marion on which is written "To the best friend a girl ever had." The writer has profited by her membership in Willie's official family, for she has made it pay and pay and pay and pay.

Her salary is said to be $500 a week for writing the tripe which is printed in all Hearst papers and syndicated in many others through Universal Service. As toastmistress on the "Hollywood Hotel" radio hour, she draws another huge figure from Campbell's Soup, sponsors of the program. The "side money" she makes is enormous. When she married Dr. Harry Martin, Hollywood physician, she was given at least a quarter of a million dollars' worth of wedding presents. There is a "Parsons Shelf" in practically every major studio on which are placed her literary efforts. Every once in a while—too often for skinflint producers—Louella writes a scenario. Geniuses may stand ragged and starving outside the gates of Hollywood, but Louella has no trouble selling her scenario ideas. It is not within my knowledge that any of her stories has ever been made into a picture, but worldly wise producers pay her well.

Dr. Martin has profited also by being a son-in-law in Willie's official family. His knowledge of medicine, not to mention the fact that his wife is the powerful Louella, makes him much sought after as a technical director on pictures dealing with any phase of the medical profession. His "social position" has also given him a wide acquaintance among rich actors and actresses. He is a specialist in social diseases and his clients are many.

Harriet Parsons, Louella's daughter, is another beneficiary of her ma's power. For some time after finishing school Harriet found no trouble selling stories to fan magazines. Now she works at Columbia, supervising *Screen Snapshots*, intimate glimpses of stars in their relaxed moments. When Louella leaves town for a vacation "Parsons, Jr." takes over the column. To do the Parsons spawn credit, when Louella is away the writing becomes almost literate.

As I said earlier, Louella's chief job is to misrepresent Marion Davies to the American public. Her latest effort in this conspiracy against film fans is best shown by contrasting her review of *Page Miss Glory* with a review of the same opus in the *Hollywood Reporter*. The *Reporter* is a trade daily, written for businessmen. In order to survive it cannot lie too freely, although it is subject to pressure through purchase of its advertising space. Louella, unfortunately for the public, knows no such limitations. Take a look at this:

Louella's view:

> No picture in a long time has been more eagerly awaited than Marion's first Warner Brothers production, principally because she is the most important comedienne on the screen today and because this is her first picture under the Warner Brothers aegis. The consensus of opinion of the boys and girls who attended the preview of *Page Miss Glory* is that here is a picture that will speak for itself at the box office.

The *Reporter*'s view of Marion's box-office appeal:

> With every resource of the Warner First-National studios put at their disposal, it's a sad commentary that this picture turns out to be barely fair program entertainment that will have to depend on the drawing power of Dick Powell for its grosses.

Louella's view of the humor:

> All of the critics agreed that there is a delightful feeling of spontaneous, natural comedy throughout the story which never lessens or becomes forced. I do not think it amiss to say that seldom has any picture brought forth so many honest chuckles as this hilarious comedy. The whole picture is fun. There is a delightful combination of fast action and snappy dialogue that has been happily directed by Mervyn Le Roy.

The *Reporter*'s view:

> What actually comes forth is a long, drawn-out affair that relies on well-worn gags for laugh getters and with one or two exceptions—the old reliables that never fail—the laughs don't come off. Exhibit "A" of the humor: "Let's talk turkey." "I like steak." Miss Davies makes her first screen appearance in many months and tries real hard, but the net result is some pretty bad overacting and a conception of light comedy delivery that only needs a custard pie to bring back Mack Sennett.

Louella's view of Marion's beauty:

> Only a girl as beautiful as Marion Davies would be willing completely to disguise her lovely self in a makeup that is so entirely original as that of the chambermaid. But when Marion blossoms out with a wardrobe that is a triumph of the modiste's skill and in her own natural beauty she offers a contrast that is so exciting that she brought forth oh's and ah's that could never have been achieved had she started without this ridiculous preliminary makeup.

The *Reporter*:

> George Folsey's photography is excellent and so are the sets, but the gowns are something that not even a movie star could make you like.

Aside from her conspiracy with Marion to make people think Willie's bosom friend is an actress, Louella has taken it upon herself to give out more misinformation than any other newspaper or magazine writer in Hollywood. The job is one that comes naturally to her, for Louella's is a bland, invincible stupidity. She misspells names, gets details of happenings on the business side of the industry wrong, and makes some of the most incredible mistakes. Many of her boners are due to ignorance, many to her own carelessness, for she is a poor reporter and a wretched writer.

When RKO announced it would make *Green Mansions*, Louella immediately rushed into print with the inside information that Radio would bring W. H. Hudson to Hollywood to help write the screen version of his famous book. The author, of course, had been dead for lo, these many years.

In writing of Warner's decision to use music with *Midsummer Night's Dream*, Louella had this to say:

> Shakespeare or no Shakespeare, there should be some entertainment in films of this kind.

Several years ago when Warners chose Alan Mowbray for the part of George Washington in *Alexander Hamilton*, Louella, with a startling and amusing display of Hearst's "Buy American" stupidity which even she has seldom topped, delivered herself of this:

> It seems strange to me that an Englishman would be cast as the father of our country.

Probably because she can utter such ridiculous things she is kept pretty well off the subject of labor. Even during the Equity strike of 1929 in Hollywood when Conrad Nagel, the Christian Science reader, sold out his fellow workers, Louella steered clear of troubled waters except to say patronizingly that the striking actors didn't know how lucky they were and that "personally, the producers have always been very lovely to me." At that time the *Los Angeles Examiner* and other Hearst papers were so bitter against the striking actors and gave so many columns of space to attacks upon them in their news sections that Louella didn't have to bring her popgun into play.

The Parsons column is devoted largely to plugging Marion Davies; to praising Hearst-Warner Brothers for their vicious antilabor and war-fostering films, and as a receptacle for all the cheap drivel that clutters up Hollywood drawing rooms. However, Louella can write upon a social theme, in her own inimitable way, when her pocketbook is threatened. Once she wrote an attack upon the income tax system, pet hatred of the patriotic Willie, and I leave it to you, gentle reader, whether you have ever seen anything in print to rival this piece, in which she bellows with all the indignation of a Holstein heifer that has just been slapped athwart the buttocks:

> "Taxation without representation is tyranny." Those words have rung down the years since the historical Boston tea party was the first stepping stone to America's glorious independence. Today these words have come to have an ironic meaning to some of our motion picture people in Hollywood, who have been so flagrantly and unfairly treated by the income tax collectors.
>
> Our own American Revolution was caused directly by taxation when King George failed to listen to the pleas of the long-suffering colonists. Injustice is bad enough in any class, or individual, but it is particularly outrageous in the case of motion picture people because the whole system of income taxation is an unjust one; and when the exactions of the tax collector are added to the injustice the situation is doubly unjust and intolerable. All the motion picture folk are taxed on their big incomes and no provision is allowed for the lean years.

Then there is this revealing closing argument:

> Everyone has an innate love for his country and certainly no one more than the motion picture player. The first profession to rally to the cause when Uncle Sam declared war against Germany was the motion picture industry. Mary Pickford, Douglas Fairbanks and Charlie Chaplin dropped their work and made a tour of the country selling Liberty Bonds. The motion picture screens were opened to propaganda. The Division of Films was formed so that the right messages might be disseminated to the people. Can Uncle Sam so soon forget?

Louella's spitefulness is well-known in Hollywood. Let an actor imply, as Leslie Howard did by gracefully backing out of the lead in a second picture opposite Willie's girlfriend, that Marion is a ham actress and Louella will "let him have it" in her column. Let anyone cross her, as Tallulah Bankhead did once, and there is nothing she will not do to get revenge. She nags spitefully in her column at people she doesn't like. As for her indifference to the old adage about "glass houses," you should read the way she publicly takes to task certain Hollywood actresses who occasionally go to dinner with married men! Once a new ticket taker on the door of Loew's State theatre in Los Angeles didn't recognize her as she swept through the door. How could he see in this waddling bovine the same radiant vision of the faked published photographs? He stopped her, thinking of all things that she might be the kind of person who would want something for nothing, and he almost lost his job. Louella did her best to have the youth fired, but a fair house manager took the boy off the door and saved him his job.

Laughter burns in the heart when one realizes what Louella's position in Hollywood indicates. She is Hollywood's sacred cow. The feeling of reverence, fear, and awe she inspires in leaders of the motion picture industry speaks for itself. That this waddling drivel-monger, this venomous, disagreeable woman can be respected by the big shots, is a sad, sad commentary upon the industry. There is some hope, however, that the increasingly successful boycott of Hearst's papers will greatly weaken the influence of "the best friend a girl ever had."

THREATS AND NEWS FROM INSIDE THE HEARST PRESS EMPIRE

BEFORE we decided to risk printing "Louella Parsons: Hearst's Hollywood Stooge," we had considered the probability of a costly, dangerous,

HOLLYWOOD EXTRA! MAN
SUPPOSED TO KNOW THE REAL
IDENTITY OF JOEL FAITH
MOBBED AT PARTY
—*James Kelly*

and difficult-to-contest libel suit. Sure enough, the very day *New Theatre* difficult-to-contest libel suit. Sure enough, the very day *New Theatre* appeared—and sold out—on Los Angeles newsstands, William Randolph Hearst prepared to strike back. He had a good case to charge defamation of character. Bill Gropper's sardonic cover had pictured Hearst as a puppet master holding Louella on one knee and his mistress, actress Marion Davies, on the other, adding insult to the injury to him of the article's accusations. I received a number of long-distance calls from Hollywood writers and directors congratulating us for our courage in taking on this despotic multimillionaire, who a few years later would be depicted by Orson Welles in *Citizen Kane*—with pious denials from Welles that there had been any intent to depict Kane as Hearst. But "Joel Faith" had not held back any punches in his article, and we could make no denial of the intent of his blistering attack on Hearst and the two ladies who served him in their different capacities.

That night I received a phone call in the small Hell's Kitchen apartment I shared with George and Louise Redfield.

"It's for you, Herb," George said, "some guy who sounds like he's muffling his voice with a handkerchief."

I answered the phone. "This is a call from Mr. J. F. Pseudonym," the voice said. I turned and whispered to George and Louise, "Joel Faith, who else!"

The magazine was "selling like bootleg booze at five dollars a copy," Joel said, and the movie colony was betting Hearst would turn all his power and influence to close us down. Joel gave us the "inside info" that his call was to advise us of a summons to be issued in New York which would force me to face charges in court of libel and defamation of character. He warned us that a judge could force me to reveal his identity—and complicity.

I assured our "secret agent" he could sleep safely. I would get legal advice to handle the summons and suit. And I would go to jail if necessary to protect his identity.

Early the next morning, George and I went to the office figuring I would receive the summons in time to break the news to the press and radio and thus get a head start lining up public sympathy and support for our defense. My desk was the nearest one to the door, so when the expected knock came I said to George, with resignation and acceptance of what was to come, "Here's the bad news." At the door, I hesitated a moment apprehensively since I had never received a summons before.

I opened the door. A tall, distinguished-looking man of about fifty stood there, carrying an attaché case. The conversation as I recall was close to the following:

"Good morning, sir," the man said, "I'd like to speak to the editor, Mr. Kline."

"You're looking at him," I replied. "And this is George Redfield, our managing editor."

The man smiled, then took an envelope from his attaché case.

I took the envelope and said, "I suppose your summons is in my name alone, as we don't have 'Joel Faith' on the premises and have no idea of his whereabouts."

"You suppose wrong, young fellow. Just open the envelope."

I did. In it were five crisp, new $20 bills. "What is this for?" I asked, wondering if it was some kind of bribe. One hundred dollars then was worth five times as much as now and was harder to come by.

"Well, you may not believe it," the man said, "but I'm a Hearst Syndicate editor. Four of my colleagues and I decided on a contribution of twenty dollars each to pay our respects to an editor with guts enough to tackle old man Hearst's and Louella's lawyers. We decided we loved your exposé as much as we hated the big boss and his sacred cow, Louella. Also we admire your 'Joel Faith,' whoever he may be. It's muckraking at its best, but a judge would be more likely to side with a famous press lord than with a radical editor. He could force you to disclose Faith's real identity in court."

I told him that the threat had already reached us, but that Joel's identity was safe and not known to George or anyone besides myself and the author. If it meant going to jail to protect my source, I wouldn't be the first editor to be put behind bars, nor the first whose constitutional rights had been disregarded.

The man nodded and smiled. Then he asked if he could buy ten copies of the magazine. George grinned and gave him the ten, plus some back issues, asking him slyly if he'd like a free subscription in someone else's name—since it was assumed he'd been careful not to give his own.

"No thanks," he replied. Then he said somewhat ruefully, "I had real guts when I was a young writer like you fellows, but after twenty years in a safe, well-paid job, I guess you could classify me, like Louella, as 'a Hearst stooge.' I'll just leave now that I've expressed our editorial respects."

George and I looked at the $20 bills in disbelief. Then we decided to call our key staff members for an emergency meeting, hoping we could decide what to do before the inevitable summons came. Soon we met and excitedly discussed different courses to follow. Dave Crystal, Bob Steck, George, Leo, and Mark all urged that I should get out of town fast, even for a few days' delay, to evade the process server until we could line up our own legal help, perhaps through the International Labor Defense. I remained undecided until Molly Thacher had a bright idea: I should head for the center of the maelstrom, Hollywood, and take along an extra suitcase containing a few hundred copies of the magazines. I could use them to contact rich "sympathizers," who would be encouraged to contribute to a defense fund. Then Mark added that I should also take Irwin Shaw's typed manuscript of *Bury the Dead* with me and try to set up a New Theatre Night à la *Lefty* to attract whoever in the movie colony wouldn't be afraid to show up.

I hadn't been to the West Coast since my trip laboring with the black gang in the engine room of the SS *Colorado*. I was easily persuaded to escape to Hollywood as fast as I could get to the airport.

We figured there was enough money on hand, plus the $100 from the Hearst editor, to cover my plane trip and a few weeks of modest living costs. I said if I ran out of funds I could "bum" my way back as I'd done in my other wanderings. But Manny Eisenberg, our newest and only comparatively well-off editorial associate, was outraged at my suggestion. "It would be undignified for the editor of *New Theatre* to bum his way and maybe get clobbered in jail by police as a vagrant," Manny said. He offered to pay his own way out so he could help with his Hollywood contacts and also, if need be, see that I would get back at his expense.

We packed quickly and hurried to the airport, feeling elated to be en route to a wonderful adventure. Just before the call to board, I phoned the office to check if a process server had shown up. Instead, I was told there had been a call from "Mr. Pseudonym," first asking for me, then confiding "inside info" that Hearst bigwigs had persuaded their boss not to sue. They had convinced him that a suit would only give *New Theatre* greater publicity and do more damage to Louella, Marion, and the Hearst image. "Mr. Pseudonym" had responded to the news of my coming out with Manny, and said he'd arrange for someone to meet us. We went off, wondering what would be next in our lives.

The trip out in the smaller planes of that time was a bit turbulent, especially as I passed over Iowa and my old hometown where I'd gone to the movies since childhood, never dreaming I'd ever see the glamour of Hollywood. Manny proved a delightful companion, making the fellow passengers nearby and the stewardesses laugh at his mostly self-deprecatory stories.

When we arrived we were greeted by two people: playwright and screenwriter Arthur Kober, who had invited Manny as his houseguest, and "Lou Norden," the pen name for our magazine's Hollywood editor. "Lou" said he couldn't resist coming to meet me for the first time after a year of correspondence and despite the risks to his job at Paramount. He drove me to Lionel Stander's house, where the character comedian, who was a *New Theatre* fan, greeted me warmly. Lionel had a day off from studio work and proved a friendly, generous, and amusing host who also had writing talent and contributed many witty lines to his roles. He was also very serious and deeply concerned about social issues and had been courageous about publicly expressing his strong Left sympathies.

The first night was fun. Lionel took us for a trip downtown to hear Jumping Joe Turner and the great jazz at Central's Avenue's celebrated Club Alabam. But from then on, it was hard work. Manny and I divided the tasks of contracting "sympathizers" among the writers, directors, and actors who had been so enthusiastic about the magazine. We were welcomed especially for exposing Louella Parsons's blackmailing them for guest-appearances on her radio show. Besides promises of articles and inside material for more slashing "Joel Faith" exposés, some volunteered "anonymous" donations—twenties, fifties, and even $100 bills. Sylvia Sidney got me to two wealthy men: William K. Howard, the highly regarded director, who gave me $250, and B. P. Schulberg, the head of Paramount Studios, who said he'd match Bill Howard's $250 plus $50 more—then he called his radical son, Budd, at Dartmouth, introduced me over the phone, and said he was giving the $300 in Budd's name to cover his own tracks as Paramount couldn't afford to tangle with Hearst.

Soon Manny, with help from Kober and S. J. Perelman, and I, with help from Dudley Nichols and Donald Ogden Stewart, had raised almost

$2,000. We had also arranged a reading performance of *Bury the Dead*, but our stars, Fredric March and Florence Eldridge, who had just read the play and loved it, would not be able to do the reading for four weeks. So we arranged a symposium to take place as soon as possible, where Clifford Odets, myself, and whoever else would join us as main speakers would discuss theatre, film, and particularly the influence of *New Theatre* magazine in filmland. We planned to charge a $2 admission and hoped to clear some profits on the evening. But our main purpose would be to show the industry that important film talents would not be afraid to associate with Odets, the revolutionary playwright, and the editor behind the publication of Joel Faith's sensational exposé. We set the date for a week later. Afterward Manny and I planned to follow up leads for donations during the few days before our return to New York.

The week before the symposium, although I was officially barred from the studios, I visited several with the aid of several stars, directors, and writers who obtained personal guest passes for me. James Cagney invited me to Warner Brothers. He was warm, friendly, and immediately agreed to a *New Theatre* feature article on him. It was subsequently written by "Forrest Clark," a pen name Lincoln Kirstein sometimes used when he was not writing on dance. And Dudley Nichols and John Ford invited us to have lunch and visit them at RKO (after the initial difficulties that Manny describes in his interview). On the set Ford showed us the bright red socks he was wearing in honor of the Parsons-Hearst-Davies article. But he refused to believe my denial of being Joel Faith. Ford said he hated giving interviews. Still he gave one to Manny anyway, saying, "I'll do it just to prove I'm not scared of Louella."

Groucho Marx left a studio pass at the gate, which got me into MGM. We hit it off so well that Groucho invited me to dinner at his home that night, together with a friend, screenwriter Norman Krasna. The dinner was marvelous and so was the conversation, mostly serious at first. Groucho described the Marx Brothers' trip to Moscow and their favorable reaction to the theatre masterpieces and to the way artists were held in the sort of esteem reserved for sports heroes in America. Then Groucho's brothers came over, one by one. Harpo brought a small, beautiful painting he had just completed, and it was fascinating for me to hear the "silent" brother talk. There was a lot of kidding that evening, including some at my expense. But it was all in good-natured fun, and I got to meet a different kind of "Marx Brothers" than the public clowns they joked with me about. When Norman was getting ready to drive me to Stander's home, I asked Groucho if he would write an article for *New Theatre*. He promised to do so but never did—and in later years, when we'd meet by chance in Hollywood, he'd pretend he didn't recognize me, then say, "Oh, yeah, you're the guy who kept turning down my articles without even the courtesy of sending me a rejection slip." Once, though, Groucho confessed that afterthoughts about trouble with Hearst had kept him from writing what I still regret never reached our magazine.

But the most surprising development of that week before the symposium came from my supposed close resemblance to John Garfield—which had been noticed during Julie's Group Theatre days in New York. I was introduced to a very successful producer of low-budget films for RKO, a writer whose "B" picture hits had earned him an executive job with a free hand in his productions. I was amazed when, after describing himself as a "closet radical," he made me an incredible offer to star in his films as "RKO's poor man's John Garfield." The studio had urged him to find a young leading man who could play "Garfield" roles, "strong but vulnerable," as he put it. He thought I'd fit the bill. I wouldn't even have to wait for "test" approval. He would put me in a small role the next week and could arrange an option deal for a seven-year RKO contract starting at $300 a week. My salary would go up $200 a week each year until the last two years when I would get $1500 a week. I wouldn't need to give ten percent of my earnings to an agent, so I could give it to *New Theatre* for years to come. Great for the magazine; high earnings and a life of luxury for me.

I asked him if this was a joke. He insisted it was real. I thanked him, but said I'd rather be a low-paid, "A" quality editor of our magazine than a highly paid "B" picture actor making a fool of myself as a Garfield imitator. The producer said I was "a crazy idealist" but that he admired me for my convictions. Then he asked me a favor—that he not be mentioned in anything I'd write about my Hollywood trip in *New Theatre.*

Soon came the evening for the symposium—a sellout with quite a few Hollywood notables in the five-hundred-seat auditorium. Rouben Mamoulian, the Theatre Guild director of *Porgy and Bess* and film director of *Queen Christina, Blood and Sand, Becky Sharp,* and *Love Me Tonight,* joined Clifford Odets and me as one of the main speakers. Clifford started things off with his characteristic flamboyant eloquence. He said *New Theatre* would stimulate efforts by moviemakers of conscience and talent to emulate the theatre of social protest with low-cost, independently produced films. He suggested that even people like himself working for the major studios should volunteer part-time to help create entertainment of social significance.

The audience was still applauding Clifford when Mamoulian's turn came. But Clifford took a moment more, waving a copy of the *Bury the Dead* script and praised the magazine and me for discovering and planning to produce this play by a great new talent, a twenty-two-year-old youth named Irwin Shaw. These remarks were met with added applause. Then Mamoulian spoke and credited *New Theatre* with making a significant contribution to theatre arts in America. Regretfully, he expressed his doubt that any magazine could influence the money-making purposes of the Hollywood industry, but he felt that the magazine should continue urging creative artists to try. He also revealed he had been warned by his agent not to appear with "notorious radicals like Odets and Kline." But he had decided as a liberal and a naturalized citizen that he would dare to live up to his American constitutional rights and join with us to say what he pleased. The audience cheered him then and again when he finished speaking in support of the Directors' Guild against the recent efforts to destroy it.

When my turn came, I announced that the magazine would soon feature other articles telling the truth about various practices we opposed in the industry. However, our main purpose was to emphasize positive articles about film artists that we admired. I said we were particularly interested in coming out strongly for their Screen Guilds. Also that I hoped our reviews by Robert Stebbins and others would help the sort of dedicated filmmakers Clifford Odets had spoken of. Stebbins's name, like Joel Faith's, elicited loud, approving applause.

The symposium turned out a considerable success. We cleared almost $1,000 above expenses—in admissions, subscriptions, and donations, some given rather furtively as fear in Hollywood of open identification with the Left ran deep. Together with other money Manny and I had raised, we returned to New York City a few days later with almost $3,000, to the cheers of our staff. The funds enabled us to pay the printer's back bill and get new credit to produce our biggest issue, the April 1936 issue containing *Bury the Dead*, a sellout of 35,000—equal to the heavily financed and advertised *Stage Magazine* and double *Theatre Arts Monthly*. Also we had lined up new contributors in Hollywood, some of whom are reprinted here.

I didn't confide to anyone, even to Manny during the trip or to my brother Mark, the real identity of Joel Faith. I avoided much questioning over the years while he was still rightfully fearful of permanent blacklisting. Now, however, long after his death, I will reveal he was a man I came to know, like, and admire for the courageous risks he took in writing for *New Theatre*. He was Charles "Chuck" Daggett, a skilled newspaperman who had turned to film PR work and was engaged by Hearst and Louella Parsons as her main rewrite man and close associate. When Chuck saw at close hand how Louella was doing her vicious blackmailing of celebrities, he decided to quit. But he stayed on briefly confiding only in "Lou Norden" as he collected the material for his sensational exposé. He had grinned mischievously as he told me how he had done his best to seem sympathetic when Louella had asked him plaintively, "Tell me, Chuck, who do you think could find out so much about me?"

John Ford: Fighting Irish

BY EMANUEL EISENBERG

MR. FORD wasn't in to anybody, the information clerk assured me; the secretary had just told him so. But I had been granted an appointment the day before. The clerk shrugged and called the secretary again. All right, I could go into the office, and he pressed a releasing button with an expression that said: for all the good it'll do you.

The secretary was extremely considerate and greatly concerned for my sanity. See Mr. Ford *today*? Did I know that he was making tests of Hepburn? That the filming of *Mary of Scotland* was to begin the day after tomorrow? She could conceive of no urgency impressive enough for disturbing him. I really must have made a mistake. Or Mr. Ford had not been aware of his own involvements in suggesting the appointment. It was quite hopeless. No one could see him today.

I walked on the mock streets of the enclosed studio city. Deserted. What would I do with the morning? I had made no more than two turns when suddenly, incredibly, there stood the unobtainable Mr. Ford, chatting leisurely with a couple of men. It was too good, too much like the mechanical ending of a joke with an overheavy buildup. I managed to catch his eye; he winked in recognition; we strolled over to the office; Dudley Nichols soon joined us; and we sat for almost two hours in an easy, informal, wandering talk. Officially he could be located or approached by no one in the studio, yet a stranger wandering illegitimately around the lot might bump into him and attract him away from schedule for a period. The nongiver of interviews found NEW THEATRE and its point of view so challenging that he stretched five minutes to 120 and extended a further invitation to come down to the set next week and watch him direct (something Dudley Nichols described as a distinct rarity).

For Ford is Irish and a fighter. He has fought for this way of living within the film industry and he has had to fight for the stories that interested him and the methods he believed in.

Pictures like *The Informer* do not come into existence lightly. To the frantic but still hopeful devotee its appearance—or the appearance of any other film on such a high level—is revelation, oasis, and consummation, a sudden reward in the stoical pilgrimage of picturegoing; but to one whose eyes have been exposed ever so briefly to the mechanics and finances of Hollywood production, the sheer physical emergence of *The Informer* is a small miracle. It began over the dead bodies of all the money lads; it was permitted to carry through in the periodic embarrassed concession to Art, an essence relied upon to secure the equally obscure quality of Prestige; and when it broke across the tape not only with high critical acclaim but with $100,000 of profit, almost the sum it had been expected to lose, confusion was intense. Such reckless and audacious efforts are not supposed to make good.

John Ford is among the startling handful of men in films who believe that a picture, to make any sense, must be conceived from the first day of action by a fixed group of workers dedicated to seeing it through from beginning to end. This is so violently in contrast to the anarchist principles of putting anybody to work who happens to be around and never quite knowing the next week's program of operation (creatively speaking) that Ford is considered something of a forbidding fanatic and accordingly permitted—but not too often—to function severely in his own way.

He has been in pictures since 1914, thinks entirely in terms of cinema, and works as a craftsman. The conception of a frame, a composition, and a camera angle is rarely something he simply hands over to the highly skilled technicians around him; it has validity and completeness only after he has scrambled up the ladder to the platform and studied the actual register inside the box. His consistent participation in all of the aspects of production sometimes makes it difficult to distinguish him from among the property men, electricians, and camera workers. Ford's high talent for simultaneous leadership and collaboration is conceded by everyone who has ever worked with him to be almost without parallel in the movies.

"After all, there's nothing surprising about the difficulty of doing things you yourself believe in in the movies," he said, "when you consider that you're spending someone else's money. And a lot of money. And he wants a lot of profit on it. That's something you're supposed to worry about, too."

"Trouble is, most of them can't imagine what'll make them money outside of what's already been made and what's already made them money before."

"Exactly! That's why it's a constant battle to do something fresh. First they want you to repeat your last picture. You talk 'em down. Then they want you to continue whatever vein you succeeded in with the last picture. You're a comedy director or a spectacle director or a melodrama director. You show 'em you've been each of these in turn, and effectively, too. So they grant you range. Another time they want you to knock out something *another* studio's gone and cleaned up with. Like a market. Got to fight it every time. Never any point where you can really say you have full freedom for your own ideas to go ahead with."

"How do you explain such a crazy setup?" I asked. "By block booking? The star system? The fact that it's first an industry and second an art?"

"I used to blame it largely on the star system," the large genial Irishman told me. "They've got the public so that they want to see one favorite performer in anything at all. But even that's being broken down. You don't think *The Informer* went over because of McLaglen, do you? Personally, I doubt it. It was because it was *about* something. I'm no McLaglen fan, you know. And do you know how close *The Informer* came to being a complete flop? It was considered one, you know—until you fellows took it up. You fellows *made* that picture. And that's what the producers are going to learn, are already learning, in fact: there's a new kind of public that wants more honest pictures. They've got to give 'em to 'em."

"How do you think they'll go about it?" I wanted to know. "That is, if they go about it at all."

"Oh, they will," he assured me. "They've got to turn over picture making into the hands that know it. Combination of author and director running the works: that's the ideal. Like Dudley Nichols and me. Or Riskin and Capra."

The point startled me. "I thought directors were running the works completely now."

Ford snorted, amused. "Oh, yeah? Do you know anything about the way they're trying to break directorial power now? To reduce the director to a man who just tells actors where to stand?" He proceeded to describe a typical procedure at four of the major studios today. The director arrives at nine in the morning. He has not only never been consulted about the script to see whether he likes it or feels fitted to handle it but may not even know what the full story is about. They hand him two pages of straight dialogue or finally calculated action. Within an hour or less he is expected to go to work and complete the assignment the same day, all the participants and equipment being prepared for him without any say or choice on his part. When he leaves at night, he has literally no idea what the next day's work will be.

"And is that how movies are going to be made now?" I asked, incredulous. "Like a Ford car?"

He smiled wryly. "Not if the Screen Directors' Guild can help it, boy. Hang around and watch some fireworks."

This Guild, of which Ford is one of the most embattled members, if and when it aligns itself with the Screen Actors' Guild and the Screen Writers' Guild, a not-too-distant possibility, will offer the autocratic money interests of the movies the most serious challenge of organization they have known to date.

Talk shifted to *The Informer*. Ford spoke of the great difficulty of persuading the studio that it ought to be tackled at all. He and Nichols arranged to take a fraction of their normal salaries for the sheer excitement of the venture; also, of course, to cut down production cost. Now, of course, the studio takes all the credit for the acclaim and the extraordinary number of second runs and for the Motion Picture Academy award—although Dudley Nichols's formal rejection of the award created considerable ructions. Nichols, it need scarcely be added, is one of the leading spirits of the Screen Writers' Guild.

But what about the ending of the picture? I asked. Wasn't that a concession? So many of the criticisms had objected to it. Yes, said Ford, it was a compromise: the plan had been to show Gypo dying alone on the docks, and this had been just a little too much for the producers. Still, the religious ending was so much in keeping with the mystical Irish temperament, Ford maintained, that it was pretty extreme to characterize it as superimposed sentimentality.

How about more such pictures? What were the chances?

"If you're thinking of a general run of social pictures, or even just plain honest ones, it's almost hopeless. The whole financial setup is against it. What you'll get is an isolated courageous effort here and there. The thing to do is to encourage each man who's trying, the way you fellows have done. Look at Nichols and me. We did *The Informer*. Does that make it any easier to go ahead with O'Casey's *The Plough and the Stars*, which we want to do after *Mary of Scotland*? Not for a second. They *may* let us do it as a reward for being good boys. Meanwhile we're fighting to have the Abbey Players imported intact and we're fighting the censors and fighting the so-called financial wizards at every point."

"Actually tackling social themes would be marvelous, of course," I put in at this point. "But what seems to us almost as important right now is to give the straight version of any aspect of life the movies *do* choose to handle. To avoid distortion and misrepresentation in favor of one interest or another. Don't you think that can be managed *within* this setup?"

"It can and should!" he exclaimed. "And it's something I always try to do. I remember a few years ago, with a Judge Priest picture, putting in an antilynching plea that was one of the most scorching things you ever heard. They happened to cut it, purely for reasons of space, but I enjoyed doing that enormously. And there can be more things like that."

"Then you do believe, as a director, in including your point of view in a picture about things that bother you?"

He looked at me as if to question the necessity of an answer. Then: "What the hell else does a man live for?"

Ford, who is on record as having directed about a hundred pictures, selects *Men Without Women* as his favorite. His desire is to do a film about the men and women workers in the wings of film production; they are the only people in "the industry" who interest him at all. That this is not remotely near being the affectation it may sound like to some is attested by Dudley Nichols, who admires John Ford as one of the most fearless, honest, and gifted men in Hollywood. Ford's house, says Nichols, is the same one he has lived in for fifteen years now: it has never occurred to him to "gold it up" or change it. No movie star or executive may ever be found visiting it. Electricians, property men, and camera men are the people invariably hanging around—and in this choice of unprominent and unsung companions may very well be found the key to the fighting Irishman's life as a clear-eyed craftsman.

The Films Make History

BY ROBERT STEBBINS

THE EXTENT of a poet's obligation to respect the facts of history, assuming that a certain objectivity is possible, has never been established. Nor is it the purpose or within the power of this paper to establish it. There was a time when any condensation, corruption, or falsification was considered quite appropriate to the historical romance and romantic drama. We can only say that at present there is a movement away from such a tendency. Maxwell Anderson's *Mary of Scotland*, in its approach

*Drawing by
Aline Fruhauf*

to history, belongs unfortunately to the former period. Even a cursory reading of Scotland's affairs during the years of his play, 1561–87, discloses a bewilderingly large list of factual variances. So crossed and crisscrossed is this period with diverse and clashing interests, with a simultaneity of dozens of actions and conflicts, that regardless of a poet's skill, it would appear impossible to be compressed within the framework of the conventional three-act play. *Mary of Scotland*, it would seem, was inevitably doomed to failure.

Under these circumstances, the film version of *Mary of Scotland*, directed by John Ford and authored by Dudley Nichols, was defeated before the battle began. The film not only inherited all the ills of the original play, and in several instances added faults of its own facture, but even deprived itself of several of the original's virtues. Like the play, the film has no directives, no point of view, is entirely unclear as to its purpose. Certain matters are touched upon but never knitted together to make a consistent fabric of ideas—religious intolerance, the warmth of France, the sourdoughs of Scotland, Catholicism against the Protestant Rebellion, Spain against England, Stuarts against Tudors, idealism against practical statesmanship. The flow of time is halted. The events of twenty-six years are telescoped into one or two years, it would seem. There is a stereotyped second-act episode in which Mary implores Beaton, her lady-in-waiting, to marry for love that is on the low ideational plane of *Graustark* or *The Merry Widow*. The play was wordy to begin with, and the change from verse to prose only increases the talkativeness, which was to be expected when one considers the ability of verse to put things more succinctly. Significantly enough, the one scene that really got going, the death of Rizzio, played beautifully by John Carradine, was comparatively underwritten.

Chiefly, however, the play and even more the film go to pieces on the reefs of faulty characterization. Mr. Anderson has gone to such embarrassing lengths in taking sides against Mary's enemies that as a consequence they possess no credible characteristics and no dimensions. But the movie goes beyond Mr. Anderson. In the play John Knox is human enough to answer Mary's plea for help with "Your Majesty, I should be untrue to myself and my calling if I refused counsel where it is asked." The movie makes him an old goat and nothing more; the chieftains—a pack of dogs; Elizabeth—a spinster with the green disease; Darnley—almost a homosexual. There is no conflict of sympathies. We detest Mary's opponents but at the same time cannot regard her with more than pity. She is a will-less creature far removed from Swinburne's characterization: "forgiveness of injuries was as alien from her fierce loyal spirit as forgetfulness of benefits."

Mary fails for many reasons—her idealism and trust—"For there is judgment somewhere in the air, what I am will be known, what's false will wash out in the rains"—her frankness in a hypocritical age, religious intolerance, loyalty to Catholicism, her family pride and obligations—"I abate not one jot of my good blood's lien on the English throne"—but chiefly she founders on her love for Bothwell. Now here was something for a movie to sink its teeth into. It does and bites the remaining life out of the theme. Miss Hepburn of the quivering lip helps complete the ruin of our sympathies. At least in the play Mary had her moments of strength—"I too have a will—a will as strong as your own, and enemies of my own and my long revenge to carry through. I will have my way in my time though it burn my heart out and yours." This aspect of Mary never emerges convincingly in Hepburn's investment of the role. It is manifestly absurd to say, as did the *New Republic*'s Mr. Otis Ferguson in the course of as purple a patch of pussyfooting as we've seen, that if the movie didn't give us Mary of Scots it gave us Hepburn and they are both great ladies. Great ladies, perhaps, but at loggerheads. Hepburn is undeniably beautiful to look at with her twisted if monotonous mask, but for all intents and purposes her Mary is Alice Adams and the heroine of *Morning Glory*—tentative, weak, jittery, full of nerves and enervations.

As cinema, that vague entity, the movie fails. John Ford, who, of all his Hollywood confreres, has the ability to give his work intensity, as witness *The Informer* and *The Prisoner of Shark Island*, is here mannered and stylized—a sure indication that he was not at ease in the play. His lighting effects seem forced and repetitious. The action is slow and segmented. Furthermore he leans on the work of other men. The courtroom scene was obviously conceived with a long backward glance at Carl Dreyer's *The Passion of Joan of Arc*. The upward pan that concluded the film was borrowed from *A Tale of Two Cities*—the telepathic communion between Mary and Bothwell from *Dark Angel*, *Peter Ibbetson*, and innumerable Hollywood essays in the mystical. The whole enterprise is a regrettable one and should serve as a warning against the indiscriminate taking over of unsuitable stage successes to the screen.

Month of Bounties

BY ROBERT STEBBINS

MARCH was a month of bounties, however mixed they proved on examination. Seldom has the moviegoer had the opportunity of observing within a limited period such varied productions as *You Only Live Once*, *The Plough and the Stars*, *Lost Horizon*, and *The Good Earth* and the work of such distinctly divergent talents as Fritz Lang, John Ford, Frank Capra, and Sidney Franklin.

Of the directors, Fritz Lang proved far and away the most individualized and absorbing. The scenario of *You Only Live Once*, which Gene Towne and Graham Baker banged out with brass knuckles, may have been bloated beyond decency by overripe coincidences, but the film from a directorial point of view provided an occasion of intense pleasure. All the mastery that went into *M* and *Fury* was in evidence, though sadly handicapped by a script that lacked social grounding and strained credulity to the breaking point. Nevertheless, the director, through a highly developed sense of social awareness, subtle implication, and sheer drive managed to eke out a temporary victory over his material. Few scenes in recent films possess greater cogency of comment than the attempt of the state to save the life of Eddie Taylor so that it can execute him at the appointed hour. Everything that medical science has stored up during the ages is called upon. We see a brief flash of a modern sterilization tunnel. A foot steps on the foot pedal of a wash basin. The doctor's hands are being rubbed together. A split second later the Warden has Doctor Stanton on the phone.

Doctor Stanton (into phone): "He's weak, but he'll be strong enough by then. I'll keep him in the hospital where we can watch him—until the time comes." (Hangs up)

Warden: "Thanks, Doctor. (Hangs up and turns to Halsey) The execution will go on as scheduled—at eleven o'clock."

Previously in the film, Lang has arraigned our institutions most bitterly for refusing the ex-convict the right to rehabilitate himself as a worthwhile member of the social organism. The conceptual penetration that goes into the episode where Eddie pleads in vain to get his job back is overwhelming.

Instances of Lang's ingenuity abound throughout the film. We need but mention the newspaper office with the editor awaiting the verdict, or the use made of the rifle sight in the last sequence to create great tension. Lang's ability to achieve dramatic effectiveness by the use of objects, although this is but one of his methods, is possessed to equal degree by no director save possibly Alfred Hitchcock. There is this difference. In Hitchcock, this *Sachlichkeit* seldom justifies itself beyond pure virtuosity. What one gets in his case is almost always shock for shock's sake. We make this distinction only to point out a similar danger that lies before Fritz Lang in the event that the scripts available to him deteriorate even beyond *You Only Live Once*. We devoutly wish this eventuality never to become fact.

You Only Live Once was considerably marred by an unpleasant, mawkish last-minute addition to the end of the film, probably through Hays office insistence. Father Dolan, whom Eddie has murdered, appears from out of a misty heaven to open the gates for the slain couple. But this is mere child's play in light of the tampering *The Plough and the Stars* endured.

It would not be too extreme to state that, all things considered, *The Plough and the Stars* is not the work of Dudley Nichols, John Ford, or Sean O'Casey. The running time of the picture—sixty-seven minutes—should be some indication of what a murderous hacking was here! There is hardly a "quickie" that would attempt to make its points in as little time. Who is specifically to blame one cannot say. Certainly the fact that Ford has steadfastly refused to see the film and that after he left the lot much of the film was reshot "to get more love interest," as the trade papers put it, clearly indicates whence the odor rises. To some extent, however, it is possible to discuss *The Plough and the Stars* as the work of Ford and Nichols on the basis of the material that appears both in the film and the original scenario.

The Plough and the Stars must have presented grave difficulties to the scenarist, Dudley Nichols—practically insoluble difficulties, in our opinion. To begin with, the play, whatever one may think of its point of view, possesses the validity and prerogatives of a work of art and therefore a great degree of scenaric fidelity was required. But O'Casey obviously regarded the 1916 revolt as a tragic and needless waste of life. On the other hand, Nichols felt strongly, and justifiably so, the great glory of the Dublin uprising. Consequently he was faced with reconciling two dichotomous points of view and the very structure of the film—the awkward shifting back and forth from tenement to the besieged post office—bears out this duality.

Apart from scenario, the direction of the film discloses certain fundamental weaknesses. In the main, these result from John Ford's reliance on excessive stylization—a tendency he first betrayed most noticeably in *Mary of Scotland*. The funeral procession of Mollser may be taken as a case in point. This took on almost the character of a slow dance, the three shawled women going through their paces as for a choreographer. Or consider his habit of fading out on a group of people frozen rigid—almost like architecture. Although Ford's desire to invest the character of James Connolly with great nobility was in evidence, his directives were so generalized that the great Irish leader took on the proportions of a stock character. The occupation of the post office, though more fully treated in the scenario, still emerged as a sequence of great expressiveness. The undeniably effective chase across the roofs was partly weakened in grip by the unrealistic character of the mise-en-scène. In this respect the choice seems to have been deliberate, for the scenario reads ". . . this roof is only an eerie impression of chimney pots, different roof levels, and smoke."

One might go on with an analysis of *The Plough and the Stars* if the thought that the film is really not the work of Ford and Nichols did not continually present itself. To all intents and purposes Ford and Nichols have yet to make *The Plough and the Stars*. No one in his senses, for example, could hold either one of them to account for the nauseating drool that splashes out of Barbara Stanwyck in the course of a performance as inept as any the screen has seen.

Unlike Ford, whose connection with *The Plough and the Stars* would appear comparatively slight, Frank Capra, from all evidence we have been able to gather, is solely responsible for *Lost Horizon*, having supervised every stage of its vast production. And great must the blame be. After *Mr. Deeds Goes to Town*, the all-pervasive triteness of *Lost Horizon* is a disagreeable shock. From the novel by James Hilton we had learned what to expect. Capra's enthusiasm for the novel and his selection of it for filmization was entirely in keeping with his psychological development. From *Broadway Bill* through *Mr. Deeds*, Capra plainly showed his distress that the world was out of joint, that mass misery is the foundation of the fortunes of the few. His distress was manifestly sincere, his concern genuine, and remains so even on the basis of *Lost Horizon*. He obviously wished he could do something about it. In *Broadway Bill*, Walter Connelly sells his huge interests, gives up money grubbing, and goes off with his favorite son-in-law to follow the ponies. Mr. Deeds gives most of his millions to several thousand dispossessed farmers and retires to "Mandrake Falls, where the scenery enthralls, where no hardship e'er befalls, welcome to Mandrake Falls."

Shangri-la is Mandrake Falls without the United Cigar Store. It has more books than the Congressional Library and a shady approximation of a Tibetan horn that hardly compensates for Mr. Deeds's tuba. As for authentic feeling for the Tibetan scene, one is reminded of a British critic's comment on *Mary of Scotland*, "the inaccuracies must have involved tremendous research." One would require but a single sequence, almost a single frame, from *Storm Over Asia* or *Son of Mongolia* to shame the highly publicized "fidelities" of *Lost Horizon*.

Some time last year we concluded our review of *Mr. Deeds* with a fervent wish that in his next picture, *Lost Horizon*, Capra would "in some unaccountable way avoid the chauvinist, jingo pitfalls" that would face him. It is among the more regrettable features of *Lost Horizon* that he fails completely. As evidence we can point to the Chinaman who leers lasciviously at the film's shady lady, Isabel Jewell, during the refueling scene. In his treatment of the reception Edward Everett Horton and Thomas Mitchell get from the native women, Capra fails to add one single nuance that distinguishes the scene from any number featuring the amorous exploits of Victor McLaglen and Edmund Lowe. Add to these the incomprehensible singing class conducted by Jane Wyatt and her final "Bob, Bob, you've come back," and you've only got an exciting airplane crash to save from the wreckage of the film. At this date, it is perhaps unnecessary to discuss so completely an escapist philosophy as that summed up in Shangri-la (a refuge for all the delicate perishable beauties of the world to which men will turn after their civilization is destroyed). It is perhaps supererogatory to point out that today the preservation of culture is a progess of complete participation in the struggles of the world. The Spanish workers who at this moment are defending with their lives their great artistic heritage understand this.

We do not wish to be unfair to *Lost Horizon*, and least of all to Capra, whose craftsmanship makes itself felt in the tidiness of the film. But we expected more of him and of his scenarist, Robert Riskin. In general, criticism is a tricky affair. We often find ourselves praising a poor film on the basis of a single surprising sequence and conversely damning a good film because of certain unexpected defects. *Lost*

Horizon unfortunately is not in the latter class. We mention this common pitfall of criticism specifically in connection with *The Good Earth*. However involved we get in tortuous faultfinding we ought to make it clear that *The Good Earth* is an extraordinarily fine work. Sidney Franklin has labored long and well to achieve his results. Attention must also be called to the highly creditable screen adaptation of the novel by Tess Slessinger, Talbot Jennings, and Claudine West.

The film's defects are chiefly attributable to the shortcomings of Pearl Buck's novel, as are its virtues. True, there have been some modifications. The film ends with the death of O-Lan. Wang's further life with Lotus and later with Pear Blossom is obviously untouched so as to conform with Western notions of marital propriety. For the same reason—conformity with Western ideas—O-Lan and Lotus exchange physiques, O-Lan becoming the petite Louise Rainer, who, incidentally, delivers herself of a remarkable performance, and Lotus assuming the person of Tilly Losch. The finding of the jewels is an unnecessarily labored elaboration. For the most part, however, the film is an unusually faithful transcription, even to the extent of retaining the murder of O-Lan's fourth child, born during the drought, an episode profoundly moving and subtly conceived.

With all its limitations, *The Good Earth* is the most humane and truest representation of Chinese life that has come out of a studio outside of the Soviet Union. Pearl Buck, however, in her novel seems to have made a conscious effort to shut her characters in a vacuum isolated from everything save her scrutiny. This she undoubtedly did with the mistaken notion that thereby she was attaining universality. But death and taxes are also universal. They are always with us. It is a source of wonder that nowhere in her novel is the matter of taxes considered. China, the worst tax-ridden area on the globe and no mention of it! This may appear a small point, but I believe it indicative of Miss Buck's entire approach to her subject, an approach which is naturally reflected in the film. I would say that the consequence of her approach is *generalization* and not universality, which can only accompany completest reality. This feeling of generalization pervades the entire production. It is largely responsible for the vague, unrealized quality of Paul Muni's performance.

Thousands of feet of film were shot in China for background, not a frame of it appearing in the final result. Instead, generalized replicas were created by landscaping a ranch in California as an equivalent. The story itself is that most generalized and unsatisfactory of situations, man's struggle against "nature." Wang's enemies are not man-made, only the drought, the sun, the flood. Remove the revolutionary sequence and you have another *Man of Aran*, which won the Mussolini prize. Indeed, it has been suggested with perfect justice that *The Good Earth* would have been impossible without the early work of Flaherty. I would have preferred more of man's world in *The Good Earth*, but the novel does not permit of it. True, the novel is decidedly more specific about the revolution, but then the film contains one brilliant condensation that almost repays you for the lack of detail. Wang asks one of his fellow workers the meaning of the word revolution. "I don't know," is the answer, "but it has something to do with food."

Reinhardt's *Dream*

BY CHARMION VON WIEGAND

MARTIAL, the Roman satirist, once said to an actor: "When I wrote those verses, they were mine; when you read them, they are yours." This is usually the case whenever anyone produces a classic, especially Shakespeare. The text becomes the material out of which the producer hews an image as the sculptor hews a statue out of marble. And just as Booth's Hamlet is another man from Henry Irving's, so the play takes different shapes in the hands of a Granville Barker or a Gordon Craig.

Shakespeare we always have with us; the new element is always the director who interprets and the actors who execute.

Hence the current show at the Hollywood Theatre is significant only as an alloy of Shakespeare, the Warner Brothers, and Max Reinhardt.

Before the war Reinhardt was a progressive and creative force in the European theatre. Like Meyerhold and Stanislavsky, he began his theatrical career as an actor; he was trained in Otto Brahm's naturalistic theatre in Vienna. This acting experience was one of his chief assets as a producer; he always retained a special sympathy for the actor, and knew how to transform the drab naturalistic theatre of Ibsen into a frame of luxurious color and life and three-dimensional reality in which the actor could function at his best.

Contrary to common belief, Reinhardt was never interested in ideas; his chief qualities were an exuberant sensuousness, a lusty humor, and a lyric sensitivity to externals. This was his quintessence as a showman, and it was shell-shocked by the war. From the moment the cannon began to roar across Europe, Reinhardt receded into his soul; from that moment he ceased to contribute anything new to the stage internally. Reinhardt stretched out old plays until their structure cracked apart. His sensuous love of color and ornament degenerated into ostentatious display; his lusty humor became vulgar clowning; and his lyric sensitivity became vaudeville bathos. Since his theatre no longer represented a new idea, Reinhardt's immense artistic and technical skill could serve no real purpose; it could no longer advance into undiscovered territory. Reinhardt was surpassed and overtaken by new directors in postwar Germany —Georg Jessner, Jürgen Fehling, and Erwin Piscator.

I saw Reinhardt's production of *Midsummer Night's Dream* in Berlin in 1913; I saw his production of the same play in New York in 1924; now I have seen the Warner Brothers version of it on the screen. The film version is by no means worse than the Berlin productions, yet it *seems* infinitely worse.

The world has changed radically since 1913. Reinhardt is more or less the same, the production is more or less the same—but the audience is not the same and the theatre is not the same. Both the art of the theatre and the technique of the movies have advanced far beyond the once-revolutionary revolving stage, but Reinhardt has not kept pace with that advance. He could not advance because he has never followed a consistent set of ideas. His theatre was composed of a coat of many colors, patched all over with brilliant borrowings. He never had the integrity and singleness of purpose which marks the Stanislavsky theatre, and which enabled it to flourish not only after a world war but after a mighty revolution which changed the whole fabric of society.

The naturalistic theatre of Stanislavsky and of Reinhardt had two things in common, however. They both emphasized the actor, and they both alternated sharply between naturalistic and mystic plays. On the eve of the World War, both theatres tried to peer into the face of contemporary reality and to escape it. Both theatres spoke for the middle classes, whose only refuge from the impending cataclysm was art. At the moment when Stanislavsky was taking the Russian intelligentsia into Maeterlinck's mystic forest in search of the Bluebird, Reinhardt took the German *Spiessbürger* into the enchanting glades of *Midsummer Night's Dream*. This was in 1905—the year of Russia's first social revolution. Germany understood the meaning of that event, yet this was the moment Reinhardt chose to present Shakespeare's eternally glamorous and lovely world, the free life of the imaginary forest, the joys of love and summer and dream, of music and tender lyricism—all opposed to the harsh world of the time. In the same way, Reinhardt later offered the stained-glass beauties of *The Miracle* with its maidens and jongleurs and banquets and jousting and feudal lords and prelates—all on the eve of the World War, when everyone who knew anything knew it was inevitable.

So now in 1935, thirty years after the first production of *Midsummer Night's Dream*, the Hollywood magnates have wakened to the charms of this production. In the sixth year of the economic crisis, with millions of unemployed and with a second world war looming on the horizon, the politicians and bankers are ballyhooing another era of "prosperity," and Hollywood prepares the path to that promised land with the dulcet music, the dreams, and the verbal delights of Shakespeare.

For such obvious propaganda it is very useful to have a cultural label; Shakespeare serves better than Dick Powell or Ginger Rogers. And a famous European director, the embodiment of the best Continental "art," is more effective than one of the Warner Brothers. But what about the production itself? It is the screen equivalent of the substitute foods which the Germans ate during the war blockade. Neatly adulterated by Hollywood, Shakespeare is reduced to Ziegfeld's Follies in a forest. Had these Follies been *intentionally* executed they might have had their charms. There is nothing wrong with transposing Shakespeare into the terms of our own times. If these times are characterized by Follies girls, jazz, and wisecracks, let's have them; *Midsummer Night's Dream* is, after all, pure entertainment; it need not be set up on a transcendental pedestal.

But Reinhardt was not content with pure entertainment. He tried to go in all directions at once and ended by going nowhere. He wanted to offer an "artistic" sop to the sophisticates, crude burlesque to the "vulgar," and cute effects to the children. Shakespeare was sacrificed to the box office in a fantastic way.

The "art" in this film is a complete flop. The sloppy sentimental interludes, the pompous "arty" settings, the pseudomysterious German folklore effects in the forest are about as artistic as Maxfield Parrish. Fortunately the horseplay is good; even Reinhardt cannot ruin Joe E. Brown. When the true artist gets a good part he gets his opportunity. Shakespeare did write good parts, and Joe E. Brown is a true artist. There is a grand style in clowning as there is in tragedy, and Joe E. Brown has style, and within its limits it is a grand style. He shines like a diamond in a pile of paste jewels. I would be ready to suffer through the show again in order to see the part where the artisans are rehearsing their play of Pyramus and Thisbe. These comic interludes are the best scenes in the entire elaborate production. They are played in the full-blooded manner common both to the Elizabethan theatre and to Broadway, although in the performance before the Duke the worst side of

Broadway triumphed in the form of pure slapstick. Joe E. Brown plays Thisbe perfectly; he has not been bluffed by the bardolatry of the pseudointellectuals into acting unnaturally. In these scenes, James Cagney seems to have been badly directed; yet, strangely enough, there is one scene in which he reveals a new aspect of himself. When Bottom finds the ass's head is gone, when he feels his face and knows he is a normal man again, the effect Cagney creates is not at all funny, but pathetic rather than wistful. Perhaps Cagney has emotional possibilities which Hollywood, specializing in "types" as Ford specializes in cars, has not begun to fathom. Perhaps Cagney is more than a comic tough.

The other actors were unfortunately cast or unintelligently directed. With the exception of Ian Hunter none of them appears to be familiar with Shakespeare's language. What is left of the poet's text is lost in naturalistic hysteria or swallowed like hot soup. In Shakespeare's play the lyric poetry is of great and unusual beauty; in the film it is wholly lost. This would not have mattered, perhaps, if Reinhardt had succeeded in translating verbal magic into visual imagery; we might not miss the words if we got their visual equivalent.

The photography, the one field where you might expect Hollywood to triumph, is a dismal failure thanks to Reinhardt's lack of a central idea. The production is a mass of unrelated scenes lumped together without rhyme or reason. The first and last acts in Athens are done in a pompous baroque manner; the Elizabethan costumes fail to create an Elizabethan style. The forest scenes—the body of the play—are in this film a potpourri of historical artistic styles.

Here is a ballet of beautiful girls who look like dancers rather than the fairies they are supposed to be, despite the invisible wires which waft them across the sky. Here are the fantastic gnomes of the conventional German fairyland with papier-mâché masks, and real live bears and a unicorn somewhat less real. Here is a vaudeville dance act where a beam of moonlight is captured by Darkness, while her twisting white arms gradually disappear into the starry sky in the best Roxy style. In fact, everything is here—except a firm directing hand and a sharp eye to hold the film together in some unity.

In this, his first film, Reinhardt still works with the methods of the revolving stage. But the screen is a much more flexible medium than the stage: it permits infinite distances and plastic effects which cannot be achieved in the theatre. Then why attempt to transfer the technique of the stage to the screen? The camera is relentless; it exposes all the trickery of the stage props and makes them utterly unreal and unconvincing.

Incidentally, the camera compelled Reinhardt to abandon one of his greatest contributions to the contemporary stage. Reacting against the drabness of the Ibsen theatre as directed by his old teacher, Otto Brahm, Reinhardt introduced brilliant and sensuous colors. The black and white screen robbed him of this advantage; but it also revealed that Reinhardt understood color only in its decorative and external values rather than its plastic values. For, if you really understand plastic, you can suggest color even in black and white. In *The Whole Town's Talking*—Edward G. Robinson's remarkable film of a petit bourgeois dreaming of power—there was a shot of a room with blank walls, a table, a chair, and a hanging light which suggested the quality of a Cézanne canvas.

To film *Midsummer Night's Dream*, you must either stylize the forest and its fairy dwellers or else make the whole thing appear naturalistic. You cannot mix the two in such grotesque contrasts of style as mark the scenes between Puck and Oberon. Poor Mickey Rooney is directed to play Puck in a manner so hysterical that you cannot hear a word he says; the spirit of the forest, the Elizabethan Pan, emerges as a guttersnipe. Victor Jory as Oberon effectively conveys the quality of almost sinister otherworldliness; but the Reinhardt trappings ruin his performance; his talent is buried behind that ubiquitous starry curtain. Often in the scenes between Oberon and Puck, the edge of the starry curtain ends in the exact middle of the screen. Behind the curtain, on one side, stands Jory-Oberon; on the other, in a naturalistic set, free of gauze, stands Mickey-Puck. They speak to each other across the border which separates the mystic stage style of prewar Germany and the realistic style of Soviet film, and you suddenly realize how thoroughly Reinhardt has mixed his hash. Mickey Rooney is not Puck at all; he is a homeless waif from *The Road to Life*.

Does this dualism of style mirror Reinhardt's own artistic dilemma? The theatre of the German petite bourgeoisie has been killed by Hitler. That theatre was liberal, literary, and artistic—and these things are taboo in the Nazi theatre. Reinhardt has lost his natural audience, and, despite his guest productions here, he does not yet know his American audience. It also is a petit-bourgeois audience. Undoubtedly he has been told that the American petite bourgeoisie is culturally behind the German; he should also have been told that it is technically in advance of anything Europe has known. Hollywood's technique, however, is sterile for lack of men who can use it in the service of a great, creative idea. Such men exist, but the principles upon which Hollywood is organized frustrates them, as was abundantly evident in the case of Sergey Eisenstein.

The Animated Cartoon and Walt Disney

BY WILLIAM KOZLENKO

THE ANIMATED CARTOON, as exemplified by Walt Disney's successful film creations, occupies a singular place in the affections of moviegoers today. It would seem necessary, therefore, to determine the reason for its appeal, and especially for its appeal to adults, since most of its story plots are based on fairy tales, fables, myths, and similar extravagant narrative. The psychologist will undoubtedly tell us that this interest in make-believe reveals a desire to revert to an adolescent state; an inclination to escape from the rigors of a disordered existence. From another point of view, this interest may be traced to a latent desire on the part of adults to relive the imaginative experiences of their childhood. In either case, however, the element of escape is perhaps the touchstone of the whole matter. The uniqueness of the animated cartoon lies in the fact that, of all film forms, it is the only one that has freed itself almost entirely from the restrictions of an oppressive reality. Its whole conception of life and of movement is based on fantasy.

It is true that, though the characters of the animated cartoons are mainly zoological (as in Disney's films), they reflect in many ways the behavior patterns of human beings. But, in action, they continue where we leave off. The characters walk on air, fly over rooftops, swim under water, ride on clouds, and carry on other extravagant maneuvers which transcend the limitations of earthly life. The artist crosses the bridge from a world of limited movement to one of unlimited movement, which is, of course, *the dream*. Like in a dream, our actions are unrestricted and free: we do what we wish and how we wish it. And what is a frustration in real life is a consummation in a dream. All our biological and material difficulties are solved: we win the girl, we suddenly find ourselves wealthy, we overcome obstacles that would be almost impossible to surmount in conscious life, we vanquish the "villain" (in whatever guise he may assume, such as our boss, or our neighbor, or our family, or even our environment). Like in a fantasy situation, our movements during the process of a dream are determined, as it were, by miracles. We get to places, not by walking or riding, but by flying; we find ourselves in situations that have neither antecedents nor causes. But, whereas there is a story plot in fantasy which holds its situations coherently together, this coherence or logic is absent in a dream. Things happen because we wish them to happen. In such a way do the incidents in an animated cartoon fulfill, in some measure, many of our unrealized objectives. What takes place before our eyes on the screen takes place similarly in our dreams, and the pleasure we get from witnessing how easily Mickey Mouse, for instance, solves the most difficult problems in an almost haphazard and miraculous way is a pleasure transferable to ourselves.

In order to achieve a free interpretation of life, the method of fantasy must consequently be free. It cannot be tied down to laws that would tend to hamper its exploitation of fancy. To realize this exploitation to the fullest extent, fantasy must necessarily employ the technics of metamorphosis. Thus, in an animated cartoon, a tree comes to life and starts running; a flower begins to dance; the wind, in the shape of an old man, is seen chasing a rabbit; a cloud is suddenly converted into an umbrella; a fish appears from the water and begins to strut. Metamorphosis is indeed the perfect instrument of fantasy; and fantasy is the romantic realization of our dreams and wish fulfillments.

This transition from a mythical place to a real one, this change from a hypothetical situation to an actual one, helps explain why so many of Disney's cartoons attain a certain contemporary significance. The unusual success of *Three Little Pigs*, for example, is a good case in point.

The story, though based on fable, was at once associated with the economic situation. Its lesson—if one wants to call it that—stressed the necessity of "sticking together," and suggested that only by building an "impregnable house" can the "big, bad wolf" be beaten. The wolf—long a symbol of hunger and privation—was accepted by all as representing the prevalent economic distress. This interpretation took on additional emphasis since it came at a time when President Roosevelt was asking for almost dictatorial powers; when bank failures and bankruptcies were rife; and when the President issued his famous appeal to the public to "stick together" (that is, with him) and "not give up hope." The verse—"Who's afraid of the big, bad wolf?"—became a national hit. The public apprehended the subtle argument of the film, and the cartoon, which originally started out to delineate in color and animation a popular children's tale, was seized upon by the canny politicians and used to disseminate a heartening message (so-called) to the people. And here fantasy succeeded where realism no doubt would have failed, especially the kind of trumped-up realism which emanates from Hollywood. And why would realism have failed? Obviously because on the plane of reality audiences would have refused to accept the conclusion that they weren't afraid of "the big, bad wolf."

Since Disney's animated cartoons are not the only ones being shown today, it would be well to scrutinize the content of another type of animated cartoon: one almost as popular and representing a different aspect of psychological portraiture. I refer to the Popeye films. These films translate wish fulfillment into terms of pure physical force: they are glorifications of strength and violence. Popeye evinces no niceties of character. He is a tough, though apparently kindhearted, pug. The salient features of his personality are illiteracy, stupidity, gruffiness, and a pair of powerful muscles. (How versatile and refined, by comparison, is such a subject as Mickey Mouse, who can play the piano, ride a horse, conduct a band, fly an airplane, build a house, and do other constructive things with equal proficiency.) In fact, every cartoon character of Disney's is distinguished by some personal trait. We identify little Donald Duck, who gets under everybody's feet, with a helpless irascibility; Pluto, the dog, is a good-natured, though clumsy, bumpkin; the wolf is a sly and incorrigible character, etc. In short, each of Disney's animal subjects is an intelligent being, reflecting the essential characteristics of his own species. What, conversely, does Popeye represent in human nature? Here is a man who, after swallowing the contents of a can of spinach (a remarkable symbol, incidentally, of metamorphosis), goes completely berserk and with a series of powerful punches destroys buildings, knocks down trees, and annihilates men normally stronger than himself. His philosophy of action is the doctrine that with physical strength man can overcome every obstacle; and his justification for this display of unbridled power usually takes the form of saving his girl from the unsavory clutches of the gargantuan villain. We are speedily convinced by all this that if a man cannot get satisfaction by persuasion, he can certainly get it by a knockout blow.

In this connection we must deplore the recent tendency of Disney to glorify violence for its own sake, as exemplified by such cartoons as *Mickey's Polo Game* and others. Not only do *Mickey's Polo Game* and *Who Killed Cock Robin?* (in the latter we have in mind the treatment accorded Jim Crow) revel in unmotivated fury, but they depart entirely from their true character as fantasy by introducing screen personalities —Mae West, Bing Crosby, Laurel and Hardy et al.

When an artist of the caliber of Disney can successfully remove himself to another world, and take us along with him, we do not have to give up anything of our organic world in order to share with him the pleasures and realizations of his world of fantasy. In short, he creates for us a world of image and fiction which is related to some extent to our own dream world and which entails no unhealthy distortion of the world of fact. And, in this regard, we can say with Constant Lambert, the eminent British music critic, that: "There must be few artists of any kind who do not feel abashed when faced with the phenomenal inventive genius of Walt Disney, the only artist of today who exists triumphantly in a world of his own creation, unhampered by the overshadowing of ancient tradition or the undercutting of contemporary snobbism."

Disney's art is determined by many factors, as regards its processes of creation and production, but the most significant, in my opinion, is the fact that, though he is the governing spirit of his organization, the final creation of every cartoon is the result, not of one man—Walt Disney—but of the collective efforts of more than a hundred men who work with him. Each cartoon, whether a Silly Symphony or a Mickey Mouse adventure, possesses those distinct qualities which distinguish Disney's work from any other in the same genre.

Disney allows his fellow workers complete freedom in their creative tasks. He neither attempts to hamper them in the projection of their own ideas nor does he seek to force upon them his own conceptions and treatment thereof. Disney himself, though the "boss" of the organization, willingly submits to the opinions of his fellow workers. If his idea is rejected in favor of another, he either discards it or changes it according to their specifications. For instance, *Three Little Pigs* was submitted by Disney to the members of his studio for a year before they finally approved it.

A cartoon, from its inception as an incomplete story idea to the final process of filming, involves about four or five months of actual work. About half that time is devoted to the preparation of a carefully detailed scenario. For this specific function there is a story department, which consists of about a dozen writers. It is their job to conceive new ideas, rewrite old stories—such as fables, fairy tales, myths, romances—and work on material already accepted. It is here, in this department, that Disney's influence is most pronounced. Undoubtedly, the outstanding feature of a Disney film—apart from its remarkable craftsmanship, its schematic integration, its story coherence—is the extraordinary confluence of plot detail, treatment, music, and animation.

When a story has been found satisfactory for picture purposes, Disney and members of his story department get together, study all the possibilities for pictorial and musical exploitation, and, after thoroughly going over all the details, the story is then assigned to one of the dozen scribes to rewrite in the form of a page synopsis. This synopsis, when finished, is distributed to several score members of the studio: animators, the musical director, and all other persons connected with the production of this particular cartoon. Each member studies the draft, concentrating on his particular angle of the story, although everyone is at liberty to contribute gags, work out new little actions, and suggest new embellishments of the plot.

After about a fortnight, all the workers involved in the production of the cartoon get together and go over the pile of suggestions which each has brought with him. These suggestions, mostly in the form of rough drawings with written annotations, are presented, criticized, and discussed by Disney, a few associates of the story department, the director in charge of the cartoon (a sort of coordinating foreman), the layout man, the musical director, and several animators. Hurried sketches are made and passed around for criticism during this conference. A composer, trying to correlate a particular rhythm or melody to a specific action sequence, rattles off a musical idea while another member rhythmically enacts an animal episode.

As soon as all the various phases of the work have been organized into a working prospectus—including a rough design of the action, a skeletal plan of the musical score, etc.—the actual work of assembling all this begins. A writer, having worked out a plan of the story, submits a detailed scenario which is illustrated by approximately fifty sketches of the main incidents in the action. The scenario is then turned over to the director of the production, who, with the aid of Disney and his associates, formulates a detailed time sheet of every single movement. The time sheet is developed further on the basis of beats in synchronization with the music, which is composed simultaneously with the script. In this manner, each movement has been synchronized with the music before either the music is recorded or the action animated.

Now begins the process of animation. Inasmuch as an animator cannot make more than several drawings a day—equal to about six feet of film—it therefore requires about a month to complete the animation alone. The animation is divided in several ways. The backgrounds, for instance, are made by regular scenic artists, and only the moving figures are animated. Each animator is assigned to that phase of the animation for which he is best fitted.

Now, what essentially distinguishes an animator from an artist? There are, of course, many subtle and indivisible differences, but the one most prominent is that the animator, besides being something of an imaginative artist himself, must be able to inject a spirit of life in the characters and their movements which he draws. These characters must be able not only to lend themselves to movement, but their movement must have the semblance of real life. It is not enough to animate them; their animation must reflect the viability of men or animals. So, in order to portray this verity of movement, the animators frequently resort to various devices for their portrayals. They may watch their own mirrored reflections as they imitate the movements of their subjects, they may study similar motions simulated by other persons, and, when the subjects are animal, in order to endow them with real zoological characteristics as well as human traits, they frequently observe animals go through their antics in the zoo or on the screen. With all this experience garnered at first hand, they thus are able to reflect in their cartoons many elements of real life.

After a section is sketchily animated, it is photographed and studied by Disney and his aides as to its verity or authenticity. If it is satisfactory, then girls copy the drawings (of which there may be thousands) on celluloid with black paint, or if it is a colored cartoon then it is done in color.

The shooting takes about four or five days, and it is done by a mechanically complex stop-motion camera. The final endorsement of approval, as in the larger studios, is made at a preview at some local movie house. If a particular sequence fails to evoke a favorable response from the audience, the film is taken back to the studio and that sequence changed; although this happens very rarely. Because of the carefully planned and synchronized scenario, there is little that requires changing after the consequent filming of the cartoon.

And so, after about four months of labor, involving the efforts of hundreds of persons, the animated cartoon is ready for its few minutes of life on the screen.

The Movie "Original"

BY WILLIAM LORENZ

"ORIGINAL" is the word they use in Hollywood when they mean a story written directly for the screen. There seems to be some mystery about the writing of screen originals. Even experienced writers are curiously naive. Because no originals have been published, people think some mystery formula exists. Are originals written in dialogue or straight narrative form? Should quoted speeches be included? Past or present tense? Can description be used? Should characters and forces be analyzed? Are lists of characters and locations unnecessary? Must the writer be familiar with camera technique, indicate fade-outs, dissolves, close shots?

All this concern with style is unnecesary. There is no mystery formula. A screen original is written like a short story and built like a play. The only yardstick for measuring it is a sense of dramatic construction. If, in order to clarify the play you intend to write, you were to put it on paper in brief narrative form, including all incident and stage business that contribute to character and to dramatic development, you would have a manuscript very much like a screen original. In your play outline you might show that certain offstage action is indicated by dialogue whereas in your movie original you would move your characters about freely, describe the scenes suggested by dialogue in the stage version, and, instead of merely saying that a rumble is heard offstage, you would let your howling mobs howl.

Originals are considered easy writing because the physical limitations of the stage are not present to make necessary the use of ingenious devices to keep the action within a space bounded by three walls and the footlights. This freedom from stage limitations generally results in rambling stories, lack of unity, flabby structure. The usual way of writing an original is to think of a wow of an opening, spread fireworks and drama all over the first three pages, and then taper off into a thin and pointless narrative.

A well-built original intended for the screen must have a beginning, a middle, an end, must show cause and effect, build logically, maintain tension, mount from crisis to crisis until the final climax is achieved. Characters should be sharply and definitely drawn, the mood sustained, every incident should contribute to the expression of a unified idea.

This sounds pedagogic and a little absurd when you consider the pictures you sit through so often at the neighborhood theatre. Construction? Mood? Unity? Idea? And the result is *Colleen* or *The Flame Within*. But let's remember that in writing novels we do not derive our standards from the masters on the Godwin list, and in studying the drama we do not use the works of Anne Nichols as examples of style and structure. Only in thinking of movies is it our habit to compare our efforts with the worst.

It is the style among screenwriters to get very holy about the books and plays they are going to write. But usually when these sacred documents reach the public they are not as good as the same writers' originals and screenplays. The essential difference between an original and a book or play written with the hope that the movies will buy it is that the book or play uses more white paper.

The selling of originals is getting to be less and less of a racket, too. In the old days a writer got an idea, submitted it in two or three hastily typed pages, and sold it to Hollywood. Alas for us, the cinch ended.

When Hollywood puts money into twenty or forty pages of white paper, it wants a lot of story. Plays that have three nights on Broadway and books that sold two hundred copies have proved their worth because people outside "the industry" have already invested money in them.

Thus the original is a sort of stepchild to the industry. Since an original can never be a classic, no publicity department will gush, no advertising office spend on exploitation when such epics as *Little Lord Fauntleroy* and *The Return of Peter Grimm* have proved their right to the ballyhoo. And writers, therefore, approach the original with a defeatist attitude, knowing that stories written directly for the screen are accepted condescendingly by directors, doubted by the producers who buy them, rejected by important stars.

It is this defense mechanism, perhaps, which allows competent writers to send the studios stories that would shame fan writers. Studio editors have shown me manuscripts that I would think had been written by correspondence-school students if I hadn't seen in the upper left-hand corner names that get four-figure checks from the magazines. These writers may defend sloppy work with the arguments that sentences cannot be photographed and that the people who buy pictures are a lot of ex-buttonhole makers completely lacking in appreciation for pure prose style. This rationalization defeats its own purpose, for every writer knows that lusty prose can sell a tepid story and that charm can hide that big hole in the plot.

Sometimes writers, born fools, fall in love with material, work with gusto when speculating on an original. It is a shame that the sale of such stories depends as much upon producing schedule, the need for stars' vehicles, the digestion of executives as upon their merits.

There are very few people in the business who consistently sell originals. Gene Towne and Graham Baker, John Bright and Robert Tasker, working as teams, and Norman Krasna, soloist, seem to be mentioned most frequently in the *Hollywood Reporter* as having "placed" another original.

All originals are not written as speculative ventures by free-lance scribes. Sometimes an idea begins with a writer who tells the story to an executive and is then paid by the studio for putting it on paper. More frequently an executive buys or gets an idea, hires writers singly, in teams or quartets. These studio-born ideas may be as vague as the demand made by a producer who asked for a real love story between a father and son, or it may be as concrete as a file of clippings on Black Legion activities.

The first thing a writer must produce is an "angle."

"What is your angle on such a story, Mr. Alden?"

"My angle, Mr. Standish, is that the Black Legion is controlled by a madman. He's not really an unsympathetic character, only a little crazy because he thinks a motor tycoon cheated him out of some invention years before. The story develops with the old nut's daughter falling for the tycoon's son, and the old man, insanely jealous, puts on a mask . . ."

"You've got something there, John. Revenge motivation."

"That's not the half of it, Miles. Family differences. Intrigue in the love story, a sort of Romeo and Juliet situation . . ."

"It's in the bag, Jack. When do I see a first script?"

Thus the angle is developed. Romeo and Juliet enter the Black Legion accompanied by Jiggs and Maggie for comedy relief and Charlie Chan to cover the race prejudice aspects of the story. The first writer's angle may be followed or discarded, as many as twelve authors compete on the script, the victors emerging with screen credit. No matter whose name appears on the screen, no matter which of the twelve is responsible for the final angle, it is certain at the start that social implications will be elaborately disregarded or cunningly tortured to create sympathy for a robust, splendid industrialist; that a villainous individual will be responsible for the conflict necessary to plot and background; that love will avert tragedy in the end.

Originals born in the studios are usually more daring than the scripts offered by free-lance scribes. But writers know that a subject which would be considered too dangerous in a speculative script will be passed by the executives if a safe "angle" is developed within the studio. Originals turned out for the Hollywood market by knowing writers respect the taboos of a system as full of complexes as Freud's most advanced case. Not only the prejudices of the producers, but the interests of the stockholders must be held sacred. Neither the tenets of the Legion of Decency, the attitudes of the women's clubs, nor the ethics of the censors are as constricting as the theories of film executives who have become thoroughly infected with the spirit of Hollywood.

"This is a fine idea," they say, "but the public won't understand. It's above their heads. Too highbrow." Perhaps they're right. But I have sat in movie houses in Bridgeport, Connecticut, Marshalltown, Iowa, Milwaukee, Wisconsin, and Encinitas, California, and I have never found any audience as dull as the big shots who attend story conferences solemnly believe.

In spite of these handicaps the stepchild flourishes. Library shelves are not loaded with enough classics to make the yearly producing schedules vital and varied.

The family trade prefers the contemporary sturdiness of *Fury* to the dead sentimentality of *Peter Ibbetson*. The industry is clogged with corpses looking backward for Belasco's secret, but the moviegoing masses want more and more original melodramas like *Public Enemy* and *Little Caesar*, and more comedies like *The Richest Girl in the World* and *A Night at the Opera*. The Marx Brothers, I hear, have quite a taste for literature but, good showmen that they are, they never try to give the public an adaptation of *The Rover Boys*. René Clair's best pictures were written for the screen, and Charlie Chaplin prefers originals, too.

There does exist today the hope of pictures produced without Hollywood gold and free from the belief that the audience mass is half-witted. Small dramatic and workers' theatre groups are dreaming of unpretentious pictures that can be made for less than a million dollars and without benefit of Janet Gaynor. Independent producers are roving around, looking for unusual material. In New York the Nykino Group, which is just completing a film with a labor theme, needs scripts for both short and feature films. They want more than a new title for *The Easiest Way*. Writers who have been given inhibitions by Hollywood's prohibitions will have a chance to use the beautiful, elastic medium of the screen for telling honest stories.

Naturally these will not be supercolossals. The lushness, ease, and elegance of Hollywood backgrounds cannot be produced for pennies, but how much of lushness, ease, and elegance are necessary when conflict is real, when story, background, and characters are authentic? The same is true of stage productions. *Stevedore* and *Waiting for Lefty* click in spite of amateur casts and makeshift sets. But try to produce *The Great Waltz* without spectacular effects or to interest an audience in *The Distaff Side* without silky actors, elegant furniture, flawless production. In some of the good amateur movies today you can see crowd effects, natural bits, incidental atmosphere snapped on street corners that carry more conviction than all the elaborate pageantry in *The Crusades*.

Hollywood art is Wildean. It imitates nature. But when director, writer, and producer are obliged to substitute reality for white drawing rooms, authentic incident for the inevitable yacht sequence, a newer and more rugged art will flourish. The makeshifts of cheap production are not so much of a handicap to the writer as the fear of a million taboos. When real situations can be used, when truth can be simple, conflict will be authentic, drama logical, and there will be no need for the tortured devices of mechanical plot structure. A straight story of an American working girl would not depend on the twists and cuties of *Wife versus Secretary*.

It would sound affected and pretentious to speak of the original as an art form, but it certainly should be as respectable a form of writing as any other. Think of *The Youth of Maxim* as a novel, of *A Nous la Liberté* as a satirical comedy written for the stage. For myself I would prefer the original to stay humble and not become an art form. That would bring in the snobs and the cultists, and we who write directly for the screen would have to consider not only the people who buy and produce, those who direct and act in our stories, the audiences who look at them, but the aesthetes, too.

Notes on Hollywood

BY JORIS IVENS

To us in Holland, and in the whole of Europe, Hollywood appears a strange empire, with embassy palaces and consulates in every country, city, and hamlet. Whoever enters one of these palaces (and he must pay for it) is on neutral ground: on the outside are sorrows, insecurity, protests—demonstrations, struggles, war. Inside is darkness. An endless series of false illusions flicker across the screen, and the cunning producer, with the help of a Clark Gable, Jeanette MacDonald, and Shirley Temple, tries to prove to the whole world—the American coal miner as well as the Dutch peasant—that human nature never changes.

It is clear in whose interest such a perversion of fact and reality is perpetuated. Who owns the screen? The talkie? The loudspeaker? Think of the thundering yell of culture over the world each evening—and think also of the following story.

In British India there lived a strong isolated tribe of mountaineers who didn't like continually paying taxes to the London bankers. They took their rifles and marched against the authorities. A bright English officer proposed to his general that he send an aeroplane with the world's most powerful loudspeaker over the camp of the mountaineers who were so audacious as to defend their liberty. A well-paid Hindu priest, assuming the voice of the God of the Mountains, announced through the silvery amplifying tubes that he wished the tribesmen to bring all their rifles, weapons, and powder to the river bank. The people complied and were conquered. Today, some of their young warriors are studying radio engineering and aviation in order to be able to deliver their own message.

I

Hollywood seemed to us in Holland very far away, much farther than the film centers of London, Moscow, Paris, Berlin. With these centers our own independent film groups and audience organizations like the film leagues maintained regular contact. Celebrated Continental directors spoke at our public meetings on their conceptions of film art and their methods of work: René Clair, Pudovkin, Renoir, Eisenstein, Pabst, and others. But Hollywood remained far removed. Our only contact with it through the years was its many mediocre and bad pictures. You can imagine what a distorted idea of American life the Dutch, the French, the English received. A country full of gangsters and G-men; every office girl with the chance to marry her boss; the old fairy tale that every boy has the opportunity to become a millionaire; Negroes who were merely clowns with nothing to do but dance and sing the whole day long. All this time and time again.

Things took a turn for the better much too slowly. Every year four or five good works (of course far too few) came out of this dream factory where films—500 per annum, 65 percent of the world's production—were made on the conveyor belt. Names like King Vidor, Milestone, Mamoulian, Von Sternberg—later John Ford, Capra, Cukor, Hawks, La Cava and Le Roy—and those of a few good actors and actresses appeared. Pictures began to be made which could no longer be derisively labeled "box office," "religion and sex," "war and sex." One had to differentiate. We now saw some good pictures. Hence there were some good people in the field, creative forces, artists who wanted to create something beyond cheap entertainment.

II

During my first few weeks in Hollywood, as a craftsman I naturally concentrated on the marvelous working places. Hollywood is indeed a magnificent place in which to produce pictures—a mild, even climate, for many a bit too monotonous—a lot of sun, little wind, scenic variety, and, in addition, the best technical equipment in existence. People from all over the world come to watch the studios in operation and to study their perfected methods of production. (Shumiatsky, for instance, the head of the Soviet cinema industry, came to Hollywood preparatory to the building of a gigantic film center in the south of the Soviet Union.) Visit these studios for a few hours and compare them with London or

Paris, the sureness, the speed and calm of the directors, cameramen, stage and electrical workers and carpenters. Here one finds a working method of the utmost efficiency, systematic mass production, a concentration of the whole population of a city for one end—to produce films.

Technically, everything is possible. The lenses move over the scene faster than the eye of the interested visitor. The microphone hears more acutely than the ear of the snooping publicity agent. In twenty minutes one passes through twenty different streets, through a few thousand years of human history. Indeed, a marvelous place in which to produce pictures.

Then, after a week, one suddenly remembers that this apparatus, technically so marvelous, only produces four or five good pictures a year. It is not as efficient as we thought! One realizes the discrepancy between the technical possibilities and the result. Why?

In the scenario department the inbreeding of ideas proceeds on an unprecedented scale. Every year an endless row of variations on boy meets girl or the Cinderella story. Experiments in direction and shooting by director or cameramen are impossible, or emerge mutilated from the cutting room. An actor has to fight for his life to escape standardization; once a dancing girl, gangster, butler, always a dancing girl, gangster, butler. In Hollywood one is not permitted to change. One is not permitted to make use of the rich life outside—American life. And it lies right next door—all around. Do not forget: Hollywood borders on Los Angeles, a city of two million, with the greatest aviation industry in the United States, the greatest fruit orchards of America, the second greatest center for rubber and oil. But between Hollywood and Los Angeles lies a boulevard which separates the motion pictures from reality.

In the scenario department the last word in contact with life is a short story from the *Saturday Evening Post* or a book. Sometimes even a good book. But the pages are juggled, and often wiped clean of their words, leaving a blank white sheet to be used as a movie screen!

III

There are certain things in Hollywood, however, which are not hampered by restrictions. One is the censors. You get the feeling that these all-powerful and ignorant midwives got in on each film from the very birth of the idea, that they hover over each meeting of boy and girl armed with the vetoes of religious and moral decency.

The curiosity of the public is similarly unlimited and unhampered, stimulated by the fan magazines, whose myrmidons scurry, like rats, in and around private life. Diaries, bedrooms, gardens are all open to them. They dutifully help to make the atmosphere of Hollywood deadly for true talent. Life in Hollywood makes the writer soft. "Of course, I only came for three months, to make a pile. Soon I'll quit and do what I want —write a book—a play—or study—or make my own film." But if you ask these writers (or actors) how long they have been in Hollywood, they answer, "Three years—four years."

Among them there are those who really had something to say. But after three or four years they dried up—like the sea in Holland—slowly, painlessly, in a marvelous climate, in a house with a view and a good car. Only a few of them can indulge in the luxury of permitting themselves individuality. With these, the producers have their troubles! The better type of production requires strong, original talent. The producers engage writers who are known to possess it and then have to nullify the very qualities they need so badly, because in most instances the writer turns up with a scenario far too powerful, too original, too honest. ("Controversial topics are barred.")

The producer has other troubles. He has to get writers into some sort of collective relationship, because it usually takes more than one to turn out a script on a picture. I experienced one typical case. The collective didn't form itself around the theme or the idea of the picture but around the prospective title: four words. (The producer assured me, "Every letter is worth gold.") I shall not divulge it, it was something like *Love on the Moon*. Four writers, the producer, and the title—a brilliant gathering!

The writers are divided into various categories. After the *Love on the Moon* collective has done its work, the gagmen and the heavy dialogue men are called in. ("And I have three idea men—fine fellows. No, they always do the same kind of work.")

IV

Instead of resorting to such travesties of the creative process, Hollywood should turn to the rich, full life at its door, life in which a Balzac or a Zola would revel! I saw a fruit-pickers' strike—three thousand Mexican workers—which offered material for at least two *Viva Villa*'s. In La Habra I was present at the birth of a fighting song, the circumstances of which, if incorporated in a film, would have had ten times the strength and directness and optimism and probably have been more of a popular hit than the usual Hollywood epic. Yet how many Hollywood film workers were aware of this heroic primitive struggle in the fruit orchards, where trees seem to be better cared for than men?

Fuller and richer scenarios would not have to wait for good directors and actors; they are there; they *want* to make better films. There are great artists and experts available. I realized it again when I saw Capra shooting *Lost Horizon*. It is the love of an artist, of a craftsman for his profession that guides him. He notices with equal acuteness the mistakes of five extras in a mass of a thousand, or an incorrect fold in Ronald Colman's Chinese gown. And he corrects everything himself. He doesn't trust his eye, and controls the screen picture in the finder of the camera. I asked whether he cut the film himself. "Of course. I consider that part of the director's job." Capra is one of the few directors in Hollywood free from front office interference. In his studio there reigns the quiet, the intense atmosphere of devotion essential to the making of good pictures, which I also found with René Clair in Paris and Pudovkin in Moscow. The same is true of others here whom I watched at work: Vidor, Milestone, Mamoulian. The calm sureness of men who are complete masters of their art, their craft. One becomes furious at the thought that such talent has not the freedom necessary for the further development of the filmic art.

One might think that Hollywood would be a marvelous green-house for actors. On the contrary. I have already commented on how each actor is typed. Only with the help of courageous directors or perhaps an intelligent producer can they escape this fate. All too rarely do they work earnestly at their profession. They always have time and energy for a physical work-out, tennis, polo, etc., but only rarely to study their roles, the character they are playing, before work on the film is begun. I had expected a great deal; I had thought that at least something of the methods of the Russian film actors had reached Hollywood, or that the modern American theatre had exerted some influence. Such was not the case.

At home their calendar is full of engagements. I tried to remain calm when a star with a yearly income of at least two hundred thousand dollars complained earnestly to me: "Thursday night and Saturday night, no date, no invitation!" (Invitations are the barometer of popularity.) One mustn't wait! Call up your friends! Organize a party yourself! That's the first straw one clutches at. (Modern court atmosphere.) Publicity manager. These are her troubles. Her final goal is a footprint in the concrete at the entrance to Grauman's Chinese theatre. Madam has worries indeed!

The young cameraman working for years without advancement has greater worries. No promotion possible. In certain companies a small group of older cameramen is in control and effectively blocks the way. No younger man however talented is allowed to get a chance. Tired musicians tell me of overlong working hours and bad pay. Matters are even worse among the army of extras. The Central Casting Bureau reports that of the 15,275 people given work during the first six months of 1936, 13,463 earned less than $200. This is the Hollywood about which the fan magazines never write.

V

When I said that Hollywood was shut-in and isolated, I did not mean that it was not completely dominated and controlled from the outside, and that it was not being used as a powerful medium to reconcile the masses to the insecurity of their daily work and life, by giving them cheap entertainment as an escape from reality. To my mind Hollywood is the world's greatest center of agitation and progaganda. One has only to remember how in 1917 the war spirit was worked up with miles of celluloid and a few telegrams and meetings. Would not such a thing be possible again today?

The mental attitude of those who work in this center of progapanda is not simple. Meeting different people in Hollywood taught me to understand better what Donald Ogden Stewart said at a public reading of *Bury the Dead* about the profession of screen writing. There are many fine, charming people in Hollywood. At home they play with their children, read a great deal, take an interest in art. But at the office they write and produce bad films that their own children and the rest of the world as well, will see. They distort, consciously or unconsciously, the fundamentally healthy illusions of human beings and project them on the screen as a new kind of reality. Their work constitutes a moral disarming of the masses.

All those who wish to raise the American screen to a higher level should heed the example of the young new theatre movement in America. No other country except the USSR can show such a steady growth of the modern theatre as America. (In Germany, by contrast, the theatre has withered away under the Nazi dictatorship.) Playwrights, directors and actors in New York sense a great task. The American screen must follow their example; the days of merely cursing or deploring Hollywood are over.

Hollywood can produce such pictures as *The Informer, Modern Times, Mr. Deeds Goes to Town, Fury, Pasteur*. Good artists in Hollywood need the help of the public in order that the box-office risk of such pictures can be reduced. The producer must sense a new terrain with new possibilities. Educational, youth, peace, and labor organizations could support such productions, could stimulate the demand for progressive films and form a bulwark against antilabor, fascist, and war tendencies in pictures.

It must be made possible for Hollywood writers, directors, and actors, and with them the public, to face the real problems of life. The film must take part in the cultural development of the people as must the theatre, literature, music, painting, and the radio.

Why shouldn't directors, screenwriters, and actors found an experimental studio for a systematic examination of the fundamental laws of the art of the film? This is essential. This studio would shoulder the cost of the experiments which the producers of feature films do not want to assume. Special studio films intimately associated with the reality of the world would enrich their aesthetic sensitivities and give new vitality to their work.

Independent film groups are engaging in courageous pioneer work with already excellent professional quality: Nykino's *Labor March of Time*, American Labor Films' *Millions of Us*. It must go on. For the public good pictures are indispensable in its struggle for life.

Pictures with the power, the artistic level, and the social function of books like *Don Quixote, Uncle Tom's Cabin* are now due in America. A young film movement must open the way.

A New Approach to Filmmaking

BY RALPH STEINER AND
LEO T. HURWITZ

(An article based on a report given at
the conclusion of Lee Strasberg's course)

LAST WINTER Lee Strasberg, one of the directors of the Group Theatre, gave a course in theatre direction at the Theatre Collective school. We, as filmmakers, with no opportunity to learn the principles of our craft except by (expensive) trial and (mostly) error, derived so much benefit from his patient, brilliant, analytical lectures that we are moved to present something of what we have learned to other filmmakers. With no film school in America led by an Eisenstein, we feel that the revolutionary moviemakers must go for help to theatre workers like Strasberg and others who have thought deeply on the problems of films.

Although we filmmakers have problems some of which relate to those of the theatre and others which are of necessity different, since we work in a different medium, this course has given us what amounts to a completely new approach to both. In addition it has given us concrete methods of attacking a number of these basic problems. Not only did we get a clearer view of the main objectives toward which we have been groping but also an equally clear indication of the means by which they can be achieved in terms of the screen.

In the first place Strasberg emphasized the necessity of getting at the basic meaning of the scenario—of defining with the utmost clarity what must be said with the film as a whole. For instance: two theatres in Moscow produced Gorky's *Yegor Buletchev*, and though in both the actors spoke the same lines each theatre gave the play an entirely different meaning; the Moscow Art Theatre produced a play about the death of a man by cancer; to the Vakhtangov Theatre the same play was not only about the death of a man but also the disintegration of a whole class of society. Strasberg gave us a method of research to determine the basic idea of the script when it is not discoverable from the scenario itself. This research tries to determine what in the life and time of the author led to the writing of the scenario and effected and conditioned its contents.

Secondly, with the basic idea determined, Strasberg suggested a method of applying it to the production in order to obtain interest and reality: how the basic idea determines the style; how to work on the problem of the sets and background in relation to the idea; how to work with the actor and how to invent his activities.

Third, he made us conscious that every step in filmmaking must be related to an audience. He made us realize that the film is *theatrical*—that is, it communicates its meaning by the re-creation of dramatic situations in filmic time and space, and depends for its effectiveness on the emotional involvement of the audience in these situations. That unless this audience response is obtained, films, however profound and socially important in subject, will be lifeless and socially ineffectual.

The significance of this whole approach to us and to other filmmakers can be better understood by indicating our previous histories as filmmakers and the major influences which affected our point of view. There were three main factors in our development, each of which contributed influences of definite positive value but each of which also warped our basic attitude toward the film medium.

THE FORMAL REVOLT FROM HOLLYWOOD

During the twenties we grew disgusted with the philistinism of the commercial film product, its superficial approach, trivial themes, and its standardization of film treatment: the straight-line story progressing from event to event on a pure suspense basis, unmarred by any imaginative use of the camera, unmarred by any freshness in editing or any human or formal sensitivity. Our reaction, which we shared with the young generation of experimental filmmakers, was a more or less aesthetic revolt from the current manner of film production. The important thing, we felt, was to do those things which the film was capable of, but which the commercial film didn't and couldn't possibly do. There seemed unbounded possibilities for the use of the films as a visual poetry of formal beauty.

The potentialities of the camera were explored: angles, lens distortions, camera tricks; the play of light, the magnificence of objects and objects in motion; the eloquence of things, rhythmic possibilities, and symphonic treatment. . . . It was a period in which much was learned and explored about the technical resources of cinematography and montage, but the whole emphasis was on the beauty, the shock, the effectiveness of OBJECTS, THINGS—with no analysis of the effect on an audience. In fact, the quick demise of this movement is proof that the audience got next to nothing out of it, though, certainly, technical advances were made. It could lead to nothing else but ivory tower aesthetic films, unrelated to contemporary life. The film had been depersonalized, inhuman; the THING, technique, and formal problems were supreme. Even people were considered externally, as objects rather than as human beings. Those who went through this period had for a time a definite mark left on them even though they came out of it disillusioned into a more salutary field.

PUDOVKIN'S FILM TECHNIQUE

The second main influence was Pudovkin's book, *On Film Technique*. The book itself, one of the first and best theoretical analyses of the film medium, satisfied an important need in the young and immature art of the movies. But its whole concern quite naturally was with the special problems of film technique, those problems that *differentiate* the film from any other medium. It did not concern itself with the basic dramatic principles that are *common* to all the theatrical arts. We made the error of overlooking the fact that Pudovkin was presupposing this base, and we considered the book a bible of *film principles* rather than a series of collected essays on *film technique*. It is easy to see what errors might flow from laying the entire emphasis, as we did, on the secondary principles of film technique without grasping or even realizing there exist the primary dramatic principles without which a theatrical art cannot affect and involve an audience.

Pudovkin's concern with the end problems—the detailed shooting script, the taking of the shot, and the final editing—did not give us the basis for the primary step—the conception and rendering of the story, mood, or idea in dramatic terms (theatricalization).

What we came away with from Pudovkin was briefly this: The basic thing in moviemaking is *editing* (montage). Editing gives life and meaning to dead strips of film by virtue of the context—just as a sentence in a poem vitalizes and gives new meaning to the individual words that, taken by themselves, are lifeless and without overtones. The content of a shot is relatively unimportant; its effect is the result of what comes before and after, the elements that react with it. You can take a shot of a man with a blank expression, as Kuleshov did, and edit the same piece of film with a shot of a plate of soup or of a woman lying partially nude on a bed—and the same piece of film takes on two different meanings in the different contexts. In the one he appears hungry; in the other he appears lustful. The whole series of Kuleshov-Pudovkin experiments in cutting and the principles that were deduced have a tremendous value, but, insofar as they taught us that the content of the shot was unimportant, that the meaning of a sequence depended on editing, they gave us an approach which led us off on the wrong track.

This point of view "made it unnecessary" for us to think about the main problem of filmmaking: the theatricalization of human ideas and situations (mise-en-scène)—in the words of Lee Strasberg, ". . . the creation of circumstances which make a scene possible, alive and full of suspense . . . the building up of the circumstances, character, etc. so that the action becomes not only plausible but necessary. . . ." Pudovkin, as a movie director, is brilliant in his invention of such circumstances and activity, but in his book he is concerned not with the problem of their invention but largely with the technical problem of how they are executed in production and editing. For example, in his book Pudovkin describes how he made an extraordinary scene in *Storm Over Asia*, the scene at the trading post where the hero brings in the valuable silver fox, which is envied by all the other trappers. Pudovkin does not tell us the process of the theatricalization of the scene with all its circumstances from the scenario; he rather describes *how* he got the special effect that he wanted by using jugglers and magicians to fascinate the crowd of trappers with their tricks, and photographing their hypnotically fascinated faces without their knowledge. He edited this piece of film with some shots of the valuable silver fox, and the effect in the film was to make the fox appear tremendously valuable in their eyes. It can easily be seen what the effect of this type of emphasis on the *technique of execution* (the results obtained by placing together unrelated pieces of film to create a new unity) would have on filmmakers who did not first understand the primary dramatic problem of constructing the scene in space and time from the words of a scenario. Our whole orientation was toward editing or montage and toward special filmic techniques, without understanding that these were only the *means* for the shaping and communication of a *basic dramatic stuff*. It reemphasized our already formal approach.

As a result of this attitude we were unable to understand or utilize the problems that were sent to us from Eisenstein's classes in the Moscow Film School. One of the problems was to stage, to create, the mise-en-scène of a situation in which a soldier comes back from two years at the front to find his wife with a newborn baby. We could see no profit in attempting to conceive this situation for the stage, nor how it would aid us in the making of films. Had we been asked to do a shot-by-shot camera script of the incident we would have seen some point in it. We did not realize that the staging—the invention of activity and circumstances to recreate the scene in space and time—was a necessary step before a shooting script could be made. Without this step a shooting script might result in an interesting camera and montage treatment but would never bring the situation to life for an audience.

THE DOCUMENTARY FILM

It is natural, out of this background, after the first flush of excitement in the purely formal experimental film, and after we arrived at our conception of the movie as a class weapon, that our interest would be concentrated in the documentary film—the film that catches reality on the wing as it passes by. In making a documentary film, as we then conceived it, you photographed the event and the things that were relevant to it, and then by means of clever editing you could do most anything in making the film effective. In brief this was our approach: You were going to do a film about the Scottsboro case or New York harbor. You knew what the film was going to say. Then you took your camera and attempted to capture as completely as you could the most meaningful visual aspects of reality. Then, to the cutting room, where you pieced the film together in a brilliant and cogent montage to make it a moving document of life. Only somehow it was never really moving. At best it turned out to be a conceptualized statement, a film concerned with objects and the purely external manifestations of people without their emotions or motivations, a pamphlet on the screen, to which you could say "yes" with your mind but your emotions weren't involved.

In our documentary films, we relied on the idea that photographed reality contained its own dramatic punch, and while it is certainly true that documentary material has a finality and incontrovertibility and carries with it a special persuasiveness, we did not realize that this was not enough to involve an audience's emotions, to create drama. We did not realize that even in a documentary film it is still necessary to use theatrical means of affecting an audience—suspense, build, dramatic line, etc.

With this background and the feeling that something was missing, we entered Strasberg's course in direction. The specific techniques applicable to all phases of filmmaking, from scenario writing to directing the actor, which we found there, we have tried to indicate briefly. But most important of all we found a basic approach toward filmmaking which, if put into practice, can raise the revolutionary film far above its present low level. We learned that the film as a dramatic medium cannot merely concern itself with external happenings even though they be revolutionary happenings, but must embody the conflict of underlying forces, causes. That to achieve this, the making of a film involves not merely (1) knowing what you want to say, (2) a scenario, and (3) shooting and cutting it, but the intermediate steps of theatricalizing the events through the invention of circumstances and activities which transform concepts, relationships, and feelings into three-dimensional happenings that are plausible, effective, and rich in significance. Only in solving problems does it seem likely that a film conduit can be constructed which can carry our revolutionary viewpoint to an increasingly receptive audience, one that is really moved because in the life on the screen it finds its own aspirations and struggles, its own failures and successes, its own truths.

DOCUMENTARY FILMS IN *NEW THEATRE* AND IN MY LIFE

I LIVE the life of a globe-trotting "film gypsy" with no home except where the work is. I have been writing these pages while finding hours from filming at the Moscow Art Theatre, the Paris Peter Brook Theatre, the Dublin Abbey, and preparing to film with Sir Peter Hall at the London National Theatre. Although I don't have a permanent residence, moving wherever the film work takes me, I am writing now in the historic Chelsea Hotel on 23rd Street in Manhattan. It was here that I first met the dean of American documentary, Robert Flaherty, who encouraged my early career. Nearby is an office I share when in town with two veterans of the Film and Photo League days, Arnold Eagle and Lewis Jacobs. (Arnold worked with Flaherty on *Louisiana Story* and with Hans Richter on *Dreams That Money Can Buy*; among his own films is *Isamu Noguchi*.)

My other office mate, Lewis Jacobs, recently published *The Documentary Tradition*, which included articles by Flaherty, Ivens, Lorentz, Van Dyke, Hurwitz, Steiner, and one Lew urged me to write, about filming *The Forgotten Village* with Steinbeck and Hackenschmied, entitled "Films Without Make-Believe." My article on nonactors was influenced by the Pudovkin selections in *New Theatre*.

Some days and nights Arnold's office fills up with students from the film courses he teaches for the New School for Social Research. At the office there is an area big enough to stage and film commercials and small scenes. Whenever someone asks, I give time gladly to answer a student's questions if Arnold is busy with someone else. I never say no because I remember painfully that a few already established documentarians could have found more time to bestow on me some of their know-how and give encouragement to the start of my own youthful learning process.

Sometimes, when Arnold and I have completed our professional editing work, students who are hanging around apart from class time ask that eternal question, "How should we go about getting the chance to work in filmmaking?"

I urge them to get all the preparation they can with class work. But, most important, if they can't afford to continue, to go out with any film group they can attach themselves to. Then they ask the inevitable question, "How did you get your first chance in films?"

I tell them I was lucky to get an opportunity with Geza Karpathy in the Spanish Civil War. Geza was a skilled photographer but confessed that he didn't know how to load the Eyemo movie camera. We decided to pretend that it had broken down and watched a mechanic at a camera-parts store load so we could count the correct number of sprocket holes. That's how *Heart of Spain* began, with Joris Ivens's encouragement whenever he could be free from his own work on the nearby Jarama front filming with Ernest Hemingway *Spanish Earth*. Later, editing work with Paul Strand and Leo Hurwitz aided my filmmaking career. I collaborated with David Wolff (Ben Maddow, actual screenwriting name) on writing a film to which Alex North contributed his first movie score. Next I worked with another *New Theatre* contributor, the great photographer Henri Cartier-Bresson, on another Loyalist film, *Return to Life*.

All these highly talented people relate to the selections on documentary. In fact, John Grierson, who coined the term "documentary," became a good and helpful friend through our article on "England's Documentary Films." Only two years later, on the eve of World War II, Robert Flaherty was in London while Alexander "Sascha" Hackenschmied and I worked with Peter Mayer and Rosa Harvan on *Lights Out in Europe*. Flaherty and Grierson arranged a screening of our rushes for Basil Wright, John Taylor, Edgar Anstey, Paul Rotha, and other English documentarians. Their enthusiasm that our work exposed the dangers of the Chamberlain appeasement policy resulted in my filming the invasion of Poland with the then-unknown photographer Douglas Slocombe, who later became famous for *Julia, Raiders of the Lost Ark*, and others.

These selections on documentary are especially dear to me as I didn't realize when we published them how they and the pioneers I admired would influence and figure importantly in the rest of my life.

Robert Flaherty's Escape

BY IRVING LERNER

IN TWELVE YEARS Robert Flaherty has made three films; at least only three he cares to remember: *Nanook of the North, Moana of the South Seas,* and *Man of Aran*. In these years Flaherty might have become one of the great film artists. But it is unfortunate that he has become a cult: the savior of the documentary film and chief rebel against the Hollywood cesspool. The latter is true perhaps, but the former is a title that Flaherty would be the first to deny. However, the acclaim received by *Nanook* and *Moana* evidently convinced Flaherty that he was following the correct aesthetic line. Some of us are as guilty of this false praise as the arty groups that revolved around *Close Up, Experimental Cinema*, and the London Film Society. Excepting that we hoped, as Mike Gold put it, "if he should ever decide to give up this whoring after strange gods, and dare to work in the Soviet Union, we would find we had another Eisenstein or Pudovkin."

This is very unlikely. Flaherty insists that he is on the right track; that if he did go to the Soviet Union (and he has expressed a desire to go) he would employ the identical methods that he used in his other films. He has no use (in filmmaking) for the sociological implications of the subject matter that confronts him. He recognizes the existence of the class struggle; but to him it is a thing of banality and has no place in his films. This bit of philosophy is the clue to the estimation of Robert Flaherty's work. This position becomes understandable upon a chronological examination of his career.

He was born and brought up in mining towns. The desire to pioneer and explore new places is a social inheritance from his father, who was an exploring mining engineer in northern Michigan. Later Robert became a mining geologist. It was in this capacity that he became associated with Canada's chief Robber Baron and railroad builder, Sir William Mackenzie. He made a motion picture record of his work for Mackenzie and in 1916 set out to assemble and edit it. As a result of a fire which destroyed the film, Flaherty resolved to go back to the North to make another. Every motion picture company turned him down, but he managed to talk Revillon Frères, the fur company, into financing the job as an advertisement for their product. The result was *Nanook of the North* (1923). It established the formula that Flaherty would follow (although at that time it wasn't obvious) in the rest of his works. *Nanook* opened with a quiet sequence establishing the family in their "normal" environment. It made the blizzard the protagonist. And Nanook's "heroic" struggle to overcome the elements (his will to live) was the central theme. Flaherty used natural phenomena in building his continuity. There was the great climax: the blizzard out of which Flaherty's superman emerges with success, and the film ends on a note of rest.

In 1923 that created quite a stir. From a technical point of view the film was an advance. It was made in the out-of-doors and it didn't smell of Hollywood. The photography was clean, sharp, and interesting. It was hailed as Art and gave the American film (and Pathé, the distribu-

Robert Flaherty's Escape 309

tors) some prestige. It also convinced Flaherty that the future of the art film was in the hands of individual capitalists, be they from Hollywood or a fur company.

But nowhere did the film show the social life of the Eskimo. There has been a whole school of romantic anthropologists in literature, but this was the first time it occurred in films. Even his Nanook was a Robinson Crusoe in furs. As far as the film was concerned Nanook and his family were the only Eskimos in Canada. And of course there was no class struggle, there was no exploitation, there was no oppression! It was too obvious; too banal for Robert Flaherty.

Still trying to escape Hollywood, and his horrible childhood memories, always looking for the ideal race, the graceful and gentle, but brave, people, Flaherty got Jesse Lasky of Paramount to finance *Moana* (1926). Here again he used the identical formula, the same situations. Only the scenery was changed to the Samoan Islands. Nanook is Moana, as much as he is the Man of Aran. *Moana* got Hollywood interested in Robert Flaherty. He was asked by Metro-Goldwyn-Mayer to film O'Brien's apotheosis of the "noble savage," *White Shadows in the South Seas*. That deal was a fizzle. W. S. Van Dine, explorer-in-chief for MGM and director of *The Thin Man*, made the film, instead.

Later Flaherty met Fred Murnau and a new partnership was started. They both complemented each other. The result in *Tabu* (1931) was only a suggestion of what might have resulted from the partnership. At least, it contained a slight recognition of the social implications of imperialism in the South Seas, in the effect of Chinese and English traders on the life of the natives. That in itself was an advance over *Moana* and *Nanook*. Left alone, Flaherty went back to his search for Atlantis. Of course, not being able to find any, he had to create one.

Thus we come to the *Man of Aran* (1934). There is no need to go into a detailed analysis of *Man of Aran*. It is an Irish *Moana* or *Nanook*. It follows the exact formula. For a fine critical appraisal I suggest Brian O'Neill's article in the *New Masses* of October 30, in which the gross disparity between Flaherty's Aran (stark struggle with the sea) and the real Aran (struggle against landlords and British imperialism) is brilliantly exposed. Actually Flaherty wasn't blind to the social implications on the Aran Islands. He confessed to me that since British capital was financing the film he was limited. He shot over 200,000 feet of film: scenes of evictions; of the native customs; of British imperialism as exemplified in the following sequence:

> Two men in canoes are struggling over something in the water. We can't identify the object. They come back to shore and engage in a fist fight.

Then we see that they were fighting over a piece of driftwood, a very valuable commodity in the Aran Islands. Just as the ownership has been agreed upon, the Coast Guard intervenes and confiscates the piece of wood, claiming it as the property of His Majesty.

This sequence was cut out to make room for the artificial shark-hunting sequence, because, as Flaherty explained, it would ruin the "composition of the film"!

It seems that in seeking things at the ends of the earth, Flaherty avoids the life around him when he gets there. Thus, what should be a documentary film (the creative treatment of the actual, honest reality) is transformed into a "poem" of pseudosymphonic structure. Even the thrilling sequence in *Man of Aran* of the sea breaking against the rocky shore resolves itself into glib "abstract cinema," visual excitement for its own sake.

Robert Flaherty has now reached a crucial period in his creative life. "What supreme pictures of the working class this man Flaherty is equipped to make!" says Mike Gold. And what an appreciative audience that same working class would be!

Or else—he can continue to thrill the boiled shirts of London and New York with another abstract film of man against the elements. Such films will continue to serve the imperialists faithfully; Mussolini will continue to award them silver cups; and Hitler will continue to distribute *Man of Aran* because it "illustrates the principles of simple living and strenuous endeavor which Hitler wishes the German people to adopt."

Too Much Reality

BY FRIEDRICH WOLF

WHEN Joris Ivens wanted to present his great film *The New Land* (the film is based on the draining of a part of the Zuider Zee in Holland) in Paris, the presentation was forbidden by the censor with the sentence: *trop de realité*—"too much reality." The Paris censor thus unwittingly paid Ivens the greatest tribute that could ever have been made to a modern cinema director.

Wherein lay the incriminatory nature of this "excess of reality"? The subject of the film, featuring as it does an outstanding engineering feat, is, though very unusual, throughout of a "newsreel" character, never intentionally aggressive. On the contrary, this gigantic work of the "peaceful conquest" of an enormous slice of land, wrested from the sea with the help of Dutch finance capital and the latest technical equipment, might have become a convincing demonstration in favor of the existing social order. And this is the very essence of Ivens's achievement: What might have been a justification has finally developed into a forceful indictment. As Lenin said, "Things have a way of speaking a language all their own." All that is necessary is a "mere trifle" to make the facts speak.

How did Ivens accomplish it? As far as the first part of the film is concerned, he managed to get some private citizens interested, who financed it as a sort of "industrial film." The picture shows how the monster elemental force—the Sea—repeatedly breaks through powerful dams, erected at the price of tremendous efforts, only to be subdued finally by that greatest of all elemental forces—Man, armed with his newest stupendous weapon, modern engineering technique. This struggle of the Titans of our time—Nature, Man, Technique—Ivens portrays in a clear, austere, magnificent montage. Only a past master in the field of film montage could have handled this material with such consummate skill. This conflict of giants—Man, Sea, Technique—forms the first part of the film. With the help of a dam 34 kilometers long a new land is born. Already wheat is growing in the fields, rows of neat houses are springing up as if by magic, telegraph poles, fertile land—a new world. But simultaneously, growing by leaps and bounds, a third (social) Monster Power is coming into being—the Crisis, the World Economic Crisis. And while Man, by virtue of giant effort, wrested this land from the sea in order to have wheat grown on it, one at the same time sees catastrophic fall of prices on the world wheat exchanges; one beholds the amazing spectacle of a world suffering from a *surplus* of grain—too much to keep the price level up. We then see thousands of tons of grain thrown into the sea in an effort to stem the precipitate downfall of prices. At the same time we witness a terrible scarcity of bread for millions of destitute workers, starving children in New York, Paris, Berlin, London—all presented in clear, natural, *factual* montage. That is where the "excessive realism" starts. Here "things begin to speak their own language." For there is nothing more actual, more demonstrative, than this proof—plainly confronting the eye and possessing the irrefutable logic of a mathematical proposition— this proof of the senselessness and barbarism of this much-vaunted system of "peace and order." "Demonstration" (demonstratio—quod erat demonstrandum) in its original meaning, as used by philosophers and mathematicians, stood for "what was to be proven." For the thematics such as this, the film—the montage film—possesses, as no other medium of art does, the power of conclusive proof. It is literally and figuratively—a "Demonstration."

His second great film—*Borinage*—Ivens produced under much more difficult conditions. The film pictures a miners' strike in the Belgian coal mines and triumphant socialist labor in the Don Bas (coal mining region in the Soviet Union). Only one who has himself gone through a great strike, facing the terror of guards, police, and even troops, can realize the skill, knowledge, endurance, and courage necessary to film these events correctly and on a mass scale, especially under conditions of illegality. Such scenes as the wholesale eviction of entire miners' communities from their miserable colonies—permeated with an appalling implacability and yet presented without a trace of sentimentality—cannot be "staged." There is about them an atmosphere of actuality that no "art" could possibly reproduce. The first part of *Borinage* unrolls a picture of suffering of the "damned on this earth," almost inhuman in its cool clarity—something we have never before witnessed in such setting. Yet in the midst of this deep, dull, monotonous oppressiveness, there appears a lightninglike perspective, a bright, keen, flaming ray of light: the miners, slow to move, but unyielding throughout, oppose the eviction of a comrade and are finally driven out of the mine; still unconquered, they demonstrate, carrying before them a picture of Karl Marx painted by one of them. This scene bears the imprint of almost childish primitivity and conveys a sense of unmistakable reality. At the same time it bears the mark of having been produced by a man who profoundly understands the art of realistic montage. For, it is clear, that sheer "true to Nature" presentation, "naked reality," does not in itself contain the compelling force of proof: the emotional appeal inherent in facts has to be brought out. We are not mere onlookers, we want to change this world! The manner in which the arrow is poised and let loose will determine whether the spectator is to remain neutral or to be profoundly stirred. In this sense, Ivens reached greater heights in *Borinage* than in *New Land*, for in some portions of the latter he still shows traces of being dominated by the material he is handling.

The second part of *Borinage* takes place in the Soviet Union; it shows the new way, the way out for humanity. As in the case of that other great master of the montage film, Dziga Vertov, the development of Ivens proceeds in a very laborious, in the beginning not very apparent, but, on the whole, entirely consistent manner, leading up to the highest achievements in his latest productions.

Translated by LEON RUTMAN

The Plow That Broke the Plains

BY IRVING LERNER

WHEN the Resettlement Administration announced last year that it was planning to make a film which would dramatize the tragedy of the western "Dust Bowl" area and depict the Administration's efforts to reclaim the wasted grasslands, no one was particularly affected one way or the other. The government had used the commercial studios to make films before, and they had all been bad. But when Ralph Steiner, Paul Strand, and Leo Hurwitz were engaged as members of the production crew for the projected picture, it was impossible to maintain an air of detachment toward the venture any longer. Here was an opportunity for a group of talented young filmmakers to produce a film of social significance which would have government backing and receive commercial distribution, something no film-art group had ever attained before. But the Hollywood producers were yet to be heard from.

In an effort to keep the screens of America safe for private investment, the motion picture industry not only attempted to block the progress of *The Plow That Broke the Plains* during production by refusing to sell the government the stock shots necessary to round out the narrative, but on completion of this, the first important American documentary film, summarily refused to distribute it. One studio executive was quoted as saying, "I wouldn't release any government picture, not even if it was *Ben Hur*."

Why this sudden prophylactic attitude toward government films? Only a week previous to the premiere of *The Plow That Broke the Plains* in Washington, the Capitol Theatre in New York (key house of the Loews-MGM chain) had shown *Around the World with Coffee*, a government film released by the Department of Commerce. And not so long ago the entire motion picture industry was producing and distributing gratis New Deal propaganda in the form of NRA shorts. The answer undoubtedly lies in the industry's fear that the government might go into the picture business in earnest.

The original scenario of *The Plow That Broke the Plains*, as written by Steiner, Strand, and Hurwitz, embodied a concept of epic implications: capitalism's anarchic rape of the land, and—by extension—the impoverishment of all the natural resources of America: mines, forests, men. This scenario was approved by Pare Lorenz and John Carter (Jay Franklin), supervisors of the project. Once out in the field, Steiner and his associates drew up a shooting script which made explicit the aims of the scenario. But at this juncture the Administration realized what it had on its hands, and Lorenz substituted a scenario of his own making, which, while keeping a great many of the *pictorial* ideas and transitions of the script, completely vitiated the integrity of the original concept. It might be all right for Rexford Tugwell, Resettlement Administration director, to assert, in *Today* magazine, that the dust storms and despoliation of the Great Plains were but one instance of the general unheeding exploitation of America's natural resources for private gain. But Lorenz evidently felt that as film fare such meat was too strong!

Steiner, Strand, and Hurwitz were already in the field. They did not want to disrupt the entire project, and therefore notified Mr. Lorenz that they would continue as photographers, accepting responsibility only for the photography. *Time* magazine of May 25 grossly misstated the facts when it gave the impression that the photographers had withdrawn their objections on seeing the finished job. The film, as put together in its present form by Mr. Lorenz, is a pale imitation of what it was intended to be.

Superficially it does show how a primeval land, a huge grass country which became a huge cattle country and later a wheat area, that great section of the continent known as the Great Plains, became the "Dust Bowl." It ends pessimistically with dust and sand blowing over the stunted grass—the Great American Desert. There is an epilogue, unnecessary and a little silly (done in the standardized manner of the regular commercial film), which makes a sorry attempt to show what the Resettlement Administration wants to do—and has done. Millions of people are homeless; and by means of an animated map you are informed that 4,500 families have been resettled!

A great deal of footage is devoted to the war boom. The film cuts back and forth from the Great Plains of the west to the battlefields of Europe, from tractors to tanks, destroying and defacing the land in the war to end war. This is partially successful irony. But where is the major tragedy—the vain sacrifices that generations of struggling men had made to build homes for themselves and their children in the Great Plains? As *Variety* says, speaking of how the farmers are portrayed in the film, ". . . they aren't called upon for any histrionics other than staring at the sky or whittling sticks to indicate complete resignation to fate."

In the beginning you are shown fat healthy cattle. Where are the shots of the cattle now starved by the lack of grass and made thirsty by the lack of water, their bones sticking out of their thin-skinned hides? Where is the sequence from the original scenario:

"Great herds are driven in on the range. Countless heads of cattle feed on the sea of grass. Steers grow fat. The cattlemen grow rich. The range is free. More ranchers drive in their herds. The herds increase. Scramble for water rights and control of range, and speculation in cattle. More stock men! Each after what he can get—no responsibility to safeguard the great resource—*the grass*."

Such was the tone and concept of the *original* scenario. It was forthright, and its implications were inescapable. Mr. Lorenz's film protests eloquently enough, but it is incoherent and unbalanced. The lack of a clear message or a decisive point of view weakens the structure of the film and makes it rhetorical and literary instead of dramatic. Evasion has never helped the documentary. There is no point in trying to make the documentary show a world that does not exist. If you do, you get an abstract film on the struggle between Man and Nature—you get a *Man of Aran*.

Nevertheless, with all its faults of bad scenario, unimaginative cutting, and unclear viewpoint, Mr. Lorenz's film still commands attention because in the various stages of its development he managed to secure the services of talented artists. *The Plow That Broke the Plains* is endowed with the finest musical score of any American film; it is the work of Virgil Thompson, who wrote the score for *Four Saints in Three Acts*, and it is simple, robust, and distinctive. It contributes more to the film than the spoken text. The photography—the sequences taken by Steiner, Strand, and Hurwitz—is superb. These sequences are brilliantly conceived and executed, especially the shots of the cattle in the early part of the film. But the stock shots are definitely inferior; when the picture companies were finally forced by government pressure to let Lorenz have such material as he needed, he failed to select shots which were up to the photographic level of the rest of the film.

Although *The Plow That Broke the Plains* is not a completely realized film, it does set a new standard for the American documentary. Its most important achievement is that it gave an opportunity to real talent. Paul Strand, Ralph Steiner, and Leo Hurwitz were not selected at random. They are members of Nykino, a group which is devoting its time to the production of progressive social films. At the moment this organization has in production a documentary film on a labor theme. Not that they have any intention of limiting themselves to the documentary; there is also a dramatic film in preparation.

Yet these films can do no good unless they are distributed. What the moving picture industry did to the government-made *Plow That Broke the Plains* is only a sample of what it will do to keep *all* independent films of merit out of its theatres. It is imperative that a strong noncommercial outlet, in addition to those already in existence, be organized through the trade unions. It is encouraging to note that in spite of the Hollywood ban, many independent theatres are booking the "Dust Bowl" film. A greater demand by the motion picture-going public will force more and more theatres to show independently made films.

Redes

by Robert Stebbins

THE EMERGENCE of the film *Redes* (*Nets*) from the welter of world film production is an event of incommensurable importance. Not only is *Redes* the first full-length film made in America on a working-class theme embodying the aspirations of the great masses of men, but it is moreover extraordinarily beautiful and moving as few films in our experience have been.

We saw *Redes* in the usual tiny, bare projection room, in its original Spanish, a language unfamiliar to us. Nevertheless, in spite of these handicaps and the unfavorable advance reports of acquaintances who had previewed the film on the Coast, our wonder at what was unfolding before us increased from moment to moment. The old thrill one gets when present at the "beginning" of things was there, but more than that was the joy that *Redes* should have risen so high above the tyranny of circumstance that usually dooms "beginnings" to mediocrity.

Redes was produced in Mexico. The project, under the supervision of Paul Strand, was initiated by Carlos Chavez, the Mexican composer and conductor, when he was chief of the Department of Fine Arts in the Secretariat of Education in 1933. Full credits for the production follow: Production (save for synchronization of the sound): Paul Strand; story: Paul Strand assisted by Velasquez Chavez; screen treatment: Henwar Rodakiewicz; direction: Fred Zinneman assisted by Gomez Muriel; photography: Paul Strand; edited by Gunther von Fritsch; music by Sylvestre Revueltas; stills by Ned Scott.

The setting of *Redes* is Alvarado, a fishing village on the Gulf of Vera Cruz.

There, in the midst of strangulating poverty, the fishermen make an heroic pilgrimage from abject, suicidal resignation to conscious, full-statured protest against their lot. As the film opens we see a village exhausted by inanition and poverty. There has been no catch for months. Miro, one of the fishermen, has lost a child because he has been unable to afford medical attention. The child is buried. Miro, himself, takes a spade from the hands of the gravedigger and throws earth on the coffin in a last self-imposed agony. He speaks for the first time in the film to say, "It isn't right—it isn't just for a man's child to die because he has no money to cure it." Miro is led away by his companions. After an interval of time, fishermen rush into the village telling that a school of fish has entered their waters. Then follows the fish hunt, frenzied yet grave, surely among the greatest single sequences in the history of films. The men take their catch to a nearby city. The local dealer, a wealthy padrone, gives them a meager handful of pesos in return. The men stand overwhelmed with shame and misery. But Miro, already embittered by the death of his child, is aroused to action. He calls a meeting at which some of the men decide not to sell unless they receive higher prices. But not all of them are persuaded. A group under the leadership of Miro's friend, Miguel, hold that action against the dealer can only lead to further disaster. They attempt to scab. There is a struggle. A politician, Juan Garcia Sanchez, hating Miro for his influence over the men, and currying the favor of the padrone, takes advantage of the tumult and shoots Miro, wounding him fatally. At the sound of the shot the battle ends. Miro's followers take him to his home. The others are confounded by the event and slowly perceive the folly of their dissension and the consequences of their cowardice. They return to Miro to find him dead. Miguel, through the death of Miro, has quickly come to realize the need for unity. He speaks the funeral oration over the body of his dead friend. Miro is placed on a boat on a stretcher of oars. The fishermen row back toward the city. Other crews gather; two boats become many. As the film ends we see a phalanx of ships which suggest the power of the waves as they rise higher and higher, rushing in to break on the shore.

Here we have a story of utmost simplicity, told directly, with almost a complete absence of symbolic digression.

I tried to think of the people who had made *Redes* and chiefly of Paul Strand, who had conceived and guided it to completion. I thought of Paul Strand's still photographs, perhaps the most beautiful created in our time. It seemed strange. How could a man who had spent most of his life arresting the fugitive nobility of real things, whose photographs arouse such elusive ideas and feelings in the onlooker, how could this man give voice so completely and unerringly to the forthright statements of *Redes*? And the answer came—there was no essential difference between the stills and the film. From his earliest works, like the blind woman in Stieglitz's magazine, *Camera Work*, to *Redes*, Strand has spoken of one thing predominantly—the dignity of human life and of the things man has made that reflect his image. But in addition, *Redes* was under the necessity of pointing to those relationships that stand in the way of man's rightful assumption of a desirable and dignified life. Hence the difference in approach. But the substance is the same.

Strand moved toward this simplicity with conscious deliberation. In the course of a statement prepared for the Secretariat of Education of Mexico, he declared: "We assume that these pictures are not being made for subtle and sophisticated people or even very sensitive minds accustomed to follow the intricacies of aesthetic nuance. On the contrary, we assume that these films are being made for a great majority of rather simple people to whom elementary facts should be presented in a direct and unequivocal way; a way that might even bore more complicated sensibilities, though we believe otherwise. We feel that almost a certain crudeness of statement is necessary to achieve the purposes of these films." Yet, despite this foreknowledge, there is in *Redes* not the slightest trace of condescension or the quaint archaism that results from the self-conscious turning of a sophisticate to simpler modes. This we can only attribute to Strand's complete belief in what he was saying. The dialogue of the film, for example, strikes the ear with the true ring of authenticity.

In the weighing scene:
Miro: We sure got a haul this time.
Fogonero: If it keeps up this way I'll hitch up with Elena.
Antonio: Which is more of a fool, a man or a fish?
Yi-yi: Who knows? You're asking me?
Miguel: Any man who lets a woman hook him—
Fogonero: How well yours caught you.
Or later:
Miguel: There's no use griping—the sharks always eat the robalo.
Miro: Yes—but don't forget—we are not fish.

But after the vigor of much of the dialogue has been noted one must always return to the visual expressiveness of the film. In a conversation with Mr. Strand some time ago he conveyed his surprise that so few films were visually beautiful, particularly since the film was a visual medium. He pointed out that even so majestic a work as Dovzhenko's

Frontier was photographically indifferent; that seldom did the photography begin to approach the heights of Dovzhenko's conception. *Redes* makes it easy for one to agree with him about *Frontier*.

In thinking over *Redes*, two films inevitably come to mind—Flaherty's *Man of Aran* and Eisenstein's unfortunate *Thunder Over Mexico*. This, not only because both films possess great photographic beauty but because Strand has admitted the influence of Flaherty and of the Russian school. As early as 1933, however, Stand pointed out certain shortcomings in Flaherty's aesthetic. Talking of *Nanook of the North* and *Moana*, he said: "It was necessary for Flaherty to more or less reconstruct the past since all these people are already undergoing changes from the contacts of so-called Western civilization. And unless Flaherty widens the scope of his work this dramatic theme of elemental struggle for survival would seem to be a limited one." In other words, the true enemies of man were the man-made social and economic relationships. These were the things you had to struggle against. Undoubtedly, Flaherty, by taking himself off to the Arctic, the South Sea Islands, or the Islands of Aran, was, in his way, expressing dissatisfaction with modern life. But in so doing he was utilizing symbols that no longer obtain today, symbols that men couldn't believe in. As a consequence, *Man of Aran* was merely *picturesque*.

In *Redes* Strand turned his back on the purely picturesque. To quote further from his letter to the Secretariat of Education: "In a world in which human exploitation is so general it seems to me a further exploitation of people, however picturesque, different, and interesting to us they may appear, to merely make use of them as *material*." True, Mr. Strand was himself, as he admitted, in a not-altogether-impregnable position, but he was confident of defending himself. "As to the criticism that the people will know and always accept the injustice of their lot, this one does not know. It is well to remember that new generations are being born and that children may have other feelings and ideas from those of their parents." As in the phrase of André Malraux, the artist "has created an illusion of conquest for the reader."

Thunder Over Mexico, mutilated in America by blind and unknowing hands, is certainly not to be thought of as the work of Eisenstein. Therefore is it only possible photographically to compare *Thunder Over Mexico* with *Redes*. On that score Strand is more human, simple, closer to the people than Eisenstein's photographer Tisse. Perhaps, the gigantic scale on which *Thunder Over Mexico* was conceived militated against complete success. Thesis and antithesis run through every frame. Not only did Tisse have to show the Mexicans as they are today but he also had to point out that they came of an ancient race of great cultural achievements, a race brought to a point just short of annihilation by imperialist oppression.

Whether *Redes* will or can be followed by films of a similar nature is open to question. In times like these, with great numbers of men blind to their true interests, perhaps a more oblique introduction of progressive thought is necessary in films—the greater use of melodramas like *The General Died at Dawn* and *Fury*, social comedies like *Mr. Deeds Goes to Town*. Yet it is difficult to believe that so complete an affirmation of a man's faith as *Redes*, so rich an intimation of a more desirable world, will fail to move audiences wherever it is shown.

THE FOREIGN FILM, YESTERYEAR AND NOW

ALTHOUGH foreign films in the 1980s are still seen mainly in small art houses in a few cosmopolitan cities, they have wielded great influence on American moviemaking. Whether it was Ernst Lubitsch, Sacha Guitry, or René Clair with their brilliant satire and comedy, or the Germans, Lang and Pabst, with their extraordinary emphasis on studio decor, or especially the great Russians, Eisenstein, Pudovkin, Dovzhenko, and Ermler, who influenced Vidor, Wyler, and Milestone, among others, American film writing and directing owed a great deal to the foreign artists. The achievements of some are covered in part from their writings or ours in these selections from *New Theatre*.

For the 1980s and other recent generations, it is important to understand how difficult it was in the mid-1930s to see the great foreign films. At that time there were comparatively few university and museum film theatres or film societies. It was an era long before TV and video cassettes helped somewhat to balance Hollywood's distribution domination. For example, in our Tri-City area with Hollywood movie palaces in towns of 40,000 like Rock Island and Moline, Illinois, or Davenport with 50,000, there was not one single theatre showing foreign films, or, for that matter, reviving the work of great American directors like D. W. Griffith, Von Stroheim, Cruze, Neilan, or others.

In 1933, the year before I went to New York City as a playwright and ended up an editor, I shared with Mark, George Redfield, and our close friends, Bill Jordan and Bob Lorenz, a desire to see and show foreign film classics. It was during the Depression, and we didn't have much money, but we rented portable equipment and set up showings with a small screen at our hall. We managed to rent films by René Clair, Jean Renoir, Luis Buñuel, Fritz Lang, and G. W. Pabst that caused us no trouble. However, we ran into difficulty when we arranged to show works of Eisenstein, Pudovkin, and Dovzhenko. That brought angry opposition from the American Legion, who threatened an injunction closing us down for showing "foreign propaganda" and "stirring up trouble with red plays and movies," as they put it. Fortunately, my Uncle Lou had fought in France in World War I and had been a commander of the nearby Burlington (Iowa) Legion post. My father called for his help and Uncle Lou came to town immediately. He persuaded his Legion buddies that it was wiser to leave "a bunch of crazy kids" alone than cause a clamor that would bring more attention to our theatre and film showings.

The Films of René Clair

BY LEWIS JACOBS

SINCE the movie is a medium dependent upon multiple technicians and artisans, few directors are capable enough to both create and control their films' manifold destinies. René Clair is one of the few who, until his most recent film, *The Ghost Goes West*, had the distinction of realizing his conceptions intact, brooking no interference in the questions of content or style. He not only supervised his cutting but also wrote the stories and constructed the scenarios for his films. None of his pictures which we have seen shows evidence of a producer's or corporation's tampering. Consequently with a director as earnest as Clair and as talented, questions of content and structure assert themselves, calling to be weighed, analyzed, criticized instead of merely being superficially dismissed.

Practically all of René Clair's films deal with the foibles of the middle class. He has a knack for swift characterization (the stock-in-trade of every caricaturist) on the intellectual level of a Leech or Gavarni. A deeper insight into the basic social and economic incongruities would inevitably lift his comedy to social satire. As it is, his humor, with rare exceptions, springs from the same cynical detachment as the *New Yorker*'s, with results just as socially ineffectual.

Clair's first films—*The Crazy Ray*, for which he still has a sentimental attachment, *Entr'acte*, made to be shown between the acts of the Picabia-Satie ballet, *Phantom of Moulin Rouge*, and *The Imaginary Voyage*—were all excursions into whimsy. Nevertheless they served as a discipline for his first feature and most penetrating film, *The Italian Straw Hat*. This was one of the first films of social satire—although in a discussion of the film with him, Clair said satire was not his purpose—a piercing cross section of the middle class. Coming from such a young director, *The Italian Straw Hat* was especially remarkable. His images were so telling that the bourgeoisie retaliated by forbidding its showing, a censorship Clair could not understand in view of the fact that he said his aim was only comedy. Notwithstanding, he was dismissed by his producers and the stigma of "intellectual" was attached to him and has remained ever since.

Although Clair has praised the films of Chaplin for their "movement," it was not until *The Italian Straw Hat* that he based his method on Chaplin's. (Upon asking Clair if he would like to make a film with Chaplin, Clair replied, "I? How could I make a film with Chaplin? He has a genius! The rest of us have only facility.") However, Clair's film revealed a feeling for social caricature as against Chaplin's poignant little-man-what-now frustrations. Where Chaplin was content with slapstick, Clair achieved ridicule. While Chaplin was concerned with an individual, Clair was concerned with a class. This feat preceded by several years Sergey Eisenstein's formulation of the "class villain."

A year's idleness was the penalty Clair paid for *The Italian Straw Hat*. His promise to behave was rewarded with another picture. In *Two Timid Souls*, as it was called, Clair concerned himself solely with plastic problems. Since honesty in content was frowned upon, Clair grappled with the Beelzebub of structure—no simple problem.

But cinema style and structural form have always been concerns of Clair. In 1923–24, with Picabia, the French painter and dadaist, Clair made the film *Entr'acte*, which helped to foment the avant-garde movement in the cinema. Experimental films such as *Ballet Mechanique*, *What Are the Young Films Dreaming*, *En Rade*, *Emak Bakia*, *Montparnasse*, together with *Entr'acte*, introduced the plastic problem to film structure. The directors of these films insisted that the film's artistic integrity lay in the correct use of the camera's resources: angles, dissolves, fades, optical distortions, tempo and space distortions, image duration, transitions and their rhythms. This engagement with the grammar of the film had a far-reaching effect. In Soviet Russia, under the tutelage of Kuleshov, the conclusions drawn from these avant-garde experiments were later put to a dynamic social use.

Entr'acte gave Clair a keen perception of the possibilities of the movie's instruments. But whereas in that film he used the means solely as an end in themselves, in *Two Timid Souls* he attempted to utilize the medium's resources as an integral basis for expression. The separation of movie from stage or even literature, the individuality of the movie as a distinct mode of art, with methods of expression peculiar to it alone, was the problem which intrigued Clair. How well he succeeded can be illustrated by several instances from the film.

A young lawyer is describing the happy home life of his client. This is the lawyer's first case and he is a bit nervous. Instead of showing his nervousness by a photograph of him in jitters—the typical Hollywood fashion—Clair lets us see a close-up of the lawyer pleading, and as he talks there is superimposed across his forehead what he is describing: the husband with flowers enters in slow motion. The nervous lawyer forgets his speech and the superimposition of the husband, still in slow motion, backs out. The lawyer then recalls his speech and the husband comes forward again. Suddenly the entire image stops and appears like a still. After a moment the still explodes, leaving the screen blank. From then on the entire speech of the lawyer is told without his presence on the screen. Here is an instance of the camera's means utilized filmically, psychologically, an integration of content and form.

Later in the same film, Clair shows two rivals indicating what they will do when they confront each other. Instead of showing one image following the other, Clair divides the screen in two and the audience sees the action of the two rivals simultaneously with each performer oblivious of the other. Of course the result is twice as effective. It is by such intelligent use of film craft that Clair lifts his material from the conventional.

Two Timid Souls ends with perhaps one of the cleverest uses of the fade-out ever recorded. The screen is split into three panels. In the left is seen the defeated suitor. In the right is "the timid soul." The center panel contains the newlywed couple in bed. Slowly the left panel goes blank, then the right. Now there remains only the center panel holding the mischievous eyes of the audience upon the bride and groom. The groom stretches out his hand and presses the electric light button. The room darkens, the panel blackens and the picture ends. This is a superb instance of the "Clair touch," illustrating again his instinct for cinematic values, values which act as a corridor for his humor or fantasy. Yet upon what puerile subject matter does he lavish his resources! The reprimand resulting from *The Italian Straw Hat* had indeed reduced Clair to grappling with windmills.

The advent of sound brought a problem Clair disdained. "Sound is the death of film," he said. However, he soon realized that the sound film was here to stay and *Under the Roofs of Paris*, his first sound film, ironically established the reputation of René Clair internationally. Craftsman as he was, he worked out a mixture where sound and image could run parallel, in this way overcoming the immobility of dialogue by relying on the mobility of the camera. But whereas in his silent films his humor was heightened by its filmic aspects, Clair was hindered when confronted with a microphone and he actually became sound struck. His camera participated in his chase patterns by dollying continually and for no other reason than to infuse an artificial sense of life to offset the deadening influence of dialogue. Often he resorted to music to overcome the language barrier for the international market. The financial success of the film, however, did not offset its structural looseness.

In his second sound film, *Le Million*, Clair's fancy has become richer. The behaviors of his characters are as grotesque and unreal as those in a musical comedy. This unnaturalness is deliberate. Treating his material as fantasy—a far cry from the social criticism of *The Italian Straw Hat*—*Le Million* could become as madcap and daring as Clair chose. Clair tries to solve the problem of sound and image by having his characters sing and dance at the slightest pretext. Only one man has been successful in this respect: Walt Disney. With Disney in mind, Clair made *Le Million*. By the nature of his films—animation—Disney has contracted and expanded sound related to image so as to create counterpoint. He juggles sound with the same dexterity as images and relates both to a rhythmic continuity which emerges as an integrated and complete sound-image unity, each dependent upon the other for life and meaning. The result of such an interdependence is form. Disney's films alone since the introduction of sound to film can be said to have form.

The predominant motif of *Le Million* is the chase, and in Clair's eagerness to out-Disney Disney his microphone is given seven-league boots. Staccato dialogue, snatches of songs, sudden refrains, a deliberate attempt to animate sound is apparent throughout. But in the meantime, the camera means, Clair's feeling for film structure, has been pushed aside. Instead of a blissful union between camera and microphone as in Disney, Clair exploits one at the expense of the other. Whereas in his silent films the very subject matter was molded and built by camera means, in *Le Million* his camera has become a spectator. Consequently his material emerges lopsided: photographed musical comedy spotlighted with mobile sound effects.

A Nous la Liberté, his next film, was an advance upon *Le Million*.

Clair's use of sound became more structural. The film has many instances of counterpoint, image-sound effects. The similarity between the jail and the factory systems was heightened by the same martial sound overtone of both. Likewise his use of sound flashback to recall an image in the office of the industrialist confronted by his former pal, the ex-convict, is structural progress. Again in the courtyard of the factory, high-hatted officials are interrupted by falling treasury notes. Their speeches suggest one thing, their greedy glances at the money another. (Eisenstein, in talking of sound film, said, ". . . thus does conflict between optical and acoustical impulses produce the true sound film.") In this instance Clair solved the problem of sound in a filmic way, an international way. One need not understand French to appreciate the meaning.

As a statement of social position, *A Nous la Liberté* lacks conviction. Poking fun at rationalization and factory methods is not enough; we must know whose rationalization and which society's factory methods. Unfortunately there was never any clue as to what Clair was joshing: democracy, the factory, the worker—everything? Somewhere in the film, Clair's sense of extravaganza got the upper hand. Allowing his fancy to rule and his camera and microphone to follow, he became a buffoon and as such was often dazzling. His technique had sharpened, his raillery distilled.

July the Fourteenth was a reversion to the sentimentalisms of *Under the Roofs of Paris*, both as to content and style. Though the film has the newspaper critic values "gaiety," "charm," and Clair "touches," his style has become a manner, the fun repetitive. The film might almost have been made in Hollywood, cut from a Clair pattern.

René Clair has often been called a great stylist. Trained as a journalist, his filmic structure partakes of journalistic simplification. Especially is this apparent in his portrait of a dictator: *The Last Multimillionaire*. From the very opening, the remarkable mock travelogue of depression-dampened Casinario, to the end, the film is a *comédie humaine* in terms of a comic strip. And as such, one would expect a great success for it. The reverse was true. Clair attributes its failure—at the box office—to its injudicious presentation. It opened in Paris at the beginning of the Stavisky affair and a few days after the assassination of King Alexander and Minister Barthou. Paris was seething with excitement. As luck would have it, the assassinated minister resembled the minister in Clair's film. A sardonic coincidence: the film was made some six months before. Demonstrations against the picture broke out. During its first showing, fascist sympathizers were pleased at the early scenes of the multimillionaire taking over the reins of government, only to become angered when later in the film he becomes mad. Shouts of disapprobation, breaking of theatre seats, and a general commotion followed. Subsequent showings were held in turmoil. The producers had to recall the film. "A tremendous failure," said Clair. But was it? Would it have had such a startling effect if it did not strike at dictators? "My films are not satire," says Clair, "they are comedy." I wonder.

The Ghost Goes West, his latest film, made in England, gave Clair a chance to prepare himself for the Hollywood factories. *The Ghost Goes West* abounds in gags. Not the kind Clair is noted for—innuendos of camera treatment—but polite drawing-room gossip where everyone is on his best behavior. For these gags we have Robert Sherwood to thank; he adapted the story from one in *Punch*. This is the first time that Clair has allowed someone else to do his screen story. Is this forced collaboration a first concession to the Hollywood system?

During the making of *The Ghost Goes West*, Clair said in discussing dialogue with Robert Herring in England, "It is the first time I have been able to [use a good deal of dialogue]! Before, I had to use music and songs, and I had to find ways to avoid dialogue, because much French dialogue would have meant the pictures could have been sold only in France. But this language [English] I make a picture in now means that it can be understood here and in America, and many places, so I can use more." Almost everything Clair has learned about film structure has been thrown to the lions of "Bob Sherwood's brilliant dialogue." Clair told me he was so delighted with the dialogue that he often altered his shots to point Sherwood's wit. A sad mistake.

A bit of the old Clair is the sequence in which he employs a sliding screen showing Edinburgh and Washington separated by the Atlantic Ocean. Offscreen voices accompany these sliding images, proclaim their country's attitude toward the "ghost going west." A simple yet imaginative treatment.

Despite Clair's denial of satirical intent, the extravagant welcome given the ghost in New York is a sly takeoff on national gullibility. A procession of autos goes triumphantly up Broadway; amidst falling confetti and tumultuous acclaim, we see a luxurious automobile driven by a liveried chauffeur. In the honored seat is a huge placard: "Reserved for the Ghost!"

However, for the craftsman Clair, the film as a whole is his most self-conscious work. Handicapped by a new language, a new technical crew, ignorant of national mannerisms in which he had to deal and which are such a vital part of his French films, *The Ghost Goes West* emerges heavy-laden. Although amusing, it is static in the stage tradition. Unless he is careful, it may not only be true, as Evelyn Gerstein said, "Hollywood is ready for Clair," but that Clair may soon be ready for Hollywood. And this would be a sad loss indeed!

PRODUCERS, ATTENTION!

Whether you realize it or not, films like *Riffraff, Red Salute, Fighting Youth,* and the constant antilabor and prowar bias of the newsreels are reactionary influences conditioning the public mind toward fascism. Not only have you failed to produce a single antifascist film, but by your cancellation of the production of *It Can't Happen Here* you have revealed your fear of antagonizing existing fascist governments. Today reaction and anti-Semitism are growing in the United States at an alarming rate. This article by Carl Dreher gives an accurate and disquieting account of what happened to the German motion picture industry when Hitler came to power. In the debacle that ensued, not only the trade unions (which *you* are fighting so savagely in this country) but all producers who did not subscribe to Nazi tenets, or were "non-Aryans," went down to ruin.

—The Editors.

Parade-Ground Art

THE GERMAN FILM UNDER HITLER

BY CARL DREHER

"FILM and microphone have done their part to bring the Man to the People and the People to the Man."

This birthday salute to the Führer does scant justice to the German film, which has performed untold prodigies in hallowing the mystic union of the Leader and the led. Nor is its work at an end, for the bond between folk and Führer requires assiduous rewelding. To this end all the forces of German movie art and science were dedicated on and after January 30, 1933.

Keeping them so dedicated requires a corporative setup to which even the native German genius for complex organization would scarcely be equal were it not for the invention and application of the unifying führer principle. Never before has the world seen, regulating a single industry, such an array of massive titles: *Reichsminister, Staatskommissaren, Reichskulturwarter, Oberregierungsräte, Hauptstellenleiter, Kontingentenleiter, Amtsleiter,* and *Geschäftsführer,* down to simple *Doktoren,* storm troopers, and policemen. Never before has history witnessed such a proliferation of governmental chambers, boards, associations, administrations, bureaus, and fronts; such a multiplication of decrees, followed by later decrees to interpret or rescind the foregoing decrees; such collection of dues and fees; such promulgation of regulations and prohibitions; such an issuance of official certificates, permits, cards, and badges; such a holding of congresses, meetings, and confabulations; such a universal furor and searching of the national soul. Withal films are made, but now they are "German" films, not things like *Mädchen in Uniform, M, The Blue Angel, Kameradschaft, Westfront 1918,* or *Congress Dances,* which formerly aroused the interest of a decadent world.

The authoritarian line descends from the Führer to the Minister for Public Enlightenment and Propaganda, Dr. Goebbels, often referred to by his adoring subordinates as "The Protector of the German Film," thence to the Reich Film Chamber, hereafter referred to as the RFK, which is divided into an employees' group, the *Reichfachschaft Film,* and associations of producers, distributors, exhibitors, etc., each with its leader and subleaders. At the same time the National Socialist Party, through its film division, has liaison officers operating between its district headquarters and the regional authorities of the RFK. This enhances the virtue of the führer principle, and perhaps facilitates the collection of a little quasi-legal graft on the side. Good Germans should be glad to pay for the blessings of totalitarian law and order.

The RFK regulates, by decree, everything and everybody pertaining to films. To trade or work in the film business, one must belong to the RFK and the appropriate suborganization, and hold a permit. One may not work even with a permit, but certainly not without one. A sample decree in this category:

"*EXPULSION FROM REICHFACHSCHAFT FILM.*

"By order of the President of the *Reichsfilmkammer,* the actor Herbert Grunack, also known as Bert Gussy, is excluded from the *Reichsfilmkammer* and thereby from the *Reichfachschaft Film.* His permit No. 320 is hereby canceled."

The innocent have nothing to fear. Thus Jenny Jugo, a brunet featured player and leading woman, keeps her permit:

"*AGAINST JENNY JUGO—RUMORS.*

"Rumors having recently been circulated that Jenny Jugo is non-

Aryan, we certify that she has furnished proofs of her Aryan descent to the office in charge."

The RFK specifies admission prices in theatres, clearances and rights to plays, rentals and accounting methods, and whether pictures may be shown at all. At one time it specified the makeup of main titles and told the producers who should get screen credit, but this proved too much of a headache even for the führer principle, and the decree was withdrawn.

Such slight setbacks mean nothing to seasoned Nazi administrators. Their führer complex knows no bounds in time or space, and they extend it conceptually to all countries. Thus a German film journal refers to "Kardinal Hayes, the führer of the well-known clean-film movement in the U. S. A...."

II

The chief expositor of Nazi cultural philosophy is, of course, Dr. Goebbels himself. When he speaks his thoughts on German film art, the entire industry prostrates itself. In reporting his speeches, the trade press has standardized certain phrases: the Doctor's words are always awaited tensely (*mit Spannung*); during his address the audience is filled with enthusiasm (*begeistert*); and at the close bursts into roaring applause (*brausenden Schlussbeifall*) followed by a triple *Sieg Heil* to the Führer. This unanimity is another achievement of the führer principle.

In the course of a weighty speech before the International Film Congress held in Berlin in April 1935, Dr. Goebbels, like Luther at Wittenberg, propounded a series of theses, but a mere seven instead of ninety-five. With rare profundity, he showed that "the laws of the film are not the laws of the stage," and that "public taste is educable for good as well as evil." He denounced pictures which offer "mere mass entertainment," but cried, "Away also with pale aestheticism!" On an earlier occasion, he warned, "Do not come to us with the story that Art must serve Truth."

The worshipful Doctor has cited four non-Nazi films as meriting Nazi approbation, at least in some respects. These are *The Cruiser Potemkin*, directed by the Bolshevik Eisenstein; Fritz Lang's *Niebelungen; Rebel*, codirected by Trenker and Kurt Bernhard; and *The Last Company*, also a Bernhard production. Bernhard is a Jew. Lang, a certified Aryan, was, with Pabst, also an Aryan, and Lubitsch, the most notable contributor to the international renown of pre-Hitler German pictures. With astounding ingratitude, he left Dr. Goebbels for Louis B. Mayer. Pabst and Lubitsch are also in Hollywood.

As for Eisenstein, the unmannerly Russian said, in the course of an open letter to Goebbels:

"*Get back to your drums, Master Drummer-in-Chief!*

"Stop disporting yourself with ritual pipings on the magic flute of National-Socialist realism in the cinema.

"Stop imitating your idol, Frederick the Great, and on his own flute, too.

"Just stay at your more congenial instrument—the ax."

III

Since the führer principle unifies by purification, the ferreting out and casting forth of non-Aryan elements have been a cardinal task of the Nazi film administrators. One gifted analogist calls this "lifting off the dross." The more common expression is *entjudung*—"de-Jewing." When de-Jewing has been accomplished, an organization is said to be *judenrein* —"cleansed of Jews," or, conversely, *rein arisch*—"pure Aryan." Thus, on October 1, 1935, the joyful news was published that the Protective Union of Film Distributors was finally *rein arisch*. The *entjudung* was complete to the last drop of blood.

The magnitude of the task of de-Jewing the German film will be understood if we contemplate its state when the National Socialists took power. Before this time, as *Oberregierungsrat* Raether points out, there was no German film. *Volksfremde*—"strangers to the people," aliens— dominated it. The German industry was then as Hollywood is now. Decency and honor, as well as jobs, were at stake. The situation cried to high heaven for correction, and it was corrected. The German film was purged of Reinhardt, Czinner, Schach, Kortner, Ludwig Berger, Pommer, Bergner, et al. Their jobs went to German-blooded men, and now the industry breathes the pure atmosphere of 100 percent Aryanism. The only remaining trouble is with the pictures.

To combat recurrences of vitiation, in July of last year Dr. Goebbels appointed Hans Hinkel special commissioner of purification. Some of the perverse Jews had persisted in trying to continue earning a living in the film business. And—it would be unbelievable if Special Commissioner Hinkel himself did not testify to it—these Israelites had succeeded in seducing a certain number of German-blooded individuals. It would appear that, while pure Aryan blood insures honesty, race pride, and nobility in *almost* every individual through whose veins it courses, there are some exceptions.

The method used by the Jews was *Tarnung*—"masking." The Jew became a silent partner, concealed behind an Aryan facade. While Special Commissioner Hinkel proclaimed himself as inflexibly determined to root out the renewed activity of non-Aryans in cultural life, he disclaimed any intention of "employing informers or listening at keyholes." Such measures were unnecessary. Before the hunt was well under way the editor and publisher of the *Licht Bild Buehne* found it necessary to announce that "communications and notices in reference to the Aryan or non-Aryan character of person, firms, or corporations can be received by us only when officially confirmed." This is an indication of the vigilance with which the Nazi businessman watches his competitors for possible redefilement of the industry.

The net result of the chase, as far as reported, was, however, somewhat disappointing. One Berlin film house was closed by the police, on the ground of masked Jewish ownership and the *Tarner* "nabbed," together with others implicated. In a more extraordinary case, one Willi Zeyn was expelled from the *Reichfachschaft Film* for acting as a *Tarner* for a Jewish film director. The mechanics of director-*Tarnung* are not clear; perhaps television and radio telephony are employed, for the Jew certainly could not show himself on the movie set.

IV

Dr. Goebbels's discovery that public taste is no unalterable fact reverberates in the halls of the German film administration. Hans Wiedemann, the youthful vice-president of the RFK, carries the doctrine a step further: "There is no such thing as public taste; we can shape that as we will. We have determined political taste; we can do the same with artistic taste!"

The concept of State-determined public taste is coupled with that of State-determined mental hygiene. Under the Weimar republic, it seems, the film and its patrons were alike very sick. Thus on July 11, 1935, *Oberregierungsrat* Arnold Raether, reviewing the achievements of the Chamber over the past two years, reported that it had almost fully restored the film business to health, by permeating it with National Socialist consciousness. Evidently it suffered a relapse, for on November 17 the president of the RFK, SS *Oberführer* Prof. Dr. Oswald Lehnich, appeared before a meeting of the Cultural Senate to prescribe numerous measures for the recovery of the industry. And on December 13 Hans Weidemann, at a private showing of the French *Les Misérables* before the *Reichsfachschaft Film*, said:

"While we must reject the material of this film and the manner in which it is presented, let it not be denied that we know and recognize its artistic achievement. It is essential for the German artist to see such foreign art; the public on the other hand must have quiet, until it is once more entirely healthy and strong."

At this meeting Nazi speakers attacked *Les Misérables* on the ground that it "portrays the criminal as innocent, as morally justified, while the State and its institutions . . . are portrayed as guilty of the misfortunes of the criminal. This whole theme is carried out in a very reprehensible manner, which taints every spectator. On these grounds the film had to be rejected for German exhibition."

From this it would appear that in Germany, as in other countries, film professionals, especially censors, acquire immunity to moral poisons which would fell the general population.

As in the United States, censorship begins at the beginning, before the picture is shot, "to prevent treatment of material contrary to the spirit of the time." In the early part of 1934 Dr. Goebbels created in the propaganda ministry the post of film dramaturgist, and appointed to it the editor of the *Angriff*, Willi Krause, who thus became the first Joe Breen of Germany. American producers, however, take liberties with the Hays office which would scarcely be safe under the führer principle. The official dramaturgist has full power over scripts and stories, including authority to inject himself into the actual production process and to direct the director. Recently, after defending himself against a slanderous rumor that he had received 65,000 marks from a producer, Herr Krause resigned. He was succeeded by Hansjürgen Nierentz.

If a finished picture is banned on the recommendation of the examining board, an appeal may be made to a superior examining office. In practice it is considered healthier to refrain from such a procedure. Where the showing of a picture is judged undesirable on political grounds, Dr. Goebbels has independent authority to forbid exhibition.

Among foreign films which received the fatal "V" (*Verboten*) in 1935 were *Nana*, *Flying Down to Rio*, *The Thin Man*, and *The Iron Duke*. Currently *Modern Times* has been barred on the ground that it is "contrary to the spirit of the New Germany of Chancellor Adolf Hitler"; thus Chaplin's mustache will not compete with the Führer's on German screens.

The German film mentors issue two kinds of exhibition permits, covering pictures which juveniles may attend and those for adults only.

Among American pictures which the Hitler Youth had to forgo in 1935 were *Naughty Marietta, Queen Christina, Eskimo, Anna Karenina, It Happened One Night, Mutiny on the Bounty, Peter Ibbetson, Broadway Melody*, the Sol Wurtzel-Dante *Inferno*, DeMille's *Crusades*, a Harold Lloyd feature, several westerns, and—Shirley Temple in *Our Little Girl*. The preponderant cause for juvenile exclusion was "moral," i.e., sexual, or in bad taste. Children are encouraged, or compelled, as a school activity, to see military films, war being considered in good taste.

The censorship has its positive as well as its negative aspect. Producers compete for official ratings of merit, which confer remission of theatre taxes and other benefits. The most honorable distinctions are *vob.* (*volksbildend*—educational), *kü.* (*künstlerisch wertvoll*—artistically valuable), *staw.* (*staatspolitisch wertvoll*—politically valuable), and *stakü.* (*staatspolitisch und künstlerisch besonders wertvoll*—of extraordinary political and artistic merit). Since the film critics take their cues from the censorship ratings, the producers of a *staw.* or *stakü.* feature are free from worry about reviews, but unfortunately no infallible way has yet been found to make the cash customers follow the reviewers. Thus a highly rated film, *Das Mädchen Johanna*, did a nosedive at the box office.

V

Entertainment films, purveying, as in other countries, the tender emotions of love and romance in safe form for the masses, are not permitted to divert the public from the serious objectives of the cinema, which are (1) protection against "enemies of the State" and (2) promotion of the patriotic virtues: loyalty to State and Party, obedience to authority, and especially *heroism*. The forte of the new Reich film producers is, in fact, the heroic film, and nothing, of course, is more heroic than War.

In order that the masses may not die on the wrong side, it is necessary to apprise them of their enemies: the Marxists and Jews. *For Human Rights*—Arya-Film—performs this mission. The writer, Hans Zoberlein, is said to be one of those "who emerge only once in centuries from the fermentation of *Weltanschauung.*" It is the time of the "Munich Freicorps," seventeen years ago. The revolutionaries are villainous-looking sailors and thugs, drunk and armed, led by a commissar who is a ringer for Trotsky. "On the one side there is the will to destroy, on the other the attachment to the land and the will to keep it." After the battle, in which right triumphs, "the clear way is seen, which leads to justice and faith." The censor decorated the picture with the order of *kü.*

German Fate on Russian Soil—Delta-Film—"tears the mask from the face of Bolshevism in Russia." The commissar with his knout is even more sinister-looking than his predecessor in *For Human Rights*. The girl who falls in love with him expiates her misstep by dying in a swamp, the God-fearing peasant leader is slain, and the survivors burn their village and flee. The censor's rating is *stakü*.

Next to the Marxist, the Jew (when they are not identical) is the enemy of the State. *Petterson & Bendel*, the Swedish film which precipitated the July 1935 riots in Berlin, deals with the Jew. This was the first foreign film in the original version to receive the censor rating *staw*.

The film depicts the rise of Bendel, a penniless East European Jew who through a series of swindles becomes a power in business. Among those whose trust he betrays is the young, frank, honest Nordic Swede, Petterson. The contrast was not to the taste of some of the Jewish customers. They hissed. The SA legions were called out, and all the Jews, male and female, who happened to be in the neighborhood paid dearly for their arrogance.

Over a month later it was found that several theatres were running prints of *Petterson & Bendel* from which scenes unpleasant to non-Aryans had been cut. The secret police put things to rights again.

Petterson & Bendel, although it inspired the heroic action of the storm troopers, is technically a comedy. *Heroism and Death Struggle of Our Emden* is a specifically heroic film released on the twentieth anniversary of the sinking of the cruiser *Emden* by the Australian cruiser *Sydney*. It is "at the same time a memorial to the heroes of 1914 and an admonition to our generation to do the same in love of the Fatherland and fulfillment of duty to the last breath. The dead arise, and show the living of today how in blood and suffering they knew how to die for the Fatherland . . . The aim of this film is to show, in one glowing hour, what Germany is—and what it means to be German."

An heroic film glorifying an earlier epoch is *The Old and the Young King*—NDLS—starring Emil Jannings. The young king is Frederick I (the Great), the old one, his father Frederick William I. In appreciation of this production, General Göring, as Prussian Minister-President, received in audience the star, the director, and two officials of NDLS. The General modestly "stressed the similarity of the statesmanlike tasks which the great soldier-king [Frederick the Great] and he himself had undertaken, wherein lie the foundations for the artistic greatness of the Fatherland."

The National Socialist party itself produces, or initiates the production of, the finest brands of heroic films. Some, like *The Road to Freedom* (freedom to arm and conscript), are merely regional in scope. The

Parade-Ground Art: The German Film under Hitler

latter, labeled "educational" as well as "politically valuable," commemorates the lives and labors of the Nazi workers in Thuringia when National Socialism was struggling to power. "The old comrades-in-arms of the Führer hurry from town to town, enlightening the citizens on all questions of politics, industry, and German *Kultur*, counteracting the racially alien elements who would defeat them." The comrades triumph, and the film ends with excerpts from the Führer's speeches.

But beside the Reich Party Day film, a review of the annual goings-on at Nuremberg, all other heroic Nazi movies appear dwarfed. The Führer himself baptized the 1935 edition, *Triumph of the Will*—his will. Leni Riefenstahl, now at work on another mammoth production showing the Olympic games "in the framework of the New Germany," was the creator of *Triumph of the Will*, which was photographed by nineteen cameramen and their assistants to an original length of 400,000 feet.

The gala premiere of this "Epochal Film Document" made a Hollywood first performance look like the opening of a delicatessen store. The *Licht Bild Buehne* broke into Gothic type to describe it:

"Majestically the sparkling eagle spreads its great wings over the marque of the UFA *Palast am Zoo*, a red sea of waving swastika flags emblazon the wide facade of the theatre, golden bands glitter from the flagpoles, everything is bathed in color and brilliant light and invites joyfully and festively to the first performance of the Reich Party Day Film."

Great crowds stand for hours to see the arrival of ministers, diplomats, high army officers, the authorities of State and city, leaders of the SA and SS and the officials of the Movement. At 8:30 the car of the Führer drives up. The square rings with deafening *Heil*-shouts. Between lanes of SS-men the Führer, escorted by Rudolf Hess, SA Major General Brueckner, and Dr. Goebbels, proceeds to the middle loge of the festively decorated theatre.

The entire house rises and salutes silently with upraised arms. The lights are dimmed, the curtains part, revealing the orchestra of the SS Bodyguard Adolf Hitler, which plays the *Crusaders March* and the *Badenweiler March*, beloved by the Führer. Then the film begins with a shot of the aerial flotilla bringing the Führer to Nuremberg, shows his welcome in the streets, the subsequent speeches and assemblies, and, above all, marching and reviews. At one time, 52,000 men of the Labor Service march by. Hitler salutes in the picture with straight arm, proving that even the best actor benefits by good direction. In person, he sits in the loge between Hess and Brueckner, looking spastically earnest, and as usual in need of a haircut. Nevertheless "Whoso still doubts, will be convinced by this film that Führer and public has in Germany become one, ruled by one will, which has triumphed over everything that in the past blocked its way, and which will triumph over all obstacles." So spoke Rudolf Hess at the close of the meeting (in the picture): 'Hitler is Germany, and Germany is Hitler.'"

VI

Even in the symphonic uproar of Nazi film production an occasional sour note is audible. Since the press, operating on the führer principle, prints only what it is good for people to know, rumors fly through the studios, the distribution offices, and the film cafés of the *Friedrichstrasse*, thence spreading abroad to "besmirch the reputation of every honest film worker." In spite of threats and decrees, rumors continue to circulate, and it has even been necessary for the propaganda ministry to deny a report that Emil Jannings is a Jew, and as such has been barred from further participation in film activities.

Unfortunately, also, the German film, as a business, is none too prosperous. While Tobis paid a 4 percent dividend for the year 1934–35, the largest German film company, UFA, passed its dividend, and between October and December its shares fell from 66 to 48, with much dissatisfaction and protest among the stockholders. Only 94 features were produced in 1935, as compared with 122 in 1934 and 151 in 1931, consequently, in spite of exchange difficulties, more foreign films had to be imported.

The economic difficulties at home are in large part repercussions of travail abroad. The German motion picture, next only to the American, was an international business. According to Dr. Scheuermann, former president of the RFK, the boycott reduced Germany's film exports 33 percent. "From all sides Germany is attacked." When the British make a picture about the sinking of the *Lusitania*, the Germans complain of it as a persecutory film (*Hetzfilm*). "Machinations against the German Film in Jugoslavia." The Jugoslavs are turning to American pictures, on the ground that "Germany today cannot boast of important pictures which might be in a position to win worldwide success. The excessive control of German officialdom prevents this. . . ." In Romania, where 104 German films were imported in 1932, 48 were all they would take in 1935. Hungary showed about the same ratio, 100 a year before 1933 and 55 in 1935. *Storm Days of 1919*, after provoking a tumult in Budapest, flopped at the box offices. In Belgium: "Dirty Brussels Hands at Work"—the Communists hiss German films permeated with "a high ethical message." The most intolerable situation is in Holland, where the Dutch Prof. Dr. Cohen, "representing a committee of predominantly Jewish interests," criticizes the German film over the radio in a manner which "transgresses the bounds of international decency." He compares the persecution of the Jews in the Frankfurt ghetto at the beginning of the nineteenth century, depicted in the American picture *The House of Rothschild*, with conditions prevailing in Germany today. Even the colossal *Triumph of the Will*, the Führer himself imbuing the photographic emulsion, while a success in Venice, provokes disturbances. *Variety* calls *The Old and the Young King* German propaganda posing as historical narrative. Only the Japanese seem to be kind to the German film, and they do not count for much in cash.

Striving valiantly to stem the tide, the Germans called an International Film Congress in April 1935, out of which developed the International Film Chamber, with Dr. Scheuermann as president. Everything possible was done. The Führer received the delegation leaders and expressed himself on the art of the film. Dr. Goebbels laid down his immortal theses. The Kroll Opera House was splendidly decorated with the flags of all nations, blazing between banks of white and blue chrysanthemums. The nations, however, did not all follow their flags into the IFK. Among those currently abstaining are the United States, Russia, England, and Holland, while others, such as France and Sweden, have participated only after making objections and reservations exceedingly painful to the sensitive Nazi spirit. Thus the privately expressed hope that the IFK might help the German film to regain its earlier "mighty place" in the international market seems illusory.

"Everywhere the press writes of the decline of German culture under National Socialism. The world must be shown that it is wrong." That, indeed, is the problem. Germany is right, the world is wrong, but it is a large world.

HOW HITLER AFFECTED THE LIVES OF TWO *NEW THEATRE* CONTRIBUTORS

ON THE European tour, I had met two of Germany's greatest film directors, G. W. Pabst and Max Ophuls, in their new roles as successful leading figures of the French movie industry. G. W. Pabst had won world fame for *Kameradschaft, Westfront 1918*, and *Threepenny Opera*, while Ophuls had directed *Liebelei, Divine,* and *Werther*. Both men were noted opponents of Hitler and trusted by the French Popular Front. They were subscribers to *New Theatre* and kept their promises to write the articles I have selected here. This relationship led to deepening friendship during my 1937 and 1938 stopovers for Paris work on my anti-Nazi documentaries.

This "memoir" will suggest to 1980s readers how swiftly lives at the top of French movie industry fame and fortune were changed as Hitler made one advance after another in his drive to realize world conquest. When England's Chamberlain and France's Daladier betrayed Czechoslovakia at Munich, life in France became perilous for foreigners suspected of opposing the government's deal with Hitler. During this time, with the aid of two courageous, talented Czechs, cameraman Alexander Hackenschmied and Hans Burger, the stage director I'd met on the *New Theatre* tour, I had managed to deceive the Sudeten Nazi Party that my fiancée, Rosa Harvan, and I were American sympathizers. A forged letter supposedly signed by Fritz Kuhn, the New York Bund leader we had marched against in Yorkville and fought during the SS *Bremen* demonstration, was accepted without question by the Sudeten leader, Konrad Henlein. We worked in fear of discovery and the consequences but got away with it, feeling like actors in an anti-Nazi drama.

By the time the Munich betrayal of Czechoslovakia came, all main filming was done, and we went "underground" to complete the editing, match the negative, make a work print, and have a score written. The only problem was how to escape if the Nazi Gestapo, now active throughout Czechoslovakia, found out about our film. We decided I should smuggle it out with help Hackenschmied and Burger arranged from anti-Nazi Czech customs officials at the airport. I played my "role" as an American tourist leaving for Paris, with the customs men ruffling my piled-up clothes and laundry that covered the cans of film at the bottom of two suitcases, so heavy I could barely lift them to the plane.

Soon, after a terrifying flight in which the sky was blackened out by an eclipse, the sun came out as we saw glittering bayonets of French gendarmes. Daladier had just decreed martial law against indignant, accusing protests and demonstrations of the Popular Front against the Munich sellout. As with the Nazis, I had prepared another false letter stating I had with me travelogue films for *The March of Time* and was only stopping one day in Paris en route to New York. The customs officials were so harassed by the heavy traffic of people leaving the martial law crisis that I got the film through to a small hotel on the Left Bank where I knew the staff was "Popular Front" and wouldn't turn me in. I phoned the noted American foreign correspondent, Vincent Sheehan, who had seen the footage in Prague and had agreed to add his international authority to replace the commentary I had written to guide our clandestine editing. I then tried to reach Ophuls but found he was away on vacation with Helga and his little son, Marcel, probably to avoid the troubles of martial law. But Pabst was home and welcomed my call. I showed Pabst and Sheehan the film at a private, confidential screening with only a few other trusted friends present: Henri Cartier-Bresson, Louis Aragon, and the visiting Mexicans, David Alfaro Siqueiros and his wife, Angelica. All were enthusiastic, and Sheehan promised to write the commentary within two weeks as I stressed the need to get the film completed and out to counter the Chamberlain-Daladier-Hitler "Peace in Our Time" propaganda we regarded as another step to realizing Hitler's aims we had warned against in *New Theatre*.

After the screening I went to Pabst's home. With his wife's approval, he offered me $5,000 to cover the cost of recording the score while Sheehan completed writing the commentary. This would speed my return with the film ready for final lab work and effects in New York, along with a narrator I expected to find among my Group Theatre friends. To avoid any direct connection, which could mean arrest and deportation for himself, his wife, and young son, Pabst drew the $5,000 in cash and gave it to me the next morning. If I would get backers to repay this amount, I should hold it in his name, as he hoped to emigrate to America and have me work with him there to learn feature direction. Two weeks later I was on my way to New York with Rosa, who had arrived as Sheehan started the commentary and had aided him on the timing.

Soon after arrival, we screened the work print for the Group Theatre, and the enthusiasm of Clurman, Crawford, and Odets led to a new Group actor, Leif Erickson, recording Sheehan's powerful commentary. Arthur Mayer and Joe Burstyn undertook to prepare distribution. But before the opening of what we titled *Crisis*, a White House showing was arranged for the President by Mrs. Roosevelt. My only previous visit to the White House had been with a group of tourists as a runaway boy on my fourteenth birthday. Now Rosa and I were invited to meet the President and show him the first feature documentary made against the Nazis.

We were thrilled to meet FDR and hear his warm response at a screening attended by members of his cabinet and several members of the State Department. "This is the first time in my life I have seen what the Nazis are really like, how they succeeded in overthrowing a democracy, then hoodwinking the west into believing it would be 'Peace in Our Time,'" said the President. "You must show this film everywhere in our country to help counter the America Firsters' propaganda calling me a warmonger!"

The night before the film was to open in New York City, I spoke on a radio program called "We the People" and predicted Hitler would break the Munich Pact by taking power in Prague in the very near future. He did so the day of the film's opening, on my birthday, March 13, 1939, and the *New York Times* ran a story suggesting that I had timed the opening to go with my prediction.

Meanwhile, in Paris, Pabst was reportedly ill. But in fact Hitler's unopposed takeover in Prague had frightened and disillusioned him. I tried in vain to reach him; later I learned that he had "disappeared." No one knew quite when or where. Friends feared he had been kidnapped with his family by the Nazis. But months afterward, while I was filming the German invasion of Poland in September 1939, I learned that Pabst had become a Nazi officer. He was directing a Wehrmacht film unit on the Polish front while Rosa and I were filming Luftwaffe strafings with Douglas Slocombe as cameraman for *Lights Out in Europe*, which became the first film on the Allied side in World War II. In 1940, when Hitler's forces occupied Paris, there was Pabst in German uniform filming the fall of the city that had given him sanctuary. After Germany's defeat, Pabst tried to make amends by filming the first film made about Hitler's last days and suicide. Pabst thought *The Last Ten Days* would make up for the betrayal of all his ideals, but it didn't, and I never saw him or heard from him again.

My other *New Theatre* contributor friend, Max Ophuls, was not "Aryan" like Fritz Lang and Pabst. As a German Jew, Ophuls had felt part of his country and people. He had believed the Germans would reject the Nazis, but the burning of the books and attacks on Jews and all who opposed Hitler made Ophuls realize his life was in peril. Before the war began, Max volunteered for the French army. He fought bravely and well as the Wehrmacht and Luftwaffe disregarded the Maginot Line and swept into France. Max was in great danger, having done a series of radio broadcasts from the trenches that were personal attacks ridiculing Adolf Hitler. He changed his army uniform for civilian clothes, sneaked back into Paris to get his wife, Helga, and their small son, Marcel, and managed to escape to a small village on the Swiss frontier.

At his hotel he saw on a table in the lobby a copy of the *New York Times* forgotten by a tourist who had left hurriedly, like so many, to escape the chaos and dangers of the German occupation. As Max said later, "I could hardly believe my eyes . . . an article by Bosley Crowther about Herbert Kline, having completed the John Steinbeck film *The Forgotten Village*, being signed by MGM to a feature directing contract. We were down to our last money, and I grasped this straw of fate, telling my wife and child, 'Herbert will help us. He will send money to bribe our way across the frontiers.'"

A strange cable, signed Marcel, reached me via MGM. At first, Rosa, Sascha, and I couldn't figure out what to do. But it referred to urgent need of $400 for an "immediate operation," and gave the name of a village bank. We didn't have $400 as I had just started at the studio, but I went to MGM and told them I needed an advance to pay for an emergency operation for my father. MGM was not the sort of "heartless corporation" often portrayed in our *New Theatre* plays of social protest. They advanced the money and soon the Ophuls family left occupied France and arrived in America a few weeks later by a neutral boat safe from Nazi submarine sinkings. They arrived in Hollywood in a new Chevrolet given Max along with some money to start writing on a film project. We had a marvelous reunion, and saw them frequently during the next years in Hollywood. Marcel was a charming eight-year-old then.

Many years later I saw little Marcel's grown-up masterpiece, *The Sorrow and the Pity*, which dealt with the same kind of collaborators that would have betrayed the Ophuls family to capture and death in the Holocaust. Instead, they found a safe haven in our country, where Max Ophuls renewed his career with fine films like *Caught* and *Letter from an Unknown Woman*, and where Marcel grew up to become as celebrated in documentary direction as his father in fiction films. Someday I hope to meet Marcel again and find out how much he remembers of these events when he was the little boy we were so fond of.

These are the real-life stories behind such articles as Ophuls on *Der Kampf* and Pabst on *Peasants*.

Der Kampf

BY MAX OPHULS

I WANTED to sit down and write the director a letter:

Dear Gustav von Wagenheim! Yesterday, together with a couple of German refugees living in Moscow, I saw your film, *The Struggle*. The sound was bad, the lighting poor—but the picture was strong. So strong, so powerful, that I, as your colleague, must say "Thank you." It has nothing to do with criticism, with professional or personal esteem. You have achieved something for which the great united front of film workers who were driven from Germany must be grateful, and will be, someday. You have been the first to redeem their honor.

The literary talents who have emigrated from Germany have long found a place in the world. It is harder for the cinema. With the exception of the Soviet Union, it cannot find a "publisher." The international producer anxiously avoids any political avowal. Let us not be unjust; perhaps he is compelled, by censorship, the danger of diplomatic complications, the requirements for labor permits, to take such a stand.

But from all these limitations you are free. It was you, therefore, who shouldered the task of making a Dimitroff picture. A great and heavy task! And one which you have carried out with such a sense of responsibility, with such integrity, that your enemies, who honored you by depriving you of citizenship, may well take a lesson from you.

This picture is no cheap glorification of a hero. There are countries today in which the head of the state must issue ordinances against the too frequent use of his portrait on handkerchiefs, powder boxes, playing cards, and beer tankards. Your film is free from any such excesses. The great man who, at his trial, faced the gigantic might of National Socialism unarmed and alone, hardly appears at all, excepting for several close-ups at the end. Yet he is omnipresent, in every foot of the film! Often one hears him speaking at the trial, as a background to other scenes. And with the invisible Dimitroff, who laboriously wrestles with the words of a foreign tongue, there is present the *idea* which was supposedly crushed during those days, the belief which made Dimitroff victorious, and which will not die—the belief in the other, new Germany. In *The Struggle* this belief shows itself repeatedly, often in a joyous, optimistic guise. There is one scene which lasts hardly a minute. Nazi automobiles are pursuing a young worker, one of the underground opposition, in the early morning. He runs around a curve in the road. Road workers are shoveling stone. In a flash the boy has sized up the situation. He comes rushing up to them laughing. Laughing, he tears off his coat, one of the unknown comrades pushes a shovel in his hands, and, laughing exultantly, he begins to heave stone, and they all shovel together—and the comradeship which is forever reaching out its hand, in hope—a solidarity which never falters, which flares up, like lightning, in countless places and situations, and, when pursued, dies down with the same suddenness. And in this film it is not shown as a secret underground organization. It is present—a great, heartwarming brotherhood—in every conversation, every handclasp, every look.

Nothing in the picture is shown in sheer black and white. No matter how grim the subject matter—imprisonment, concentration camps, assault, blood purges—the figures of the other side are never overdrawn, never caricatured or depicted with blind hate. Often there is a residue of humanity shown, which may lead them back, someday, where they belong, on the other side.

There is still another aspect to *The Struggle*. It is a memorial to the onetime unpolitical, nonpartisan, respectable Germany, which was taken unaware and overwhelmed by the Hitler regime. There is, for instance, Dr. Hillstedt. He is supposed to certify a death—one of the "suicides." He resists. Later he sits in the comfort and intimacy of a small beer hall, at the table reserved for patrons of long standing, waiting for his friends, gentlemen of the law, of science. They do not come. Instead, a young storm troop leader and his new comrades, in new uniforms, surround him, sit at his table, propose a toast. The doctor is saddened. Later he helps a fugitive. The man comes to him in his office hours, for a first-aid dressing. Suddenly there is an uproar on the stairs, the doctor steps to the door and opens it—and is struck down by a revolver shot. Respectable Germany.

Dear Gustav von Wagenheim, it was for all these things that I felt I had to thank you. I think that many in our profession will be thankful too, and not judge this film as they do others, by the photography, the dialogue, the cutting alone. They will see in it something no one else has achieved. And this achievement, conceived by you and executed by all the actors, who speak and play, not as if they were living in Moscow, but as if they had just taken the city tramway from Wedding or Schönberg to the studio, will not be limited in its appeal to any one class, party, or country.

Your film is called *Der Kampf*. May it not some day be entitled, with far greater right than the superfilms generated by Leni Riefenstahl and Goebbels, *Der Triumph des Willens* or *Sieg des Glaubens?*

A Letter to F. Ermler on *Peasants*

BY G. W. PABST

My dear Ermler:

At last my wish has been fulfilled: I have seen your *Peasants*. I left the theatre full of gratitude and joy. Joy, because my heart could once more hear its own language, which, for such a long time, it has had to forgo. Gratitude, because you gave the only answer possible to the many fruitless words and discussions with which we have been squandering our time—a deed, an accomplishment.

You have created a work of art. You were given a problem of particular importance: the struggle of the revolutionary peasants against the kulaks. This theme was of historic significance because the fate of the Russian revolution depended in such great degree on the triumph of the collective idea over individualism. And this theme has been transformed by your creative hands into vivid facts. What was purely conceptual you have turned into the flesh and blood of your characters. You have opposed the group to the individual, the former kulak, Gerasim Platonovich, but you have given him so much warmth that he, the villain, gains our sympathy and understanding. By so doing, you have made the victory of the collective idea more noble and real.

The world of the bourgeoisie in which we live and work insists that the film must not be a means of propaganda. Of course, by propaganda they mean—opposition. Every attempt to use the film as a forum for the discussion of the burning issues of the day runs up against the "morale." Today, every living problem is declared outside the "morale." The world, by this prohibition, proves both its weakness and its knowledge of that weakness. It has dragged down to the level of the peep show the finest instrument for the cultural advancement of humanity since the invention of the printing press. No regard is ever paid to the vulgarity and barbarousness of the film so long as it maintains the present order—the profit system.

Now, along comes your picture diametrically opposed to our ways of filmmaking. Your film has no "tempo." That is because it has an *idea* to convey. The scenes have an *intellectual* basis. The lengthily cut shots serve to guide the mind of the audience and to permit identification with the action and actors of the film. On the other hand, *our* insane insistence on "tempo" originates in the fear that a slight pause would inevitably reveal the emptiness of both words and scene. Your picture doesn't have a love story and doesn't require one because its subject *is* love. You have more beautiful people than the bourgeois film has ever found. Their bodies are clad in dirty work-perspired rags. No misguided desire to please the senses has obtruded on the gray appropriateness of these clothes. But the eyes of your people are wide-opened windows through which their souls, pregnant with the future, call to us. The humor of your picture grows organically out of the circumstances of the story. It does not consist of laboriously invented gags. But over and above all, the chief beauty of the film, to me, is to see how one great thought flows like a smooth stream through the body of the entire collective: to see that the value of an individual is determined by his value to the whole, and how it is grievous punishment not to be permitted to participate in the activity of the group.

What intensity emerges from the struggle of these men for an idea! It is essentially their unity, and their unity alone, that makes the kulak the enemy of the muzhiks . . . one may feel pity for his tragic destiny . . . but he is doomed because he struggles to fence his life and goods from the collective.

Often the picture achieves the quality of a parable. For example, the old peasants search for the truth by raising their hands in oath, calling on heaven to witness their innocence. Thus they express a belief in an order outside of themselves, while the youth—and how beautiful is the grave face of the young Communist—finds law in himself and his party! When the new life, in the form of the community's first bathhouse, overcomes the accustomed dirt of centuries, Anisim, the village elder, in consequence of his wager that the village would never see a bathhouse in *his* time, must surrender his dearly fostered tress; in other words, his beard. And that accursed rascal, the head of the local politbureau, cuts it off in person. How this manly scene warms the heart! The happiness of this intimate circle of perspiring heads and bodies scatters the old man's anger as the spring sun melts the snow.

As your picture finally fades out on the friendly face of the soldier, you have succeeded in proving that the mass is no more than the sum of the millions of these youthful peasants, and you make us believe that their future will be more beautiful than the dreams and songs of a people ever were.

I thank you for the pleasure and the beauty you have given us. If I have failed to mention the many who helped you with the very best they could give, you will understand that my thanks go to the whole group as much as to you.

I send you my heartfelt greetings.

(Translated from the German)

A FILM DIRECTOR HERO OF THE SIEGE OF LENINGRAD

OUR *New Theatre* tour to meet Eisenstein, Dovzhenko, and Pudovkin had missed fire with all three away on location, but we did get to meet Friedrich Ermler. Like all other Russians we met, Ermler fearfully evaded questions on the treason trials of Communist leaders also going on in Leningrad. However, he was forthright about his personal experiences and proved a marvelous storyteller. His fascinating background included fighting Cossack pogroms as a teenager in the impoverished Jewish shtetl village of his birth. Then, later, after the Cossacks' anti-Semitic leaders were killed or imprisoned by the Bolsheviks, Ermler fought as a volunteer in a Communist Cossack battalion against the foreign armies that joined the White Guards trying to crush the Russian Revolution. He had won the equivalent of our Congressional Medal of Honor for bravery in battle and was offered any civilian post he wanted as a reward. He asked, to the surprise of the military commanders, to get a chance to write and direct a movie. They offered instead to send him to a film school, but he insisted and, against all doubts, persuaded the authorities to let him start without special training, aided by a professional cameraman. The result astounded the Soviet film world. Ermler's *Fragment of an Empire* became a classic and is so ranked to this day.

But when we met in Leningrad, never in his dreams, or ours, was it conceived that a few years later, Ermler had still to play an even more heroic role in real-life drama, in defending that great city, which had previously withstood the forces of Napoleon. When Hitler's Wehrmacht surrounded and cut off Leningrad, its fall was imminent due to the shortage of both arms and food for its starving soldiers and citizens, whose terrible suffering and deaths ran into the tens of thousands in their resistance to Nazi cannonfire, Wehrmacht assaults, Luftwaffe bombings. In the midst of all this, Friedrich Ermler was appointed to one of the three-man committees to head the resistance. His heroism won highest Soviet honors as he fought on the Russian front against the Germans. Only this time, Leningrad, like Moscow and Stalingrad, helped destroy the Nazi invaders, and, unlike his friend and mine, Afinogenov, Friedrich Ermler survived to continue his filmmaking career.

Dovzhenko's *Frontier*

BY IRVING LERNER

ALEXANDER DOVZHENKO'S *Aerograd*, released here as *Frontier* (Amkino), cannot be isolated from the earlier films of that extraordinary Ukrainian director. *Arsenal, Soil,* and his first sound film, *Ivan,* have all been shown in the United States. All of them provoked discussion both here and in the Soviet Union. They were difficult to understand because of their extreme complexity, their intense subjective quality, and their original directorial technique.

Dovzhenko's people are unusual and his themes are not petty everyday ideas. His film heroes represent social groups, and also express the director's personal philosophy. All his films lack solid story sequence, but they are rich in ideas, facts, and theories. A Dovzhenko film is a synthesis of an enormous quantity of rich obeservation of natural phenomena. In *Soil* and *Arsenal* he attempted to express, among other things, the complexity, the manifold richness (material and human) of contemporary Soviet life. *Soil* was too mystical and steeped too deeply in obscure Ukrainian folklore. *Ivan* was a determined effort to get rid of that trend. It represented the Ukrainian agrarian and his gradual adjustment to industrial life; but the film displayed a tentative quality that was symptomatic of Dovzhenko's personal development, at that time still confused. Nevertheless, *Ivan* was the brilliant work of a genius. Even though it was a failure from the popular point of view, Dovzhenko was presented with the Order of Lenin for merit. It was Karl Radek, I believe, who remarked on the occasion of the award that *Ivan* was a magnificent failure. *Frontier*, however, is mature and firm and is a tribute to the director's increasingly creative powers.

Like *Ivan* and *Soil*, *Frontier* is an analysis of the old and the new. The new life is not only epitomized by the youth, by the Communists, the Red Army men, but by the ancient taiga, the great Siberian forest; by the militant partisans and revolutionary traditions; and finally by the symbol of Russia's great industrial and defensive development, the airplane. The old is symbolized in the kulaks, the clergy, the Japanese imperialists who attempt to incite an uprising in Soviet territory.

Not only is there the new life of the present, but the *future* in the person of the young Chukchi native who hears of the new city of the Far East, Aerograd, where one will be able to learn and study. Hundreds of miles he travels: on foot, on skis, over snow and ice, through streams, following the roar of the airplane motor, only to find upon his arrival no city, but a ceremony: "Hail to the city of Aerograd, which we Bolsheviks are founding today on the shore of the Great Ocean."

"That means," says the native, "the city is not yet. I came to study in the city. I heard, I went eighty suns. I understand, it must be built. Good, and when we build it, then I will speak. There will be many, many people, like the trees in the taiga."

The film's ideas are embodied in a simple and tenuous story. The old partisan, Glushak, known as "The Tiger's Death"—now a member of the collective—and his lifelong friend Vasil, the animal breeder who turns traitor, are the two protagonists. Vasil is a staunch individualist and is opposed to collectivization. He assists a Japanese officer in the organization of the kulaks for an armed uprising. The uprising fails. When the two old friends meet in the enemy's camp it is the occasion for the film's most dramatic sequence and one of the most memorable that has ever been recorded.

The screen is silent as Glushak leads his prisoner, Vasil, into the forest. During this death walk, which is similar to the walk of the mother whose son is killed in *Ivan*, the emotional tension is so great that time seems suspended. Finally the silence is broken with Vasil's "Here." He fixes his shirt, smooths his coat, adjusts his hat. Glushak simultaneously adjusts his rifle and says, "Good-bye." Then he addresses Vasil through the audience: "I am killing the traitor and enemy of the workers, my friend, Vasil Petrovich Kudiakov, sixty years of age. Be witness to my grief, Vasya." Then just before the shot is fired Vasil utters three terrific cries, each time waiting for the echo to answer: hearing for the last time his voice in the great forest where he and his friend lived for more than half a century.

More important than the story is the progress of the various moods. They determine the structure and style of the film. The opening is joyous and lyrical. It serves to establish the general theme: that life is beautiful. Offscreen voices sing the "Song of the Aviators" as the plane weaves its way in and out of white clouds, over endless forests, and turbulent seas. Suddenly we are thrown into a manhunt. A series of titles like decrees is projected:

In the East, Beyond the Amur River

On the Shore of the Japan Sea Known by the Name of Karl Marx

The Old World Contracts and the Great Ocean Narrows Down

Across the Amur Border, Strangers Carry Dynamite—Five Russians, Two Non-Russians

Attention! We'll Kill Them Immediately!

Glushak fires upon the invaders. He kills the five Russians but the two Japanese escape. The chase that follows is a masterpiece of film architecture; the cutting gets swifter and the shots closer. The only sounds from the sound track are the moans of the hunted men, which increase in intensity as the chase narrows down. Finally the Japanese imperialist is caught in his trap and he explodes:

"I hate your whole country and your nation and your calm and your cheerful sweat and collective labor . . . the whole taiga is millions of meters . . . Great Asia is mine and the fish and the animals and the cities from the sea to Baikal."

The mood continues on this realistic note until the introduction of the second Japanese. Here we get another picture of the imperialist: the ruler of Asia by divine right. We see him inspired by a holy ritual. The sequence is stylized—a performance of a high war dance of death. Compare this with the similar idea in *Soil*: just before the kulak murders the hero he goes into a death dance, a ritual based on Ukrainian folklore.

Then ensues the battle between the partisans and the kulaks. Dovzhenko returns to the realistic manner. It is here that Glushak executes his friend. It is here that a young Chinese member of the collective meets his death. The old partisan carries the body of the young hero to his son's plane. The plane soars into the air. Its motor again sings the "Song of the Aviators," which has now become a dirge. But the plane is joined by other battalions from all parts of Siberia and Russia until the sky is filled with them. The song, the funeral march, is once more joyous. The sequence is allegorical: like the endings of *Soil* and *Ivan*. But here it becomes a clear and definite statement: an integral part of the film.

It is difficult to be coldly critical of a film that is unlike any other film and unlike any other form of art. In his silent films, Dovzhenko achieved a lyric-poetic quality with purely cinematic methods: more fundamentally, more cinematically than any abstract, avant-garde film. Each sequence and shot within that sequence was so beautifully controlled that you were absorbed in it almost without knowing it; they were so accurately timed that they expressed fully what the director wanted to say with them.

Dovzhenko's use of sound in *Frontier* places the film years ahead of anything that has been produced so far. It is not burdened with the formalistic approach that was apparent in Pudovkin's *Deserter*; it isn't a "talkie" in any sense of the word. The director has blended the sight-sound image so cleverly that the use appears perfectly natural. Yet when there is straight talk it isn't like any other kind of dialogue. It is literary, highly poetic, and in keeping with the individual shot. Most striking of all is Dovzhenko's use of silence in a sound film. Some years ago he stated, "We shall strive to attain an artistic creation on the basis of the relations and proportions of sound to image." Dovzhenko has unquestionably achieved this with *Frontier*.

To attempt to compare *Frontier* with such dramatic films as *Youth of Maxim*, *Peasants*, or *Chapayev* is unfair. It simply isn't that kind of film and it doesn't have the same emotional appeal that the straight dramatic film possesses. Moreover, it is unfortunate that Dovzhenko has for the first time neglected the photography. Somehow the sustained photographic beauty of Dovzhenko's earlier films is lacking. Except in one or two places Tisse's camera work is too realistic, too prosaic for the mood of the film. Camera work to the contrary, *Frontier* emerges as something more than an unusual film; it is a profound intellectual document that demands your attention. It requires *active* audience participation; it requires repeated seeing. Some persons will raise the point that such a form is not good movie and entertainment: therefore bad drama. But certainly it can't be judged by any present standards of motion picture entertainment. To Dovzhenko *Frontier* is not only a work expressive of his love for new Russia and its vast taigas, but a prophecy:

"I became convinced that the existing administrative and economic centers in the Far East are inadequate—that a road should be found through the Sakhalin Ridge to the sea, and a socialist, Bolshevik city built on the shores of the Pacific Ocean. That city should be called Aerograd and the title of my film I regard as a forecast of the future. I soon decided that this film should be a defense film and so it turned out."

The Youth of Maxim

BY V. PUDOVKIN

THESE are days of triumphant joy for all workers in the Soviet cinema. We are now in the midst of a great and happy celebration. It is not merely the celebration of the fifteenth anniversary of the young Soviet cinema that is responsible for this spirit of proud jubilation. This important jubilee comes at a time when our cinematography records the greatest artistic triumphs thus far achieved. Only recently, for the first time in the history of the Soviet cinema, the *Pravda* devoted a leading editorial to the film *Chapayev*.

But then, you might say that is just a "lucky streak." A series of "accidental successes"? I recall how western reviewers, rudely propelled out of their complacency by the worldwide success of *Potemkin*, called it just a "lucky incident." They were grievously mistaken, these critics. Now, as before, it is not a matter of a few isolated instances of success, of a few individual producers hitting the bull's eye.

These successful artists are not just bright meteors suddenly and unexpectedly appearing on the Soviet cinema horizon. Each of them has a "creative biography" of his own and a good deal of experience.

A few days ago I witnessed the presentation of the new film, *The Youth of Maxim*, produced by the Leningrad directors G. Kosintzev and L. Trauberg. The plot is characterized by simplicity and clarity. During the czarist regime, in the years of darkest reaction, a young worker finds himself drawn into party work. He is driven thither by the cruelty and brutality of the capitalist hirelings and by his growing class-consciousness carefully nurtured by the party comrades. Toward the end of the picture Maxim becomes a full-fledged Bolshevik.

The enormous difficulty of the problem faced by the authors lay in the creation of an atmosphere of stirring emotion which, according to the conception of the authors, was to permeate the entire picture. This difficulty was successfully surmounted by the authors. The picture succeeds in transmitting to the audience a strong emotional impulse, a feeling, noble and austere—closely akin to the one that seizes upon us when we rise to the melancholy strains of the funeral march, played in memory of fallen revolutionary fighters, or when we look at a portrait of Lenin in his youth—tempered with a sense of joy, pride, and happiness when we compare the dark past, the glorious present, and the radiantly hopeful future. Yes, this film is a decided success! Another great achievement. After the heroic epic of *Chapayev*—the lyrical dramatization of the *Youth of Maxim*.

The picture opens with a New Year's celebration in czarist St. Petersburg, with all its merriment and abandon. Moskvin's amazing photography, Shostakovich's music, the brilliant montage all combine to produce a masterpiece of "formal" art of the very highest order. The finale is exceedingly simple: the hero, a young Bolshevik, just released from prison, is seen going down the hill into a wide plain stretching before him. Somehow this simple setting deeply stirs the spectator. In the plain lies Russia, its future hidden in the sweeping expanse of open country. The easy natural movement of the young man speaks of power, confidence, and a will to conquer.

In this transition from the formal splendor of the opening to the simple but profoundly moving finale is reflected something of the creative biography of the authors themselves, as well as most of our artists. A work of art is impossible, unless the creator is wholly and unreservedly engulfed by it, unless he is passionately in love with it. It is this love that creates the magnetic inffuence which never fails to be transmitted to the audience. To learn to love that which is of vital interest to the masses, which deeply stirs them—is to become an artist in the true and full meaning of this word.

Translated by Leon Rutman

THE RISKS OF LIFE ON THE LEFT

As I write this in 1984, "Big Brother" is not as dominant as George Orwell envisioned, although conservative pressure groups are often dangerously effective in their attempts to stifle freedom. Perhaps looking back at how we confronted similar attacks in the 1930s will encourage younger generations to continue the battle for freedom that in the spirit of Socrates and Galileo, those rebelling against "Big Brothers" have had to fight again and again.

Some, like "Joel Faith" and "Louis Norden," had to use pseudonyms to avoid Hollywood blacklisting long before McCarthyism imprisoned John Howard Lawson and Albert Maltz, two of the "Hollywood Ten." I was blacklisted as a director in 1952 after the Hearst press ran my picture between Lawson and Odets along with a Joe McCarthy attack that scared off producers. I had just written (with Abe Kandel) and directed *The Fighter*—from a story by Jack London—co-starring Lee Cobb and Richard Conte. Strangely, I was able to continue writing, but I didn't get to direct again until *Walls of Fire* in 1967. Like others dubbed "premature antifascists," I learned the risks on the Left.

Nevertheless, Archibald MacLeish challenged his employers and continued at *Fortune* while writing for *New Theatre*, even after marching with pickets in the Ohrbach strike. Fortunately, he escaped violence from both police and hired goons in that struggle the workers won. Others took risks on the picket lines, among them Albert Maltz, George Sklar, Paul Peters, Langston Hughes, Richard Wright, Waldo Frank, Irwin Shaw, and Alfred Kreymborg. People often ask me why prominent writers and artists risked their positions and incomes and sometimes their lives. My answer is always the same—we were not only American radicals but also citizens acting on our beliefs. We felt a moral obligation, whether marching against the Yorkville Nazis, boarding the SS *Bremen*, or picketing in the first strike on Madison Avenue's "Publishers Row," after office workers, who went out for better union-protected working conditions, were harassed by the police.

After the first attacks, the office workers' union called on leading writers and editors to join their pickets, hoping our "names" would mean publicity that could help forestall, or at least soften, the violence. I was among those called upon, as editor of *New Theatre*, and Mark was asked to represent the New Theatre League. We brothers joined a distinguished group of picket-line protesters, all a bit apprehensive about facing police, thugs, and probably jail sentences. About fifteen of us took part: our group included Malcolm Cowley, the brilliant literary critic and editor of the liberal *New Republic*; novelists James T. Farrell, my close friend since early *Studs Lonigan* days; Nathanael West, author of *Miss Lonelyhearts*; Edward Dahlberg, whose novel *Bottom Dogs* was praised by D. H. Lawrence as an overlooked masterpiece; Joseph Freeman, editor of *New Masses*; Mike Gold, also known for *New Masses*, his plays, and his novel *Jews Without Money*; Alfred Kreymborg, the poet-dramatist; critic Granville Hicks; and the famous author, Waldo Frank.

"New York's Finest" showed up in force, some on foot, others mounted, waving clubs menacingly and, even more frighteningly, rearing their horses high over the pickets' heads, the pawing sharp hooves a deadly danger if not restrained. The strike committee tactics worked. Evidently, the police had been instructed this time not to ride us down or use their clubs, just to frighten us into running for cover. We were scared, but no one ran, and soon the officers arrested our group after obtaining our names from informants who recognized us. We had been asked by the strike leaders not to resist arrest if no violence was used against us. The strikers yelled loudly in our support and held their ground courageously while we were carted downtown in a large police van to the Centre Street jail.

Soon we were led into one large cell and locked behind bars in the cramped quarters. There was just one sink with a few metal drinking cups, no towels, no lavatory, just a hole in the cement floor and the embarrassment of using it publicly. But no one complained, and all of us felt fortunate that we hadn't been harmed. We were also glad to be put in a separate cell from hardened criminals nearby, some of whom seemed to have heard about the strikers and admired us for "taking on the cops" on behalf of "poor people."

We told jokes and reminisced about Thoreau, who volunteered to accept imprisonment for opposing the invasion of Mexico, and who answered Emerson's "What are you doing inside bars, Henry?" with "What are you doing outside, Waldo?" But mostly it was kidding, nonpolitical, with only occasional expressions of hope that news of our jailing would reach the press and radio to aid the strikers. Soon, we heard that it did, but we were nervous about not being allowed to phone . . . neither lawyers, nor families, nor friends. Before long, however, a lawyer appeared from the International Labor Defense. He assured us that within a few minutes we would be allowed one by one to make phone calls and that he would be presenting our case to a judge very soon. I looked around at the array of writing talent and whispered to Mark that we could put together a helluva fine issue of *New Theatre* if each of our cellmates would write for us. But we agreed that under the circumstances, it would be inconsiderate to ask.

We learned soon after, to our surprise, that we were to be released. The ILD lawyer reappeared and informed us elatedly that the judge had decided to "dismiss charges" as "wrongful arrest." He had concluded that sentencing us would serve the strike with even more unfavorable publicity for the publishers and the police than our arrests had caused. It was exhilarating to think we had carried out our mission without any physical harm, and we felt proud we had acted as part of an American radical prolabor tradition dating back to the bloody Paterson textile strike and the fervent demonstrations against the execution of Sacco and Vanzetti.

We also felt a link to American writers who had taken openly radical positions: Ernest Hemingway had written for *New Masses* a scathing denunciation of General MacArthur, who had led an Army attack on the World War I bonus marchers, driving them out of their pitiful hovels where they had suffered near starvation and freezing cold within a short distance of the Hoover White House. Thomas Wolfe, like Hemingway, could hardly be condemned as "a Red" but he had also written for the *New Masses* (several years before Steinbeck's *The Grapes of Wrath*) a vivid, heartrending, indignant account of the Depression suffering of impoverished Americans he met on a cross-country trip. And Sinclair Lewis, after *Babbitt* and *Main Street* strictures against his hometown stuffed shirts, called on citizens of all classes to imagine the perils of American fascism in his memorable *It Can't Happen Here*.

Another important writer who became closely involved with *New Theatre* was Kyle Crichton, editor and highly paid feature writer for *Collier's*, a mass-circulation magazine as influential then as *Time* and *Newsweek* are today. Kyle was a "celebrity" in the publishing world, so valuable to his employers that they refused to accept his offer to resign his high-paid job rather than stop writing gratis for the left-wing press that often opposed *Collier's* conservative and sometimes reactionary views. They agreed Kyle would not be asked to write anything against his beliefs, but required his use of a pseudonym that would protect *Collier's* from advertisers' and readers' charges of involvements with the Left. Accordingly, Kyle wrote for us and other publications from *P.M.* to the *New Masses* under the pseudonym "Robert Forsythe." He was pleased that most everyone in publishing and writing knew his real identity, and he enjoyed appearing at left-wing gatherings as "Robert Forsythe" to publicly express his often hilarious put-downs of the Right. I will always remember this big, friendly, and always kidding man who would say, "Well, Herb, since you want me to take on those Goddamn censors, and the Pope himself, how many pages do you have to squeeze your loquacious pal down to?" Here is a slightly shortened version of a "Robert Forsythe" blast that got us condemned by the church and other censorship forces, but also won admiration as one of the strongest attacks on censorship in our time.

Who Speaks for Us?

BY ROBERT FORSYTHE

AT FIRST GLANCE it would seem that the extraordinary thing about the Pope's encyclical on the movies was its belatedness. It was pointed out almost immediately and with a slightly wounded air by Mr. Martin Quigley, ardent Catholic and editor of the *Motion Picture Daily*, that the Holy Father could surely not have Hollywood in mind because Hollywood had already been cleaned up by Mr. Joseph I. Breen, the Catholic layman acting as censor with the consent of the film companies. Mr. Quigley, perhaps a bit desperate, lifted one paragraph from the encyclical which went as follows: "*In particular you, venerable brethren of the United States, will be able to insist with justice that the industry in your country has recognized and accepted its responsibility before society.*"

A full reading of the encyclical, however, dispelled any such comfort for Mr. Quigley. What the Pope meant by the foregoing paragraph was not that he praised Hollywood for its success in elevating the films but that it warned the "venerable brethren of the United States," i.e., the Catholic bishops, to keep an eye on Hollywood, which had promised many things in the way of decency but needed watching. It was saying, in brief, that Hollywood, having accepted the principle of outside censorship, was not to be allowed to beg off. Mr. Will Hays was quick to point out that a recent report of the Legion of Decency revealed only four productions condemned since the industry had undertaken its own cleanup campaign under Mr. Breen. But all of the successive statements of the Beverly Hills gentry, brave as they attempted to be, gave indications of their awareness that the Trojan Horse which had been led through the studio gate by Mr. Joseph I. Breen was beginning to disgorge its occupants.

Since the church is not known for its stupidity, it could only be agreed

*Drawings by
John Groth*

that the encyclical was in no sense behind the times but was an important document foreshadowing future action. The point about censorship is that it never openly announces its destination. As Bernard Shaw noted in denouncing the English censorship of the stage, the provision by which control of the theatre is in the hands of the Lord Chamberlain (with no recourse possible elsewhere) arose from a desire of Walpole in 1737 to curb the attacks of Henry Fielding on parliamentary corruption. *"Walpole, unable to rule without corruption, promptly gagged the stage by a censorship which is in full force at the present moment."* Walpole, naturally, said nothing about protecting himself from Fielding's attacks, but placed the matter on a high moral plane. Would a father like to have his sixteen-year-old daughter sit through a play by Fielding, etc., etc.? The censorship, which was so easily imposed, has never been lifted.

The spectacle of William Randolph Hearst denouncing Mae West for immorality is not so hilarious as first appears. As an expert at perverting ideas, Mr. Hearst is not unaware of the moral position to be attained by defending the home against sin. His extramarital life with Marion Davies at San Simeon hardly entitles him to honorable mention as a Great Moral Force, but it was significant that the Legion of Decency campaign had its most fervent support from the Hearst newspapers, stories of its successes appearing on the same pages with pictures of young ladies from

MR. WELLS'S UTOPIA IS VISITED
BY A STRANGER

the Paradise or Hollywood clubs who were giving living examples of the truth that the human form, in a Hearst newspaper, is a thing of beauty.

But Hearst was not fundamentally concerned with Mae West, any more than any censorship is concerned primarily with sin. He was concerned with the censorship of ideas, just as the Catholic church, sincere as it may be, is concerned with ideas. It is interested in protecting the home, the family, and, most important of all, the status quo. If it were only on the matter of sexual relations, we might conceivably join the Pope in his crusade. We could easily do without Mae West, although we are less offended by the buxom lady than we are by most of the ideas which pass as art in Hollywood. Nothing is so immoral to us as a series of pictures calculated to show that the life of Carole Lombard will be open to anybody who yearns hard enough and learns not to complain. The half-truths, the distortions, the evasions which constitute the average Hollywood film will not offend the eye of the most moral because they pander to the desire of settled individuals to feel that we are living in the best possible of worlds.

In Catholic circles a polite fiction is maintained that the Pope speaks only to his own flock, but in truth it is assumed that he speaks as the moral conscience of the world. Is the world which has fought Catholic suppression in the arts and sciences now to accept an edict from the Vatican which seeks to control the greatest medium of expression left to man? It is only a Catholic matter because the Pope has made it so. The attempt of any religious body to demand control of the motion pictures of the world would need equally firm resistance. In writing about the backward state of various parts of New England after the Revolutionary War, Van Wyck Brooks in his *The Flowering of New England* writes: "*At the moment, the state of mind of these inland regions,— even Connecticut, which faced the sea,—seemed hardly auspicious for the man of letters. It was not quickened by the mental currents that brought new light to the towns of the Eastern seaboard. It was wrapped in an atmosphere of gloom; and its doctrines of total depravity and the utter vanity of human effort paralyzed the literary sense. . . .*" In short the effect of religious suppression and terror was as deadly as it has been in all ages. Progress has been brought about by constant warfare upon religion, magic, and superstition. The fight is as serious now as it has ever been.

The action of the Legion of Decency in condemning *Things to Come*, the H. G. Wells fantasy which even managed to elude British censors, is something to be worried about. In this case no question of sexual morality can be raised because in the first part of the film people are too busy being massacred to think of the matter and later they become too beautiful and hygienic for such nonsense. But the Legion is not pleased even with this pasteurized version of life. They list the film, Class B—Objectionable in Part, and write: *Objection*: *The Wellsian theory of a mechanical age with the exclusion of any thought of a Higher Being is expounded in this film.* Just what Mr. Wells could have done in his film short of presenting a mysterious figure waving a wand over the prophylactic characters is beyond us. The fact that we are to have, according to the British seer, air-cooled cities and rocket trips to the moon seems to have agitated nobody but the Legion. The garments of the new-fangled creatures didn't win us but they were evidently human beings despite that and for the Legion to state by implication that Mr. Wells was thinking of hatching his new people artificially from incubators rather than having them fashioned in the time-honored way is a libel on the picture and a too-patent indication of what may be expected from religious censorship of the films.

The record of American cities in which Catholic politicians and religious fervor controls public opinion is not good in the matter of the stage. The barring of *Tobacco Road* and *The Children's Hour* by Mayor Kelly in Chicago followed the action of Boston in suppressing earlier plays by Eugene O'Neill, *Within the Gates* by Sean O'Casey, and *The*

Children's Hour by Lillian Hellman. The latter play was barred before it had an opportunity of opening in Boston, the mayor rejecting it in words which led to a suit for slander being instituted against him by Mr. Herman Shumlin, producer of the play. From the agitation which arose over the incident, an amendment was passed through the activities of the Massachusetts Theatre Alliance which placed censorship control in the hands of a committee consisting of the mayor, police commissioner, and a member to be elected from the city art department instead of being in the hands of the mayor, the police commissioner, and the chief justice of the municipal court of Boston. The former bill gave the committee the right to "revoke any licence at their pleasure." The new amendment provides for a "hearing of all persons interested." It was substituted for the notorious Dorgan Bill, which would have barred any theatrical production which "contains dialogue or action in its subject matter pertaining to homosexuality, incest, the portrayal of a moral pervert or sex degenerate or *the use of subversive propaganda*." We call attention to the latter phrase, in which the defenders of the public morals give the case of censorship away. Mr. Dorgan, being a bit more frank or a trifle less careful, had stated the case in its entirety. What the advocates of censorship are interested in is not the nakedness of a chorus girl or the smuttiness of a comedian's joke but in ideas. First, last and always ... ideas!

The successive leg shows of Mr. Earl Carroll and Mr. George White and minor imitators of the Minsky order have not been bothered in Boston in years. If lust, carnality, and incitements to seduction are objects of concern, another encyclical might be written on that subject alone, but it is notorious that the censors turn a glazed eye to such entertainments and only awaken when *Waiting for Lefty* reaches town. *Model Tenement*, a play by Meyer Levin which was scheduled as the first production of the Federal Theatre Project in Chicago, was kept from the boards by the interference of Mayor Kelly acting in conjunction with Father Giles. The Project people in Washington were in no position to deny the wishes of a man who had carried Chicago and Illinois for Roosevelt. The most amazing part of Mr. Levin's experience with Father Giles was the reference to *Les Misérables*. Now there, said Father Giles, was a book which was on the *Index*. Yet the Legion of Decency has been able to recommend the film ... because the film was not like the book. In the book the church failed Jean Valjean. So, naturally, the book was on the *Index*. But in the film, well, that was another story....

Mr. Levin's comment on this is important: *"It didn't seem to occur to Father Giles that the church had actually caused the filmmakers to reverse the meaning of a world classic by an author who, being dead, had no comeback. He didn't seem to consider that a preponderant audience of non-Catholics was not interested in Catholic symbolism in their films.*

The censorship of the cinema is now being followed by action aimed at taking over the radio. *Variety* has recently published the first reports of another decency move which was to do for the air what the Legion has done for Hollywood. It is significant only as a sign of progress. The radio is already censored to the hilt by the major companies. A successful attempt at controlling both the movies and the radio will inevitably lead to censorship in all fields. If we are not mistaken New York state still has on its books the censorship law which makes it possible to padlock a theatre in which a condemned play has been presented.

The church is utterly sincere in its censorship ideas. It feels that man is better off under discipline; it feels that "a little learning is a dangerous thing"; it is earnestly desirous of protecting its people from changes which will lead away from the authority of the church and hence, in the church's view, act to their detriment.

As Robert Briffault states in *Rational Evolution: "But the revolt of the oppressed against power no more depends solely or chiefly upon physical force than does the exercise of oppressive power. Constituted power is guarded by defenses more effective than any Pretorian guard. It is protected by ideas. . . . No resistance against unjust power can take place while the sanctioning ideas which justify that power are accepted as valid. While that first and chief line of defence is unbroken there can be no revolt. Before any injustice, any abuse or oppression can be resisted, the lie upon which it is founded must be unmasked, must be clearly recognized for what it is. Hence, every advance of justice, every step in moral progress, has been not an abstract ethical inspiration, but a process of intellectual criticism, a victory of rational thought over irrationalism. Thus it is that whatever growth of justice and moral sense sets the modern age above the barbarism of preceding periods, has invariably gone hand in hand with the growth of rational thought."*

And the implications of rational thought are precisely what the advocates of censorship wish to avoid. The campaign which begins as a sortie against nudity and carnality soon becomes a mass enveloping movement calculated to stifle all novelty of thought or faithfulness of depiction. So censorship, which begins as the purest reproach of vulgarity, inevitably ends in suppression of thought.

Again I want to quote Briffault: *"When the King's permission was requested for the performance of Beaumarchais's comedy, The Marriage of Figaro, he exclaimed, 'But, Messieurs, if permission is granted to perform this play, one ought—to be quite consistent—to pull down the*

Bastille!' *Figaro went through sixty-eight performances—and the Bastille did duly get pulled down. It was by those men, Bayle, Montesquieu, Voltaire, Diderot, D'Alembert, Volney, Holbach, Condorcet and their contemporaries, who cast aside all conventional formulas, resolved to think for themselves, and, what is more, speak out boldly what they thought, to own no other sanction or criterion than rational thought, that the world has been transformed. Behind them and around them stood mediaevalism in all its ignorance and darkness and tyranny over life and mind, for all the superficial veneer of refinement laid over it by the renaissance and the 'Grand Siècle.' After them is a changed world, the modern world. It was those men who threw open the portals from the one into the other.*"

Whether the censorship comes from the Moderator of the Presbyterian Church in Pittsburgh or from the Pope in Rome or from the Caliph of Baghdad, the danger is equally great. When a single united group can capture control of the most powerful agency of public opinion the world possesses, the duty of those who cherish civil rights and the freedom of the human mind is plain. They must be prepared to fight.

There was a strange silence from the Vatican while the fascist forces of Mussolini were murdering the Christian brethren of Ethiopia, but the matter of the world cinema warrants a document of such weight that it is cabled in full to the *New York Times*, filling the better part of a page. At a time when the world is in turmoil and when the malevolent forces of reaction are determined to defeat an honest portrayal of social conditions, we have a letter from Rome which seems, at first glance, singularly outmoded.

The progress of civilization has been achieved by fighting religious suppressions. Are we prepared to give that up now at the request even of a voice from Rome? Is Hollywood, already defeated by a financial setup which prevents any but the most accidental treatments of reality, to be further smothered by the repressions of a highly interested group? The public is entitled to truth and art and honesty. Is it going to sacrifice the chance of that at the demand of a minority which is so actively engaged and directly affected that it cannot even pretend to impartiality in its judgments?

What we should like to know is this . . . Who speaks for us? And who gave them permission . . . ?

Afterword
THE BEGINNING OF THE END OF *NEW THEATRE*

Backstage

> Herbert Kline's name has been on the masthead of *New Theatre* since April 1934, first as managing editor and then as editor in chief. More than any other person he was responsible for its survival against overwhelming odds and its emergence as a real force in the theatre and film world. Kline left the impress of his individuality and his tremendous devotion to the magazine on every issue which he edited. He resigned on January 1 (after collecting much of the material for this issue) to take up correspondent work with the Loyalist forces in Spain, and the good wishes of the staff and of the readers of the magazine, go with him

My brother Mark placed this brief farewell notice from the March 1937 issue in a letter that reached me at the Jarama front, near the highway between Madrid and Valencia. Geza Karpathy and I were there filming what later became *Heart of Spain* about Dr. Norman Bethune's Canadian blood transfusion unit.

The letter began with a brother's worry for my safety, then said that *New Theatre* staff efforts to raise money in New York had been unsuccessful and that John Howard Lawson's promised Hollywood backing had also not come through as expected. Mark regretted having to tell me the magazine we had slaved so hard for would not last beyond the April issue. With Franco's fascist forces 150 yards away trying to cut the lifeline to the beleaguered Loyalists in Madrid, and scattered exchanges of rifle, machine gun, and artillery fire exploding nearby, the troubles in New York seemed very remote. But that night was a sleepless one as I recalled—what I have never revealed publicly until now—the reasons for my resignation from *New Theatre*.

In early December 1936, after my resignation (which actually occurred on December 1), rumors began circulating that John Howard Lawson's political interference had forced me out of *New Theatre*. I had evaded

JOHN HOWARD LAWSON
Phil Wolfe

telling the truth about what had happened. I felt it would harm the magazine's chances for survival; and also, because I liked and admired Lawson, I did not want to reveal anything that would cause him difficulty as a screenwriter or as a leader of the Screen Writers' Guild. I respected Jack (as close friends called him) for his fine plays, films, writings on theatre and film technique—including the many articles he had written gratis for *New Theatre*. Besides, I didn't want to say anything that would hint at the sort of "red-baiting" often practiced by those who broke with the revolutionary Left, where Jack was considered a major spokesman for the theatre arts.

It may be of value, however, to later generations concerned with guarding democratic freedoms, to learn how extremist sectarianism of the Left destroyed *New Theatre* at a time when it was most needed to fight fascism.

The conflict between Lawson and me began at an emergency staff meeting two months after I returned from the European theatre tour. As usual, *New Theatre* was in a financial crisis, but this one was more serious than usual. We needed to raise $3,000 to keep us going for six months, when, according to my estimates, we should break even. Lawson did not support me and said, quite bluntly, that we should stop publishing for two or three months after the December issue was out. He felt we should not count on raising money in Hollywood (where we had recently found some funding) since leftist sources there were involved in raising money for medical aid to Loyalist Spain.

I told Jack that to stop publishing would be a death sentence for the magazine. "Closing down for even one issue would destroy the confidence of subscribers and advertisers."

Jack disagreed with me strongly. He insisted that *New Theatre* needed not only financial reorganization but also needed to reexamine its political line and take "a less wishy-washy liberal approach."

Jack's words made me very angry, because I realized what was really going on. Jack was expressing a criticism of *New Theatre*'s "popular front" approach that had been expressed by V. J. Jerome, the so-called cultural commissar of the far Left, who had accused me of turning *New Theatre* into a vaguely leftist magazine that differed from the political positions he, as a pro-Communist, had urged me to take. I told Lawson I refused to let Jerome influence me. I believed Jerome had it in for me because I wouldn't let him interfere with *New Theatre*'s "popular front" policy and had rejected several of his submissions. I asked Lawson to admit he was acting against me under Jerome's influence.

Although Mark tried to calm us down, both Jack and I were at a stalemate. Jack wanted me to cooperate with him. If I didn't, he insisted *New Theatre* would lose financial support from the far Left. I argued that giving in to political pressure from them would kill the magazine. I told Jack that at this point my only alternative to his kind of dictatorial interference was to resign.

"Cooperate or resign!" he said. "The choice is yours."

I answered bluntly that I would leave him to preside over the magazine's future—or the failure that would certainly follow the shutdown Lawson wanted.

No sooner did the rumors of my resignation begin to spread than phone calls of concern and sympathy began pouring in from friends and contributors in Hollywood and New York. The calls were an outpouring of incredulity, questions, offers of support. To all I told the same cover story: I deeply regretted leaving the magazine but was determined to do my part in Spain.

I remember three particular calls that meant a lot to me. One call was from Bennett Cerf, generously offering a loan if I needed it or a well-paid editing job at Random House. Another was from the literary critic Philip Rahv, whom I knew and admired for his brilliant writing and coediting with William Phillips of *Partisan Review*. Phil commiserated about what he guessed was "typical Jerome political interference." He offered me a coeditorship and also asked me to write a drama and film section, which he would feature in his prestigious magazine. I confess both offers were tempting. And I was a bit fearful about going off to my first war. But I refused both Cerf and Rahv, with the same explanation I had given for my resignation—my commitment to Loyalist Spain.

The third call was from Bosley Crowther at the *New York Times*. He was then an enterprising young reporter who had not yet risen to eminence as a major film critic. Bosley wanted an interview, which, he assured me, would be on the front page of the drama section the following Sunday. I thanked him but refused as politely as I could.

Bosley, too good a reporter to give up, hurried to my office only a few blocks from the *Times*. He argued that the story should be aired in the press, especially if what had happened involved the sort of political pressure he surmised. I again refused. But I still felt disturbed about my resignation, and asked for his promise not to reveal what I told him "off the record." I told Bosley part of the "inside story." Even though disappointed he couldn't write about it, Bosley kept his word. In subsequent years he wrote favorably about me and my films, without ever mentioning what I had confided that day.

That was how and why I resigned from *New Theatre*. Years later, during the McCarthy era, Lawson went to prison for a year along with the "Hollywood Ten," and Jerome, who had protested his constitutional rights in vain, received a longer sentence under the infamous Smith Act as a "Communist subversive." Both were courageous, dedicated men who risked all for their beliefs and suffered serious illnesses from their imprisonment. Lawson was blacklisted from screenwriting and never returned to writing for the theatre, his major talent. But he continued as a writer, producing fine books on writing technique. His too-early death was a sad loss to theatre arts in America.

In 1976, the year before he died, Lawson made a sincere effort to repair our differences. It happened this way.

I was in Hollywood at the time and received a phone call from Mordecai "Max" Gorelik, who had been the Group Theatre scenic designer and a *New Theatre* contributor.

"Herb, don't hang up on me," he said. "Jack Lawson thought you might, but he asked me to call, as a mutual friend, and make an appointment for him to see you."

I didn't hang up. I could never forget it was Max who had recommended me to Ben Blake for *New Theatre*. But I told Max I didn't want to see Lawson and open up old wounds. However, Max prevailed on me to at least talk with Lawson, and I agreed reluctantly to accept Lawson's phone call.

When Lawson called, his voice, filled with emotion, broke as he asked if I would meet with him. He said he couldn't express himself properly over the phone and asked me to reconsider not seeing him. I thought of Jack in prison, of my own sleepless nights remembering our *New Theatre* days, and I didn't have the heart to refuse him.

Soon after the call, we met at a rickety old wooden house in the hills

Afterword

near Dodger Stadium. It was a far different abode than those of his halcyon days as one of Hollywood's highest-paid screenwriters.

Jack had tears in his eyes as we met, and I realized his sincerity when he embraced me in a bear hug, then said, "I know you can never forget, Herb, but can you forgive me?"

I couldn't help but respond with affection towards this remarkable man.

"I can't find it in my heart to continue resenting you, Jack. *New Theatre*'s death was long ago. But I must reproach you for giving up your writing for the theatre."

Jack nodded sadly. He admitted his life would have been happier if he had continued as a playwright and had left political action to others. He also said that, indeed, Jerome had influenced him against me. He then confided he was writing an autobiography that would express his reasons for putting political aims ahead of his theatrical career. He asked my help now to answer questions about what had gone on in the *New Theatre* movement in New York while he was busy working on Hollywood films.

After we finished, Jack said, "You've got such a wonderful memory of all this, Herb. Why don't you write a book on your life?"

"I've thought of it," I said. I even had a title and several hundred pages of rough sketches that I called "Flashbacks to My Future." But I doubted I'd ever be able to take time off from filmmaking, or have enough money, to do so.

But the thought remained with me. And here I have presented with love at least part of my story, the memories and writings of the mid-1930s, gathered together in 1984 on the fiftieth anniversary of the year I first began working on *New Theatre*.

Tables of Contents
FOR NEW THEATRE (1934–36) AND NEW THEATRE AND FILM (1937)

Listed here are Tables of Contents for the thirty-four issues of *New Theatre* that appeared from January 1934 to November 1936 and the two issues of the magazine that appeared in March and April 1937, after its name change to *New Theatre and Film*. Complete runs of the thirty-six magazines are located at the Memorial Library University of Wisconsin, Madison, Rare Books and Special Collections, and at the Theatre Collection of the New York Public Library in New York City. Please note that the first listing is for the January 1934 issue, Volume III, Number 2. The publication that was eventually to become *New Theatre* began in the early 1930s as a mimeographed magazine called *Workers' Theatre*, edited by Ben Blake. The magazine changed its name to *New Theatre* in October 1933. For its January 1934 issue, the format of *New Theatre* was redesigned and for the first time printed. It is this issue that is generally considered to be the "first" issue of *New Theatre*.

JANUARY 1934—VOLUME III, NUMBER 2

1934—Comment on Events 2
Prospects for the American Theatre 5
Scenery—The Visual Machine 9
MORDECAI GORELIK
Stage in Review 10
National Theatre Festival 18
ANNE HOWE
A Theatre Advancing 19
NATHANIEL BUCHWALD
International Scene 21
JOHN E. BONN

MOVIES
March of the Movies 13
IRVING LERNER
Workers Study the Film 14
TOM BRANDON

DANCE
Kurt Jooss 4
EDITH SEGAL
The Dance 15
MIGNON VERNE
Workers' Dance League 16
Dance Group in Trade Union 17

FEBRUARY 1934—VOLUME III, NUMBER 3

1934—Comment 2
Community House Drama 5
LEON BLOCH
National Theatre Festival 7
Meet the Theatre Union 8
EMERY NORTHRUP
Prospects for the American Theatre 10
The Artef Theatre 14
Stage in Review 15
LEON BLOCH

MOVIES
March of the Movies 20
IRVING LERNER
The Revolutionary Film 21
SAMUEL BRODY
News and Notes 23

DANCE
Mass Dance in Soviet Union 4
The Dance 17
OAKELY JOHNSON

MARCH 1934—VOLUME III, NUMBER 4

1934—Current Comment 3
"U.S. Puts 150 Idle Actors to

Work" 5
KAY SHARPE
Voice of the Audience:
On Tobacco Road 6
D. VIVIEN
Montage 8
PETER MARTIN
A Letter from the Editors 11
National Theatre Festival 12
OSCAR SAUL
Prospects for the American Theatre:
A Questionnaire 13
JOHN WEXLEY, HIRAM MOTHERWELL,
LISTON M. OAK, GLENN HUGHES,
FRANCHOT TONE, MORDECAI GORELIK
The Playwrights' Competition 15
Stage in Review 20
New and Notes 21

MOVIES
Sound and the Future of the
Cinema 7
V. I. PUDOVKIN
Massacre in Hollywood 16
ROBERT GESSNER

DANCE
A Chorus Girl's Job 10
The New Dance Group 17
What to Dance About 18
EZRA FREEMAN
Brief Dance Reviews 19
BEN WOLF
New and Notes 19

APRIL 1934—VOLUME III,
NUMBER 5

The Awakening of the Actors 2
National Theatre Festival 10
OSCAR SAUL
How to Make Your Own Lights 12
The International Workers'
Theatre Olympiad 15
JOHN BONN
Two Years of Workers' Theatre
in Canada 16
R. GORDON

STAGE REVIEWS
The Armored Train 9
PETER MARTIN
They Shall Not Die 18
BEN BLAKE
The Pure in Heart 19
JENNIE HELD

Squaring the Circle 19
VICTOR CUTLER

MOVIES
Dovzhenko, Soviet Cinema
Director 6
M. BAJAN
Hollywood or Lenin Hills 9
HARRY ALAN POTAMKIN
The Eyes of the Movies 13
TOM BRANDON
News of Film and Photo League 22

DANCE
Whither Martha Graham 7
EDNA OCKO
An Open Letter to Workers'
Dance Groups 20
BLANCHE EVAN
Brief Dance Reviews 22
BEN WOLF

MAY 1934—VOLUME III,
NUMBER 6

Cover Design by Jim Kelly
Cover—Rex Ingram as Blacksnake
in *Stevedore*
The Winter of Broadway 3
HAROLD EDGAR
From Atlantic to Pacific—2nd
National Workers' Theatre Festival 5
BEN BLAKE
America, America 7
Sketches by M. HERBST
Crowd Scene 9
FRANK MERLIN
Voice of the Audience: Impressions of
a Newcomer 10
PAUL ARRANOW
A Theatre of Action 11
ALICE EVANS
Stevedore, reviewed by 13
JACK SHAPIRO

FILM
The Revolutionary Film—
Next Step 14
LEO T. HURWITZ
Program of the International
Cinema Bureau 15
Truth Is Forbidden—Censorship
in Chicago 16

DANCE
Which Technique? 17
EZRA FRIEDMAN

The New Dance Advances—
Workers' Dance League Recital   18
Hy Glickman
Casualties: Humphrey-Weidman   19
E.O.
Workers' Dance League Festival
in June   21

JUNE 1934—VOLUME III,
NUMBER 7

Editorials   3
Take Theatre to the Workers   5
Al Saxe
Lawson Crosses the Class Line   5
Lester Cohen
Towards a Revolutionary Theatre   6
John Howard Lawson
From a Director's Notebook   8
Stephen Karnot
To Eva Le Gallienne at 33   9
Paul Romaine
Jim Crow? Oh No!   10
Facing the New Audience   11
Michael Blankfort
No Greater Treachery   13
Leo T. Hurwitz
The Stage Was Not Set   14
Anne Howe
Stevedore Cast Votes "No"   15
Herbert Kline
News and Notes of L.O.W.T.   16
Oscar Saul
Workers' Theatre: A Criticism   17
Conrad Seiler
March of the Movies   18
David Platt
What a Racket   19
Anonymous
Voice of the Audience   20
Men in the Modern Dance   21
Ezra Friedman
A Letter to Blanche Evan   22
Workers' Dance League
Brief Reviews   12, 22
Drawings and Photos by
Valente, Wally,
Phil Wolfe

JULY–AUGUST 1934 (NO
VOLUME; NO NUMBER)

Editorials   3
Krasny-Presny   6
E. Stephen Karnot
The Brookfield Playhouse   8

John Mitchell
Garbage Delivered to Your Door   9
Robert Stebbins
Hisses, Boos and Boycotts   10
Leo T. Hurwitz
Marion Models, Inc.   11
Nathaniel Buchwald
Newsboy from Script to
Performance   12
Alfred Saxe
Facing the New Audience   14
Michael Blankfort
Scenes from the Living Theatre   16–17
Film and Photo League
Sin and Cinema   18
David Platt
The Movie Front   19
Tom Brandon
Dimitroff   20
Art Smith and Elia Kazan
Diagnosis of the Dance   24
Emanuel Eisenberg
Revolutionary Staging for
Revolutionary Plays   26
Molly Day Thacher
Workers' Theatre: From Coast
to Coast   27
Reply to Michael Gold   28
Edna Ocko
Dance Convention   29
Grace Wylie
Eight Men Speak   30
Will Ferris
Drawings and Photos by
Valente, Adolph Dehn,
William Segal, James Kelly,
G. Giltinger, Phil Wolfe

SEPTEMBER 1934—VOLUME I,
NUMBER 8

Editorials   3
$6 a Week Actors   5
Elmer Rice   6
Joseph Freeman
Workers' Theatre Advances   8
George Sklar
20° Cooler Inside   9
Robert Forsythe
Rubber Stamp Movies   11
King Vidor
From a Director's Notebook   12
Stephen Karnot
The Magic of Meyerhold   14
Lee Strasberg

San Francisco 1934   16
PHILIP STERLING
Perspectives of the Dance   18
HARRY ELION
The Shadow Dance   20
SIMON BREINES
On the New Season   21
EDNA OCKO
Revolutionary Movie Production   22
RALPH STEINER
Films of the Bourgeoisie   23
BELA BALASZ
Revolutionary Drama   25
VIRGIL GEDDES
Send Us Scripts   26
International Theatre   27
BEN BLAKE
Nijinsky's Tragedy   27
LYDIA NADEJINA
Shifting Scenes of Workers' Theatre   28
Five Month Plan   29
The Movie Front   30
Drawings and Photos by
Del, Charles Dibner, William Gropper, M. Levy, Esther Krieger, Phil Wolfe, Hosen, Raphael Soyer

OCTOBER 1934—VOLUME I, NUMBER 9

Editorials   3
An Appeal to Playwrights   5
VIRGIL GEDDES
Film into Fascism   6
BELA BALASZ
It Makes You Weep   8
JANET THORNE
A Playreader on Playwrights   9
JOHN GASSNER
Theatre of Action   11
MARK MARVIN
Revolutionary Ballet Forms   12
LINCOLN KIRSTEIN
Nebuchadnezzar by the Yard   16
ROBERT FORSYTHE
Judgment Day   17
BEN BLAKE
Drama in Dixie   18
MOLLY DAY THACHER
Why Makeup?   20
LEWIS LEVERETT
Winesburg, Ohio   21
LESTER GLASS
From Palmer Raids to Vigilantes   22

DAVID PLATT
The Star-Spangled Dance   24
BLANCHE EVAN
Voice of the Audience   25
Building of the New Audience   26
MARGARET LARKIN
Workers' Films   27
LEO T. HURWITZ
Shifting Scenes   29

NOVEMBER 1934—VOLUME I, NUMBER 10

Editorials   3
Columbia's Call to Arms   5
Continuous Performance   6
ILYA EHRENBURG
Punch Goes Red   8
LOUIS BUNIN
A Play With Two Smokes   9
VIRGIL GEDDES
Three Songs About Lenin   10
J.L.
Straight from the Shoulder   11
JOHN HOWARD LAWSON
Shock Troupe in Action   13
RICHARD PACK
Hollywood Sees Pink   14
RICHARD WATTS, JR.
The Folk Dance   15
SOPHIA DELZA
Merrily They Roll Along   17
MOLLY DAY THACHER
Scenes from the Living Theatre—
Sidewalks of New York   18
BEN SHAHN
Observer or Partisan   20
MIGNON VERNE
The Artef   21
SAMUEL KREITER
Ungrateful for Gift Horses   22
ROBERT STEBBINS
Shifting Scenes   23
Facing the New Audience   25
MICHAEL BLANKFORT
Technical Advice to Movie Makers   27
RALPH STEINER and IRVING LERNER
New Dance Group   28
EDNA OCKO
Dances Notes   29
The Movie Front   30
DAVID PLATT
Voice of the Audience   31
We Gather Strength   32
HARRY ELION

Tables of Contents

DECEMBER 1934—VOLUME I, NUMBER 11

Editorials 3
Dramatist in Exile 5
RICHARD PACK
A Little Child Shall Read Them 6
ROBERT FORSYTHE
The Snickering Horses 7
EM JO BASSHE
Robert Flaherty's Escape 9
PETER ELLIS [IRVING LERNER]
Below Chicago's Mason-Dixon Line 10
ALICE EVANS
Stanislavsky's Method of Acting 12
M. A. CHEKHOV
Piscator's First Film 14
BELA BALASZ
Blood on the Moon 15
JOHN HOWARD LAWSON
Paul Sifton Replies 16
The Mass Dance 17
JANE DUDLEY
Open Letter to Jasper Deeter 18
CURT CONWAY
The Plays of the Month 19
BEN BLAKE
Play Contest 20
English Theatre of the Left 21
MARIE SETON
Writing for Workers' Theatre 22
HERBERT KLINE
Films of the Month 24
ROBERT STEBBINS
The Movie Front 25
The Voice of the Audience 26
Return from Moscow 27
L. DAL NEGRO
Dance Reviews 28
Shifting Scenes 29

JANUARY 1935—VOLUME II, NUMBER 1

Editorial 3
HAROLD EDGAR
Yesterday 4
ANATOLI GLEBOV
Soviet Theatre Today 6
HEINRICH DIAMENT
Theatre for Young Spectators 7
The State Jewish Theatre 8
LEON MOUSSINAC
The New Soviet Cinema 9
SERGEY EISENSTEIN
Meyerhold's New Theatre 10
H. W. L. DANA
An Epic of the Ether 13
SERGEY TRETIAKOV
A Theatre Director in the Soviet Cinema 14
ERWIN PISCATOR
Animated Films 15
A New Generation 16
MARIE SETON
The Soviet Dance 17
CHEN I-WAN
New Soviet Movies 20
What They Said About the Cinema 21
Workers' Dance League Soloists 22
The Revolutionary Solo Dance 23
STEVE FOSTER
Plays of the Month 24
LEON ALEXANDER
Books Received 25
The Movie Front 26
DAVID PLATT
Shifting Scenes 27
ANNE HOWE
From Agitprop to Realism 28
BEN BLAKE
Voice of the Audience 29

FEBRUARY 1935—VOLUME II, NUMBER 2

B'way Inc. vs. The Theatre 5
BLACK TAYLOR
Stanislavsky's Method 6
M. A. CHEKHOV
The Artef on Broadway 8
NATHANIEL BUCHWALD
Ladies of the Revolutionary Dance 10
EMANUEL EISENBERG
Will Hays—Puppet Dictator 11
TOM LANGELY
Waiting for Lefty 13
CLIFFORD ODETS
Shows for Sale 21
HAROLD EDGAR
Voice of the Audience 22
Life Will Be Beautiful 23
ROBERT STEBBINS
Dramatizing Our Times 24
FRIEDRICH WOLF
The Dance League Recital 25
EDNA OCKO
The Dance Front 26

Shifting Scenes 27
Dance Reviews 28
DAL NEGRO & SKRIPP
Backstage 30
Drawings and Photographs by
George Price, I. Russack, Mackey,
Alfredo Valente, Pavelle, F. Zachnoff,
and Lapchek

MARCH 1935—VOLUME II,
NUMBER 3

Editorials 3
Paul Muni Denies All 5
EMANUEL EISENBERG
Our Hall 6
MARK MARVIN
The Youth of Maxim 8
V. PUDOVKIN
Too Much Reality 9
FRIEDRICH WOLF
Fragments from *Panic* 10
ARCHIBALD MACLEISH
German Theatres Underground 12
Why Improvisation? 14
MOLLY DAY THACHER
The Living Theatre 15
ALICE EVANS
Let Us Have Dance Critics 16
EDNA OCKO
Recording Dance Scripts 18
ELISE HAROLD
Time Marches Where 19
RAY LUDLOW and EVA GOLDBECK
Awake and Sing! 20
MARY VIRGINIA FARMER
The Dance and Acting 21
TAMIRIS
The New Plays 22
HERBERT KLINE
A Revolutionary Gentleman 24
Against Fascism 25
Backstage 26
Shifting Scenes 27
Drawings and Photos by
Pearl Binder, Phil Bard, Philip Reisman,
Siskind, Wm. Gropper
Cover—Morris Carnovsky in *Awake
and Sing*. Photo by Ralph Steiner

APRIL 1935—VOLUME II,
NUMBER 4

Editorials 3
Entertaining the Army 5
EMANUEL EISENBERG

Stars and Stripes on Broadway 6
HIRAM MOTHERWELL and
HELEN REYNOLDS
Drama on the Western Front 10
H. W. L. DANA
Dance of Death 11
PAUL LOVE
The Movies in Wartime 16
TOM LANGLEY
Did You Hear Their Voices? 18
PHILIP STERLING
Black Pit 20
HERBERT KLINE
New Found Land 21
STEPHEN FOSTER
Consider the Red Octopus 22
JULIAN LEE
An Editorial Appeal 23
Films, Current and Coming 24
LOUIS NORDEN
The Lay Dance 26
RUTH ALLERHAND
Dance Reviews 27
The New Dance League 28
Writers' Congress 29
Shifting Scenes 30

MAY 1935—VOLUME II,
NUMBER 5

Editorials 3
The Censors See Red 5
RICHARD PACK
Coal Diggers of 1935 8
ALBERT MALTZ
A Scene from Floridsdorf 10
FRIEDRICH WOLF
The Little Theatres 12
PAUL ROMAINE
I Work on the Drama Project 14
ANONYMOUS
Till the Day I Die 16
RUDOLPH WITTENBERG
Luck Comes to the Proletariat 17
LOUIS NORDEN
Pie in the Sky 18
RAY LUDLOW
The Dance as Theatre 20
LINCOLN KIRSTEIN
Directing the New Dance 23
EDITH SEGAL
Dance Reviews 24
Moscow Dance Week 25
Current Plays 26
Shifting Scenes 28

Tables of Contents

JUNE 1935—VOLUME II, NUMBER 6

Editorials 3
Sketches from "Parade" 5
The Law of Conflict 10
JOHN HOWARD LAWSON
Pescados Photographs 11
PAUL STRAND
Two Scoundrels Die Hard 12
LOUIS NORDEN
Plays of the Month 14
MOLLY DAY THACHER
The Third Stage 16
PAUL LOVE
Men Must Dance 17
GENE MARTEL
Men's Recital 18
Color in the Films 19
ROBERT EDMOND JONES
Movies About Us 20
ROBERT GESSNER
Voice of the Audience 21
New Theatre League Schools 22
The People's Dance 23
RICHARD CHASE
Actor's Forum 24
Waiting for Lefty 25
A $200 Prize Play Contest 25
Backstage Notes 26
Film Front 27
Film Checklist 29
Cover photo by Paul J. Woolf
Photos by Alfredo Valente, Vandamm, Martin Harris, and Paul Strand

JULY 1935—VOLUME II, NUMBER 7

Editorials 3
I Breathe Freely 5
PAUL ROBESON
Trouble With the Angels 7
LANGSTON HUGHES
Imitation of Life 9
ROBERT STEBBINS
On the White Man's Stage 11
AUGUSTUS SMITH
A Negro Community Theatre 13
ROWENA WOODHAM JELIFFE
Scenes from "John Henry" 14
HERBERT KLINE
Uncle Tom's Cabin to Stevedore 21
EUGENE GORDON
Negro Players in Southern Theatres 24
J. O. BAILEY

Nuthin' But Brass 25
EDWIN ROLFE
Martha Graham 26
EDNA OCKO
Correspondence 27
Boycott Hearst Films 28
LOUIS NORDEN
The Young Go First 30
"Bring 'Em In on Stretchers!" 31
Two Prize Play Contests 32
The Dance Festival 33

AUGUST 1935—VOLUME II, NUMBER 8

Editorials 3
Mary Wigman—Fascist? 5
NICHOLAS WIRTH
The Cult of the Flag 6
ILYA EHRENBURG
Louella Parsons—Hearst's Hollywood Stooge 8
JOEL FAITH
Columbia, Gem of the Drama 10
ROBERT FORSYTHE
Soviet Diary 12
HAROLD CLURMAN
The Drama in Transition 13
JOHN W. GASSNER
$300 Prize Play Contests 14
Concerning Paramount's Mr. Wilkie 15
ROBERT STEBBINS
Can We Use Stanislavsky's Method? 16
V. ZAKHAVA
Hollywood Goes In for Color 19
GEORGE LEWIS
American Dancers in Moscow 21
CHEN I-WAN
The Dance Unit 22
LEONARD DAL NEGRO
Theatre and the Trade Unions 23
ALICE EVANS
Revolt of the Actor—1935 24
ARTHUR HACKETT
Correspondence 25
Backstage 30
Cover by William Gropper

SEPTEMBER 1935—VOLUME II, NUMBER 9

DRAMA
Editorials 3
Preview 5

FRED J. RINGEL
The Quest of Eugene O'Neill   12
CHARMION VON WIEGAND
Midsummer Revue   21
JOHN R. CHAPLIN
Prospects for the New Theatre   24
MARK MARVIN
Shifting Scenes   25

FILM
Louella Parsons: Reel Two   4
Footlights in Filmland   20
RICHARD SHERIDAN AMES
Mayer of MGM   6
JOEL FAITH
Kino-Walpurgis Night, 14th St.   10
EDWARD DAHLBERG
Directing the "Nonactor"   18
V. I. PUDOVKIN
A New Approach to Filmmaking   22
RALPH STEINER and LEO T. HURWITZ
The New Film Alliance   29
Film Checklist   33

DANCE
The Fokine Ballets   26
BLANCHE EVAN
Martha Graham's *Panorama*   27
EDNA OCKO
Redder Than the Rose   28

OCTOBER 1935—VOLUME II,
NUMBER 10

DRAMA
Editorials   3
Children's Theatre on Tour   8
BEN GOLDEN
New Musical Revues for Old   2
JEROME MOROSS
Let Freedom Ring   16
ALBERT BEIN
The Art of Makeup   26
TAMARA DAYKARHANOVA
Building a Mobile Stage   28
EDWARD EDMAN
Shifting Scenes   30

FILM
A Letter on *Peasants*   5
G. W. PABST
Hollywood's *Riff-Raff*   6
JOEL FAITH and LOUIS NORDEN
Music in the Film   14
GEORGE ANTHEIL
Films of the Month   22
ROBERT STEBBINS

DANCE
Music for the Dance   10
ELIE SIEGMEISTER
Burlesque Strike   15
DEL
I Dance for Moscow   24
DHIMAH

NOVEMBER 1935—VOLUME II,
NUMBER 11

DRAMA
Editorials   3
A Letter from Hallie Flanagan   6
A Letter from H. W. L. Dana   7
Broadway Tries Again   9
JOHN W. GASSNER
Taming of the Shrew   11
MOLLY DAY THACHER
Shifting Scenes   28
Trade Union Notes   30

FILM
Salute to War   5
RAY LUDLOW
Charlie Chaplin in *Modern Times*   12
JOHN R. CHAPLIN
Lighthorse McLaglen   14
WARREN STARR
Reinhardt's *Dream*   18
CHARMION VON WIEGAND
Private Hicks   20
ALBERT MALTZ
Shifting Scenes   28
Film Checklist   33

DANCE
Ballet Russe   8
The Swastika Is Dancing   17
EDNA OCKO
Modern Dance Forms   26
PAUL DOUGLAS
Dance Front   33

DECEMBER 1935—VOLUME II,
NUMBER 12

DRAMA
Editorials   3
New Plays by Odets and Peters   4
Duke Ellington on *Porgy*   5
EDWARD MORROW
"Formation Left"—Los Angeles   6
The Theatre in Mexico   7
EMANUEL EISENBERG
Hope for Poetry in the Theatre   9

Tables of Contents

Archibald MacLeish
The Play's the Thing 10
John W. Gassner
An American People's Theatre 24
Mark Marvin
The Prize Play Contests 25
Theatre Workshop—
Art of Makeup 30
Tamara Daykarhanova
Shifting Scenes 33
With the Stage Unions 37

FILM
James Cagney 14
Forrest Clark
Will Hays: Film Enemy No. 1 16
Joel Faith
"The New Gulliver" 20
Louis Bunin
In Praise of Hollywood 22
Robert Stebbins
Film Checklist 23

DANCE
The Dance Season Begins 26
"Revolutionary" Dance Forms 28
Irving Ignatin
Dance Front 32

JANUARY 1936—VOLUME III, NUMBER 1

DRAMA
Editorials 3
The Awakening of the American Theatre 5
Clifford Odets
Paradise Lost and the Theatre of Frustration 8
John W. Gassner
Hymn to the Rising Sun 11
Paul Green
Interpretation and Characterization 21
Harold Clurman
Shifting Scenes 32
Book Reviews 37
New Theatre's Second Anniversary 40
Backstage 46

FILM
Stills from *Borinage* 6
English Documentary Films 7
Evelyn Gerstein
Love 'em with Bullets 22
Robert Stebbins
Dovzhenko's *Frontier* 24

Peter Ellis [Irving Lerner]
Uncle Tom, Will You Never Die? 30
Arthur Draper

DANCE
The Dance in Mexico 26
Sophia Delza
Dance Reviews 28
Elizabeth Ruskay
Dance Front 36
Cover by William Entin

FEBRUARY 1936—VOLUME III, NUMBER 2

DRAMA
Ethiopia 4
A Scene from the Censored Play 4
Editorials 5
Katakombe Cabaret-Berlin 7
I Can't Sleep 8
Clifford Odets
The Person in the Play 14
John W. Gassner
Vaudeville Fights the Death Sentence 17
Philip Sterling
Drama of Negro Life 26
Herbert Kline
Book Reviews 29
New Theatre in Philadelphia 30
Molly Day Thacher
Shifting Scenes 32

FILM
Eddie Cantor Likes Peace 10
Emanuel Eisenberg
The Films of René Clair 12
Lewis Jacobs
Air Raid Over Harlem: Scenario for a Little Black Movie 19
Langston Hughes
Gentlemen, Place Your Bets 22
Robert Stebbins
Film Checklist 22
Harry Alan Potamkin 28
David Wolff
Trade Union Notes 34

DANCE
Trudi on the Road 6
Muriel Rukeyser
The Solo Dance Recital 20
Norma Roland
Dancers, Take a Bow 24
Edna Ocko

The Dancer Organizes 25
TAMIRIS
Cover by A. Birnbaum

MARCH 1936—VOLUME III, NUMBER 3

DRAMA
The Man from Brinks 9
ERNESTINE FRIEDL
The Federal Theatre Presents 10
JOSEPH MANNING
Ethan Frome and the Theatre of Fate 12
JOHN W. GASSNER
The Obligatory Scene 18
JOHN HOWARD LAWSON
Eva Le Gallienne—Ten Years 20
WALTER PELL
Shifting Scenes 30
Five-Finger Exercises 31
BOB LEWIS

FILM
Little Charlie, What Now? 6
CHARMION VON WIEGAND
The Pair from Paramount 14
ALFRED HAYES
The Movie: 1902–1917 22
ROBERT STEBBINS
Hollywood's Hundred-Grand Union 25
GEORGE MANSION

DANCE
From a Dancer's Notebook 16
BLANCHE EVAN
Dance Reviews 27
ELIZABETH RUSKAY
Cover by Miguel Covarrubias

APRIL 1936—VOLUME III, NUMBER 4

DRAMA
"Patriots" on the Project 5
RICHARD PACK
Drama versus Melodrama 8
JOHN W. GASSNER
The New Theatre Conference 11
MARK MARVIN
Bury the Dead 15
IRWIN SHAW
Playwright into Critic 35
CHARMION VON WIEGAND

Play Reviews 38
Five-Finger Exercises—II 39
BOB LEWIS
Shifting Scenes 40
Backstage 46

FILM
John Ford: Fighting Irish 7
EMANUEL EISENBERG
Film Forms: New Problems 12
SERGEY EISENSTEIN
The Academy's Last Supper 32
HERBERT KLINE
Film Checklist 33
ROBERT STEBBINS
An "Outside Reader" Looks In 41
FRANCIS ROBUR

DANCE
From a Dancer's Notebook 31
BLANCHE EVAN
Dance Reviews 37
EDNA OCKO
The National Dance Congress 37
Books on the Ballet 39
ELIZABETH SKRIP
Cover by George Grosz

MAY 1936—VOLUME III, NUMBER 5

DRAMA
The Equity Elections 5
RICHARD PACK
Idiot's Delight 9
DAVID SHEPPERD
Perspectives—Past and Present 10
JOHN W. GASSNER
American Writers Organize 13
ELEANOR FLEXNER
Moscow Rehearsals: A Review 19
LEE STRASBERG
Soviet Theatre Festival 21
The Negro Theatre *Macbeth* 24
ROI OTTLEY
A Worker Looks at Broadway 25
JOHN MULLEN
The Theatre Collective 27
Backstage 38

FILM
Bury the Dead: A Hollywood Preview 6
The Trade Paper Racket 14
S. F. VAN BUREN
Mr. Capra Goes to Town 18

Tables of Contents

ROBERT STEBBINS
Film Forms: New Problems 28
SERGEY EISENSTEIN

DANCE
Danse Macabre 22
EMANUEL EISENBERG
Dance Reviews 30
NORMA ROLAND
The Dance Guild Recital 31
Open Letter 31
Detroit Dance Festival 31
Cover by Willard Van Dyke

JUNE 1936—VOLUME III, NUMBER 6

DRAMA
German Theatre Front 5
ELEANOR FLEXNER
The Living Newspaper 6
MORRIS WATSON
End of Season 9
JOHN W. GASSNER
Theatre for Children—Moscow 13
LUCILE CHARLES
Burlesque 18
PHILIP STERLING
The Los Angeles WPA Theatre Project 22
SANORA BABB
Play Reviews 24
Ten Million Others 29
BEN IRWIN
Five-Finger Exercises—III 31
BOB LEWIS
Shifting Scenes 32

FILM
Parade-Ground Art 10
CARL DREHER
We Are From Kronstadt 15
ROBERT STEBBINS
"Ain't Hollywood Romantic?" 16
CLARA WEATHERWAX
Union Smashing—Hollywood Style 25
HERBERT KLINE
Film Forms: New Problems 27
SERGEY EISENSTEIN

DANCE
A Museum of Ballet 20
LINCOLN KIRSTEIN
English Letter 30
LESLIE DAIKEN
John Bovingdon 32

ELIZABETH SKRIP
Answer to an "Open Letter" 32
BLANCHE EVAN
Cover
WILLIAM GROPPER

JULY 1936—VOLUME III, NUMBER 7

DRAMA
Case of the Group Theatre 5
NORMAN STEVENS
Federal Theatre Plays 6
JOHN W. GASSNER
A Call for a National Theatre 7
MARK MARVIN
François Villon in Prague 16
CHARLES RECHT
Toward a One-Act Theatre 20
JOHN W. GASSNER
A $200 Prize Play Contest 21
Pins and Needles 24
BEN IRWIN
Shifting Scenes 25
Backstage 30

FILM
Fritz Lang and *Fury* 11
ROBERT STEBBINS
A Night at the Movies 13
ALFRED HAYES
Theatre and Film 14
HERBERT BIBERMAN
The Plow That Broke the Plains 18
PETER ELLIS [IRVING LERNER]

DANCE
The Dance Congress 23
EDNA OCKO
Cover
AUGUSTUS PECK

AUGUST 1936—VOLUME III, NUMBER 8

DRAMA
Maxim Gorky—Dramatist of the Lower Depths 10
H. W. L. DANA
Ernst Toller—The Playwright of Expressionism 13
CHARMION VON WIEGAND
Turpentine Workers 18
PHILIP STEVENSON
Kids Against War 19
HELEN KAY

Shifting Scenes 26
Jewish Play Contest 27
Backstage 30

FILM
Who Speaks for Us? 6
ROBERT FORSYTHE
The Animated Cartoon and
Walt Disney 16
WILLIAM KOZLENKO
The Movie "Original" 20
WILLIAM LORENZ
Film Checklist 22
ROBERT STEBBINS
Wanger, Love and Mussolini 23
MARCIA REED

DANCE
The Dance Project 24
MARION SELLERS

SEPTEMBER 1936—VOLUME III,
NUMBER 9

DRAMA
Maxwell Anderson: Thursday's
Child 5
PHILIP STEVENSON
Smirnov's *Shakespeare* 10
BERNARD D. N. GREBANIER
Impressions of Nazi Drama 14
H. W. L. DANA
Injunction Granted! 20
HARRY ELION
Shifting Scenes 24
Backstage 30

FILM
Dancing in Films 11
LINCOLN KIRSTEIN
Who Owns the Movies? 16
PHILIP STERLING and DOROTHY DANNEN
The Films Make History 21
ROBERT STEBBINS

DANCE
Spain Says "Salud!" 8
ANGNA ENTERS
Texts for Dancers 19
EDNA OCKO

OCTOBER 1936—VOLUME III,
NUMBER 10

DRAMA
Preview 5
Designs by Moi Solotaroff 6

Ten Million Ghosts 7
ELEANOR FLEXNER
Portrait of a Man with a
Headache 11
EMANUEL EISENBERG
Memorandum on Hedgerow 13
MARY VIRGINIA FARMER
The Project Workers Serve
Notice 15
MORRIS WATSON
Historians to Come 19
IRWIN SWERDLOW
Atkinson on the Soviet Theatre 24
JAMES BURKE
Shifting Scenes 26
Backstage 30

FILM
Notes on Hollywood 8
JORIS IVENS
Der Kampf 16
MAX OPHULS
Film Miscellany 17
ROBERT STEBBINS
Educational Films 21
LOU KENDRICK

DANCE
Russia Dances 22
PAULINE KONER
Cover
HARRY STERNBERG

NOVEMBER 1936—VOLUME III,
NUMBER 11

Cover by John Groth
Reinhardt Hails a Popular Front
Play 5
ELIZABETH MEYER
D. W. Griffith 6
RICHARD WATTS, JR.
A Festival of People's Art 9
HERBERT KLINE
Kids Learn Fast 11
A. B. SHIFFRIN
Hollywood Story Conference 17
ARTHUR KOBER
Heroism in the Theatre 18
JOHN W. GASSNER
Redes 20
ROBERT STEBBINS
Film into Poem 23
DAVID WOLFF
Let Freedom Ring on Tour 24

LAURENCE SPITZ
Moi Solotaroff's Exhibition 25
NORRIS HOUGHTON
Theatre Workshop 26
HAROLD CLURMAN
Massine 27
IRVING DEAKIN
Plays on Parade 30
Shifting Scenes 32
Theatre Books 37
Backstage 38

MARCH 1937—VOLUME IV, NUMBER 1

The Silent Partner 5
CLIFFORD ODETS
Gorky on the Films, 1896 10
So You Want to Go Into the Theatre? 12
WILLIAM GROPPER
Marching Song 13
ALBERT MALTZ
Teatro Español 14
RALPH BATES
Lillian Hellman 15
JOHN HOWARD LAWSON
WPA Plowed Under? 17
An Open Letter to Darryl Zanuck 27
IVOR MONTAGU
The Diluted Theatre 30
JOHN W. GASSNER
Give All Thy Terrors to the Wind 33
CLAIRE and PAUL SIFTON
The Reign of the Director 43
LEWIS MILESTONE
Runs, Hits, Errors, 1936 44
ROBERT STEBBINS
Film Checklist 46
Plays on Parade 47
Artist and Audience 48

EDNA OCKO
Editorials 50
Shifting Scenes 52
Books in Review 53

APRIL 1937—VOLUME IV, NUMBER 2

Sit-Down Theatre 5
MORRIS WATSON
Which Way the Federal Theatre? 7
WALTER PELL
Tsar to Leon 11
WILLIAM LORENZ
Are Newsreels News? 12
ROBERT STEBBINS and PETER ELLIS [IRVING LERNER]
Editorials 16
Wings Over Broadway 19
JOHN W. GASSNER
Soviet Scene Design 22
MORDECAI GORELIK
The Living Theatre 24
Month of Bounties 26
ROBERT STEBBINS
Billy Bitzer: Ace Cameraman 29
PHILIP STERLING
Road Show—CIO Style 31
RICHARD PACK
Wage Scales for Dancers 32
LOUISE MITCHELL
Books in Review 34
You Can't Say That! 37
VIOLA BROTHERS SHORE
Shifting Scenes 38
Photographs and drawings by Lewis Jacobs (cover), Adolf Dehn, James Kelly, John Groth, Florence Sachnoff, William Hernandez, Sophia Delza, Vandamm, Martin Harris, Ben Shahn, Dorothea Lange.

Chronology
OF SELECTIONS IN THIS ANTHOLOGY

The selections appearing in this anthology have been presented thematically. The following chronology dates the selections in the order in which they first appeared.

Peace on Earth, Jack Shapiro, January 1934
They Shall Not Die!, Ben Blake, April 1934
Whither Martha Graham, Edna Ocko, April 1934
Lawson Crosses the Class Line, Lester Cohen, June 1934
Revolutionary Ballet Forms, Lincoln Kirstein, October 1934
It Makes You Weep, Janet Thorne, October 1934
The Artef, Samuel Kreiter, November 1934
Robert Flaherty's Escape, Irving Lerner, December 1934

Gorky on the Films 1896, March 1935
Our Hall, Mark Marvin, March 1935
The Youth of Maxim, V. Pudovkin, March 1935
Too Much Reality, Friedrich Wolf, March 1935
Black Pit, Herbert Kline, April 1935
Men Must Dance, Gene Martel, June 1935
On the White Man's Stage, Augustus Smith, July 1935
From *Uncle Tom's Cabin* to *Stevedore*, Eugene Gordon, July 1935
Trouble with the Angels, Langston Hughes, July 1935
Soviet Diary, Harold Clurman, August 1935
Louella Parsons: Hearst's Hollywood Stooge, Joel Faith, August 1935
Theatre Against War and Fascism, Archibald MacLeish, August 1935
Footlights in Filmland, Richard Sheridan Ames, September 1935
The Fokine Ballets, Blanche Evan, September 1935
The Quest of Eugene O'Neill, Charmion Von Wiegand, September 1935
Anti-Nazi German Theatre in Yorkville, N.Y., Molly Day Thacher, September 1935
A New Approach to Filmmaking, Ralph Steiner and Leo T. Hurwitz, September 1935
A Letter to F. Ermler on *Peasants*, G. W. Pabst, October 1935
A Letter from Hallie Flanagan, Hallie Flanagan and Herbert Kline, November 1935
Broadway Tries Again, John W. Gassner, November 1935
Reinhardt's *Dream*, Charmion Von Wiegand, November 1935
The Hope for Poetry in the Theatre, Archibald MacLeish, December 1935

Interpretation and Characterization, Harold Clurman, January 1936
Dovzhenko's *Frontier*, Irving Lerner, January 1936
The Awakening of the American Theatre, Clifford Odets, January 1936
A Statement by Elmer Rice, February 1936
A Scene from the Censored Play, Arthur Arent, February 1936
The Films of René Clair, Lewis Jacobs, February 1936
The Federal Theatre Presents, Joseph Manning, March 1936

Eva Le Gallienne—Ten Years, Walter Pell, March 1936
The Movie: 1902–1917, Robert Stebbins, March 1936
Little Charlie, What Now?, Charmion Von Wiegand, March 1936
John Ford: Fighting Irish, Emanuel Eisenberg, April 1936
Bury the Dead, Irwin Shaw, April 1936
Perspectives—Past and Present, John W. Gassner, May 1936
Idiot's Delight, Anatomy of a Success, David Shepperd, May 1936
Parade-Ground Art: The German Film Under Hitler, Carl Dreher, June 1936
François Villon in Prague, Charles Recht, July 1936
The Living Newspaper, Morris Watson, June 1936
Pins and Needles, Ben Irwin, July 1936
The Plow That Broke the Plains, Irving Lerner, July 1936
Who Speaks for Us?, Robert Forsythe, August 1936
The Animated Cartoon and Walt Disney, William Kozlenko, August 1936
The Movie "Original," William Lorenz, August 1936
Shifting Scenes, August 1936
Impressions of Nazi Drama, H. W. L. Dana, September 1936
Spain Says "Salud!", Angna Enters, September 1936
Texts for Dancers, Edna Ocko, September 1936
The Films Make History, Robert Stebbins, September 1936
Memorandum on Hedgerow, Mary Virginia Farmer, October 1936
Notes on Hollywood, Joris Ivens, October 1936
Der Kampf, Max Ophuls, October 1936
Reinhardt Hails a Popular Front Play, Elizabeth Meyer, November 1936
Redes, Robert Stebbins, November 1936
D. W. Griffith, Richard Watts, Jr., November 1936

Marching Song, Albert Maltz, March 1937
Month of Bounties, Robert Stebbins, April 1937
Billy Bitzer, Ace Cameraman, Philip Sterling, April 1937